THE LATIN L

THE
LATIN LANGUAGE

BY

L. R. PALMER

University of Oklahoma Press : Norman

Library of Congress Cataloging-in-Publication Data

Palmer, Leonard Robert, 1906–
    The Latin language.

    Reprint. Originally published: London: Faber and Faber, 1954.
    Bibliography: p. 342
    Includes indexes.
    1. Latin language—History.   2. Latin language—Grammar, Histori-
cal.   I. Title.
PA2071.P26   1987   470'.9   87-40564
    ISBN 0-8061-2136-X

Published by arrangement with Faber and Faber Limited, London.
Copyright © 1954 by L. R. Palmer. All rights reserved. Manufactured
in the U.S.A. First printing of the University of Oklahoma Press edition,
1988.

          7   8   9   10   11   12   13   14   15   16   17   18   19   20

CONTENTS

PART I

AN OUTLINE HISTORY OF THE LATIN LANGUAGE

PART II

COMPARATIVE-HISTORICAL GRAMMAR

PREFACE

I N this book, one of a series not primarily addressed to specialists, I have tried to summarize for classical students, for fellow scholars working in other fields, and for the interested laity the results reached by research into the history of Latin from the Bronze Age down to the break-up of the Roman Empire. No previous knowledge of the principles and methods of comparative philology has been assumed, such matters being elucidated in the discussion of the various problems to which they are relevant. My aim has been to state the *communis opinio* where one exists and elsewhere to set forth as fairly as I could the evidence and the divergent views which have been expressed, although I have not everywhere been able to conceal the fact that I have opinions of my own.

To keep the bulk of the book and its cost within reasonable limits it has been necessary to make a rigid selection of topics. This was especially the case in the chapter on syntax, which should be taken as a running commentary on the standard school grammar books. Expediency has prompted certain unorthodoxies, which I hope will make the book easier to use. Thus for early Latin literature I have referred to E. H. Warmington's *Remains of Old Latin* rather than to less accessible texts. I have not been able to reconcile all my friendly critics to the use of consonantal *v*, but this distinction is philologically useful and I have been content to follow the example of Leumann–Hofmann. Quantities have been marked only when the length of the vowel is relevant to the discussion.

I have profited from the learning and advice of many friends and immediate colleagues. In particular my thanks are due to Mr. J. Crow, Professor W. D. Elcock, Professor D. M. Jones, Mr. S. A. Handforth, Professor W. S. Maguinness, Mr. A. F. Wells, and Professor E. C. Woodcock, who read the proofs in whole or in part and removed many blemishes of fact and presentation. Apart from this my obligations are to the general body of scholars. Detailed acknowledgement of my indebtedness was not practicable in a work of this nature. I have tried to make some slight amends in the bibliography, but this has the restricted aim of helping those who wish to pursue their studies further to find their way into the specialist literature on the subject. As a statement of my debts it is quite inadequate, and in general I must apply to the author of this work the words *si in tanta scriptorum turba mea fama in obscuro sit, nobilitate ac magnitudine eorum qui nomini officient meo consoler.*

L. R. PALMER

Languages
of
Ancient
Italy

LEPONTIC
GALLIC
RAETIC
VENETIC
LIGURIAN
ETRUSCAN
EAST ITALIC
UMBRIAN
SABELLIAN
FALISCAN
LATIN
VOLSCIAN
OSCAN
MESSAPIC
SICEL

PART I

AN OUTLINE HISTORY OF THE LATIN LANGUAGE

CHAPTER I

LATIN AND THE OTHER INDO-EUROPEAN LANGUAGES

His constitutis rebus, nactus idoneam ad navigandum tempestatem
III fere vigilia solvit equitesque in ulteriorem portum progredi et navis
conscendere et se sequi iussit. a quibus cum paulo tardius esset admini-
stratum, ipse hora diei circiter IIII cum primis navibus Britanniam
attigit atque ibi in omnibus collibus expositas hostium copias armatas
conspexit. CAESAR, *de bello Gallico* 4. 23. 1–2.

THIS passage, in which the great Roman statesman and stylist
C. Julius Caesar describes the first onslaught of Roman armed
might on our island, has represented for many generations of
Englishmen the first shock and impact of the authentic Latin
language. A British scholar and patriot standing among the ex-
pectant warriors on the Kentish hills may well have wondered
what manner of men these invaders were and whence they came.
Less than a hundred years later a British king was carried off to
the invaders' capital and there is credited by Tacitus with a speech
of such dignity, accomplished rhetoric, and impeccable Latin as
to win him respect and an honourable captivity. In the city of his
conquerors he might have read in Livy the proud story of Rome's
legendary beginning and rise to imperial greatness. His modern
descendant, though encouraged by the reflection that he studies
in the country of Caratacus, must approach with humility the task
of tracing even in outline the history of the language which these
Romans gave to so much of the Western world.

It is called Latin because it is basically merely one of the dialects spoken by the Latini, a group of related tribes who settled in
the territory of Latium, in which Rome occupied a dominating
position (see Chapter III). The historian of the Latin language will
primarily be concerned with the successive forms of the language as
it is revealed in a series of texts reaching (for our purposes) from
the fall of the Empire back to the earliest extant documents. It
must at once be said that as thus conceived the Latin language
has little history. Certain changes of sounds, forms, syntax, and

meaning have been faithfully and diligently recorded. But there is an almost complete absence of texts earlier than the third century B.C. In Plautus, whose plays present us with the first considerable body of latinity, the language of the Romans emerges in a form which in fundamentals differs little from the Latin of the Golden Age. There is no evidence which has for the historian of Latin the significance which *Beowulf* has for the student of English. Since, then, the historical study of the monuments of the Latin language fails us at a point far short even of the legendary foundation of the city in 753 B.C., to say nothing of the still remoter origins, recourse must be had to another method—the comparative method— about which we must first say a few words.

Languages are basically systems of vocal signals which human beings use to communicate with one another. These utterances or sound-complexes produced by the speaker evoke certain responses in the hearer which we call understanding. But not every hearer can understand; for the understanding of a language requires a long and elaborate training in the use of this particular system of signals. Such training, 'learning the language', is made necessary by a fact which is of fundamental importance for the science of language: there is no natural or necessary connexion between the sound-signals and the meanings they convey. The arbitrary nature of the allocation of meanings to sound-signals has an important theoretical consequence. If two (or more) groups of people use identical or similar sound-signals, we must regard it as highly improbable that this similarity is due to chance or independent invention. The more arbitrary the connexion between sound and meaning and the more far-reaching the similarities of the systems compared, the greater is the degree of improbability that the resemblances may be accidental. In the case of signal-systems so arbitrary and so complex as languages, any far-going similarities must lead to the conclusion that the two systems are historically connected, that is to say either that one has arisen from the other or that both are descended from a common parent. In German, for instance, signals such as *Mann, Gras, Hand*, etc., occur with much the same meanings as English *man, grass, hand*, etc., and the hypothesis of independent creation is infinitely less probable than one of historical connexion. The similarities of vocabulary and grammatical structure are such as can be accounted for only by postulating a common ancestor from which they are both derived. We now propose to apply this comparative method to discover possible relatives of the Latin language in the hope that this will enable us to trace the history farther back than the time of the earliest extant written evidence.

The Italic Dialects: Osco-Umbrian

Among the inscriptions of ancient Italy are those written in the so-called Oscan language. *Osci*, earlier **Opsci*, was the name given by the Romans to the inhabitants of Campania whom the Greeks called 'Οπικοί. But the language spoken by the Samnite tribes with whom Rome later came into conflict turned out to be more or less identical with that of the Oscans. Thus the Romans came to designate this group of dialects by the name of the tribe among whom they had first encountered it, much as the French use the tribal name *Alemanni* to designate the language we call German: e.g. Livy in his account of the war against the Samnites (10. 20. 8) writes: 'gnaros Oscae linguae exploratum quid agatur mittit.'

Inscriptions written in Oscan occur in those parts of Italy which were occupied by Samnite tribes—Samnium, Campania, Apulia, Lucania, and Bruttium. The language was also introduced into Messana when it was captured by the 'Mamertines', the Campanian mercenaries recruited by Agathocles. The inscriptions, which cover a period of some five centuries from the earliest coin legends to the *graffiti* of Pompeii written after the first earthquake in A.D. 63, are written in various alphabets. The majority exhibit the Oscan alphabet, which is traced through Etruscan to the Chalcidic Greek alphabet. But the most extensive text, the *Tabula Bantina*, a bronze tablet found at Bantia in 1793 containing municipal regulations, is written in the Latin alphabet, while a Greek alphabet is used in inscriptions from southern Italy. Oscan was the chief language of central Italy until its subjugation by the Romans, and it remained in use in official documents until the Social War of 90–89 B.C. The fact that the inscriptions show few dialect variations despite the wide area over which it was in use suggests that in this official Oscan we have a standardized common language.

Closely related to Oscan is the language known as Umbrian. The only extensive document is the famous *Tabulae Iguvinae*. Discovered in 1444 at Gubbio (ancient Iguvium) in Umbria, these nine bronze tablets (two of which have been lost since their discovery) contain the acts of a religious brotherhood resembling the Roman *Arvales Fratres* (see pp. 63 f.). Written partly in the Latin alphabet and partly in the native Umbrian (derived like Oscan from a western Greek alphabet through Etruscan intermediacy), the texts range in date from roughly 400 B.C. to 90 B.C. Apart from these tablets the Umbrian language is known only from a few meagre inscriptions from various towns in Umbria, but there is evidence that the Umbrians once occupied an area extending to the western sea-board.

In addition to Oscan and Umbrian we have some slight evidence of the dialects of the lesser tribes of central Italy which are sometimes conveniently grouped under the name 'Sabellian'. These include the dialects of the Paeligni, the Marrucini, and the Vestini, all of which closely resemble Oscan. The dialect of the Volsci, which is known only from a short inscription from the town of Velitrae, appears to occupy an intermediate position between Oscan and Umbrian.

These so-called 'Italic dialects' indubitably show many resemblances to Latin, but the precise degree of relationship is difficult to determine. Scholars are undecided whether they are to be regarded as different dialects of one and the same language, 'Italic', or as two separate languages. This is largely a dispute about terms which have no precise scientific definition. A language is a system of vocal signals used by a given community of human beings. Any person who makes intelligible use of that system becomes *ipso facto*, at least for such time as he makes use of it, a member of that linguistic community. This factor of intelligibility may be used to attempt a rough definition of dialect. Within the given system local and personal varieties may occur, but as long as intelligibility is not seriously affected such variation is not felt to involve exclusion from membership of the linguistic community. These local and individual forms of speech are regarded merely as subvarieties of the system used over the whole area. The term 'dialect' thus implies both difference and similarity, a sense of exclusiveness and yet of solidarity. Where the sense of linguistic solidarity is broken by organization into separate political states speakers tend to dignify their own variety of speech by the name 'language'. Thus Norwegians, Swedes, and Danes are quite capable of carrying on a conference with each member using his own 'language', though by the test of intelligibility they might all be regarded as dialects of 'Scandinavian'. It remains to add that intelligibility forms only a rough-and-ready means of distinguishing between language and dialect. It may vary with the tempo of speech and from sentence to sentence. Moreover, in a series of dialects spoken over a given area those geographically contiguous may be mutually intelligible while those occupying the extreme positions fail to satisfy this test. The real difference between the two terms is that 'language' is an absolute term while 'dialect' poses the problem of relationship: dialect = a variety of x.

If we now apply this test to Latin and the Italic dialects, and compare an Umbrian text with a Latin translation, e.g.

I A 7 ff. pusveres Treplanes tref sif kumiaf feitu Trebe Iuvie ukriper Fisiu, tutaper Ikuvina = *post portam Trebulanam tris sues gravidas facito Trebo Iuvio pro arce Fisia pro civitate Iguvina.*

it will be evident at the first glance that the two are mutually unintelligible languages. It has been calculated that 60–70 per cent. of the words contained in the Iguvinian Tables are different from Latin, whereas for Greek only 10–15 per cent. of the words occurring in the Cretan Gortynian Laws are not found in Attic. To these decisive differences of vocabulary we must add far-reaching divergences of phonology and morphology.

Phonology

1. The labio-velar consonants (see pp. 226 f.) are treated differently: thus to Latin *quis* and *vivus* Oscan responds with *pis* and *bivus*.

2. The Indo-European aspirated stops (see pp. 227 f.) *bh, dh* appear medially in Latin as *b* and *d*, in 'Italic' as *f*: *tibi, media* = U. *tefe*, Osc. *mefiai*.

3. *kt* and *pt* of Latin appear in Osco-Umbrian as *ht* and *ft*: *Octavius, scriptae* = Osc. *Uhtavius*, Osc. *scriftas*.

4. Syncope of short vowels in medial syllables (see p. 212) is more thoroughgoing than in Latin: *agito* = Osc. *actud, hortus* = Osc. *húrz*.

5. Final *ā* > *ō* in 'Italic': *viā* = Osc. *viú, atrā* = U. *atru*.

Morphology

In the first and second declensions Osco-Umbrian has the original nominative plural endings *-ās, -ōs* (see p. 242), which Latin replaced by the pronominal forms *-āi* (*-ae*) and *-oi* (*-ī*). In the consonant-stems Oscan shows the original inflexion *-ĕs* for which Latin substituted *-ēs* (see pp. 245 f.). In the genitive singular of the *o-* and consonant-stems respectively Latin has *-ī* and *-is* whereas Osco-Umbrian has *-eis* in both these declensions. The conjugation of the verb, too, shows considerable divergences. The characteristic *-bo* future of Latin is unknown to Osco-Umbrian, which has made its future tense from an old subjunctive formation: e.g. *deivast = iurabit, ferest = feret*. The present infinitive active of Italic ends in *-om*: Osc. *ezum*, U. *erom = esse*. The future perfect shows the formant *-us*: U. *benust = venerit*.

In view of these great differences between Latin on the one hand and Osco-Umbrian on the other there can be no doubt that we should recognize them as separate languages. The degree of unintelligibility is far greater, for instance, than that between Italian and Spanish. But, as we have said, the use of the terms 'dialect' and 'language' is a matter of definition, and scholars like A. Meillet who regard Latin and Osco-Umbrian as different dialects of 'Italic' base their conclusion on certain important resemblances which we must now examine.

Phonology (see pp. 209 f.).

In both groups (1) IE. *ə* becomes *a*, (2) *eu > ou*, (3) *r̥* and *l̥ > or, ol*, (4) *m̥* and *n̥ > em, en*, (5) the voiced aspirates *bh, dh, gh*, become voiceless fricatives, (6) intervocalic *s* is voiced, (7) *t-t > ss*, (8) words of the syllabic pattern *p—qʷ > qʷ—qʷ* (e.g. **penqʷe > quinque*), and (9) final *-t* becomes *-d*.

In assessing this evidence we must remind ourselves once more of the fundamental principle of comparative linguistics: that relationship is established by the existence of similarities of such a nature as to rule out the possibility of independent development. Similarly the postulate of an exclusive 'Italic unity' from which Latin and Osco-Umbrian have developed would be necessitated by the establishment of striking similarities which these languages share to the exclusion of other more distantly related languages. Now (1) represents a development shared by all Indo-European languages except Sanskrit, (5) occurred separately in Hellenistic Greek, (6) is a widely occurring phonetic phenomenon without significance for the question of relationship, (7) occurred in Germanic and Celtic, (8) is also a feature of Celtic. But when these have been eliminated, phonetic evidence remains an insecure basis for an hypothesis of relationship, for it has often been observed that languages in geographical proximity exhibit similarities of phonetic and phonemic structure even when they are not related. Thus Sapir has pointed out that a number of unrelated 'Indian' languages of the Pacific coast of North America, from California to southern Alaska, 'have many important and distinctive features in common'. In the above list the change of *eu* to *ou* occurs not only in Latin and Osco-Umbrian but also in Venetic and Messapic. Similarly the change *r̥*, *l̥* > *or*, *ol* is also a feature of Venetic and Illyrian. Such similarities may thus be a product of contiguity rather than relationship and so have no cogency for the question of an Italic unity.

Of greater importance are similarities of morphology, since it is a rare occurrence for one language to borrow devices of declension and conjugation from another. Now in both Latin and Osco-Umbrian the ablative in -*d*, which in Indo-European was confined to the *o*-stems ('second declension'), was extended to other types, e.g. Lat. *praidad*, Osc. *toutad*, Lat. *loucarid*, Osc. *slaagid* (= *fine*), Lat. *castud*, etc. The same ending also appears in those adverbs which are formally old instrumentals in -*ē*; e.g. Lat. *facilumed*, Osc. *amprufid* (= *improbe*). The formation of the dative singular of the personal pronouns is also strikingly similar in both groups: OL. *mihei*, U. *mehe*, OL. *tibei*, U. *tefe*, OL. *sibei*, Osc. *sifei*. Turning now to the verbal system, we find that the conjugational types are the same in both groups: that is to say the verbs are organized into the four conjugations familiar from Latin grammars. Further, the Osc. *fufans* = *erant* suggests that Osco-Umbrian had created an imperfect indicative of the type represented by the Lat. *amabam* (see p. 270). The formation of the imperfect subjunctive is also identical: *foret* = Osc. *fusid* (**fu-sē-d*). A distinctive passive system (see pp. 264 f.) had been created along the same lines from elements present in the most ancient Indo-European: thus *sacratur* = Osc. *sakarater*. Further resemblances are to be observed in the formation of the supine (U. *anzeriatu* = *observatum*) and the gerundive (*sacrandae* = Osc. *sakrannas*). Finally we may mention the fusion of IE. aorist and perfect into a single 'perfect', and the fusion of the original subjunctive and optative moods evident in the sub-junctive forms of Latin and Osco-Umbrian.

Such far-reaching resemblances in the reorganization of the nominal and verbal systems bring Latin into closer relationship with the 'Italic dialects' than with any other Indo-European languages, though in a recent paper D. M. Jones has argued that the facts fit better 'into a scheme of western Indo-European relations [see below] than the development of a uniform common Italic'. The interpretation of this closer relationship in historical terms is, however, disputed.

The simplest hypothesis which would account for the observed facts is to assume that at some time in the past there existed an 'Italic' community within which the common features we have observed in Latin and the Italic dialects were developed, the very considerable differences being the product of independent develop-ment after the break-up of this linguistic community. But a German scholar, A. Walde, in a paper on the relationship between Italic and Celtic which we shall have occasion to discuss below, maintained that the resemblances between Latin and Osco-Umbrian are a phenomenon of convergence, the linguistic reflec-tion of contacts between the two groups at a comparatively recent period in Italy itself. The Italian school of linguists favours this hypothesis with minor variations of emphasis. Thus Devoto main-tains that the divergences between Latin and Osco-Umbrian are ancient and that the resemblances developed at a relatively late date when the proto-Latins had already settled in Latium. From the eighth century onwards (foundation of Rome and the presence of a Sabine tribe on one of the hills) relations were established which resulted in an exchange of linguistic elements between the proto-Latins and the Osco-Umbrians ; it is this stage of progressive approximation which should be labelled the 'Italic period'. But Devoto maintains, this should not be understood in a genealogical sense implying the one-time identity of the two linguistic systems. To all this it may be objected that geographical contiguity and social and cultural contacts between people speaking different languages may well result in resemblances of phonetic system and the exchange of loan-words, but fundamental structural peculiari-ties such as types of tense, mood, and case-formation are not so easily transferable. Linguistic developments must ultimately be traced back to acts of speech, which are essentially social habits, and such social habits as evidenced in subjunctives and the like are transferable from one set of human beings to another only under such conditions of linguistic intimacy as amount to 'linguistic community'. An Oscan institution such as a 'cook-shop' may become an established feature of Roman life, and bring with it the Oscan name *popina*; but under what *speech* conditions can we imagine the exchange of a gerundive, a supine, or an imperfect subjunctive between speakers who, on this hypothesis of convergence, were even more mutually unintelligible than those of the historically attested Latin and Osco-Umbrian? The concepts of 'linguistic exchange', 'common mental schemata', 'convergence', and the like with which Devoto operates are too remote from the realities of actual speech. The linguistic facts demand the postulation sometime somewhere of some form of society comprising representatives of both the major Italic groups, i.e. the linguistic ancestors of the speakers of Latin and of Osco-Umbrian. But this need not imply an 'Italic unity' comprising all the proto-Latins and the proto-Italici. As a minimum hypothesis it would suffice to assume that one group of invading Osco-Umbrians combined with the proto-Latins, and it was this engrafting of an alien population on Latin stock which produced those resemblances between Latin and Osco-Umbrian that formed the starting-point of this discussion. The legends of the origins of Rome (Titus Tatius and the Rape of the Sabine Women) seem to imply some such historical event as we have postulated (the Sabine elements in Latin will be discussed on pp. 37 f.), and the evidence of the non-Roman dialects of Latium points in the same direction (see Ch. III). It remains to state that this conclusion agrees in the main with Devoto in that it excludes an 'Italic' community existing before the invasion of the Apennine peninsula by the ancestors of the two groups of tribes. The closer resemblances comprised under the label 'Italic', we agree, did develop on Italian soil. All we have suggested is that the concept of convergence requires translation into the realities of actual speech and the conditions of human society which these imply.

The Italo-Celtic Theory and 'The Civilization of the North-West

Turning our attention now farther afield, we may at once state briefly that the comparative method has established that Latin is one of a group of languages stretching from India in the east to Celtic and Germanic in the west. In these languages resemblances of structure and fundamental vocabulary have been detected so remarkable as to exclude all explanations except descent from a common ancestor which is known as Indo-European. This postulation of a more or less uniform parent language to account for the resemblances detected in the group of related languages must further imply the one-time existence of a group of speakers—the IE. people. Moreover, the analysis of the stock of common words has enabled scholars to build up a picture of at least some features of their civilization. Thus they appear to have been familiar with the metal copper and its working, they practised at least a primitive agriculture, and had domesticated certain animals such as the cow and sheep; they worshipped a god of the bright sky; and had a patriarchal organization of society. We must, however, not imagine them as a closely coherent political state with a uniform language: they were more probably a loose aggregate of seminomadic tribes, settling for some time to till the soil and moving again when it had been exhausted by their primitive agricultural methods, and perhaps assembling at intervals for the celebration of common religious rites. Such a 'society' would inevitably exhibit differences of dialect. Moreover, during the long period of migrations which eventually brought them to the widely scattered places where they appear in historical times, certain tribes may for limited periods have established closer associations, or marauding bands may have been created from members of different tribes. We must therefore reckon with the possibility that other 'unities' of varying duration and intensity intervened between the original IE. period and the appearance of the separate peoples in their historical habitats. These communities would have reflections in language, and the task of the linguist is to attempt by analysis to detect such closer dialectal affinities within the major group. Such analysis has revealed a number of peculiarities which 'Italic' and Celtic share to the exclusion of the other related languages.

We shall first enumerate the facts before discussing their significance, for their interpretation is still much disputed.

Phonology

1. The Indo-European labio-velars[1] (q^w, g^w, g^wh) show similar treatment in Italic and Celtic, becoming labials in Britannic and Osco-Umbrian and velars in Latin and Goidelic (e.g. the IE. interrogative stem q^wis, etc., appears in Irish as *cia*, in Latin as *quis*, in Welsh as *pwy*, in Oscan as *pis*). It has been suggested that these facts are reflections of one-time dialect relationships in an Italo-Celtic group; that at some prehistoric period the linguistic ancestors of Celts and Italici were in close proximity and so grouped that the pre-Britannic people shared with the pre-Sabellians this change of $q^w > p$. Later the whole group would have split up and re-formed, pre-Britannic and pre-Goidelic to form common Celtic, and pre-Latin and pre-Sabellian to form common Italic, Celtic and Italic henceforward going their separate ways. This hypothesis is destroyed by a simple fact: in all the Celtic languages original initial IE. *p*- has disappeared (e.g. Ir. *én* 'bird', W. *edn* < **pet-n*, cf. Lat. *penna*, etc.): this means that the change of $q^w > p$ in Britannic must have taken place *after* the common Celtic period and therefore took place independently of the similar change in Osco-Umbrian. In any case a similar change took place in Aeolic Greek, where the labio-velars also appear as labials (e.g. **penq^we* > πέμπε). The phenomenon is therefore not conclusive evidence of closer relationship.

2. More peculiar, and consequently of greater significance as evidence for relationship, is the change which took place in words where the first syllable began with a labial and the second with a labio-velar: in such words assimilation took place in both Italic and Celtic,[2] *p—q^w* > *q^w—q^w*: e.g. IE. **penq^we* 'five' > Italo-Celtic **q^wenq^we*, e.g. OIr. *cóic*, OW. *pimp*, Lat. *quinque*, O.-U. **pompe* (cf. Osc. *púmperiaís* 'quincuriis').

Morphology

1. The genitive singular of *o*-stems ends in -*ī*: Ir. *maqi* 'of the son', Gaulish *Segomari*, Lat. *domini*. Although traces of an adverbial case in *ī*- have been found in Sanskrit (see pp. 242 f.), this does not diminish the significance of this phenomenon. Its incorporation into the regular declensional system instead of the original genitive in -*osyo* is a common innovation of Celtic and Latin (Osco-Umbrian has substituted -*eis* from the *i*-stems of the third declension), but it is also shared by Venetic and the Illyrian dialect Messapic (see pp. 39 f.).

2. The impersonal forms of the verb in Osco-Umbrian and Celtic are characterized by -*r*: e.g. Umbr. *ferar* 'one must bear', W. *gweler* 'one

---

[1] See pp. 226f.   Celtic languages diverge only in treatment of q^w.

[2] See p. 225.

sees', Ir. *berir* 'one carries'. This -*r* is also a mark of the deponent and passive forms in both groups: e.g. Lat. *sequor, sequitur*, Ir. *sechur, sechithir*. These -*r* endings have been found in other Indo-European languages, e.g. Hittite, Tocharian, and Phrygian, and the evidence of these languages suggests that the -*r* ending originally figured only in the singular and in the third person plural of the present tense. Here, too, we have a significant common development of an inherited feature.

3. Verbs of the type of *amā-re, monē-re* in Latin make their future with an element -*b*- (*amabo, monebo*), which is traced to the IE. root *bhu* 'to be' (see p. 271): the formation is in fact a periphrastic tense with the meaning 'I am to love', etc. The same type is found in Celtic, e.g. Ir. *léicfea* 'I shall leave'. While it is difficult to reduce the attested forms to a single prototype, the conclusion seems inescapable that the germ of the future in -*b*- existed in the dialects from which Latin and Irish have developed. A striking innovation, it is significant evidence of a one-time close relationship of Italic and Celtic.

4. In Indo-European the subjunctive was formed from the various tense stems by the addition or lengthening of the thematic vowel *e/o*: e.g. in Homeric Greek indic. ἴμεν subj. ἴομεν, or indic. λύομεν subj. λύωμεν. But in Celtic the subjunctive mood is independent of the tense stem and is formed by adding -*ā* or -*s* to the root: e.g. Ir. *bera* (*ber* 'to carry'), *tiasu* (*tiag* 'to go'). The same types are present in Italic (see pp. 277 f.): e.g. OL. *advenat* with the subjunctive built on the root *ven* and not on the present stem *veni-*, and *faxo, capso* with -*s*- added to the roots *fac-* and *cap-* as distinguished from the present stems *faci-* and *capi-*. This morphological feature, found only in Italic and Celtic among the IE. languages, would appear to be conclusive evidence of close relationship. But the fact that the subjunctive is independent of the tense stems and may even be made from a different root (e.g. *fuam* as the subjunctive of *sum*) accords with most archaic features of the IE. verbal system, in which there was no 'conjugation' properly speaking but each tense existed independently of the others. It is therefore possible that the *ā* subjunctives are archaisms,[1] eliminated in the other IE. languages and preserved only in Italic and Celtic. If we take this view, these subjunctives are less cogent as evidence for relationship since, as was pointed out above, archaisms may survive independently in the various languages.

5. In the comparison of adjectives, too, Italic and Celtic show agreements which link them closely together. In Indo-European the 'comparative'[2] was formed (1) by the addition of the suffix -*iōs* to the root,

---

[1] See pp. 252 f.

[2] It is likely that Indo-European possessed no true 'comparative' but that the derivatives in -*iōs*, -*isōn*, had much the same meaning as the English *biggish*, *sizish*, which have 'relative' function as opposed to the 'absolutive' meaning of the so-called positive (see pp. 252 f.).

e.g. Skr. *náva-* 'new', *náv-yas* 'newer'; (2) by the suffix *-tero*, which had 'contrasting' or 'separative' function as in *laevus: dexter, magister: minister*, etc. Both Latin and Irish had developed and regularized the first procedure (e.g. Lat. *senior*, Ir. *siniu*). In the superlative, too, we may distinguish two types: (1) suffix *-t°mo* (Lat. *ultimus, intimus*), the original function of which was perhaps to denote the 'extreme point of a spatial continuum',[1] and (2) the type in *-is-to* (Engl. *sweetest*, Gk. ἥδιστος, etc.), which like the ordinal numbers (e.g. *first*, German *zwanzigste*, Gk. πρῶτος, etc.) denoted the culminating or completing member of a totality. This second type is not found in Italo-Celtic, which has, however, besides type (1) a complex form in *-s°mo* not found elsewhere: Lat. *maximus*, Osc. *nessimas* (= *proximae*), OIr. *nessam*, W. *nesaf*.

Vocabulary

The analysis of vocabulary reveals that there are also a number of words exclusive to Italic and Celtic. For instance the verbs *cano* and *loquor* have exact correspondents in Irish: *canim* and *-tluchur*. Among agricultural words the root found in Lat. *metere* 'to reap' occurs elsewhere in this sense only in Celtic, e.g. W. *medi*; similarly *seges* 'crop' corresponds to W. *heu* 'to sow'. For parts of the body we may note the equations *cūlus* = Ir. *cúl, dorsum* = Ir. *druim*, *pectus* = Ir. *hucht, tālus* = Ir. *sál*. To these we may add the nouns *pulvis* = W. *ulw, harēna* = Ir. *ganem, terra* = Ir. *tír, avunculus* = W. *ewythr, saeculum* = W. *hoedl*; and the adjectives *vastus* = Ir. *fota, trux* = Ir. *trú, grossus* = Ir. *bras, mītis* = Ir. *móith. vātes* 'bard', though related to Germanic words like OE. *wōp* 'song', finds an exact correspondence in Ir. *fáith* 'poet'. This mass of evidence would appear to establish a strong prima-facie case for the one-time existence of a community comprising the linguistic ancestors of the Latin (Italic) and the Celtic peoples. But before allowing this we must note that there exist elements (1) common to Celtic and Germanic, (2) common to Italic and Germanic, (3) common to all three, and (4) that the words belonging to this last group are often found also in Balto-Slavonic. This has led scholars to speak of an 'occidental' group of IE. languages including Celtic, Germanic, Italic, and Balto-Slavonic but excluding Greek. We tabulate this evidence before proceeding to evaluate it.

[1] See p. 253.

Celtic and Germanic

OIr. *oeth* = Goth. *aips* (Engl. *oath*), OIr. *orbe* = Goth. *arbi* (German *Erbe*), W. *rhydd* = Goth. *freis* (Engl. *free*), OIr. *rūn* 'secret' = Goth. *rūna*, OIr. *luaide* = OE. *lēad* (Engl. *lead*), etc. To these we must add a large number of loan-words which have been exchanged between these two groups of languages such as Gothic *reiks* from the Celtic word *rīx*.

Italic and Germanic

The following evidence has been adduced:

1. The development of *t-t* > *-s-s*; but it is also found in Celtic (see below).

2. The voicing of voiceless intervocalic fricatives (e.g. Lat. *aedes* from an IE. root *aidh* seen also in Gk. αἴθω) occurs in both groups; but this is a phonetic development which might easily occur independently, and that it did so is suggested by the fact that the change in Italic is confined to Latin. Thus no conclusion about relationship may be drawn from this resemblance.

3. The IE. aorist and perfect are combined to form a single preterite tense (see pp. 272 f.).

4. In both groups (and in Celtic) the paradigm of the verb 'to be' is made from two roots, *es* and *bhu*: Lat. *est, fuit*, Engl. *is, be*, etc., Ir. *is, biuu*, etc.

5. The perfect *nōvī* corresponds in formation to OE. *cneow*. But this *-u* appears in Germanic also in the present *cnāwan*, and the origin of the *-u-* perfect in Latin is so vexed a question (see pp. 273 f.) that this equation is too insecure a basis for the construction of theories about relationship.

6. Perfect forms with a long stem-vowel of the type of *sēdimus* occur also in Germanic, cf. Goth. *sētum*. Note, however, that in Gothic the long vowel is confined to the plural, so that Latin singular forms *sēdi*, etc., would have to be regarded as analogicall levelings (see pp. 272 f.).

7. The Latin demonstrative *is, ea, id* = Goth. *is, ija, ita*.

8. To this we may add numerous correspondences in vocabulary. Thus many verbal equations are confined to Italic and Germanic: e.g. *dūcere* = Goth. *tiuhan* (Engl. *tug*); *clāmāre* = OHG. *hlamōn*; *tacēre* = Goth. *þahan*; *silēre* = Goth. *ana-silan*. Moreover, both groups share exclusively[1] such agricultural words as *far* = ON. *barr* (Engl. *barley*),

---

[1] Possible congeners may be found in other Indo-European languages, but these words are confined to Germanic and Italic in the particular form and meaning quoted.

sulcus 'furrow' = OE. *sulh* 'plough'; and further *haedus* = Goth. *gaits* (Engl. *goat*), *ulmus* = *elm*, *annus* = Goth. *apns*, 'year'.

Occidental words

It has often been pointed out that Celtic, Italic, Germanic (and sometimes Balto-Slavonic) have words in common which do not appear in Greek, Armenian, and Indo-Iranian. These words are so numerous and such fundamental constituents of the vocabulary that the coincidences, so the argument runs, cannot be due to chance but reflect a common period of civilization, which is termed 'the civilization of the North-West'.

Among these words we find the adjectives for 'true' (*vērus*, Ir. *fīr*, OHG. *wār* = OSl. *věra* 'faith'), 'blind' (*caecus*), 'smooth' (*glaber*); the vegetation names—*corilus* 'hazel', *flōs* 'blossom', *salix* 'willow', *ulmus*, Ir. *lem* 'elm'; the zoological terms—*porcus* 'piglet' (not 'domestic pig' as opposed to *sūs* 'wild pig', as is often stated), *merula* 'blackbird', *natrix* 'water-snake', *piscis* 'fish'; agricultural words (objects and operations)—*grānum*, *faba*, *sero* 'sow', *scabo* 'scrape', *seco* 'cut, mow', *sūgo* 'suck', *molo* 'grind' (common Indo-European in the sense 'crush'), *līra* 'furrow'; sociological words—*cīvis*, *hostis*, *homo* (which contains the root **ghem/ghom* specialized to denote 'human being' as in Goth. *guma*, Ir. *duine*, Lith. *žmuõ*), *vas* 'pledge, security';—miscellaneous—*verbum* 'word' (Goth. and OPr.), *nīdus*, in the specialized sense 'nest', *mare*, *vinco*, *ferio*, *cūdo* 'strike, forge', *emo* 'take, buy'.

The facts so selected and so set out would appear to give strong support to the conclusions based on them: that the peoples who later spoke the Italic languages after the break-up of the IE. community settled or remained in Europe and for some time shared in a common civilization with the linguistic ancestors of the Celts, Germans, and Balto-Slavs. But there are other facts which should give us pause. Among these occidental words we find, for instance, the important word *teutā* 'people' (Osc. *touto* = Lat. 'civitas', Umbr. *tota*, Ir. *tuath*, Goth. *piuda* 'nation'); but this word is lacking in Latin. The same is true of the occidental word for 'house' exemplified in Ir. *treb*, Lith. *trobà*, Engl. *thorp*, which appears in Italic in Osc. *triibúm*, Umbr. *tremnu*, but is absent from Latin, for it is extremely doubtful whether *trabs* 'beam' is related to these words. On the other hand, in *domus* Latin has preserved a widespread IE. noun which is not found in Celtic, Germanic, or Baltic. Such examples underline the danger of basing conclusions about relationship on resemblances or differences of vocabulary. In every language the loss of words depends on a variety of factors, the interplay of which is so complex that the absence of a particular word or words from a language may well be accidental. For instance, *ignis* 'fire' has cognates in Skt. *agnis* and again in Balto-Slavonic; but the word is lacking in Osco-Umbrian where, however, Umbr. *pir* finds relatives in Gk. πῦρ, Engl. *fire*, and also in Hittite, Armenian, and Tocharian. Here, too, Latin has lost an ancient IE. word and so broken a link even with its nearest relatives in the Italic dialects. The same is true of the word for 'water', which Latin designates by *aqua*, which has cognates only in Germanic (Goth. *ahwa* 'river') and possibly in Celtic. Only in a different sense of 'wave' does Latin preserve in *unda* the ancient IE. word widely attested elsewhere, e.g. Umbr. *utur*, Engl. *water*, Gk. ὕδωρ, etc. Of the two IE. words for 'man' (1) *wiro*, (2) *ner*, Latin has not retained the second (except in the Sabine proper names *Nero*,[1] *Nerio*), which, however, is represented in Osc. *niír*, Umbr. *nerf* (accus. plur.), OIr. *nert*, Gk. ἀνήρ, Skr. *nár-*, etc. These examples could be multiplied, but enough will have been said to make clear the danger of arguments *ex silentio* in matters of vocabulary. Each word has its own history, and the pattern of resemblances between languages shifts from word to word. Thus *terra* is found in Celtic and Italic, but Germanic *earth* finds a relative in Gk. ἔρας and Celt. *ert*. It would, in fact, not be difficult to draw up a list of Latin words which Greek shares to the exclusion of one or other of the so-called 'occidental group'. Among the parts of the body *cutis*, for instance, has correspondences in Gk. κύτος, in Germanic (Engl. *hide*), and in Baltic (OPr. *keuto*); *inguen* 'groin' has an exact correspondent in Gk. ἀδήν, with relatives also in Germanic (ON. *økkr*); *nefrundinēs*, too, finds relatives only in Gk. νεφρός and Germanic (German *Niere*); with *pellis* we can equate πέλλα and OIcel. and Engl. *fell*; *pēnis* is related to Gk. πέος and Skt. *pásas*; for *pugnus* 'fist', Gk. πύξ, πυγμή are quoted; *iecur*, a word of a most ancient morphological type, is found in Greek (ἧπαρ), Lithuanian (*jãknos*), and Indo-Iranian, but it is absent from the occidental languages Celtic and Germanic; Germanic and Baltic again lack the word for 'bone', Lat. *os*, Gk.

---

[1] According to Suetonius, *Tiberius* 1. 2, *Nero* = *fortis ac strenuus*.

ὀστέον, Skt. *ásthi*, Hittite *ḫastāi*, etc. Certain agricultural and zoological words reveal a similar pattern: *agnus* finds an exact correspondent only in Gk. ἀμνός (both < *agʷnos*), the Celtic forms presupposing an original initial *o-* (Ir. *uan*, W. *oen*) and Slavonic either *ō-* or *ā-* (*jagnę*); *pullus* is related to Gk. πῶλος, to Germanic words represented by Engl. *foal*, and to Arm. *ul*; the word for 'egg', *ōvum*, has an element *-w-* which appears only in Doric Gk. ὤϝεον (and in Iranian), whereas Germanic and Slavonic show no trace of this internal *-w-* (e.g. German *Ei* < *aiya*); *glāns* has congeners in Greek (βάλανος), Balto-Slavonic, and Armenian (*kałin*); *vīrus* 'poisonous juice of a plant' is related to OIr. *fí*, Gk. ϝιός, and Skt. *viṣám*; in this group we may include the nouns *termen*, *terminus* 'boundary mark' cognate with Gk. τέρμα, and *vallus* 'stake' for which the only relative quoted is Gk. ἧλος (Aeolic ϝάλλοι). To these we may add the verbs *carpo* 'pluck' cognate with Gk. καρπός, with Germanic words of which we single out Engl. *harvest*, and with Balto-Slavonic words such as Lith. *kerpù*; *lego* 'pick, gather', for which congeners are quoted only from Greek (λέγω, etc.) and Albanian; another such technical verb *glubo* 'I peel' finds exact correspondents in Gk. γλύφω and Germanic words such as Engl. *cleave* (OE. *clēofan*, OHG. *klioban*, ON. *kljūfa*); *sarpo* 'prune' has a root *serp* which appears in Gk. ὄρπηξ 'shoot, sapling', in OSl. *srŭpŭ* 'pruning knife' and Lett. *sirpis*. *creo*, too, may conveniently be grouped here as a word of agricultural operations: cognate with *crēsco*, it has been equated with Arm. *serem* 'I engender', *sermn* 'sowing', and further with Lith. *šeriù* 'feed' and Gk. ἐκόρεσα, κόρος 'sate', 'satiety'. Finally the word for 'bear', *ursus*, may reinforce the warning about *argumenta ex silentio* in matters of vocabulary: cognate with Gk. ἄρκτος, Skt. *ŕkṣas*, Arm. *arj* and OIr. *art*, it is absent from Germanic and Balto-Slavonic, where it has been replaced by new words, perhaps for reasons of taboo.

Among the sociological vocabulary we may note that the word *vīcus* may claim relatives in Germanic (e.g. Goth. *weihs* 'village'), Gk. ϝοῖκος, Skt. *vēśás*, and in Balto-Slavonic (e.g. OB. *vĭsĭ* 'village'), whereas in Celtic it is absent except for Latin loan-words such as Ir. *fich*. Greek is also a member of the group which has cognates of *nurus* 'daughter-in-law' (Skt. *snuṣā*, Arm. *nu*, OB.

snŭcha, OHG. snur, Gk. νυός). ianitrīces 'brothers' wives' is similarly represented in Gk. εἰνάτερες together with Skt. yātar-, Arm.
ner, OLith. jéntė, OSl. jętry; but the important members of the
'occidental group' lack the word, as they do the word for 'husband's sister', glōs, which again has a cognate in Gk. γαλόως and
Sl. zŭlŭva (Russ. zólva). It is worth noting, too, in this connexion
that līber 'free' has its only exact correspondent in Gk. ἐλευθερός,
although a more remote connexion is possible with OHG. liuti
'people' (German Leute), etc.

Latin also shares with Greek (sometimes exclusively) important
words of religion and ritual. lībare, for instance, finds immediate
relatives only in the important Greek group λείβω, λοιβή, etc.,
though a more distant connexion may be traced to Lith. lieti
'pour'; Lat. spondeo 'vow', which presumably once referred to a
religious operation accompanying the vow, is the causative-itera-
tive form of the root seen in Gk. σπένδω 'pour a libation'—the antiquity of this word may be judged from the fact that it also occurs
in Hittite šipanti 'he pours a libation'. Another term of the religious vocabulary is voveo, vōtum: as may be seen from Umbr.
vufetes (Lat. 'votis') the word may be traced to the root form
*wŏgʷh, to which belongs Vedic vāghát 'sacrificing, making a vow'
and further Gk. εὔχομαι 'I pray'. templum 'the space marked out by
the augur' has no relative closer than Gk. τέμενος 'sacred enclosure'
from the root *tem 'cut'. nemus 'sacred grove' resembles most
closely in form and meaning Gk. νέμος, although the religious
character of the word is more strongly marked in the Celtic
representatives, Ir. nemed 'sanctuary', Gaul. νεμητον.[1] On the
other hand, Celtic does not form part of the group which presents
religious terms corresponding to Lat. daps 'sacrificial meal': this
includes Germanic (OIcel. tafn 'sacrificial animal'), Arm. tawn, and
possibly Gk. δεῖπνον.

We may round off the evidence with a miscellaneous group of
words in which Latin and Greek figure to the exclusion of one or
more of the occidental group. fāma (also in Italic) has an exact

[1] E. Laroche writes (Histoire de la racine NEM en grec ancien, p. 259): 'Le
celto-germanique nemeto- forme en face du greco-latin nemes- un groupe en appa-
rence homogène.' He points out, however, that onomatology supplies evidence for
the existence of an s-stem in Celtic, a fact which underlines the dangers of arguments ex silentio.

correspondent only in Gk. φήμη (Doric φāμā); the only certain congener of *frīgus* is Gk. ῥῖγος. Among the verbs, *ango* = Gk. ἄγχω; the root *el* 'go' occurs in *amb-ul-are, ex-ul*, in Gk. ἐλθεῖν, and OIr. *lod* 'I went'; the present stem *eo, īre* is found in Greek, Lithuanian, and Indo-Iranian, but not in Germanic or Celtic; *fugio, fugāre* finds relatives in Greek and Lithuanian; *iubeo* in Greek, Balto-Slavonic, and Indo-Iranian; *mereo* is related to Gk. μέρος, μείρομαι, etc., and the root is found in the Gaulish *Ro-Smerta*, the name of a goddess, and further in Hittite *mar-k* 'divide' (a victim); the nearest relatives of *perīculum, perītus* < (*ex*)*perior* are found in Gk. πεῖρα, etc., although Germanic, too, has derivatives such as OHG. *fāra* 'danger'; the important verb *dō, dă*, found in Greek, Balto-Slavonic, Armenian, and Indo-Iranian, is lacking in Celtic and Germanic; for *iacio* we find a relative only in Gk. ἵημι, ἧκα; *salio*, too, has an exact correspondent only in Gk. ἅλλομαι.

Among the adjectives the nearest relative of Lat. *brevis* is Gk. βραχύς, though derivatives are found also in Gothic and Avestan; *cavus* is equated with Gk. κοῖλος (*κοϝιλος) and further with Ir. *cūa* (*koϝio); it is only in Gk. δεξιτερός that we find the suffix denoting 'one of a contrasting pair' attached to the root meaning 'right' which appears in *dexter*; for *scaevus*, too, Greek provides the only perfect parallel in σκαιϝός, while *laevus* corresponds exactly with Gk. λαιϝός and OSl. *lĕvŭ*; *paucus* like *paullus* and *pauper* contains the root *pau* which we encounter in Gk. παῦρος and Goth. *fawai* 'few'; *lēvis* 'smooth' is equated with Gk. λεῖος. We may end the list with the pronoun *ambo* which corresponds exactly with Gk. ἄμφω.

The evidence presented in the preceding paragraphs is put forward to impugn the conclusions about Latin participation in a civilization of north-west Europe from which Greek is excluded. What has been maintained is that such conclusions may be nothing more than elaborate *argumenta ex silentio* resting on accidental loss by Greek of many of these 'occidental' words after the entry of the Greek-speaking peoples into the Balkan peninsula. By way of counter-argument a number of important words has been adduced which Greek shares with Latin to the exclusion of some or all of the other occidental languages. It is necessary to insist that in so doing our intention has been purely destructive. The Greco-Latin coincidences are presumably due to the independent preservation of elements of the most ancient IE. vocabulary. They do not necessarily imply any intimate relationship between Greek and Latin leading to the postulation of a pre-historic 'Italo-Greek' unity.

Italo-Greek Affinities

Such a unity has been maintained by a number of scholars who point to the following resemblances:

1. In both languages the word-accent cannot be placed farther back than the third syllable from the end (the antepenultimate), whereas in Indo-European the accent was completely free. But the conditions vary in the two languages and in any case the accentuation of Classical Latin is a comparatively recent phenomenon, since in primitive Latin there was a strong stress accent on the first syllable of the word (see pp. 211 f.).

2. In both languages the voiced aspirated plosives became voiceless (e.g. *bh* > *ph*). But this, even if it is substantiated (it is hypothetical for primitive Italic), is so common a phonetic phenomenon that it could easily have happened independently, just as in post-classical Greek the voiceless aspirate became a fricative, thus making φέρω and *fero* (< *bherō*) more or less identical in pronunciation.

3. More plausible are certain common features of morphology. Thus the nominative plural of the *o*-stems originally ended in *-ōs*, which still persisted in Indo-Iranian, Germanic, and Osco-Umbrian. Both Latin and Greek, however, have replaced it by *-oi*, which characterized the demonstratives (see p. 243).

In both languages, again, the original nominative plural of the *a*-stems *-ās* (e.g. Osc. *aasas = arae*) has been replaced by *-ai* after the *-oi* of the second declension. This contact-infection of nouns by the demonstratives which precede them is, however, a common phenomenon, and the coincidence of Latin and Greek presumably rests on independent development. We find it again in the endings of the genitive plural of the *a*-stems. In Indo-European the ending was *-ōm* < *ā-+-ōm*. The corresponding form of the feminine demonstrative was, however, **tāsōm* (cf. Lat. *is-tarum*, Gk. τά(σ)ων), and this ending was transferred to the corresponding feminine nouns (*regin-arum*, θεά(σ)ων).

In both languages we find a similar interaction between the *-ā*-nouns and the *o*-nouns in the accusative plural. In primitive Indo-European this appeared as *ā-ns* and *-o-ns*, but in the former *-n-* presumably disappeared producing the disparity *-ās*, *-ons*. Both Latin and Greek restored regularity by reintroducing *-ans* in the first declension: then in Latin and most Greek dialects (note, however, Cretan τονς ἐλευθερονς, etc.) *-n-* disappeared with compensatory lengthening of the preceding vowel, so that the ending of *vi-ās*, etc., is now identical with that of τιμάς, etc.

In the verb, too, we find an instance of independent development producing an illusory coincidence. The 'future imperative' was formed by the addition of the ablative of the demonstrative *-tōd* to the imperatival stem (e.g. *datōd*, Gk. δότω(δ)). These forms did service for any person and number, but both Greek and Latin have created forms for the third person plural, so that *ferunto* closely resembles φερόντω (see p. 277).

4. Similarities of inherited vocabulary have already been dealt with, but new 'isoglosses' (p. 30) were produced in both languages by cultural borrowings from the Mediterranean civilization with which they both came into contact (see pp. 55 ff. on *cornus, porrum, malva, vaccinium, ervum*, etc.). These, of course, have no bearing on the question of a prehistoric Italo-Greek unity.

To sum up we may say that the differences between Greek and Latin far outweigh their resemblances, which are largely due to parallel developments and independent borrowing from unknown Mediterranean languages.[1] Coincidences of Latin and Greek due to the preservation of ancient elements of the IE. parent language cannot, of course, be used as evidence indicating any close relationship in the period following the break-up of the IE. community. If their number seems comparatively large, this must be ascribed to the accident which has provided us with a mass of early texts for both Latin and Greek. If we had texts of comparable date for Celtic and Germanic,[2] the pattern of relationships would doubtless present a very different picture.

Marginal Phenomena

In the immediately preceding paragraphs we have been considering certain characteristics shared by one or more western languages, a group of dialects which may plausibly be presumed to have remained in close geographical proximity after the break-up of the IE. unity and so developed common features. But besides these, scholars have detected in Italic and Celtic other features which are shared with languages at the other extreme of the IE.

---

[1] The direct influence of Greek on Latin will be discussed in the next chapter.

[2] Gaulish or continental Celtic is known to us only from a few short inscriptions and from words quoted by Latin and Greek authors. For Gaelic the earliest evidence is the Ogham inscriptions, which date from the fifth century A.D. Germanic appears first in the Runic inscriptions of the third century A.D., the first substantial text being Bishop Ulfila's Gothic translation of the Bible in the fourth century A.D. As for Baltic, the earliest documents, the translation of Luther's catechism, date only from the sixteenth century.

C

world but are absent from the intervening languages. In other words, we have a new classification of 'peripheral' as opposed to 'central' characteristics. Here, too, an enumeration of the facts will best precede the discussion of their significance and the conclusions which may legitimately be drawn from them.

1. Latin exhibits a form of the third person plural of the perfect indicative, e.g. *dīx-ēre*, which lacks the characteristic *-nt* that figures in *dīcunt, dīcebant, dīxērunt, dīxerant*, etc. Now similar *-r* endings are found in Hittite *-ir*, in Tokharian *-ăr, -ăre*, while in Indo-Iranian, too, the perfect and the optative third person plurals are characterized by *-r* (for details see p. 275). No such endings are found in the 'central' languages, Greek, Germanic, Baltic, or Slavonic, which thus must have eliminated them in the prehistoric period.

Latin preserves two other peculiarities of the perfect which may be traced back to the most archaic period of Indo-European.

2. The familiar type of perfect in *-v-* as in *amāvit, docuit*, for instance, is thought to have developed from forms such as *nōvī*, which has a characteristic *-v-* that appears also in Skt. *jajñau* 'he has known' and again in Arm. *cnaw* 'he is born'. What is noteworthy is that this *-v-* appeared originally only in the first and third persons singular: e.g. Tokharian *prakwā* = **precāvī*, while Hittite, too, shows preterite forms in *-un* for the first person singular where the ending *-n* is attached to the characteristic *-u-*. Here, too, the conclusion has been drawn that it is from an ancient type of which only vestiges remain in 'marginal' languages, Indo-Iranian, Tokharian, Hittite, Armenian, and perhaps Celtic, that Latin has constituted its most characteristic type of perfect formation. We should note, however, that in Sanskrit the *u*-ending appears only in reduplicated perfects, e.g. *paprau* 'I filled' (IE. **plē* 'fill'), whereas no *-v-* perfect of Latin is also characterized by reduplication (see pp. 273 f.).

3. The other inflexional peculiarity of the Latin perfect which is paralleled elsewhere is the *-is-* which appears before the endings of the second person: *dīxistī, dīxistis*. In Hittite, too, the preterite sometimes exhibits an *-s-* before the endings beginning with a *-t-* but not before those beginning with a vowel, and similar facts have been noted for Tokharian and Vedic. The conclusion is drawn that here, too, Latin has preserved an archaic feature of the IE. inflexional system which appears elsewhere only in the peripheral languages. This *-is-*, however, appears throughout the other tenses and moods of the Latin perfect, e.g. *dīxero, dīxeram, dīxisse*, and again indirectly in the new third person plural ending *dīxērunt* which has replaced *dīxēre* (for details, see pp. 274 f.), and many scholars trace these Latin perfect formations to an original *-s-* aorist (see p. 275).

4. Yet another 'peripheral' feature has been detected in the fact that while other IE. languages have a separate feminine form for the participles of the present and the perfect, Latin has a single common form, e.g. *ferēns*. Since Hittite, too, makes no distinction between masculine and feminine and the same is true of Armenian, another 'peripheral' language, the conclusion has been drawn that Indo-European did not complete the process of formal gender distinction in such words until after the departure of those swarms who were the linguistic ancestors of the speakers of the peripheral languages. This, however, can be upheld only by neglecting or rejecting the alternative explanation that in this instance formal development in Latin has obscured an original IE. distinction of gender. For Hittite the most recent authoritative grammar[1] states: 'Hittite distinguishes two genders, the *genus commune* (masculine-feminine, personal gender), comprising the old masculine and feminine, and the *genus neutrum*.' Moreover, in this instance the evidence of other peripheral languages is neglected: for instance, feminine formations such as *satī*, the Sanskrit present participle of *es* 'to be', bear the marks of antiquity upon them. Yet the nearest corresponding form found is the ἔασσα (< *esn̥tiə) of Greek, one of the so-called 'central' languages. It is difficult to reconcile this pattern of facts with the postulated earlier detachment of Indo-Iranian as one of the peripheral languages from the main body of the parent Indo-European (on other common features of Greek and Indo-Iranian such as the augment and the prohibitive particle see p. 31).

5. In vocabulary, too, scholars have claimed to detect in Latin similar marginal elements shared only with Celtic and languages at the eastern extremity of the IE. world. In particular much attention has been paid to words from the sphere of religion and law. The word *rēx* 'king' occurs in Celtic, e.g. in Ir. *ri*, feminine *rigain*, in Gaul, *Dumno-rīx* in the west (also as a Celtic loan-word in Germanic, e.g. our *bishop-ric*) and apart from this only in Indo-Iranian, e.g. Skt. *rājan-*, fem. *rājñī*. Many scholars again equate *flāmen* 'priest' with Skt. *brahmán*—but here the long quantity of the Latin -*a*- causes difficulties, so that others derive the Latin word from *bhlād-(s)men and quote as congeners Goth. *blōtan* 'worship' and ON. *blōt* 'offering, victim'. *iūs*, too, has been connected with Skt. *yōḥ* 'Hail!' and the Avestan *yaož-daδāiti* 'it makes pure'. The reconstructed parent form *yevos or *yovos is given the original meaning 'religious formula which has the force of law'. Hence *iūdex* meant 'he who pronounces the sacred formula' and *ius iurare* 'to pronounce the sacred formula'. The meaning has, of course, been secularized in Latin; so that Servius on Virgil, *Georgics* 1. 269 comments 'ad religionem fas, ad homines iura pertinent'. Yet another word from the same sphere is *lēx* 'law', the word for the single ordinances the collection of which constitutes

[1] J. Friedrich, *Hethitisches Elementarbuch* i. 14.

ius. Those who uphold the 'marginal' theory equate this with the Vedic *rājani* (locative) 'under the law of' and the Avestan *rāzan-* 'religious law'. But these Indo-Iranian words are better connected with the root *reg* 'stretch out, make straight, rule', and *lēx* is linked up either with the verb *lego* 'pick, choose', which, however, leaves the semantic development unexplained, or with the root **legh* 'lie, lay' which appears in our own word *law* (OE. *lagu*, etc.). Greater plausibility attaches to the equation of another legal-religious word, *crēdo*, with the Skt. *śrád-dadhāti*, which is compounded of a root noun **kred* and the verb **dhē* 'put, make', a compound which recurs in the Avestan *zrazdā* 'believe'. The noun **kred*, so this theory holds, once denoted the magical potency of a thing and the compounded verbal expression **kred-dhē* thus meant 'to put magical potency into a thing or person', from which operation the feeling of faith or trust was produced. But here again as with *iūs* the Roman usage is secular and matter-of-fact, like the corresponding noun *fidēs*. Cato, for example, lays it down *vilicus credat nemini* 'a bailiff should lend to nobody'. To say that the religious significance apparent in Indo-Iranian is the original one is, therefore, an assumption, and one might suggest with no less plausibility that **kred* once denoted something like 'pledge' deposited with another person, thus creating and symbolizing the relationship of faith and trust, an operation which holds good also of transactions with gods, perhaps on the principle of *do ut des*. Another legal word which shows a similar 'marginal' distribution is *rēs*. We find an exact correspondent in the Vedic *rām* (accusative) signifying 'wealth'. In Middle Welsh, too, *rai* has the meaning 'wealth, property'. In Latin the original significance 'property' is still apparent in expressions such as *res familiaris.*

It will be evident that such agreements between languages at opposite poles of the IE. world rule out the possibility of their being common innovations by these languages. The resemblances can be explained only on the supposition that the languages in question have preserved ancient features of the parent language. That such preservation is due to the 'marginal' position of these languages is a more doubtful proposition and involves a point of methodology which merits discussion, all the more because there has been much uncritical use of the principle of *marginalità* especially by the Italian school of 'neo-linguistics'. This principle has been derived from the geographical study of dialects. On a dialect map, such as the map for the Gallo-Romance words for 'mare', we see that the standard French *jument* extends over the greater part of central and northern France, *cavalla*, an intruder from Italy, occupies a compact region in the south, while the ancient word *equa* is found only in the Massif Central and a few isolated places in the Pyrenees and the Alps. Thus it is preserved in marginal and isolated areas. It is such maps which have led linguists to lay down the principle that marginal areas tend to be archaic. But we must bear in mind that in most countries where such geographical studies of language have been carried out we find a congeries of local communities organized in a national state where the dialects are exposed to the influence of an all-pervading standard language radiating from a centre of culture and administration. What it is essential to grasp is that the impingement of the standard language on a dialect speaker is a phenomenon of bilingualism—the dialect speaker at least understands the standard language. If his community is isolated, he has less contact with speakers of the standard language and so is less exposed to innovations proceeding from that source. It is equally true, of course, that he is deprived of the protective conserving influence of the standard language. But what is fundamental in linguistic geography is that a given speech area is the field of linguistic social forces which operate because speech is a mimetic process. Thus, they can operate (*a*) where there is mutual intelligibility, and (*b*) where geographical contiguity and means of communication ensure the necessary contact of speaker with hearer. If we now turn to the interrelationships of the IE. languages, we find that the bottom has dropped out of the principles of dialect geography. With reference to what *centre of innovation* can Sanskrit be dubbed a marginal area or a central area? We may ask central to what? Marginal to what? In the second millennium B.C. Indo-Iranian, Hittite, Greek, Latin, Celtic, and the rest existed in widely separated geographical regions; and they were mutually unintelligible languages. Where was now the organized IE. State? Where was the standard language based on the solidarity of a ruling class? Where the career open to well-spoken talent? Where, again, the pervading bilingualism, the contact of man with man, which alone makes possible the unbroken chain of mimetic processes which underlie the spread of linguistic forms from centres of innovation? A few examples chosen from words already discussed will make clear how inadmissible it is to apply the concepts of dialect geography to an entirely different set of linguistic facts. (1) *aqua* has been declared to be more archaic than (2) ὕδωρ because the latter is found in the central, i.e. innovating, area, as set out in the following table:

	Germanic	Latin	Osco-Umbrian	Greek	Hittite	Indo-Iranian
1.	Goth. *ahva*, etc.	*aqua*				
2.	Goth. *wato*, *watins*	*(unda)*	*utur*	ὕδωρ	*watar*	*udnah* (genitive)

According to this theory, Latin is more 'marginal' than Umbrian. But the concordance of Germanic, Hittite, and Indo-Aryan, along with the highly archaic declensional type instanced in Goth. *watins*, Hittite *wetenas*, Skt. *udnas*, shows beyond reasonable doubt that this word belongs to the oldest stock of IE. words. It remains to add that Celtic at the extreme western periphery has substituted a new word—Ir. *dobur*, W. *dwfr*, Br. *dour*, a word which also occurs in the Germanic place-name *Uerno-dubrum* 'alder-water'. Again, *ignis* is said to be older than *pur* because the latter is found in a central, i.e. innovating, area with the following distribution:

	Germanic	Latin	Osco-Umbrian	Balto-Slavonic	Greek	Indo-Iranian
1.		*ignis*		Lith. *ugnìs*		*agniḥ*
2.	*fire*		*pir*		πῦρ	

This time Germanic is less 'marginal' than Latin and here, too, Umbrian is grouped with Greek in sharing a word the presence of which in Tokharian (*puwar* 'fire') shows it to be of ancient stock. Once more Celtic (marginal and archaic!) goes its own way: Ir. *ten* 'fire', W. *tân*, Br. *tan*—a word which has been linked with Avestan *tafnah* 'heat'. The point need be laboured no further. It will be clear that the fundamental concepts of 'areal linguistics', centre of innovation, marginality, and the like, largely derived as they are from study of the behaviour of dialects in centrally organized states in which a given set of social forces governs the patterning of the linguistic data, have no validity when applied to a totally different set of linguistic facts, i.e. the relationships of mutually unintelligible languages scattered over immense geographical areas.

The methods and principles of linguistic geography apply strictly only to synchronic material collected in a closely cohering system of dialects. To permit the application of such principles to the IE. dialects we should first have to reduce the available material, attested at widely different dates and under different circumstances, to a synchronic basis. We must, for instance, first reconstruct the Celtic, say of 2000 B.C., and set it in the geographical position it occupied at that date, and similarly with all other major IE. groups. How difficult and disputed such reconstructions would be has already been indicated—the available material is too fragmentary. In particular, concordances and discordances of vocabulary among the IE. languages must be treated with the greatest caution. Languages easily replace their ancient inherited stock of words because of many linguistic and historical accidents. So it is that for only a tiny fraction of the vocabulary of any IE. language have reasonably sure etymological connexions been established and very few words indeed are represented in all the branches of the IE. family. The facts of survival for particular words might be represented by punching holes in cards which might then be classified by a Hollerith machine (though the size of the holes would have to vary to represent the different degrees of etymological plausibility!). In this way statistics might be obtained for the different interrelationships, some of which have been discussed above, and once the question of statistical significance is satisfactorily cleared up, it may be possible to give a more cogent interpretation of the facts of vocabulary. Meanwhile it is permissible to doubt whether in the case of *rēx*, *lēx*, and the rest we have elements of an archaic vocabulary which was preserved only by groups detached at an early date from the mass of the IE. nation and which has disappeared in the 'central' part of the domain. We must first ask, for instance, at what date did the foreign word βασι-λεύς appear in Greek, and what word did it replace? If it replaced *rēx* in the second millennium B.C. *after* the Greeks entered Greece, this innovation has nothing to do with the 'central' position of Greek among the IE. languages. It is a fact on all fours with the replacement of the words for 'water' and 'fire' in 'marginal' Celtic and the replacement of the ancient word for 'horse' *equus*, etc., by a derivative **hrossan*, 'the leaper, runner' in West Germanic (the ancient word survives in OE. *eoh*, Goth. *aíhwa*, OHG. *ehu*). The loss of *rēx* in Greek may well be a simple accident of vocabulary of

late occurrence and no more significant than the survival of the
no less important religious words σπένδω, λείβω, τέμενος, etc. (see
above).

The same criticism applies to other attempts to determine the
dialect affinities of Latin. It has been pointed out, for instance, that
certain IE. language groups tend to confuse *o* and *a*, e.g. IE.
*oktō(u) 'eight', Goth. *ahtau*, Lith. *aštuonì*, Skt. *aṣṭáu* This tendency, apparent in Indo-Iranian, Balto-Slavonic, Albanian, and
Germanic, is not found in Celtic, Italic, and Greek, and is regarded
as an important 'isogloss' for grouping the IE. dialects. The term
'isogloss', taken over from the linguistic geographers, is commonly
used by linguists to indicate a common feature which a number of
languages or dialects share. Here, too, it will be well to consider
the implications of this term before applying it uncritically to a
totally different body of material. On the linguistic maps which
plot the dialect variants of a given linguistic feature a line is
drawn linking localities which exhibit a common feature. We do so
because geographical contiguity and the known facts of social and
political history justify us in concluding that the separate phenomena are connected by chains of mimetic processes. The line, the
isogloss, is an expression of such *connectedness*. But to apply the
term 'isogloss' to resemblances detected in widely dispersed and
mutually unintelligible languages obscures a stage of the argument:
namely that the resemblances are such as to rule out the possibility
of independent development and to require the assumption of
linguistic contact and imitation at some historical period. A brief
reconsideration of the change of *o* to *a* is sufficient to explode the
fallacy underlying the use of the term 'isogloss' in this case. It is a
comparatively minor phonetic change which has recurred more
recently in certain English dialects (*strop* and *strap* are dialect
doublets) and again in certain varieties of modern American
English. The process is, therefore, of such a nature that we must
return an affirmative answer to the question which the comparatist
must constantly put: can this be accidental? This being so, the
change *o* to *a* must be stripped of the importance it has assumed
in discussions of IE. dialect relations, and it would be wiser to
eschew altogether the use of the term 'isogloss' with its implication of 'connectedness by chains of mimetic processes'.

Of perhaps greater significance as a criterion of relationship is the change provoked by the juxtaposition of two dental plosives in such words as *vid-tos* where the Latin treatment *vīsus* (< *vīssus*) resembles Germanic *wissan* (< IE. *wid-tan*) and contrasts with Gk. (ϝ)ιστός. This -ss- is found in Italic, Celtic, and Germanic, -st- in Greek, Slavonic, and Iranian. It is this last fact which weakens the significance of the phenomenon, for Indo-Aryan *sattá* differs from the closely related Iranian *hastō* (both < IE. *sed-to-*, cf. Lat. *sessus*), which suggests that the development is comparatively recent in Iranian and independent of the similar change in Greek and Slavonic. It has been suggested that in primitive IE. *t-t* evolved to *tst*, a phonetic combination which was simplified in a limited number of ways independently in the individual languages. This is not unplausible, and if true this phenomenon, too, cannot be regarded as an 'isogloss' implying 'connectedness by chains of mimetic processes' and hence as a pointer to dialect relationship.

More firmly established is the isogloss relating to the treatment of the Indo-European palatal plosives, which in a number of language groups appear as fricatives. The example usually quoted is the word for 'hundred'. The palatal appears unaltered in Lat. *centum*, Ir. *cet*, Gk. ἑκατόν (Gothic *hund* is obscured by the action of Grimm's Law), whereas Iran. *satəm*, Indic *çatam*, OSl. *sŭto*, Lith. *šimtas*, all exhibit a voiceless fricative. The phenomenon, of which this word serves as the type-example, is used to divide the IE. languages broadly into two main groups: a *centum* group comprising Celtic, Germanic, Italic, Greek, Hittite, Tokharian and a *satəm* group comprising Albanian, Balto-Slavonic, Armenian, and Indo-Iranian. It may be doubted whether this fact is of such cardinal importance, for this division is crossed by other isoglosses. For instance, the use of the augment to characterize past tenses is found in Greek, Armenian, and Indo-Iranian (e.g. ἔ-φερε, Arm. *e-ber*, Indic *á-bharat*), a group which again concur in their use of the prohibitive particle *mē*: Gk. μή, Arm. *mi*, Indo-Iranian *mā*.

We may now summarize the conclusions suggested by the foregoing examination of the evidence for the affinities of Latin. Little remains of the formula that Latin is descended from one of the *centum* dialects which with Germanic, Celtic, and 'Italic', and with Balto-Slavonic of the *satəm* group, shared in a period of common civilization from which Greek was excluded, entered into a prehistoric linguistic community with Celtic, and later formed with the 'Italic dialects' a 'common Italic', from which Latin emerged by differentiation.[1] What we have affirmed is that Latin is an IE. language with a complex pattern of relationships, exhibiting points of resemblance, varying from detail to detail, with most other IE. languages. Few of the facts of resemblance commonly accepted have been impugned. What we have ventured to reassess is the relative weighting of these facts in the calculus of 'relationship' and the translation of these observed points of linguistic similarity into hypotheses about prehistoric communities or 'nations'. How complicated the historical events which leave their traces in language may be we can sense from the example of English, which from one point of view is the language of 'Frenchified Norsemen re-Germanized'. We do not postulate a Germano-Romanic unity to account for the considerable resemblances between English and French. Nor do the common features of Latin and 'Italic' necessarily imply the one-time existence of a 'common Italic' from which both Latin and Osco-Umbrian have emerged by differentiation. As has been indicated, the minimum hypothesis required to account for the observed similarities between the two groups is the fusion of *one* 'Italic'-speaking group with the proto-Latins. The non-linguistic evidence which supports this minimum hypothesis will be discussed in the following chapter. Finally we have affirmed that *marginalità* is a *Sondergöttin* who can claim no worship outside her special functions in the linguistic geography of centrally organized states, and even there she is not wholly free from the suspicion of being a false goddess.[2]

---

[1] The latest edition of Meillet's *Esquisse* (1948) still contains the statement 'Le vieil italo-celtique et l'italique constituent des paliers entre l'indo-européen commun et le latin' (p. 127).

[2] This point will be discussed in the forthcoming second edition of my *An Introduction to Modern Linguistics* (Faber and Faber).

CHAPTER II

THE PROTO-LATINS IN ITALY

IN the previous chapter we were concerned with those features of
the Latin language for which we can detect resemblances in other
IE. languages. Such resemblances suggested certain conclusions
about the remote origins of Latin in an IE. dialect. But Latin as it
appears even in the earliest texts has an individuality so pronounced that it must be regarded as a language separate even from
its closest IE. neighbours, the 'Italic dialects', Oscan and Umbrian. This radical transformation of a western IE. dialect doubtless took place after the entry of the 'proto-Latins' into the
Apennine peninsula. Latin is, in fact, the linguistic product of the
manifold historical experiences of these proto-Latins in their new
Mediterranean environment. Thus our next task must be to trace
as far as we can the course and stages of the route which brought
this IE. people to their historical settlements in Latium and then
to separate out the various constituents which combined with the
inherited IE. elements to form the amalgam that is Latin.

The fund of common words possessed by Latins, Celts, and
Germans discussed in the previous chapter must reflect participation in a common cultural unity. It implies that the linguistic
ancestors of these three groups once lived in more or less close
geographical proximity. Thus the evidence suggests to the comparative philologist that the Latin language was brought into
Italy by invaders from western or central Europe. The philologist
unaided can give no further precision to the picture. But a movement of peoples of such historical importance is likely to be mirrored in the remains of material culture which it is the province of
archaeology to examine. So it is to the archaeologist that we must
first address our more exacting inquiries about the stages of the
route followed by the proto-Latins southwards into Latium, where
we find them at the beginning of the historical period. We can give
the archaeologist at least one important specification: the Latin
word for bronze, *aes*, is common Indo-European, while *ferrum* 'iron'
has no cognates even among the most closely related western

languages. This means in the first place that we can rule out the neolithic settlements of Italy as possible claimants to the proto-Latin title.

The use of bronze was introduced, by eastern Mediterranean standards, at a comparatively late date into Italy from cultures of central Europe. The process seems to have begun with the infiltration of Swiss lake-dwellers who established villages built on piles in the north-west Italian lake district just before 2000 B.C. This development, however, was of no great significance[1] in the history of the peninsula as a whole, and it is in the so-called *terramara* settlements found on both sides of the river Po that many scholars have sought the beginnings of the Indo-europeanization of Italy. The *terramara* ('black earth', the name given locally to the mounds of occupation debris) has been described as 'a sort of lake dwelling without the lake'. The typical settlement was stated to be trapezoidal in shape and enclosed by a rampart of earth and a moat. The burial rite represents a departure from the inhumation practised in neolithic Italy. The remains were cremated and placed in urns, which were then deposited in pile-raised cemeteries outside the village. Use of the horse is attested by the presence of perforated cheek-bits, an invention which occurs first in Europe in the Tószeg culture of western Hungary. A recent authority has stated that 'pottery, cremation-rite and the all-important horse can be accounted for better in this quarter than anywhere else'.[2] The pile-structure peculiarity is explained by the hypothesis that the *terremare* are the products of invaders from western Hungary practising 'urn-field' burial, who fused with hut-villagers and lake-dwellers round about 1500 B.C. Another peculiarity we must now mention is that in the *terramara* of Castellazzo di Fontanellato the settlement is so laid out that the two main ways cross each other at right angles and that secondary ways parallel to these subdivide the settlement into rectangular sections. Scholars were not slow to seize on the striking resemblances to the layout of a Roman legionary camp with its *fossa* and *vallum* and the rectangular intersection of the main ways, the *cardo* and the *decumanus*. Other

---

[1] Some scholars ascribe the pile-dwellings to an indigenous Mediterranean population.

[2] C. F. C. Hawkes, *The Prehistoric Foundations of Europe*, p. 342, a work to which I am deeply indebted.

analogies to Roman practices have been found in the *templum* surrounded by a ditch found on the east side of the *terramara* and further in the small ditch sometimes found at the foot of the rampart surrounding the settlement. The Romans, too, marked out with a furrow the limits of a temple (the use of a bronze plough is an indication of the antiquity of this ceremony), and the boundaries of the city itself were also so marked out. It is, moreover, such a 'pile-dwelling' culture that seemed to provide a plausible explanation of the Roman word for 'priest'. The bridge over the moat providing the ingress to such a settlement was a vulnerable place demanding magical reinforcement no less than the gate of the more usual type of human habitation. So it was that the word 'bridge-builder', *pontifex*, became specialized to designate the priest who conducted the magical ceremonies which were the essential accompaniment of bridge-making.

This seductive hypothesis which would trace the proto-Latins via *terremare* back to the urn-field culture of central Europe is unfortunately open to a number of objections. According to Pigorini's theory the *terramara* people moved southwards at the end of the Bronze Age and subsequently occupied the whole of Italy—they were, in fact, the ancestors of the Italic-speaking tribes. But if this were true, we should expect typical *terremare* to occur south of the Po valley in a chronologically graduated series. But in fact no *terremare* exist in Italy outside the Po basin. Still worse, the 'typical' *terramara* with its resemblance to the legionary camp is a generalization from the first one discovered, which in fact has turned out to be unique, those discovered later showing variations in both plan and shape. The so-called *vallum* may be nothing more than a local and occasional solution of the problem of flooding.

A further objection will become apparent if we turn to the archaeological history of Latium. Latium and the site of Rome were only sparsely, if at all, occupied in neolithic times, and the first evidence of any considerable settlement dates from the Iron Age. This Iron Age culture is closely related to that of Etruria and that of northern Italy which is called Villanovan. Thus what is crucial to the theory of the descent of the Latins from the *terra-maricoli* is that archaeological data should establish a link between the Bronze Age *terramara* and the Iron Age Villanovan cultures.

But no convincing proof for this link has been adduced and the Villanovans are now regarded by some authorities as fresh bands of invaders from Sudetenland and Hungary, some of whom in the eleventh century B.C. settled around Bologna while others pushed on into Etruria and Latium as far as the Alban Hills. Like their *terremare* predecessors they cremated their dead, and it is this form of burial rite which is found in the earliest Iron Age cemeteries of the Roman Forum. But this simple picture is obscured by the fact that this site has also produced graves in which the corpse was inhumed. These graves are later in date, but it would appear that no long time-interval separated the arrival of these two distinct groups on the site of Rome. This picture is repeated in the Alban Hills settlements, where the cremation graves are even earlier than those of the Forum. This accords with the legends of the foundation of Rome by settlers from Alba Longa. But if we equate the cremating Villanovans with the proto-Latins, who are the inhuming people who soon joined them in Latium? It has been pointed out that a renewal of the inhumation rite is observed also in 'geometric' Greece and further in the Danubian-Balkan area, where it has been attributed to the influence of the horse-riding Thraco-Cimmerian peoples. Thus the appearance in Italy of an inhuming people would find its place in a wider movement which received its impetus from the east. Among the results of this suggested eastern influence were the intensification of horse-breeding, of horse-riding, and the introduction of iron. That these were comparatively late innovations is suggested by the Roman ritual-prohibition of iron and riding. The eastern connexion is further pointed by the etymology most plausibly suggested for the Roman word for iron—*ferrum*. It has been derived from **bhersom* or **fersom* and brought into relationship with the Semitic words *barzel* (Hebrew-Phoenician), *parzlâ* (Syriac), *parzilla* (Assyrian), which were themselves possibly borrowed from some unknown Asiatic language. To return to Italy, we may now first note that the cremating graves (*pozzi*) are found in northern and central Italy but not in the south, whereas the inhumation graves (*fosse*) are found as far south as Calabria but not farther north than Populonia. If we now add the linguistic evidence, we observe that the Osco-Umbrian dialects enclose the Latin-Faliscan group and cut them off from northern Italy. So it is difficult to resist the conclusion that the speakers of Osco-Umbrian represent a somewhat later wave of inhuming invaders whose absence from northern Italy suggests invasion across the Adriatic rather than by the northern land route. And it may well be that the legends about the fusion of Sabine and Latin tribes in the early years of the city are the survival in folk-memory of the events reflected in the archaeological evidence.

Philological evidence is not lacking for the contribution of the Italic dialects and in particular of 'Sabine' to the making of the Latin language. We have in the first place the testimony of Roman writers themselves that *curis* (= *hasta*, Ovid, *Fasti* 2. 477), *dīrus* (= *malus*, Servius auct. on *Aen*. 3. 235), *cascus* = *vetus* (Varro, *L.L.* 7. 28), *februum* (Varro, *L.L.* 6. 13) were Sabine words. To these, by using phonological criteria, we may add words which show a medial *-f-* as opposed to the purely Roman *-b-*:[1] e.g. *bufa, būfō, forfex, inferus, rūfus, scrōfa, vafer*. The dialect origin of the last word is also suggested by its survival only in certain southern dialects of modern Italy. Similarly Italian *bifolco* must go back to an ancient dialect form **bufulcus* which shows a similar phonological divergence from the purely Roman *bubulcus*. Again, IE. *g^w* produced initial *v* in Latin but *b* in the other Italic dialects (see pp. 226 f.). Thus *bōs* (< **g^wōus*)and *botulus* stand revealed as dialect intruders which have displaced the expected descendants **vōs, *votulus*. Again IE. *q^w* yields Latin *qu-* but 'Italic' *p-*, a criterion which singles out *lupus, popa, popīna* (Roman *coquīna*), and *nefrundines* (Fest. 342. 35) as non-Latin dialect elements of the vocabulary. Among the aspirated consonants *gh* > *h* in Latin (p. 229), but a number of dialects of Latium exhibit *f* for *h*, e.g. Sabine *fircus, fēdus* (= *haedus*), *fasēna* (= *harēna*). (The ascription of *fel* and *fēnum* to Sabine rests on dubious etymologies.)

Sabine was further distinguished by its retention of intervocalic *-s-*, which became *-r-* in Latin (*ausum* = *aurum, fasēna* = *harēna*). Thus there is at least a presumption of Sabine origin for such Latin words as *caesar, caseus*, etc. The different treatment of the diphthongs provides yet another series of words of presumed Sabine origin. Thus from *ou, au*, and *ai* the Latin equivalents *ū, au, ae* contrast with Sabine *ō, ō, ē* respectively. Hence we might list as

[1] See pp. 227 ff.

Sabine such words as *rōbus, rōbīgō, lōtus* (as opposed to purely Roman *lautus*), *ōlla* (= *aul(l)a*), *lēvir* (< **daivēr*, cf. δαήρ 'husband's brother'). This last word yields yet another phonological criterion, the *l-* for the expected Latin *d-*. This phenomenon is seen also in *lingua* for *dingua*, *lacrima* for *dacruma*, and in *oleo* as contrasted with *odor* and *solium* as against *sedēre*.

It remains to add that for most of the phenomena discussed in the preceding paragraph we can achieve no more than 'a presumption of Sabine origin'. The words listed may have entered Latin at widely differing dates; and many of the characteristics we have used as criteria were shared by the country dialects of Latium, so that the words discussed may equally well be of rustic Latin origin (see below). Furthermore, we have little knowledge of peculiarities of the Sabine dialect which would enable us to distinguish this dialect from the mass of the Osco-Umbrian group. In fact the few remnants preserved of this dialect show that it was so strongly influenced by Latin at a very early date that its classification with the Osco-Umbrian group is itself a matter of doubt. However, that this is the correct classification is made probable by such Sabine names as *Pompilius* (which shows O.-U. *p-* for Lat. *qu-*) and *Clausus* (for *Claudius* with the non-Latin assibilation of *-di-* exemplified also in the word *basus = badius* 'chestnut-brown'). The name *Sabini* epitomizes the whole problem. Like *Sabellus* (**Safnolos*) and *Samnium* (**Safniom*) it contains the root *Saf*; and the presumption is that they called themselves *Safini*, whereas the form of their name familiar to us from the Roman writers embodies the typical Roman sound change *-b-* discussed above. Despite the meagreness of the evidence attempts have been made to trace not only a 'Sabinizing' vogue in Latin but even an 'anti-Sabine reaction'. This remains no more than an interesting speculation.

We may now attempt to draw up a provisional balance. It would appear that the IE. speech which we know in the historical period as Latin is an amalgam of two IE. languages introduced into Latium about 1000 B.C. by groups of invaders who had found their way by different routes from central Europe. These were doubtless considerably differentiated in language before their separate entries into Italy, but an approximation took place as the result of contiguity and fusion in the settlement of Latium and Rome in par-

ticular. It is this complicated series of events which lies behind the
linguistic affinities which comparative philologists have projected
into the more or less remote past as the period of 'common Italic'.

Illyrian

We must now complete our picture with a brief mention of
other IE. invaders of Italy and discuss what contributions they
made to the Latin language. Besides what we may describe as the
proto-Latin invasion of cremators by the northern land route and
the slightly later 'Osco-Umbrian' invasion of 'inhumers' across
the Adriatic, archaeologists list a third influx of people who show
distinct eastern influences and whose arrival brought a knowledge
of horse-riding as distinct from horse-driving and the intensification of horse-breeding.[1] The climax of this 'easternizing' influx
came in the second half of the eighth century B.C. The philological
counterpart of this archaeological evidence is provided by the
remnants on the east coast of Italy of dialects which are classified
as 'Illyrian'. The evidence for the Illyrian affinities of these dialects consists largely of place-names and personal or tribal names.
Thus the Iapyges are equated with the Iapydes of north Illyria,
the Calabri with the Illyrian tribe Γαλάβριοι. The Poediculi are connected with Ποίδικον in Noricum, the Apuli with Apulum in Dacia.
It is in ancient Apulia and Calabria that we find the densest agglo-
meration of such Illyrian names, more than half of the zoological,
place, river, mountain, and tribal names of this region having been
assigned to this source. Examples are *Brundisium*,[2] the harbour of
which is described by Strabo as resembling a stag's horns. Hence
the name of the town, for the gloss βρένδον· ἔλαφον is found in
Hesychius and elsewhere and a form of the word appears to survive in Albanian *brį-ni* 'horn'; *Salapia* and *Salapitani* are connected with the Illyrian Selepitani and contain the words *sal* 'salt'
and *ap* 'water'; *Odruntum* (Otranto) contains a Messapic word
odra 'water' (cf. ὕδωρ, etc.). From this focus in Apulia and Calabria Illyrian settlers appear to have reached Lucania and the
ager Bruttius, where considerable Illyrian elements have been

---

[1] See J. Wiesner, *Die Welt als Geschichte*, viii, 1942, pp. 197 ff.

[2] Other town-names derived by a similar suffix from animal names are *Ulcisia*
(Pannonia) < *ulc* 'wolf' and *Tarvisium* (Treviso) < *tarvo* 'bull'. See Bertoldi,
Colonizzazioni, p. 167.

detected in the onomatology: e.g. *Amantia* and the river name *Apsias* (closely resembling the Illyrian *apsus*). Moreover, Croton was established in territory said to have been earlier in possession of the Iapyges. Similar evidence is not lacking in Sicily, too, where, for instance, *Segesta* and *Egesta* contain the characteristic Illyrian suffix in -*est*- (cf. Τένεστ-ῖνοι and *Iadest-ini* in the Balkans). On the other hand, there appear to be no such Illyrian traces in Samnium and Campania. Thus the philological evidence supports the testimony of ancient authorities about the Illyrian origin of certain tribes of ancient Italy (e.g. the Daunii, the Peucetii, the Paeligni, and the Liburni). The direct evidence for the 'Messapic' or 'Iapygian' language consists of some 200 inscriptions, the majority of which are epitaphs containing only proper names, many of which are also found in Venetia (see below). Among the grammatical features we may single out for the nouns the genitive singular in -*ihi*, the dative plural in -*bas* (e.g. *logetibas*); the verbal system exhibits middle forms but no augment, and both the subjunctive and the optative moods are preserved. Important points of phonology are the change of IE. *o* to *a* as in Germanic, and the representation of *bh* and *dh* as *b* and *d*. Whether Illyrian was a *centum* or a *satəm* language is a matter of some dispute, but the balance of probability is on the *centum* side. This is further supported by the fact that the labio-velars were represented in Illyrian by labials.

A small number of Illyrian (i.e. Messapic) words has been detected in Latin: they are *blatea* 'swamp' (Illyrian *balta*), *deda* 'nurse' (cf. Gk. τήθη), *parō* 'a small ship' (derived via south Italian Greek παρών from Messapic), *gandeia* (a word, with the Illyrian suffix -*eia*, related to the Venetian *gondola*, which descends via Vulgar Latin *gondula*, ultimately from Venetic), and *hōreia* 'a small fishing-boat'. The importance of the horse is evidenced by the loan-word *mannus* 'pony' (Illyrian *manda*-), and the same word is contained in the name of the Messapian God Menzana, identified with Jupiter, to whom live horses were sacrificed (cf. further Virgil, *Aen*. 7. 691 *Messapus equum domitor*). It seems likely that Illyrians acted as intermediaries in the transmission of certain Greek words and culture to Italy. The very name *Graeci*, it has been suggested, was possibly an Illyrian name for a Greek tribe with whom they were in contact in north Epirus. The puzzling

Latin form of the name of Odysseus, *Ulixes*, may also find its explanation along these lines. (In this connexion we may note that it has been argued that the legends about Aeneas came to Italy and Rome through Illyrian intermediacy.) Similarly *lancea* 'spear, thrown with a thong', a word ultimately of Celtic origin, cannot be directly equated with Gk. λόγχη, though the resemblance can hardly be accidental. The change of *o* to *a* would be explicable if the word passed into Latin via Illyrian. In this way, too, an etymological relationship might be established between Gk. θώραξ and Lat. *lōrīca*, but the latter word is with greater probability connected with *lōrum*. The phonological difference between Lat. *ballaena* and Gk. φάλλαινα has also been explained by the postulation of Messapic intermediacy. Finally we must mention that from the Illyrian regions of eastern Italy there came to Rome the poets Ennius, his nephew Pacuvius, and Horace. In this connexion it is worth noting that *lāma* 'a swamp', a word attested only in Ennius and Horace, occurs as an element in place-names of the Illyrian areas of Italy.

Venetic

At the head of the Adriatic we find evidence of another people, the Veneti, whose language and culture show close resemblances to those of the Illyrian tribes just discussed. Famous for their horse-breeding, they sacrificed images of horses to their goddess Reitia. Like the Thracians they worshipped the hero Diomede, to whom they sacrificed white horses. The high boots worn by them are also ascribed to Thracian influence. Cremation with subsequent urn-burial is attested in this culture from the ninth century onwards, and it has been suggested that this people immigrated from the north-east under the pressure of the Thraco-Cimmerians. Onomatological study has revealed traces of the Veneti as far as Liguria (*Iadatinus, Crixia, Segesta*) and even in Latium, where the Venetulani (Pliny, *N.H.* 3. 69) are the people of **Venetulum*, a place-name meaning 'the place of the Veneti', just as *Tusculum* is 'the place of the Tusci'. *Carventum*, again, has been connected with Illyrian *caravantis* (**karvant-* 'rocky'), while *Praeneste* shows the familiar *-est-* suffix.

The affinities of the Venetic language are a matter of some

dispute. Proper names are notoriously an uncertain basis for the establishment of linguistic relationship, and in fact Venetic borrowed elements of its onomatology from Celtic (e.g. *Verkonzara*), Illyrian (e.g. *φohiios*), and Latin (e.g. *Appioi*). Recent monographs agree that Venetic had most points of agreement with Latin. The aspirated plosives *bh* and *dh* become *f* initially and *b*, *d* respectively between vowels precisely as in Latin. On the other hand, in the treatment of the palatal aspirate *gh* Venetic agrees with Illyrian, and the same is true of the sonant nasals *m̥*, *n̥* (> *am*, *an*, whereas in Latin they are represented as *em* and *en*). The sonant liquids *r̥* and *l̥*, however, show the same changes in Venetic, Illyrian, and Latin (> *or*, *ol*). Not much is known about the morphological system. In the noun Venetic shows a dative plural -*φos*, -*bos* which recurs in Celtic, Italic, Illyrian, and Indo-Iranian. The *o*-declension has the genitive singular in -*ī* which it shares with Latin-Faliscan, Celtic, and Illyrian. In the verbal system we find an aorist in -*to* (e.g. *zonasto* = *donavit*) which recalls that of Indo-Iranian and Greek (ἔδοτο).[1] In vocabulary the affinity with Latin is most striking. Thus the name of the goddess *Louzera* corresponds to the Latin *Lībera* and the word for 'free' has in both languages acquired the special meaning 'children' (*louzeroφos* = *līberis*). The Latin verbs *donare* and *faxo* are constructed precisely as Venetic *zonasto* and *vhaχsθo*, while the goddess mentioned above, Reitia, has an epithet *śahnate·i*, which, being interpreted as 'healer', finds its only etymon in the Lat. *sānare*. But yet another set of 'isoglosses' connects Venetic with Germanic. Perhaps most striking is the fact that the accusative singular of the first personal pronoun has acquired a guttural consonant from the nominative: thus *eχo*, *meχo* = Goth. *ik*, *mik* (also Hittite *uk*, *ammuk*). The pronoun of identity also shows a close resemblance in both languages: Ven. *sselboi sselboi* = 'sibi ipsi'; cf. OHG. *der selb selbo*. In the vocabulary, too, there is an important point of resemblance: if *a·hsu* is correctly interpreted as 'Herma', then it may well be cognate with the Germanic *ansu-* 'divinity'. That the Veneti were once in close geographical proximity to the Germans is suggested by the mention of *Venedi* by

---

[1] In *zonas-to* the personal inflexion has been added to a preterite form characterized by -*s*. Professor T. Burrow draws my attention to the similar forms in Hittite, e.g. *na-iš-ta* 'he led'.

ancient authorities in the region of the Vistula. The conflict of evidence suggests, then, that provisionally we should acquiesce in the verdict of a recent authority who holds that Venetic is an independent branch of Indo-European closely related to Latin and Illyrian with points of contact with Germanic, Celtic, and even Balto-Slavonic.

Sicel and 'West Italic'

The discussion of Illyrian leads now to a consideration of the Sicel language, the evidence for which consists of a few inscriptions, a considerable number of glosses, and personal and local names. While scholars are agreed that the language was Indo-European in character (the verbal form *esti* puts this beyond doubt), its closer affinities are a matter of some dispute. The onomatological evidence, suggesting links with Illyrian (e.g. the -*nt*- of *Agrigentum*, Σεργέντιον), is supported by the reference in Hesychius to Sicels in Dalmatia (cf. Pliny 3. 141). The implied movement of people from the Balkans across Italy into Sicily is, however, contradicted by the archaeological evidence, for although Sicel remains have been discovered in Bruttium, it is clear that this culture came *from* Sicily across the straits. More impressive is the evidence for a closer affinity of Sicel with Italic. According to some ancient authorities (Varro and Favorinus) the Sicels were once settled over the whole peninsula as far as Cisalpine Gaul, and these statements are supported by the widespread occurrence of certain personal and local names (e.g. *Sicilinum*). Certain items of the linguistic evidence seem to point in the same direction. Thus the name *Siculi* itself has the same formant as other early ethnica belonging to IE. tribes in Italy (e.g. *Rutuli*). The glosses (to ignore the inscriptions, the interpretation of which is a matter of guess-work in which scholars widely diverge) suggest in particular a closer connexion with Latin: e.g. ἀρβίννη 'flesh', cf. Lat. *arvina*; κάμπος 'hippodrome', cf. *campus*; κάτινος cf. *catinus, catillus*; *dōs* 'gift', cf. *dōs*; Δουκέτιος, a king of the Sicels, cf. *dux*; γέλα (= πάχνη), cf. *gelu*; πατάνιον, πατάνα, cf. *patina*. A well-defined semantic group is made up of the words referring to money and weights: μοῖτον = *mutuum*, νοῦμμος = *nummus*, λίτρα cf. *libra* (both from **liθra*), ὀγκία = *uncia*. The Sicel λέπορις, though this word was

Iberian in origin, was connected by Varro with Lat. *lepus*, with a comment which has some bearing on the present problem:

lepus quod Siculi quidam Graeci dicunt λέπoριν. A Roma quod orti Siculi, ut annales veteres nostri dicunt, fortasse hinc illuc tulerunt et hic reliquerunt id nomen (*L.L.* 5. 101).

This assertion that the Siculi were once established in Latium is supported by the fact that Sicans were among the thirty tribes who gathered annually for the worship of Jupiter Latiaris on the Alban Mount.

Now if a people of Latian origin had made their way into Sicily, we should reasonably expect to find some traces of their passage through, and perhaps settlement in, intervening territory. In fact some scholars[1] have sought to establish the existence of a 'West Italic' group of dialects comprising Latinian, Ausonian, Oenotrian, and Sicel. Campania before the invasion of the Samnites in the middle of the fifth century was inhabited by the *Opici*, whose language, it is claimed, differed in important respects from Oscan. Thus the local name *Liternum*, in Gk. Λευτερνο-, appears to be a derivative from the root **leudh*, which in Oscan should yield *Louferno*. 'Opic', further, presents the form *sum* as in Latin, whereas Oscan has *sim*. An important phonological criterion again links 'Opic' with Latin in contrast to Oscan: intervocalically it has voiced plosives where Osco-Umbrian has voiceless fricatives. Thus the names *Stabiae* and *Allibae* occur in the forms *Stafia* and *Allifae* in the Samnite period. Similarly the Mediterranean word *teba* 'hill' is later found in Samnite Campania in the form *tifa*. On the other hand, 'Opic' joins with Sicel in representing an ancient *dh* by *t* as against Latin *d/b*: e.g. *Liternum*. The Ausonians to the north of the Opici are included in this 'West Italic' group, but the only evidence offered is the tribal name *Rutuli*, which being etymologized as 'the red ones' is made to reveal the same phonological characteristic (*dh* > *t*) as 'Opic'. As for the Oenotrians of Lucania, the only linguistic evidence adduced is also a local name, *Ager Teuranus*, which apparently preserves the old diphthong *eu* and so is distinguished from 'Italic' in general where it developed to *ou*.

The evidence, then, on which the 'West Italic' hypothesis is

---

[1] Devoto, *Storia*, pp. 56 f.

erected is of the flimsiest character, nor is its interpretation un-
disputed. *Rutuli* is regarded by some scholars as Illyrian and
Λεύτερνοι as Aegean. It is certainly a plausible assumption that
the Sicule Αἴτνη means 'the burning mountain' and contains the
IE. root *aidh*, but the morphology of the postulated word **aidhena*
remains puzzling. Nor can pre-IE. place-names like *Tebae* suffice
to conjure up new Italic dialects. Sicel itself is relatively much
better attested, but even here the evidence is equivocal. In fact
it has been said that 'the resemblance (*scil.* between Sicel and
Latin) is almost too strong, so that it would be difficult to rebut
the contention that all the Sicel words which can be obviously
connected with Greek or Latin forms should be regarded as mere
borrowings'. Here we meet again the same methodological difficulty; common possession of elements of vocabulary, especially
those referring to matters of culture, trade, and commerce, does
not necessarily imply genetic relationship. The resemblances and
differences between *lībra* and λίτρα may in fact be explained by
various hypotheses of direct or indirect cultural contacts. So, too,
the common terms for weights and measures (e.g. *quincunx* appears as a 'calque' in Siceliote Greek πεντώγκιον, while τετρᾶς is
explained as a transformation of τετράς under the influence of
quadrans) may merely reflect early commercial relations between
Rome, southern Italy, and Sicily. It has, indeed, been suggested
that under the Etruscan domination of Rome there was a systema-
tization of weights and measures which influenced the other states
of Italy as a consequence of the prestige of Etruscan Rome,
evidenced, for instance, by the use of Latin letters and abbreviations
on the coins of central and southern Italy. We might compare the
use in English of the abbreviations *lb.* for 'pound weight' and £ for
'pound sterling', with their significance for Italian influences in
our commercial and financial history. Nor does the evidence of the
Sicel glosses fare better at the hands of the critics of the 'West
Italic' theory. ἀρβίννη is pronounced 'hyper-Latin', κάτινος a
Latin loan-word, while Lat. *latex* and *patina* are Greek loan-words
in Latin. Among other words often quoted as evidence for the
Sicel-Latin connexion κάρκαρον and κύβιτον are not directly assigned to Sicel and in any case they may equally well be Latin
loan-words. Thus effective doubt may be cast on all the items used

in support of the 'West Italic' theory, so that nothing more remains than the bare fact that Sicel was an IE. language.

Etruscan

Of far greater importance for the historian of Latin than these IE. occupants of Italian soil was a new people which made its appearance in Italy during the eighth century B.C. It would transgress the limits of this book to enter into the debate about the origin of the Etruscans. Let it suffice to say that both the main theses maintained in ancient times: (1) that they came from Lydia under the leadership of Tyrrhenus (Herodotus), and (2) that they were autochthonous and yet differed from all other peoples of Italy in their language and customs (Dionysius of Halicarnassus), still find their champions today. It is true the former thesis is supported by the fact that the Etruscans themselves believed they were Lydians who came by sea to Italy, that the chronology of the archaeological data shows a new civilization appearing in Tuscany during the eighth century and gradually expanding from north to south and from the coast towards the interior, not reaching Bologna for some two centuries after its first appearance, that matriarchal customs (evident, for instance, in the custom of writing matronymics on tombstones) find their counterpart in Lydia, and that the importance and technique of divination recall that of Babylonia. What is beyond doubt is that by the last quarter of the sixth century Etruscan power extended from the foothills of the Alps to Campania (where they failed in their efforts to reduce Cumae) and from Corsica to the Adriatic. Of more immediate interest to our present theme is that they were established at Falerii in the second half of the seventh century, and that subsequently they made themselves masters of a good deal of Latium, including Rome, where their rule lasted for a century and a half, their presence being attested, for instance, by the town-name Tusculum and the *vicus Tuscus* in Rome itself.

Of decisive importance in matters of town-planning, of political organization, religion, and higher cultural life, the Etruscan domination left surprisingly few traces in the Latin language[1] even in

[1] Cf. H. H. Scullard: 'Rome was never in any real sense an Etruscan city; she merely had on occasion to endure the domination of a small number of powerful families' (*A History of the Roman World 753–146* B.C., p. 37).

those spheres where their influence on Roman institutions and practices is most apparent, for all the most important political and religious functionaries are designated by Latin terms. But the intimate fusion of the Etruscan and Roman aristocracies is revealed in the nomenclature. On the Roman side the IE. system of a single compound name (e.g. *Hipparchus*) was replaced by the Etruscan custom of using *praenomen, nomen* (*gentile*), and *cognomen*, many of the names themselves being of Etruscan origin. Among these we may mention especially those in -*na*, -*erna*, -*enna*, -*inna*, e.g. *Vibenna, Caecina, Mastarna, Perperna, Velina*; cf. Etruscan *Porsenna, Porsina*. Another important group is represented by names in -*o* corresponding to Etruscan forms in -*u*; among these are the familiar names *Cato, Cicero, Piso,* and *Varro*. Many Latin gentile names in -*a* have a similar origin. Etruscan used this suffix to derive *cognomina* and *gentilicia* from *praenomina* (e.g. *velχa* from the praenomen *velχe*, cf. Lat. *Casca: Cascus*). If we now recall the fact that many localities are named after families (*Tarquinii, Falerii, Vei, Corioli*, etc.) and that many names in -*a* are used as *gentilicia, cognomina,* and place-names (*Atella, Sora, Acenna,* etc.), and further that many Etruscan parallels enable us to extract from the series *Romaeus Romatius rumate rumaθe* the basic family name *ruma*, it is difficult to resist the conclusion that the city *Roma* too, like *Acenna* and the rest, derives its name from an old Etruscan family. This conclusion is further strengthened by an examination of the name of one of the mythical founders of Rome—*Rĕmus*. First we recall that the tradition gives to the *habitatio Remi* the name *Remōna*; and the place 'ubi Remus de urbe condenda fuerat auspicatus' was called *Remora* (cf. Ennius: 'certabant, urbem Romam Remoramve vocarent'). Now *Remona* (Gk. 'Ρεμώνιον) is the 'settlement' of the **remu* or *remne*, just as Ταρχώνιον is the town of the *tarχu* or *tarχna*, and *Remoria* shows an -*r* suffix frequent in Etruscan. Thus Remus, the eponymous ancestor of the Etruscan *remne*, stands revealed as Etruscan no less than the name of the city to which history denied his name. It should be emphasized that there are no linguistic parallels which would support the view that *Rĕmus* is formed from *Rōma* by 'false analogy'. It is possible, too, that at least three of Rome's seven hills were named after Etruscan families. For the *mons Palatinus* we have the series of

Etruscan names *Palla, Palanius, Palinius*, etc. (cf. *Sulla, Sulla-nius, Sullatius; Volca, Volcanius, Volcatius; Bulla, Bullanius, Bul-latius*). The Etruscan origin of the *mons Velius* is apparent from the cluster *vel, velni, velus, velie, Velenius, Vellenius, Velianius*. For the *mons Caelius* we have the Etruscan name *caile vipinas* (cf. the name *M. Caelius Tuscus*). In addition to these the name of the valley between the Viminal and the Esquiline hill, the *Subura,* is possibly connected with the Etruscan names *Zupre, supri*.

The importance of the Etruscan contribution to the political organization of Rome is evidenced by the fact that the three oldest centuries of *equites* bear Etruscan names: *Ramnes, Tities, Luceres* ('omnia haec vocabula Tusca', Varro, *L.L.* 5. 55), and that Etruscan origin is also probable for three of the 'rustic' tribes—*Lemonia, Pupinia*, and *Voltinia*. Etruscan origin has also plausibly been claimed for the names given to the *equites* of regal times—*flexuntes* (also *flexuntae*), *celeres*, (for which formation compare *Luceres*) and *trossuli*. Morphological and semantic criteria also suggest that *satelles* 'body-guard' is an Etruscan loan-word: the institution of the bodyguard was introduced into Rome by Etruscan nobles, tradition associating it in particular with Tarquinius Superbus. Two other military terms without IE. etyma show similar morpho-logical characteristics—*mīles, mīlitis*, and *vēles, vēlitis*, the latter being attributed to the Etruscans by the ancient authorities. Apart from this Etruscan made remarkably little contribution to the vocabulary of Latin. The list which follows consists chiefly of words denoting minutiae, among which those referring to the theatre and other amusements are noteworthy: *cacula* 'soldier's servant' (Etr. **cace, *cacla*); *caerimōnia* (possibly from **caerimo*, a word resembling *lucumo* in its formation; perhaps the ancient authorities were correct in deriving it from the Etruscan town of Caere); *crumīna* (cf. Gk. γρυμέα, see below); *cupencus* 'priest of Hercules' (Etr. *cepen* 'priest'; but a Sabine word according to Servius); *fala* 'scaffolding'; *fenestra* (Etr. **fnestra*); *genista* 'broom'; *hister, histrio* ('hister Tusco verbo ludio vocabatur', Livy 7. 2. 1); *lanista* 'trainer of gladiators'; *laniēna* 'butcher's stall'; *lepista* 'drinking vessel'; *rabula* 'pettifogging advocate' (Etr. *rapli*); *satura* 'sermo' < *satir* 'speak, talk'; *servus* (cf. the Etruscan names *Serui, Serue*); *spurius* (cf. *spurcus* 'impure' and the name *Spurinna*);

sūbula ('subulo dictus, quod ita dicunt tibicines Tusci' (Varro, *L.L.* 7.35)). To these we may add the divine names *Angerona* (from Etr. *ancaru* 'goddess of Death') and *Libitīna* 'goddess of corpses', 'funeral apparatus', 'bier', etc. (cf. Etr. *lupuce = mortuus est*(?)), and two derivatives from such names: *aprīlis* (Etr. *apru(n)* from Gk. Ἀφρώ, an abbreviated form of Ἀφροδίτη) and *autumnus* (from Etr. *autu*, cf. Lat. *Autius*), with a widespread Aegean-Anatolian suffix seen also in *Picumnus*, *Vertumnus*, and further in pre-Hellenic place-names such as Αἴσυμνος, Λάρυμνα, etc. It remains to add that such loan-words contained formal elements such as suffixes which were naturalized in their new habitat and so were attached to pure Latin words. Among such Etrusco-Latin hybrids we may mention *lev-enna*, *soci-ennus*, *doss-ennus* (a character of the Atellan farce, based on *dossus*, a popular form of *dorsum*), *fav-issa* (*favea*+the common Etruscan suffix seen, for instance, in *mantissa* 'make-weight').

Besides these direct contributions from their own language the influence of the Etruscans is also apparent in the twist they gave to Greek loan-words which found their way into Latin. These will be best discussed within the framework of the whole Greek contri-bution to early Italic civilization.

Greek

Throughout their history the civilization and language of the Romans were profoundly influenced by the Greeks. We shall have occasion in later chapters to discuss the successive stages. For the moment we are concerned with the earliest stratum of the Greek elements in Latin. It was in the eighth century that the Greeks began their colonization of southern Italy and Sicily. The first settlement, doubtless preceded by trade relations, was curiously enough the most remote from the homeland, Cyme being planted about 750 B.C. by colonists from Chalcis in Euboea. Other Chalcidian colonies soon followed, e.g. Naxos, Zancle, and Rhegium. These colonists brought with them a dialect of the Attic-Ionic group. Syracuse, however, was founded by Corinthians, Gela by Cretans and Rhodians, all these speaking Doric dialects. On the east coast of Italy colonization began from the cities of Achaea on the north coast of the Peloponnese, the first colony being Sybaris, followed

later by Croton. Tarentum, on the other hand, was Sparta's sole
effort at colonization in these parts and the tradition is that the
colonists consisted of expelled pre-Dorian elements of the Laconian
population. These Greek cities with their boundless energy and
superior culture had much to offer to the other peoples of Italy, and
their influence is apparent in not only the arts of material civilization but also in religion, myth, and language. In particular the
evidence of Etruscan art reveals that many figures of the Greek
pantheon and mythology were familiar to the Etruscans by 600 B.C.
On the other hand, it has been stated that 'in no single case can it
be established that immediate contact took place between Rome
and Greece or a Greek colony'.[1] So it was through non-Roman intermediaries that the elements of Greek culture and their corresponding names reached the Romans at this early period.

Certain philological criteria applied to these words will enable us
to draw rough distinctions of chronology and dialect. In the first
place the Attic-Ionic group is distinguished from other Greek dialects by the change $\bar{a} > \eta$ (e.g. μᾱ́τηρ > μή́τηρ). This means that
the loan-words in Latin which exhibit $\bar{a}$ (e.g. *mācina* < μᾱχᾰ́νᾱ)
must derive from the Doric dialects of Italy. Another useful
chronological indication is provided by the treatment of the di-
gamma (ϝ, pronounced like the English *w*). This sound had disappeared in Attic-Ionic before the time of the earliest inscriptions;
in certain Doric dialects it was more persistent, but even here the
sound disappeared soonest in the intervocalic position. An early
date must therefore be assigned to words like *Achīvī* (< Ἀχαιϝοί)
and *olīva* (< ἐλαίϝα).

The treatment of internal vowels and diphthongs in such loan-
words provide us with further evidence of date, for such sounds in
Latin were early subjected to processes of weakening, possibly as
early as the fourth century B.C. (but on this see pp. 219 ff.). Thus
loan-words like *camera* (καμάρα), *phalerae* (φαλάρα), *trutina* (τρυτάνα),
mācina (μᾱχᾰ́νᾱ), *balineum, balneum* (βαλανεῖον), *talentum* (τάλαντον), Tarentum (Τάραντα), etc., must have entered the language
before these sound changes ceased to operate and so are clearly
distinguishable from later loan-words such as *cerasus* (introduced
by Lucullus in 76 B.C.), which do not exhibit this phenomenon.

---

[1] Altheim, *History of Roman Religion*, p. 149.

We may presume, too, that Greek words whose Latin form betrays Etruscan influence belong to the time of Etruscan supremacy in Latium. Such intermediacy is betrayed by uncertainty in the rendering of plosive consonants, as evinced, for instance, in *amurca* (ἀμόργα with a change in the internal vowel comparable to *alumnus* < *alomnos*), *gubernare* (κυβερνᾶν), *Agrigentum* (Ἄκραγας); or again by the change of quantity in *crĕpĭda* (κρηπῖδα). Here, too, as with direct borrowings from Etruscan, the only evidence of Etruscan intermediacy is often circumstantial. Thus *sporta* is obviously connected with Gk. σπυρίδα. The evidence for Etruscan intermediacy lies in the substitution of *t* for *d* and *o* for *u*, which we find again in *cotoneum* < κυδώνιον. *gruma*, again, is derived from γνῶμα (cf. *Memrun* < Μέμνων), *triumpus* from θρίαμβος, and *catamītus* from Γανυμήδης. In the case of *cisterna* (κίστη) and *lanterna* (λαμπτήρ) it is the addition of a familiar Etruscan suffix which betrays the route by which the words reached Latin. With these we may compare *crēterra* = κρητῆρα. In the case of *gutturnium* or *cuturnium* 'vas quo in sacrificiis vinum fundebatur', both phonology and morphology show that the Gk. κωθώνιον was first distorted by Etruscan speakers before reaching Rome. In the case of this word we may note further its semantic sphere, for many words denoting pottery and utensils were given to the Romans by the Etruscans. Thus perhaps both *urna* and *urceus* have a distant connexion with Gk. ὔρχη. Another semantic group we may notice here is made up of words connected with theatrical performances. We have already seen that *hister* and *histrio* derive from Etruscan, and it is likely that *persōna* is an Etruscan word in which the suffix -ōna has been added to the word φersu, itself possibly an Etruscan deformation of πρόσωπον. Even the word *scēna* may have come by the same route, for it is sometimes spelt *scaena*, and that Etruscan sometimes rendered *ā* by *ae* is apparent from *Calaina* (for Γαλάνā), and *laena*, an article of clothing, if this is borrowed from Latin *lāna*. Other confirmatory examples of the change are *Saeturnus*, *Aesculapius* (Αἰσκλαπιός) (an example of the reverse substitution is seen in *crāpula* for κραιπάλα). *paelex* for παλλακή is more complicated since the word may be of Mediterranean stock. This may be true also of *caupo*, the meaning of which corresponds exactly to καπηλός, and the substitution of *au* for *a* suggests Etruscan intermediacy. The difference of the suffix, however, rules out Greek as the creditor language and it may well be that both Greek and Etruscan have drawn on native Mediterranean vocabulary, the latter passing the word on in its turn to Latin. An interesting case has been made out for the origin of *elementum* in a Gk. **elepanta* 'ivory letter', in which the change of *p* to *m* was an Etruscan contribution for which we have at least a partial parallel in the Praenestine *Melerpanta* for Βελλεροφόντης. Yet another Latin word shows a similar affinity to Greek: *forma* has been derived from μορφή via an Etruscan **morma* with a substitution of *m* for φ, (the dissimilation of *m-m* to *f-m* is paralleled by *formica*: μύρμηξ and *formido*: μορμώ). Finally we see a linguistic indication of the part played by Etruria even in the formation of Roman legends: the cognomen of bridge-keeping Horatius, *Cocles* 'the one-eyed', is nothing more than the Etruscanized form of Κύκλωψ, again with *o* for *u*.

Celtic

Etruscan power, weakened at the centre by internal dissension, received its death-blow at the hands of yet another group of IE. invaders. The Celts, from their home around the Upper Rhine and Danube had as early as 900 B.C. crossed the Rhine into what was later known as Gallia. The Celtic invasion of Italy, however, took place not via the Western Alps (so Livy 5. 33 f.) but via the Brenner from the area of the Upper Rhine towards the end of the fifth century B.C. In Italy they made themselves masters of the Northern Plain between the Apennines and the Alps, where their remains overlie those of Etruscan civilization. They pushed back the Etruscans and the Umbrians and sent marauding bands throughout the length of the peninsula, sacking Rome itself in 390 B.C. They do not seem to have established permanent settlements anywhere in Italy except in that part known as Cisalpine Gaul, and even here they were easily absorbed by the peoples among whom they settled, so that Gallic had ceased to be spoken in Italy by 150 B.C. (Polybius 2. 35. 4). This linguistic instability combined with their ignorance of the art of writing may account for the fact that only three inscriptions written in Gallic have been found in Italy, and only one of these in Cisalpine Gaul. The Gauls, speakers of that variety of Celtic known as Mainland Celtic, which is distinguished *inter alia* by its substitution of p for IE. q^w, contributed to Latin a number of words drawn chiefly from the following semantic categories:

Riding, driving: *benna* 'a two-wheeled cart with a wicker-work body', *carpentum* 'two-wheeled covered wagon', *carrus* 'four-wheeled wagon', *cisium* 'a light two-wheeled vehicle', *covinnus* 'scythed-chariot', *essedum* 'war-chariot', *petorritum* 'four-wheeled wagon', *reda* 'travelling coach', *verēdus* 'horse' (it is from the Low Latin hybrid word *paraverēdus* that German *Pferd* is derived). *mannus* is stated by Consentius to be a Gallic loan-word, but it is more probably Illyrian (see above, p. 40, and Ernout–Meillet, *s.v.*).

Warfare: *cateia* '(sort of) boomerang', *gaesum* 'javelin', *lancea* (see above), *parma* 'a light shield', *sparus* 'spear', 'lance'. *caterva = legio* is sometimes quoted as a Gallic word in Latin (Isidorus 9. 3. 46), but it may be a native Latin word belonging to the same family as *cassis* and *catena*.

Clothing: *birrus* 'hooded cloak', *bracae* 'breeches' (this word was borrowed by Celts from Germanic), *sagus, sagum* 'tunic'.

Miscellaneous: *alauda* 'crested lark', *betulla* 'birch', *bulga* 'a leather bag' (cognate with the Germanic words of which Engl. *belly* is a representative). Of particular interest is *ambactus* 'serf', a word used by Ennius. Cognate with the W. *amaeth* 'serf', this word found its way into Germanic and it is from the Gothic *andbahti* (= German *Amt*) that the Fr. *ambassade* is derived.

Lepontic

On Gallic territory of northern Italy traces of a mysterious people practising inhumation burial have been discovered near Bellinzona and the sites have yielded inscriptions written in the so-called 'Lepontic' language. This language, unquestionably Indo-European, belongs to the *centum* group and like Gallic changed IE. q^w into p (if enclitic *-pe* is really equivalent to the Lat. *-que*). Like Celtic and Latin it forms the genitive singular of the *o*-stems in *-ī*. A further striking peculiarity is that the nominative singular of the *n*-stems ends in *-u* as in Gallic. It has further been claimed that of some seventy proper names at least fifty find some counterpart in Gallic. On the other hand, many place-names of the region exhibit the suffix *-asco, -asca*. This suggests at least a 'Ligurian' substratum (see below), but at the time of these inscriptions (second century B.C. onwards) all this part of Italy had been overrun by Gauls and some authorities maintain that 'Lepontic' should be regarded as a Celtic dialect. Other scholars lay more emphasis on the non-Celtic characteristics (e.g. the alleged preservation of the initial *p-* in *pala* 'gravestone(?)' and the difference in the system of personal names) and would describe the language as Celto-Ligurian. But this difference between the two conceptions, apart from questions of detail, would appear to be one of emphasis, for they both agree in ascribing the Lepontic inscriptions to a Celtic people who settled in what was originally 'Ligurian' territory.

Ligurian

Among the ancient peoples of the western Mediterranean we find the Ligurians. Whether they were indigenous or were yet another tribe of IE. invaders is a disputed question which we must briefly consider. In historical times they appear as a typical 'relict' people inhabiting poor and inaccessible lands to which they had been confined by the pressure of more powerful peoples. But it is evident from the combined testimony of ancient authorities and place-names that they once extended over a much greater area of western Europe, reaching into the plain of the Po and as far down as Etruria and, according to some authors, even Rome and Latium. This area corresponds roughly with the distribution of place-names formed with the suffix *-sc-* (e.g. the river-names *Vinelasca*, *Tulelasca*, *Neviasca*, etc.). We hear further of Ligurians in Corsica; and even the Siculi are stated to have been Ligurians driven into Sicily by Umbrians and Pelasgi. In both Sicily and Liguria we find the place-names *Entella*, *Eryx*, and *Segesta*. The language of the Ligurians has been described as Indo-European 'beyond all question'[1] on the grounds that the Ligurian words such as *asia*, λεβηρίς 'cony, rabbit', *saliunca* 'valerian' are all Indo-European, and many of the place-names of the district are also Indo-European: e.g. the river *Porco-bera* salmon-bearing', the mountain *Berigiema* 'snow-bearing', the town *Bormiae* 'warm springs', all of which are traces of an IE. dialect which on the evidence of phonology can be neither Italic nor Celtic. This view that Ligurian is Indo-European conflicts with the archaeological evidence, for it implies an invasion, presumably from the Italian lake district, of which there is no trace in the prehistoric cultures of the region. This throws us back

---

[1] Whatmough, *Foundations*, p. 129.

on the hypothesis that Ligurian was spoken by the descendants of the neolithic inhabitants of the region. That in fact the Ligurians were early occupants of their historical habitat is suggested by linguistic relationship to Sicel which was discussed above. So it has been affirmed with no less confidence that Ligurian is non-Indo-European (H. Krahe), and that the IE. character of some of the place-names is to be explained by the hypothesis that an IE. people superimposed itself at some stage on the neolithic population. The dispute appears to resolve itself into one of definition and date. Those who uphold the IE. character of Ligurian would presumably admit that this implies invasion and subjugation of the previous population, who for their part are held to have migrated in neolithic times from north Africa to Italy by way of Spain and France (*O.C.D.* 'Ligurians'). The only question is on whom to bestow the title 'Ligurians', and further at what date did that people arrive to whom we must ascribe the IE. words and place-names admitted by both sides. We leave the question with a word of warning. The interpretation of prehistoric place-names is largely a matter of guesswork. How uncertain it is we may illustrate from a key-example. The mountain name *Berigiema* mentioned in the *Sententia Minuciorum* has, as we saw, been analysed as *Beri-giema* 'bearing snow' (*bher*+**gheiem*). This would imply that the people who gave it this name spoke a *centum* language, but that its treatment of the aspirated stop (*bh* > *b*) excludes its membership of the Italic group. All this, however, falls to the ground if, as one authority has suggested, we must analyse the word as *Berig-iema*.

The Mediterranean Substratum

From the Ligurians we now turn our attention to the linguistic contributions made by the native Mediterranean peoples in whose land the proto-Latins established themselves. Here we are at once faced with a methodological difficulty, for we have little or no direct knowledge of the pre-IE. languages of Italy. It will not suffice to regard all Latin words without an IE. etymology as pre-Indo-European. The cognates in other languages may have been lost or the Latin word transformed by the countless forces of innovation at work in every language, nor can we ignore the possibility of borrowing from unknown languages before the proto-Latins invaded Italy, nor again, of independent creation. It is, however, possible to reach tolerable certainty with some classes of words. It has been observed that substratum words denoting features of topography and indigenous animals and plants are everywhere particularly tenacious. Moreover, such words transcend linguistic frontiers and their non-IE. character is often revealed by the fact that though they are similar they cannot be reduced to a common parent form. A particularly crass example is provided by the word for the metal 'lead'. The variations in the Greek dialect forms (μόλυβδος, μόλιβδος, μόλιβος, βόλιμος) alone are indicative of the cultural loan-word. In Lat. *plumbum* the resemblance though vague is unmistakable.[1] In the most favourable cases indigenous words also exhibit peculiar features of morphology which put their provenance beyond reasonable doubt. This is true, for instance, of the word *vaccīnium*. The corresponding Greek word is ὑάκινθος. Here we find a general resemblance in the root part of the word, but the differences are such as to exclude direct borrowing in either direction. Moreover, the Greek word has the suffix -ινθο- which occurs in many names of places and cultural objects (e.g. Κόρινθος, ἀσάμινθος 'bath tub') which are ascribed to the pre-Greek population of the Aegean. *vaccīnium* may, therefore, be attributed with a fair degree of certainty to the Mediterranean substratum. In this category of botanical names we may list *menta* (Gk. μίνθη), *viola* (ϝίον), *lilium* (λείριον), *cupressus* (κυπάρισσος with the Aegean suffix -σσο- also found in place-names), *laurus* (the Greek variants show the marks of the foreign loan-word: δάφνη, δαῦκον, δαύχνα, λάφνη), *fīcus* (σῦκος, τῦκον, Arm. *thūz*), *citrus* (κέδρος).

While indubitably ultimately traceable to a common Mediterranean source, these words make it clear that there is no justification for postulating linguistic uniformity in the shape of 'a Mediterranean language' before the arrival of the various IE. tribes.[2] In the

---

[1] *plumbum* has plausibly been ascribed to Iberian and brought into connexion with Basque *berun*. Such a 'colonial' word may assume different guises in the borrowing languages.

[2] According to H. Krahe (*Indogermanisierung*, pp. 32 ff.) we should distinguish two areas of the pre-Indo-European speech in Italy. Central and Southern Italy and Sicily on the evidence of characteristic place-names in -ss- (*Tylēssos* in Bruttium, *Krimissa* in Southern Italy, *Telmēssos* in Sicily), in -νθ- (*Kokynthus* in Bruttium), etc. belong to the Aegean-Anatolian area. Krahe links this up with the statements of the ancient authorities (e.g. Dionysius of Halicarnassus i. 23)

word for 'rose', for instance, there is a tolerable resemblance between Gk. ϝρόδον and the Iranian *wŗdi* (Persian *gul*), which appears as a loan-word in Arm. *vard*. In Lat. *rosa* the medial consonant is puzzling and implies an intermediate source in which the -*d*- had been assibilized.[1] Another peculiar feature is that this intervocalic -*s*- has been exempted from the rhotacism normal in Latin words (see p. 230).

Attempts have been made, especially by Italian scholars, to isolate the characteristics of the Mediterranean languages. Thus from the alternation of consonants exhibited, for instance, in *Padus*: *Patavium*: *Bodincus*, or *Bergomum*: *Pergamum* deductions have been made about the nature of the 'Mediterranean' occlusive consonants. But the frequent occurrence elsewhere of such alternations (e.g. in the Germanic dialects *Beet/bed*, *Ding/thing/ting*) should tighten the rein of caution on such flights of fancy. As for vocabulary, the modern dialects, especially of the Alpine regions, have been scoured for evidence of pre-IE. words and scholars have isolated a whole series referring to peculiarities of the terrain which are strikingly similar in phonetic structure. Such are *ganda* 'scree', *alba* 'rock', *balsa* 'marsh', *gava* 'watercourse', etc. These have been compared with Etruscan words such as *lada* 'woman' and the conclusion is drawn that stems of this nature were prevalent in Mediterranean languages. This is not an unplausible origin for Latin words like *bāca* 'berry', for, as we saw above, words connected with viticulture are of Mediterranean origin. Varro, *L.L.* 7. 87, tells us 'vinum in Hispania bacca' and it is tempting to recall in this connexion the name of the wine-god Βάκχος.

Similar methods have been used in the attempt to give greater precision to the notion of Mediterranean dialect areas. Thus a western Mediterranean suffix -*it*- has been isolated from place-names *Gaditanus*, *Iliberritanus*, *Panormitanus*, etc. Sardinian suffixes in -*arr*, -*err*, -*urr* have been found 'in slightly divergent forms' in Sicilian place-names like Ὕκκαρα, Ἴνδαρα, Λιπάρα, and being brought into relationship with the Roman *suburra* have suggested

about the presence of 'Pelasgians' in various parts of central and southern Italy. In the western part of the Mediterranean one pre-Indo-European people was the 'Ligurians' (see above).

[1] Assibilization of *d* took place in Oscan and Messapic.

the ascription of the ancient Latin words *acerra* 'incense-box' and *vacerra* 'post', 'log' to a western Mediterranean source.

From the confused and fragmentary evidence discussed in the preceding pages we may now sketch a tentative picture of the massive movements of peoples which led to the Indo-Europeanization of the Apennine peninsula and summarize the manifold influences which shaped the early history of the Latins and their language in their new home. The first invaders of IE. speech from central Europe were the ancestors of the Sicels. The next arrivals were the proto-Latins followed by the speakers of the 'Italic dialects'. On these peoples the various tribes of Illyrian invaders impinged, administering perhaps the shock which drove the proto-Latins from their settlements in the Po basin to their historical home in Latium. Once they had blended in their new settlements with a people of the Osco-Umbrian group, a new organizing and civilizing force was brought to bear in the shape of the Etruscans. How far, during the period of Etruscan power, this welter of peoples was drawn together into a new unity may be divined, as we have seen, from a study of personal names, on which Krahe (*Indogermanisierung*, pp. 58 f.) has written:

within the system of three names an Etruscan may bear Latin or Umbrian or Illyrian names, or a Latin may have an Etruscan or Illyrian name, an Illyrian an Oscan or Celtic or Etruscan name, and so on. Indeed it can happen, although rarely, that each of the three names, *praenomen*, *nomen*, and *cognomen* may belong to different languages. This illustrates most clearly that a process of fusion on the greatest scale was beginning and ultimately reached completion.

Finally it was under Etruscan tutelage that the Romans began that apprenticeship in the 'arts and disciplines' of Greece which was to last throughout their cultural history.

CHAPTER III

THE LATIN DIALECTS AND THE EARLIEST TEXTS

WE have now examined the evidence bearing on the prehistory of the Latin language and come to the tentative conclusion that the proto-Latins were an IE. tribe originating in central Europe which entered Italy towards the end of the second millennium B.C. Arriving in Latium about the tenth century B.C. they settled Latium in scattered rural communities (or *populi*) which combined in loose confederations. Rome itself originated in a *synoecismus* of cremating Latin and inhuming Sabine folk. In political matters these various Latin *populi* combined on terms of equality, a state of affairs which continued, except for the period of Etruscan domination, until the fourth century, when Rome gradually asserted herself over her weaker brethren, finally reducing them in 338 to the status of subject allies. It was this political supremacy of Rome which gradually led to the replacement of the dialects of Latium by the Latin of Rome. But that Roman was originally merely one of many Latin *patois* is evident from the earliest inscriptions in the Latin language.

For instance, among the inscriptions found in the territory of Falerii (Città Castellana) is one reading *foied vino pipafo cra carefo = hodie vinum bibam cras carebo*. Here we have exemplified a phonological peculiarity which distinguished Roman Latin from the country dialects and indeed from the other Italic dialects, that is the change of -*bh*- to -*b*- between vowels as opposed to the rustic -*f*-. A parallel development affected original -*dh*-, Roman -*d*- corresponding to Faliscan -*f*-, if *efiles* is correctly interpreted as *aedilis*. Despite its agreement on this point with Osco-Umbrian Faliscan was a Latinian dialect since *qu* appears for *q^w*, which in Osco-Umbrian became *p* (see above). Other phonological points distinguishing Faliscan from Latin are its treatment of the diphthongs (e.g. *ai > ē*, e.g. *pretod = praetor*; *ou > ō*, e.g. *loferta*[1] *= līberta*); and the loss of final consonants, e.g. *cra(s), zenatuo(s), sta(t), mate(r)*.

---

[1] On this word see p. 218.

In the morphology we may single out the second declension dative singular in -*oi* (*zextoi*), the secondary ending third person singular in -*d* (*douiad* = *det*), the future in -*f*- (*carefo*, *pipafo*), and the reduplicated perfect *fifiked* = *finxit*(?). Much has been made of a supposed genitive in -*osio* of the second declension. But the only example offered is *kaisiosio*,[1] and this is open to the suspicion of being a dittography, while there are many authentic examples of the normal Latin genitive in -*i*. We have reserved until the end an interesting point of phonology—the interchange of *f* and *h* at the beginning of words, e.g. *hileo* and *filea*, *haba* = Lat. *faba*, but *foied* = *hodie*. This phenomenon is found in Sabine and in Etruscan, which suggests that in Faliscan we may have a *lingua latina in bocca toscana*. At any rate the same phenomenon also appears in the Latin dialect of Praeneste (Palestrina) where yet other Etruscan influences have been detected.

From Praeneste has come the oldest text in the Latin language. On a fibula dating from the sixth century B.C. there are inscribed in Greek characters the words *Manios: med: vhe: vhaked: numasioi* = *Manius me fecit Numerio*. Here we find again the dative in -*oi* and another reduplicated perfect *fefaced* for the inherited *fēcit* preserved in Roman Latin. This perfect recurs in the Oscan forms *fefacust*, *fefakid*, a fact which perhaps may be explained by the geographical position of Praeneste on the linguistic frontier between Latin and Oscan. Both *fefaced* and *Numasioi* show the preservation of the full vowels in interior syllables. But it is possible that at so early a date Roman Latin, too, had not yet effected the characteristic weakening of unstressed vowels (see pp. 219f.). Another feature of Praenestine is the change of *i* before a vowel to *e* (*conea*, *fileai*) and in open interior syllables, e.g. *Orcevio* = *Orcivius* (cf. Varro, *R.R.* I. 2. 14: 'rustici etiam quoque viam veham appellant et vellam non villam'). On the other hand, in a closed syllable before -*r*-, *e* changed to *i* (e.g. *Mirqurios*, cf. *stircus* in Lucania and again Oscan *amiricatud* = *immercato*). Thus Lat. *firmus* as opposed to *ferme* may be a dialect form, and rustic origin may likewise be plausibly ascribed to *hircus*.

In the treatment of the diphthongs Praenestine, like other rustic

[1] Cf., however, *eco quto Ievotenosio*, 'I am the κώθων of I.' (Vetter in *Glotta*, 1939, 163 ff.).

dialects, diverged from Roman. Final *-āi > ā* (e.g. dat. *Fortuna, primocenia*); *ai > ē* (*Esculapio*); *ei > e* (e.g. *Hercole*); *oi > ō* (*coraveron = curaverunt*); *eu > ou > ō* (*Poloces < Πολυδεύκης*); *au > ō* (*Plotia*). As in Faliscan *s* is lost at the end of words (*nationu = nationis*), but it is preserved before nasal consonants where it was lost in Roman (*losna = lūna < *louksnā*). In morphology we may mention the second declension nominative plurals in *-es* (*magistere(s)*), a formation found elsewhere, e.g. at Tibur, Capua, and Falerii. Another phenomenon widespread in non-Roman Latin is the genitive singular in *-us* (*-os*) exemplified in *nationu(s)*. In vocabulary, too, we have some evidence that the country dialects differed from Rome. Thus on the word *nefrendes* Festus writes: 'sunt qui nefrendes testiculos dici putent, quos Lanuvini appellant nebrundines, Graeci νεφρούς, Praenestini nefrones'. Here we have a dialect word for 'kidneys' cognate with German *Niere*, for which Roman Latin used *rēnes*. The phonetic variants *nefrones, nefrundines, nebrundines* showing *-f-* and *-b-* respectively are noteworthy. Another ancient word preserved in rustic Latin but lost in the dialect of Rome is the Praenestine *tongitio*, the verbal noun from the verb *tongeo*, cognate with our 'think'. On this Festus writes: 'tongere nosse est, nam Praenestini tongitionem dicunt notionem.' Oscan, too, presents a cognate word in *tanginom* 'sententiam'.

Apart from Praenestine and Faliscan, the 'archaic' Latin inscriptions from other localities show other marked differences from Roman Latin in addition to those mentioned incidentally above. We may conveniently summarize the most important at this point.

Among points of phonology we may mention the change of *d* to *r* before a labial as in *arvorsum, arfuisse* (cf. Volscian *arpatitu = affundito* and Marsian *apur finem*). Hence *arbiter* may be a dialect word. The violent syncope of unstressed vowels instanced in such forms as *lubs* for *lubē(n)s*, *dedront* for *dederunt*, and *cedre = caedere*, is only apparent, for in many such instances the consonants may have syllabic value *b = be, d = de,* and *c = ce*. The dialectal treatment of the diphthongs is reflected in the declension of the nouns, e.g. the dative singulars *Locina* and *Diane* (both *< āi), Marte*, etc. (*ē < ei*).

In the first declension the nominative plural often retains the ancient ending *-ās* (*matronas, quas*), while the dative plural once appears as *-as* (*< āis*, e.g. *devas Corniscas*). On the genitive singular in *-aes* (e.g. *Aquiliaes*) see p. 241. Among the dialect peculiarities of the second

declension, the alleged plural in -ōs occurs only in gentile names preceded by two praenomina denoting sons of the same father. The forms
in -o(s) may therefore be interpreted as singular. In the verb the ending
of the second person singular middle often appears as -us instead of
classical Latin -is, e.g. spatiarus. In the deda(nt) of CIL i.² 379 we have
a reduplicated form of do as in Umbrian. The influence of Oscan may
be seen in the imperative forms fundatid, proiecitad, parentatid from
Luceria in Apulia, on which see p. 278.

Of the Latin of Rome itself we have only a few tantalizing
glimpses before the end of the third century, when texts became
more abundant. The earliest inscription is that written on a mutilated cippus found in 1899 under a black stone which was regarded
as marking the tomb of Romulus. On this cippus, which dates from
about the fifth century, there is inscribed vertically boustrophedon
a text (No. 3) whose evident antiquity and importance for the
history of Latin has stimulated the ingenuity of scholars. It has
been interpreted variously as regulations affecting the privileges of
the rex sacrorum, a law of Tarquinius Priscus composed in Saturnians, a law of Tarquinius Superbus concerning war-booty, and so
on. Of the words in the extant part of the text there seems general
agreement that quoi = quī, sacros = sacer, recei = rēgī, iouxmenta
= iūmenta, iouestod = iūstō. This adds little to our knowledge of
Latin which was not already achieved by reconstruction. No less
baffling is the inscription written on a vase comprising three compartments found in 1880 in the valley between the Quirinal and
the Viminal (No. 2). In the first line it is possible to make out the
words deiuos, qoi, med, mitat, cosmis, virco, siet, but the sense of
the whole still escapes us. In the second line nothing is certain. The
first three words of the third line duenos med feced evidently mean
Bonus me fecit. Thus, while the early evidence yields few positive
additions to our knowledge of early Latin, it does permit the conclusion that between the fifth and third centuries B.C. Latin had
changed so drastically that scholars can no longer understand texts
of the earlier period. It is likely that the Romans themselves were
in similar embarrassment[1] if we may judge by the Carmen Arvale

---

[1] This is expressly stated by Polybius (3. 22. 3) in discussing the treaty made
between Rome and Carthage in the year following the expulsion of the kings: 'I
give below as accurate a translation as I can. For there is so great a difference
between the dialect as spoken by present-day Romans and the ancient tongue that
some parts of it can hardly be elucidated even after careful study by the most

included in the record of the proceedings of the *Fratres Arvales* in
A.D. 218. Here we have a ritual text originating at a very remote
period which, handed down through successive generations of
religious functionaries, had become mere gibberish to those who
pronounced it. This text (No. 4) has been most recently interpreted by E. Norden, who translates it:

(1) Hail, aid us ye Lares. (*thrice*)
(2) Do not allow pestilence or catastrophe to afflict the people.
(3) Be thou sated, wild Mars, leap upon the boundary mark and st ind
   there.
(4) Call ye in turn all the Semones.
(5) Hail Mars aid us
(6) triumpe.

The hymn was sung at a ceremony which took place on the
boundary (*limen* used in a metaphorical sense, cf. *postliminium*) of
the *ager Romanus*. First the help of the Lares (who are *agri custodes*, cf. Tibullus 1. 1. 9) is implored. Then Mars, who is not only
the wild war-god but also the protector of the farmers' crops,
house, and buildings, is summoned to take his stand on the
'threshold' and protect the land from harm. The Semones are a
group of gods of whom little is known, but Norden suggests that
they are divine potencies, executive agents, as it were, for the
supreme gods: 'The Semones, manifestations of powers which preserve the people, will co-operate.' Points of linguistic interest are
the interpretation of *enos* as *ē* (particle of asseveration like Gk. ἦ)
plus *nōs*; the jingle *lue(m) rue(m)* (*ruēs* for later *ruina*; from the
same semantic group we may cite *lābēs, strāgēs, tābēs*); *sins* presumably stands for *sinās*; *fu* is an imperative from the root **bhu*,
which provided so much of the conjugation of the verb 'to be';
berber is a reduplicated form of a demonstrative stem seen also in
the augural formula *ullaber arbos* (Varro, *L.L.* 7. 8; see p. 66).
alternei is apparently a locative form used adverbially meaning 'in
turn'. *advocapit* is an apocopized form of *advocapite*, the future
being used imperatively. It is evident that we have in this
document a Latin text of extreme antiquity though with some
superficial modernization (e.g. *pleoris* for *pleoses*) and possibly

intelligent persons' (see Tenney Frank, *An Economic Survey of Ancient Rome*,
i, pp. 6–7).

corruption. It relates to a most ancient ceremony lying at the heart of Roman State religion. Yet Norden has adduced weighty evidence which suggests that even this ancient document of Roman latinity owes much in thought, structure, and formulation to Greek models.

The influence of Greek is apparent also in yet another document which reaches back to the fifth century B.C.—the Twelve Tables. With this we now turn to a more troubled source of information about early latinity: for our knowledge of the Twelve Tables we have no first-hand inscriptional evidence. Whether or not the original bronze tablets were destroyed in the Gallic sack of Rome in 390 B.C., certainly 'no authoritative text was in existence at the end of the republic'.[1] Our knowledge of the text of the tables comes from quotations or paraphrases by authors beginning in the first century B.C., notably Cicero and the jurists. The Romans themselves believed that when the patricians under plebeian pressure were forced to agree to the drawing up of a code of law an embassy was sent to Athens to study Solon's legislation and that after its return the *decemviri* drew up the code which was inscribed on ten bronze tablets and set up in the market-place (450 B.C.). That this legendary origin contains a core of truth is made plausible by resemblances of context and formulation to early Greek law codes, e.g. that of Gortyna in Crete. Greek origin of this fundamental document of Roman law would explain why so focal a word of legal vocabulary as Lat. *poena* is a Greek loan-word (ποινή). The immense importance of the Twelve Tables for the development of the literary language of the Romans may be gauged from Cicero's remark (*de leg.* 2. 4. 9): 'a parvis enim, Quinte, didicimus *si in ius vocat* atque eiusmodi alias leges nominare.' The significance of the fact that a text which Roman schoolboys learned by heart was based on Greek models will be more fully examined in our next chapter on the growth of literary language. The archaic linguistic features of the texts which the accident of tradition has preserved for us will be discussed in the second part of this volume. For specimens see Appendix.

Among the early texts preserved in the writings of later Roman authors there are others whose evident antiquity makes them parti-

[1] Jolowicz, *Historical Introduction to Roman Law*, p. 106.

cularly valuable for our knowledge of pre-literary Latin. Among them is the augural formula preserved in Varro, *L.L.* 7. 8. Such formulae had become largely unintelligible to Romans of later centuries and were the subject of interpretation and controversy among grammarians and lexicographers, as is apparent from Varro's comment: 'quod addit templa ut sint tesca, aiunt sancta esse qui glossas scripserunt. Id est falsum nam . . . .' I give the text of the formula in the main as it has been restored and interpreted by Norden. (See, however, the criticisms of K. Latte, *Philologus*, xcvii, 1948, pp. 143 ff.)

> templa tescaque m(eae) fines ita sunto
> quoad ego easte lingua nuncupauero
> ollaner arbos quirquir est quam me sentio dixisse
> templum tescumque m(ea) f(inis) esto in sinistrum
> ollaber arbos quirquir est quod me sentio dixisse
> templum tescumque m(ea) f(inis) esto ⟨in⟩ dextrum
> inter ea conregione conspicione cortumione
> utique eas rectissime sensi.

The augur is engaged in marking out the *templum* within which signs are to be observed. Before him is a plot of ground regarded as of supernatural character (cf. Accius 557 W. 'quis tu es mortalis qui in deserta et tesca te apportes loca' and Varro, *L.L.* 7. 10 'loca quaedam agrestia, quod alicuius dei sunt'). In the first part of the formula the augur chooses two trees to left and right and pronounces each of them to be a *templum tescumque*. *templum* here has the meaning 'limit' while *tescum* stresses that it is holy ground. Virgil seems to be echoing this augural phrase in his *limina laurusque* (*Aen.* 3. 91). The last two lines are mutilated and obscure. Varro paraphrased their sense as ' within them regions are defined within which the eyes are to view'. The three abstract nouns in -*io* may be active as in *obsidio* or passive as in *regio, dicio*, etc. The prefix *con*- in verbal compounds has completive force (e.g. *conficere*). To the same semantic group belongs *condicio* from the widespread IE. root *deik/dik* which means 'mark, point out'. Thus *condicio* meant originally 'an act of marking out' or 'the ground so marked out'. It naturally figured in contexts concerning the settlement of territorial disputes (cf. *aequae condiciones*), so that in certain contexts *condiciones* is synonymous with *pax*, another boundary-mark[1] word (*pag 'fix', cf. pāla 'stake'). Thus conregio, etc., may mean the space within certain limits set by a physical act of drawing lines (conregio), by using the eyes (conspicio), and by a mental operation (cortumio). inter has its oldest meaning. It is the separative form of in characterized by the suffix -ter (see p. 253). Like in it could originally take the locative ablative. The formula as it stands is incomplete and doubtless ended with an appeal to the god on the lines of the formula quoted by Livy 1. 18. 9: 'uti tu (Iuppiter) signa nobis certa adclarassis inter eos fines quos feci'. Linguistic points of interest, apart from the archaic technical word tesquom, are the demonstratives easte = istas, ollaner and ollaber (for -ner cf. O.-U. ner = sinister and Gk. νέρ-τεροι = inferi, sinistri; for -ber cf. the reduplicated berber above). quirquir = ubicumque with an adverbial formation in -r similar to that in the Engl. where, there, Lith. kur̃, and Lat. quōr, cūr (see p. 282).

Among other religious formulae preserved by later authors we may mention the prayers contained in Cato's instructions to the farmers (de ag. cult. 132. 1 and 134. 3). The rites described belong to the oldest stratum in Roman religion and among the prayers the most striking in phraseology are those addressed to Jupiter Dapalis and Janus when making an offering of a strues, a fertum, or wine. For example 'postea Iano vinum dato sic: "Iane pater uti te strue ommovenda bonas preces precatus sum, eiusdem rei ergo macte vino inferio esto." postea Iovi sic: "Iuppiter, macte isto ferto esto, macte vino inferio esto."' There is little doubt that we have here 'unquestionably genuine old Roman prayers, taken from the books of the pontifices and preserved in their original state word for word'.[2] A constantly recurring technical term in these prayers is the mysterious word macte. The meaning of this term, doubtless of great antiquity, was only vaguely understood even in the Republican period and had degenerated into a mere exclamation of congratulation, e.g. macte virtute 'bravo!'. Popular etymology connected macte, mactus with magnus and it was explained as magis auctus. This explanation still enjoys some vogue today, mactus being regarded as the participle of a verb *mago. However, the

---

[1] For the semantics of 'boundary' words see my 'The Indo-European Origins of Greek Justice' (Transactions of the Philological Society, 1950).

[2] Ward Fowler, Religious Experience of the Roman People, p. 182.

series of words *mactus, mactare, magmentum* when put in parallel with *aptus, aptare, ammentum* from *apio* suggest that the basic verb is *macio*. Other morphological parallels such as *lacio* from *lax, opio* from *ops* make it likely that *macio* is similarly connected with a noun *max* of which *macula* 'spot' is the diminutive. The meaning 'sprinkle' thus elucidated for *macio, mactus, mactare* as verbs applying to a concrete ritual act is borne out by the contexts in which these words are attested. For instance Servius on *Aen.* 9. 641 writes:

> Macte, magis aucte, adfecte gloria. Et est sermo tractus a sacris: quotiens enim aut tus aut vinum super victimam fundebatur, dicebant 'mactus est taurus vino vel ture'.

There is nothing surprising in the semantic development of a word denoting originally a special ritual act into the more generalized meanings to 'sacrifice', 'worship', 'bless'. Of the numerous examples from many languages it suffices to mention one from Latin —*immolare* originally 'to sprinkle sacrificial meal on the victim'. But perhaps the most striking parallel is provided by our English word 'bless', which may be used in some contexts to translate *macte* and *mactare*. *Bless* goes back (see *O.E.D. sub voc.*) to Teutonic *blôdisôjan* a derivative of *blôdo* 'blood'. Originally meaning 'to sprinkle with sacrificial blood', it had so far progressed in meaning that at the time of the English conversion it was chosen to render Lat. *benedicere* with all its associations of 'worship, praise, bless God, invoke blessings, bless a deity', etc. In view of the use of *macte* in rites addressed to Ianus the remarks of *O.E.D.* on the original meaning of OE. *bloedsian* are of particular interest:

> Original meaning (prob.) to make 'sacred' or 'holy' with blood; to consecrate by some sacrificial rite which was held to render a thing inviolable from profane use of men and evil influence of men or demons (the streaking of the lintel and door-post with blood, Exod. xii. 23, to mark them as holy to the Lord and inviolable by the destroying angel, was apparently the kind of idea expressed by *bloedsian* in pre-Christian times).

There is thus general agreement that the ceremonial sprinkling described as *mactare* was likewise a rite which transferred the victim from the sphere of the profane to the sacred. Thus a pig so treated is described by Varro as *mola mactatus* (*Men.* 2, Bue.), 'blessed with (consecrating) meal'.

It is now time to turn from these scanty remains of archaic Latin to inquire how Roman Latin gradually replaced the other patois of Latium. This linguistic process was, as everywhere, the reflection and consequence of political and social events. About the middle of the fifth century the Sabellian people of the mountains began their descent into the plains. Tradition has it that the Capitol was occupied by the Sabines and Tusculum by the Aequi. In the face of this danger the peoples of Rome and the other Latin communities were forced into politico-military co-operation, in which Rome gradually assumed the dominant role. Threats from the various enemies evoked the alliance with the Latins of 358–354, with the Aequi of Tibur and Praeneste in 354–350, and with the Faliscans in 343–339. Finally conflict broke out between Rome and her Latin allies, and by 335 the Latins were under Roman control, their cities reduced to *municipia*, their territory supervised by Roman colonies. But the Roman way of consolidation was not suppression but absorption. During this period we see families of non-Roman origin playing prominent parts in Roman affairs. The very annexation of Latium opened the consulate to the noble families of the conquered communities, while C. Marcius Rutilus, the first plebeian dictator, was of Volscian origin. It was doubtless this afflux and absorption of non-Roman elements into the Roman State which transformed the Roman patois into a metropolitan Latin, just as standard English, though basically the dialect of the educated and commercial classes of London, resulted from the fusion of elements from many different dialects. Typical of the consequences of this process are dialect doublets such as *whole* and *hale*, *skirt* and *shirt*, *fox* but *vixen*, *raid* and *road*, etc.; while in morphology the ending of the third person singular in -*s*, which replaced -*th* only in the sixteenth and seventeenth centuries, is of northern origin as are the pronouns *they*, *them*, *their*. In the same way metropolitan Latin embraced words and forms from the country districts. These reveal themselves as intruders through their divergent phonetic forms. Some of the relevant criteria have already been mentioned. The diphthong *ou* developed to *ū* in Roman but to *ō* in certain country dialects. Thus *rōbus* and *rōbigo* (< **reudh-*) stand out as rustic intruders in the metropolis. To these by the same token we may add *ōpilio* (for the urban *ūiplio* <

ovi-pilio). *domōs* is said to have been a rustic form of the genitive singular of *domus* used by Augustus for *domūs* (< *domous*). The dialect development of *au* to *ō* picks out as rustic such words as *clōdus, cōda, cōdex, lōtus, lōtium, lōmentum, olla, ollula, plōstrarius, plōstellum* (urban *plaustrum*), etc. For the rustic change of *ae* to *ē* we may quote Varro, *L.L.* 5. 97 'in Latio rure *edus* qui in urbe ut in multis A addito *haedus*'. Certain country dialects were distinguished from Roman by the absence of rhotacism which turned intervocalic -*s*- into -*r*- (*flōs, flōris*). It is to such dialects that we should perhaps assign Latin words such as *adasia* ('ovis vetula recentis partus'), *caseus*, and proper names like *Caesar, Valesius*, etc. *casa*, if correctly derived from *qatia*, must come from a dialect which assibilized *t* before *i*, cf. Osc. *Bansae* = *Bantiae*, Marsian *Martses* 'Martiis'. At any rate the intervocalic -*s*- is non-Roman. So, too, intervocalic -*f*- for urban Latin *b* or *d* reveal the following words as dialect intruders: *rūfus* (< *reudhos*, yet another dialect form corresponding to Roman *rūber* < *rudhros*), *scrofa, vafer* (also *vaber*). Finally the phonetic form of *furnus* (cf. *fornax*) and *ursus* (we should expect *orsus*, see p. 223) suggests that these words come from dialects in which *o* had changed to *u* before -*r*- in a closed syllable.

That early Rome was essentially a farmers' community is evident from Roman state religion, which, it has been said, is the adaptation of a farmers' cult, and from early Roman law which mirrors the interests and conflicts of peasant proprietors. In a suggestive paper J. Marouzeau has pointed out that the peasant's view of the world persists in many Roman words, metaphors, and proverbs. Thus *pecunia* mirrors the assessment of wealth in terms of cattle, as was observed by Cicero himself, 'tum erat res in pecore ... ex quo pecuniosi ... vocabantur'. Hence the *locuples* is one who has 'his piece of land (*locus*) full'. *emolumentum*, too, was presumably in its origin a farmer's term for the amount of flour 'ground out' (*molere*) from a given quantity of grain. (The suggested connexion, however, of the archaic term *adoria* 'military glory as reward' with *ador, adoris*, 'a kind of corn, spelt' is to be rejected.) *laetus*, too, was a rural word signifying 'fat, rich, productive' used of land and crops ('quid faciat laetas segetes', Virg. *G.* I. I; 'ager laetus', Cato, *Agr.* 6I. 2) and animals ('glande sues laeti redeunt',

Virg. *G. 2.* 520). This very concrete sense emerges clearly from the derivatives *laetare* 'to manure' and *laetamen* 'dung, manure'. In the language of augury a *laetum augurium* was one presaging abundance and prosperity, whence the common significance 'joyful, cheerful'. *fēlix*, too, originally meant 'that which produces crops' (derivatives in *-īc-, -āc-, -ūc-,* etc., are especially characteristic of rustic vocabulary) and was then used in a metaphorical sense 'happy, favoured by the gods, propitious'. *almus*, a derivative of *alere*, shows a similar trend of meaning: it is used with *ager, terra, vitis,* etc., and also of goddesses connected with fertility, Ceres, Maia, Venus. *probus* is derived from **pro-bhuos* and signified 'that which grows properly', e.g. 'probae . . . fruges suapte natura enitent' (Acc. *trag.* 199 f. W.). Thence it was used in a transferred moral sense. A similar development is seen in *frūgi*, the dative of *frux*, which was used in expressions like *esse frugi bonae* 'to be capable of giving a good crop'. The phrase was then applied to persons in a moral sense and eventually *bonae frugi* was abbreviated to *frugi*, which functioned as an indeclinable adjective. *luxus* and *luxuria* seem first to have referred to uncontrolled, disorderly growth of vegetation : 'luxuriem segetum tenera depascit in herba', Virg. *G.* 1. 112. These words have been plausibly connected with the adjective *luxus* 'dislocated' (for the change of meaning compare Gk. λελυγισμένος 'effeminate'), but other authors regard *luxus* as derived from a desiderative containing an enlarged form of the root seen in *luo* (cf. *fluxus, laxus*). *pauper*, too, was an agricultural term used of both animals and land meaning 'bearing little'. From ploughing operations have come *delirare*, literally 'to diverge from the furrow (*lira*)' thence to 'go off the rails, be mad', and *praevaricari*, which was a derivative from *varus* 'knock-kneed, crooked, bent'. In ploughing it meant to 'plough a crooked furrow' ('arator praevaricatur', Pliny, *N.H.* 18. 179) and was used in the lawyer's language of an advocate who acts in collusion with the opposing party. The interests of the herdsman are evident in the term *subigere* 'to submit the female to the male' or 'to bring the ox beneath the yoke'. *fēnus* 'interest' was derived by the ancients, too, from the same root as *fēlix*. Capital was regarded as producing offspring : 'fenus . . . a fetu quasi a fetura quadam pecuniae parientis atque increscentis' (Varro *ap.* Gellium 16. 12. 7) ; cf. Gk. τόκος. From the hobbling and unhobbling of animals have come the terms *impedire* and *expedire*. A lame animal was *peccus*, whence the derived verb *peccare* ('solve senescentem mature sanus equum, ne peccet ad extremum ridendus et ilia ducat', Hor. *Ep.* 1. 1. 8). *incohare* is literally 'to attach to the *cohum*', a part of the yoke. *stimulare* and *instigare* meant 'to urge on with the goad'. *egregius* and *eximius* both meant 'one taken out of the flock, a picked animal' ('eximium inde dici coeptum quod in sacrificiis optimum pecus e grege eximebatur', *P.F.* 72. 3). On the other hand, *contumax* was first applied to unmanageable, refractory animals. A similar notion underlies *calcitro* ('equum mordacem, calcitronem' Varro, *Men.* 479). In the language of the law we find the term *rivalis*. This, a derivative of *rivus* 'stream', acquired the metaphorical meaning in disputes about water-rights, as is apparent from *Digest* 43. 20. 1 'si inter rivales, i.e. qui per eundem *rivum* aquam ducunt, sit contentio de usu. . . .' The legal term *stipulari* derives its origin from the symbolical breaking of the straw (*stipula*) in making a covenant. The *forum*, the Roman market-place, the centre of public life, originally denoted the enclosure surrounding the farmstead. *cohors*, too, was a farming term for the yard, pen, or enclosure, either for cattle, poultry, implements, etc. ('*cohortes* sunt villarum intra maceriam spatia', Non. 83. 11). It was then applied by this nation of farmer-soldiers to a division of a military camp and then to the unit encamped there so that it acquired the technical meaning of a subdivision of a legion. A cohort contained three *manipuli*. This unit too derived its name from rustic vocabulary. Literally 'a hand-full', its technical meaning was the truss grasped in the hand by the reaper and then tied together by a few twisted stalks (*manipulos obligare, vincire*, etc.). A truss of hay was, we are told, carried by a *manipulus* as its standard and so the word came to be used for the unit itself (cf. the Greek loan-translation, σπεῖρα 'anything twisted or wound'). Finally we may mention the military term *agmen*, which was 'something driven: a herd or flock'. A drastic figure of speech such as would occur to a countryman is exemplified in *tribulare tribulatio* derived from *tribulum*, a threshing sledge provided with sharp teeth. That *aerumna*, too, must once have possessed a concrete meaning is evident from Festus' note on the diminutive *aerumnula*: '*aerumnulas* Plautus refert furcillas quibus

F

religatas sarcinas viatores gerebant . . ., itaque aerumnae labores onerosos significant', *P.F.* 22. 13. The word is perhaps of Etruscan origin as the suffix *-umn-* suggests (see p. 49). The underlying notion of 'burden' is still apparent in the earliest examples *aerumnas ferre, gerere* (Ennius). *promulgare*, too, is a picturesque farmers' term used originally of squeezing the milk from the udder. Even the common verbs *cernere* and *putare* signified the agricultural operations of 'sifting' and 'pruning' (*putare* is actually a derivative of *putus*, 'clean, pure'). *propagare* is 'to set a slip or layer' (*propago*).

Marouzeau also calls attention to the large number of proverbial expressions which in Latin refer to country-life in its many aspects. But it is questionable whether this is of any great significance, since the same is true of almost any language. Expressions such as 'make hay while the sun shines' fall easily from the lips of the most urbanized Englishman. Moreover, since the growth of industry is a comparatively recent development and the great majority of mankind since neolithic times have supported themselves by agriculture or allied occupations, it is inevitable that all languages should be eminently *langues de paysans*.

Such, then, was the language of early Rome, a language brought into Italy by an IE. people which after long wanderings finally settled in Latium. There it was crossed with the language of a separate IE. people and began its slow progress to world significance under the tutorship of Etruria and of Greece. With Rome's growing power and advance to political supremacy in Italy it received and absorbed new immigrants from Latium and eventually from the whole peninsula including Magna Graecia. It was not merely the governing aristocracy which received such recruitment. As early as the sixth century Rome had become 'the wealthiest city of Italy north of Magna Graecia', attracting and welcoming immigrants, among them 'a populous group of artisans, Greek artists and builders'.[1] A recent authority has argued powerfully that the purpose of the Servian reforms was to harness this mass of resident non-citizens to the military needs of the Roman State (H. Last, *J.R.S.* xxxv, 1945, 33 f.). The influx of these new elements could

[1] Cf. Cicero, *de rep.* 2. 19. 34: 'non tenuis quidam e Graecia rivulus in hanc urbem sed abundantissimus amnis illarum disciplinarum et artium'. Cicero quotes as an example Demaratus of Corinth (i.e. latter half of the seventh century B.C.).

not remain without linguistic consequences. In the teeming quarters of the great metropolis the language, without the discipline of a literary norm, luxuriated in riotous growth. To attempt to form some estimate of this spoken language of the early Republic must be our next task.

CHAPTER IV

SPOKEN LATIN—PLAUTUS AND TERENCE

It is in the nature of things that in the absence of recording apparatus there can be no direct knowledge of the spoken form of any non-contemporary language. All we can hope to do is to separate out colloquial features from the written documents available to us. This analysis requires a set of criteriawhich will enable us to stamp certain phenomena as 'colloquial'. Spoken language is distinguished primarily from writing by the greater intimacy of contact between speaker and hearer. The give-and-take of dialogue increases the emotional tension, which reveals itself in interjections, exclamations, forcefulness, exaggeration, insistence, and constant interruption. The speed and spontaneity of conversation reduces the element of reflection. Sentences are not organized into self-consistent logical structures, but meaning is conveyed by fits and starts with parentheses, afterthoughts, and those changes of construction which grammarians catalogue as anacolutha, contamination, and the like. Perhaps most important is the fact that conversation takes place in an elaborate context of situation which often makes detailed and explicit linguistic reference unnecessary and tedious. Hence colloquial speech is characterized by its allusiveness, by deictic elements, abbreviation, ellipse, and aposiopesis. J. B. Hofmann has applied such criteria to the language of the Roman writers of comedy and Cicero's letters and he has reaffirmed the general opinion that such documents reflect contemporary spoken Latin. This thesis we must now examine.

At first sight plausibility is lent to this view by the abundance of interjections: *vae tergo meo! heu me miserum! heus tu! hem!* etc.; many of them are taken from Greek: *attatae, babae, eugepae.* An interjection may even introduce a question: 'eho an dormit Sceledrus intus?' (*Mil.* 822). Frequent are the accusatives of exclamation: *lepidum senem, facetum puerum, bono subpromo et promo cellam creditam*; these accusatives are often combined with interjections *en ecastor hominem periurium; edepol senem Demaenetum lepidum fuisse nobis,* etc. In this connexion we may mention the abbreviated prayers and curses such as *ita me Hercules* (*iuvet*), the *infinitivus indignantis* such as '*perii, hoc servum meum facere esse ausum*' ('I'm lost! To think that my own slave should have dared to do this!'); and exclamatory sentences in general, 'ut adsimulabat Sauream med esse quam facete!' (*Asin.* 581).

The emotional tension of popular speech is evident, further, in repetition such as *abi abi aperite aperite*; *ut voles, ut tibi lubebit*; and in the constant insistence on the attention of the hearer: *tu, frater bi ubi est*; *tun, Sceledre, hic, scelerum cap ut*. Such a 'prostactic use of the second personal pronoun sometimes leads to apparent derangements of syntax: 'tu, se te di amant, agere tuam remi occasiost' (*Poen.* 659); 'sed tu, qu pro tam corrupto dicis caussam filio, eademne erat haec disciplina tibi?' (*Bacch.* 420 f.); and, still more remarkable, 'eamus, tu, in ius' (*Truc.* 840), which has, somewhat tortuously, been explained as a contamination of *eamus ambo in ius* and *i tu mecum in ius*. Colloquial speech makes much freer use of the personal and demonstrative pronouns than does written Latin. Typical examples are: 'quia si illa inventa est quam ille amat, recte valet' (*Bacch.* 192); 'pallam illam quam tibi dudum dedit, mihi eam redde'. This 'anaphoric' *is* may even refer to the person addressed: 'tu autem quae pro capite argentum mihi iam iamque semper numeras, ea pacisci modo scis' (*Pseud.* 225 f.); 'quid illum ferre vis, qui tibi quoi divitiae domi maxumae sunt, is nummum nullum habes?' (*Ep.* 329 f.) Such redundancy of expression, the product of the speaker's anxiety to hammer his point home, is particularly frequent in superlatives: *primumdum omnium*, 'first of all'; *hominem omnium minimi pretii*; *perditissimus ego sum omnium in terra*; *quantum est hominum optumorum optume*, etc. Double comparatives are no less a mark of popular speech, 'nihil invenies magis hoc certo certius' (*Capt.* 644); 'inimiciorem nunc utrum credam magis' (*Bacch.* 500); 'magis maiores nugas' (*Men.* 55). Plautus abounds, further, in examples of the universal tendency to reinforce negative expressions: 'neque ego hau committam' (*Bacch.* 1037); 'nec te aleator nullus est sapientior' (*Rud.* 359); 'neque id haud immerito tuo' (*Men.* 371). Often the negative is given a fuller form: e.g. *nullus* is used for *non* in 'is nullus venit' (*Asin.* 408); for *ne* in 'tu nullus adfueris' (*Bacch.* 90); *haud quisquam* is substituted for the more colourless *nemo*. Closely allied to this is the pleonastic use of pronouns meaning 'any one, anything' in negative sentences: 'ne quid significem quippiam mulierculis' (*Rud.* 896); 'ne dum quispiam...imprudentis aliquis immutaverit' (*Mil.* 431); 'nisi quid ego mei simile aliquid contra consilium paro' (*Vid.* 67). Pleonasm is, in fact, so natural a device of popular rhetoric that we may content ourselves with a few random illustrations: *ambo . . . duo*; *idem unum*; *par idem*; *repente...subito*; *continuo...protinam*; *omnibus universis*; *rursum . . . recipimus*; *exire foras*.

It is in vocabulary that the urge to impress, convince, and dominate the hearer produces its most powerful effects, and it is here that the colloquial tang of Plautus is most evident. Colourless words like *dico* find more evocative substitutes such as *narro, fabulor, memoro*, or, in the imperative, *cedo* 'out with it'. For *miser sum* we find *vivo miser*, for *benevolens est, benevolens vivit*. The commonplace *bonus, bene* give way to *bellus, pulchre, lepidus, lautus; minutus* and *grandis* roll off the tongue better than *parvus* and *magnus*. A rich variety of expressions does service for the notion 'very', *admodum, nimis, oppido, solide, probe, strenue*, etc. There is no mistaking the colloquial flavour of utterances like 'verum, si frugist, usque admutilabit probe' ('but if he is any use, he will fleece him good and proper', *Capt.* 269); 'epityra estur insanum bene' (*Mil.* 24). Plautus abounds in such picturesque slang: 'me . . . decet curamque adhibere ut praeolat mihi quod tu velis' ('it is right and proper for me to see to it that I get an advance whiff of your desires', *Mil.* 40); 'ea demoritur te' ('she's crazy about you', *Mil.* 970); 'mulierem nimi' lepida forma ducit' ('he's bringing a woman with a simply lovely figure', *Mil.* 870); 'sed ecqua ancillast illi? est prime cata' ('Has she got a maid servant? She has, and a winner for slyness', *Mil.* 794; cf. 'fabula prime proba', Naevius *com* 1); 'tum igitur ego deruncinatus, deartuatus sum miser' ('in that case I'm reduced to shavings, torn limb from limb', *Capt.* 641).

This last example introduces a device much favoured by the popular language, the replacement of simple verbs by more expressive compounds. Examples with the prefix *de-* are *deascio, deamo, delacero, deludifico, derogito, delucto*, etc. This prefix also serves to intensify other parts of speech: e.g. *derepente, desubito*. Perhaps the most numerous expressive compounds are those made with the prefix *con-*, of which *comedo*, which later ousted the simple verb *edo*, may serve as a type example: others are *condeceo, consilesco, commereo, commisceo, commonstro, comperco, comprecor, concaleo, condolesco, confodio, confulgeo*, etc. Less frequent are those in *ad-*: *adcredo, adformido, adlaudo, admoderor*. This prefix, too, strengthens other parts of speech: *apprime, approbe, adaeque*.

Suffixation, too, plays its part in giving greater volume and forcefulness to simple verbs. Thus *fodico, frico*, and *vellico* do duty for *fodio, frio*, and *vello*. But what is especially characteristic of the popular language is the replacement of simple verbs by their corresponding frequentative formations, a process which continued throughout the history of Latin down to the Romance period. Plautus abounds in verbs like *essito, fugito, sciscito, ducto, minitor, quaerito, negito, dormito, loquitor*. But the diminutives are the most important class of emotionally charged words. Such formations do not, of course, merely denote smallness as in *catillus*, a small *catinus*, but, with the added connotations 'dear little', 'poor little', and the like, express a whole range of emotional attitudes—endearment, playfulness, jocularity, familiarity, and contempt. A *muliercula* is not a little woman, but 'a bit of a hussy', and is generally used with reference to a courtesan. When Hegio in the *Captivi* says 'ibo intro atque intus subducam ratiunculam' (v. 192) the savour is much like our modern phrase 'a spot of accounting'. In the *Miles Gloriosus* the shifty and ingratiating tone of Lurcio when under cross-examination by Palaestrio is apparent from the diminutive in 'sed in cella erat paullum nimi' loculi lubrici' ('a patch just a wee bit too slippery', v. 852).

Familiarity not unmixed with contempt is evident in 'quis haec est muliercula et ille gravastellus qui venit?' ('who is this female and that little fellow with gray hair?', *Epid.* 620). The mock auction scene in the *Stichus* provides some examples of the euphemistic use of the diminutives, some of the articles offered for sale being 'cavillationes adsentatiunculas ac peiieratiunculas parasiticas' (vv. 228 f.). But it is, of course, in the language of love that the diminutives find their most congenial and profuse employment as endearments: *mi animule, mea melilla, meus ocellus, meum corculum, melculum, verculum, o corpusculum malacum, mea uxorcula, edepol papillam bellulam, belle belliatula.* An extravagant example is provided by the much-quoted love letter, *Pseudolus* 64 ff.:

> nunc nostri amores, mores, consuetudines,
> iocu', ludus, sermo, suavisaviatio,
> compressiones artae amantum corporum,
> teneris labellis molles morsiunculae,
> nostrorum orgiorum . . .—iunculae,
> papillarum horridularum oppressiunculae. . . .

The same style is parodied in *Asinaria* 666 ff.:

> dic me igitur tuom passerculum, gallinam, coturnicem,
> agnellum, haedillum me tuom dic esse vel vitellum,
> prehende auriculis, compara labella cum labellis.

It should be noted that such diminutive formations are found not only in nouns but in adjectives (e.g. *vetulus, dicaculus, primulo diluculo, minutulus,* etc.), adverbs (*pausillatim, pauxillisper,* etc.), and especially comparatives (*plusculum, ampliuscule, liquidiusculus, maiusculus, nitidiuscule, tardiuscula*). We even find a verbal derivative in *missiculare* (*Epid.* 132), with which we may compare *pensiculo* (Gellius and Apuleius).

We now conclude this rapid survey of the colloquial characteristics of Plautine Latin by considering some phenomena which reflect the speed and spontaneity of dialogue. The attention of the hearer is invited by introductory phrases such as *quid ais? quid vis? viden? scin? quid tu?* The utterance then proceeds in short disconnected phrases without explicit marks of subordination: e.g. *nunc quid vis? id volo noscere; dic mihi, quid lubet*; cf. 'sed volo scire, eodem consilio quod intus meditati sumus gerimus rem?' (*Mil.* 612). It is such juxtapositions which gave rise to the unclassical use of the indicative in indirect questions: 'scio iam quid vis dicere' (*Mil.* 36). Such paratactic constructions (see Syntax, p. 328) abound in Plautus: 'sed taceam, optumum est' ('I'll be quiet, it is best', *Epid.* 59); 'iam faxo hic erit' (*Mil.* 463); 'adeamus appellemus' (*Mil.* 420); 'ibo . . . visam' ('I'll go and see', *Bacch.* 235); 'hoccine si miles sciat, credo hercle has sustollat aedis totas' (*Mil.* 309); 'hercle opinor, ea videtur' ('I certainly think it looks like her', *Mil.* 417). All kinds of logical subordinations may be implied by such juxtapositions: consecutive as in 'tantas divitias habet, nescit quid faciat auro' ('he's so rich he doesn't know what to do with his money', *Bacch.* 333); 'nam nimi' calebat, amburebat gutturem' (*Mil.* 835); 'sed me excepit: nihili facio quid illis faciat ceteris' (*Mil.* 168). In the following example the question represents a conditional clause, the apodosis being expressed in the deictic phrase which follows: 'opu'ne erit tibi advocato tristi, iracundo? ecce me!' (*Mil.* 663).

Colloquial utterance is often interrupted by parentheses: 'nam vigilante Venere si veniant eae, ita sunt turpes, credo ecastor Venerem ipsam e fano fugent' ('if they came while Venus was awake, so ugly are they, it's my belief they would scare Venus herself out of the shrine', *Poen.* 322 f.). Such parentheses are particularly frequent with expressions of politeness (e.g. 'sed, amabo, advortite animum', *Mil.* 382) or diffidence *opinor, credo*, etc. But the full explanatory parenthesis seems rarer in Plautus than in Terence, from whom Hofmann takes most of his examples: e.g. 'dictum hoc inter nos fuit (ex te adeo ortumst) ne tu curares meum neve ego tuom?' (*Ad.* 796 ff.); 'minis viginti tu illam emisti (quae res tibi vortat male): argenti tantum dabitur' (*Ad.* 191); 'nimium inter vos, Demea, ac (non quia ades praesens dico hoc) pernimium interest' (*Ad.* 392). It is a frequent occurrence, too, in colloquial speech that a speaker completes the scheme of a sentence and then strings on a series of afterthoughts Such supplementation is seen in 'ait ... sese illum amare, meum erum, Athenis qui fuit' ('she says she loves him, my master, the one who was in Athens', Pl. *Mil.* 127); 'dedi mercatori quoidam qui ad illum deferat, meum erum, qui Athenis fuerat, qui hanc amaverat' ('I gave [the letter] to a merchant to deliver to him, my master, the one who was in Athens, the one who loved this girl', *Mil.* 131 f.). Both these examples are, of course, from the quasi-prologue (Act II, Scene i) of this play, but they illustrate a typical procedure of oral exposition. It is supplementation by afterthought which gives rise to a particularly frequent syntactical colloquialism—the proleptic accusative. Sentences like 'viden tu hunc quam inimico vultu intuitur?' (*Capt.* 557) lead naturally to constructions of the type 'qui noverit me quis ego sum' (*Mil.* 925); 'dic modo hominem qui sit' (*Bacch.* 555).

The spontaneity of speech which gives little time for reflection

or correction leads, as we saw, to illogicalities and syntactical dislocations which grammarians catalogue as anacolutha. A language
may offer a variety of alternatives for expressing a given meaning.
In the course of the sentence the speaker may forget which one he
has started with and change over to a different construction. It is
in this way that contaminations arise, a phenomenon extremely
common in everyday speech. Thus in 'triduom non interest aetatis
uter maior siet' (*Bacch*. 461) the speaker has blended two modes of
expression: 'there is not three days' difference in their ages' and
'you could not tell which of the two is the older'. Similarly 'ut
edormiscam hanc crapulam quam potavi praeter animi quam
libuit sententiam' ('so that I may sleep off this hang-over which I
got through drinking more than I wanted to', *Rud*. 586) appears
to be a blend of *praeter animi sententiam* and *praeter quam libuit*.
A particularly frequent syntactical anacoluthon is occasioned by
the desire of the speaker to focus attention at the outset on the
particular point of interest at the moment. This he achieves by
mentioning it at the beginning of the sentence, which then moves
into another construction. This results in anacolutha of the type
called *nominativus pendens*: 'nam unum conclave, concubinae
quod dedit miles . . . in eo conclavi ego perfodi parietem' (*Mil*.
140); 'plerique homines, quos quom nil refert pudet, ubi pudendum
est, ibi eos deserit pudor' (*Epid*. 166). Sometimes a substantival
clause introduced by *quod* occupies the same position of syntactical neutrality: 'istuc quod das consilium mihi, te cum illa
verba facere de ista re volo' (*Mil*. 1114), which is equivalent to a
colloquial English sentence beginning 'about that advice you gave
me . . .'; cf. 'quod apud nos fallaciarum sex situmst, certo scio,
oppidum quodvis videtur posse expugnari dolis' ('what with the
combined trickery of the six of us I'm pretty certain any town can
be stormed by guile', *Mil*. 1156 f.). In both these examples the
topic of the *pendens* clause is later brought into the construction:
e.g. *de ista re, dolis*.

   It will now be clear that there is strong prima facie evidence to
conclude provisionally that the plays of Plautus represent a spoken
idiom and it would seem reasonable to suppose that this was the
colloquial speech of his own day. We may now briefly survey its
main characteristics. The first impression is of the overwhelming

fecundity of the vocabulary—the *ubertas sermonis Plautini* for which he was famous in antiquity and which led Varro to his judgement 'in argumentis Caecilius poscit palmam, in ethesin Terentius, in sermonibus Plautus' (*Sat. Men.* 399 B.). Law, religion, warfare, intrigue and love, vice and virtue, luxury and debauch, flattery and abuse, on all these topics Plautus dilates with boisterous gaiety and aggressive ebullience. To this seemingly inexhaustible flood of words Greek had continued to make its contribution. Among nautical terms we note *prora, nauta, nautea, nauclerus, celox* (κέληξ transformed by association with *velox*), *carina* (if this is really from καρύϊνος), *lembus, stega* 'deck', *exanclare* (ἀντλεῖν). It will be convenient to add here some other nautical words not actually attested in Plautus: *aplustra* (plur.), a word found in poetry from Ennius onwards (= ἄφλαστον), *campsare* 'to round (a cape, etc.)' (κάμψαι) and *pausarius* 'rowing master', i.e. one who gives the signal to stop (παῦσαι). Business and finance are represented in Plautus by *danista, logista, trapessita, symbolum, syngraphus, exagoga* 'export', etc.; medicine by *glaucuma*, education and learning by *paedagogus, syllaba*, etc.; technology by *architectus, ballista, machaera, pessulus* (πάσσαλος). The word *contus* (κόντος) does not occur in Plautus, but its existence is guaranteed by the colloquial verb *percontor*, which presumably once had the sense 'to sound or probe with a pole'. Greek influence on the organization of town life is evident in loan-words like *platea*, from which our word *place* is descended, and *macellum* 'provision market'. Greek also contributed many terms in the realm of zoology: 'edepol haec quidem bellulast. :: pithecium haec est prae illa et spinturnicium' (*Mil.* 989). Others are *cantherius, balanus* a shellfish, *ballaena, concha, narita* (νηρίτης), *scomber*. Particularly numerous are the words for wine vessels and household equipment: *ampulla, batioca* (βατιάκη), *cadus, cantharus, cyathus, gaulus, lagona* (λάγυνος), *patina, scyphus, cista, culleus* (κολεός), *marsuppium*, etc. Of particular interest is the word *clatri* 'lattice' (Cato) which may be traced to a Doric word κλᾷθρα and is presumably a very ancient borrowing. Plautus has a derivative in 'neque fenstra nisi clatrata' ('and on window without a lattice', *Mil.* 379). But it is especially in the sphere of pleasure, luxury, extravagance, and debauchery that the Greek made his contribution to Roman life and language. That

Roman women looked to the Greeks in matters of fashion as ours do to the French is evident from passages such as:

> quid istae quae vestei quotannis nomina inveniunt nova?
> tunicam rallam, tunicam spissam, linteolum caesicium,
> indusiatam, patagiatam, caltulam aut crocotulam,
> subparum aut subnimium, ricam, basilicum aut exoticum,
> cumatile aut plumatile, carinum aut cerinum.   (*Epid.* 229 ff.)

On *cumatile* Nonius comments: 'cumatilis aut marinus aut caeruleus; a graeco tractum, quasi fluctuum similis; fluctus enim graece κύματα dicuntur'. We may cite further the names of luxury craftsmen listed in *Aulularia* 508 ff.: *phyrgio, patagiarii, murobatharii, diabathrarii, molocinarii, strophiarii, zonarii, thylacistae, corcotarii.* Ornaments and cosmetics also derive their names from Greek: *spinter* (σφιγκτήρ 'choker'), *fucus* 'rouge', *cincinnus* 'curl', and *schoenus* 'a cheap perfume' (cf. Varro, *L.L.* 7. 64: 'schoenicolae ab schoeno, nugatorio unguento'). Finally we may illustrate the adjectives and adverbs of fashion like our *chic, soigné*, etc.:

> eugae, eugae! exornatu's basilice.
> tiara ornatum lepida condecorat schema.
> tum hanc hospitam autem crepidula ut graphice decet!
> (*Pers.* 462 ff.)

Greek influence is apparent also in the field of sport (*palaestra, discus, athletice, pancratice*) and the theatre (*scaena, choragium*; for *encore!* the Romans shouted πάλιν), while even the word for 'cheerful' *hilarus* is Greek. But the less innocent influence of the Greek is apparent in *sycophanta, parasitus, moechus, moechisso, comissor* (κωμάζω); and in what light the Roman regarded his Greek tutors in debauchery is evident from the meaning attached to the words *graecor, pergraecor, congraeco* which is illustrated in the following passage: 'aurum . . . quod dem scortis quodque in lustris comedim congraecem' ('money for me to spend on prostitutes and to squander in gluttony and debauch in brothels', *Bacch.* 743).

Some of these Greek words may, of course, be due to the Greek originals which Plautus followed. Thus *exenterare* occurs four times in the *Epidicus* but nowhere else in Plautus or Terence. But even if the suggestion is correct that this word is a calque of ἐξεντερίζειν, no comic author would use a word wholly incomprehensible to his audience. It may well be that Roman audiences found Greek as irresistibly funny as French in general or the German word for 'five' appears to English music-hall patrons. But there can be little doubt of the ability of the Roman audience to understand at least some Greek. This is implicit in the play on Greek words in which Plautus often indulges: 'quis istic est? :: Charinus :: euge iam χάριν τούτῳ ποιῶ' (*Pseud.* 712); 'quis igitur vocare? :: Diceae nomen est :: iniuria's, falsum nomen possidere, Philocomasium, postulas; ἄδικος es tu, non δικαία, et meo ero facis iniuriam' (*Mil.* 436 ff.). It should be realized that most of the numerous Greek loan-words found in the Latin at this period were not introduced by the educated classes. There can be little doubt that many of them were picked up by the Roman plebs in their intimate contact with Greeks who had settled in the city, and formed an integral part of the everyday speech of the lower strata of the population. This is strongly suggested by the fact that in the plays of Plautus Greek words and expressions occur predominantly in the passages spoken by slaves and low characters.

A further indication is the frequent use of Greek in slang words and expressions: *morus, bardus* (βραδύς), *blennus, logi* (equivalent to *fabulae*), *graphicus servus* 'a bright, clever slave'; 'benene usque valuit? :: pancratice atque athletice' ('Is he still keeping well?' 'Champion and fighting fit', *Bacch.* 248). *massa* (Gk. μᾶζα 'barley cake', later (LXX) 'lump, mass') is also used in a strikingly modern phrase: 'argenti montes non massas' ('mountains of money not just masses', *Mil.* 1065). *harpago*, an adaptation of ἁρπάγη in slang denotes 'a grab-all'. In 'aeternum tibi dapinabo victum, si vera autumas' ('I'll stake you for the rest of your days if you are telling the truth', *Capt.* 897), *dapino* = δαπανάω, although its Roman meaning may have been influenced by false association with *daps*. The popular word κόλαφος 'clout on the head', which is attested from Epicharmus, the writer of Sicilian comedies, as a proper name, also found its way into Latin. Plautus has the transcribed form *colaphus*, but that the spoken language possessed a form *colopus* is evident from Petronius' derived verb *percolopare*. This popular form was the ancestor of Italian *colpo*, Fr. *coup*. Finally as evidence for the Roman populace's capacity to pick up even the most curious Greek words we may quote Livy 27. 11: 'quos androgynos vulgus ut pleraque faciliore ad duplicanda verba Graeco sermone appellat'. Even a common Greek verbal suffix was transplanted into Latin and became productive: *malacissare, cyathissare, purpurissare*, etc., are modelled on Greek loan-words in -ίζω, the ζ becoming -ss- in the Latin phonemic system (cf. *massa* < μᾶζα). How independently this suffix developed in Latin is apparent from *patrissare* 'to take after one's father' (though a πατριάζω in this sense is attested by Pollux), *graecissare, drachumissare, comissari* (κωμάζειν).

In grammatical structure there is little which distinguishes Plautus' language from Classical Latin. Certain syntactical usages were later avoided: the accusative with *utor*, the prepositions *ex* and *in* with the names of towns, the indicative in indirect questions, the infinitive of purpose—all might cause pain but certainly no difficulty to the purist. In morphology certain divergences from the classical norm stand out: we find a vocative *puere*, the genitive singular of fourth declension nouns is regularly of the type *senati*, the locative of the fifth declension appears as *die* in *die crastini*, and Plautus does not make the classical distinction in the ablative singular of -*e* for participles and -*i* for adjectives (e.g. *malevolente*). The pronouns offer forms like *ipsus, eumpse, eampse, eapse*, nominative plurals *hisce, illisce*, the ablative singular *aliquī, quī* (interrogative, relative, and indefinite). In the verb we may single out the imperatives *face, dice*, the perfect *tetuli*, aorist subjunctives and optatives like *faxo, capso, faxim, dixis, induxis*, and the infinitive passive in -*ier*, e.g. *adducier*. Certain verbs belong to the third conjugation which were later transferred to the second: *olĕre, fervĕre, intuor*. Impersonal verbs have a perfect passive: *puditum est, miseritum est, pertaesum est.*[1] Some classical deponent verbs appear in the active: e.g. *arbitro*. Certain periphrastic forms occur: *carens fui, sis sciens, audiens sum*, etc. Among the adverbs archaisms are also found: *antid hac, antehoc* (Plautus does not use *antea*), *interdius*. We may add the verbal prefix *indo*: *indaudio, indo-tueri, indupedio*.

In pronunciation *vor-* had not yet changed to *ver-* (the spelling of *vert-* for *vort-* is said to have been introduced by Scipio Africanus (Quintilian 1. 7. 25)); the long vowel was preserved in final syllables.

---

[1] *puditum est* also in Cic. *pro Flacc.* 22. 52; *pertaesum* in Cic. *ep. ad Q. fr.* 1. 2. 4.

e.g. *dicāt, dicēt, audīt, dicār, matēr, oratōr*; final -*s* after short vowels was weakly pronounced and had no prosodic value (we know from Cicero, *Or.* 48. 161 that this pronunciation was regarded as *subrusticum* in his time); final -*d* was still pronounced in *mēd, tēd*; and intervocalic *v* was eliminated in words like *obliscor, dinus, controrsia, aunculus.*

Some of these divergences from the classical norm may be exemplified from inscriptions of the same age. Thus the *Senatus Consultum de Bacchanalibus* of 186 B.C. (Appendix No. 8) offers *arvorsum, sēd, figier, gnoscier*, and the periphrastic *scientes esetis* (cf. *sis sciens* above). This might be regarded as some confirmation that Plautus in his comedies used the spoken idiom of his day. But closer observation of the archaisms used by Plautus should give us pause: many of them are confined to the end of the verse. The infinitives in -*ier*, for instance, occur almost invariably at the end of the verse (some 168 examples) or at the end of the hemistich (6). Greater licence is observed in the cantica. Much the same is true of the subjunctives *fuam* and *fuas* and the optatives *duim* and *duis* which appear only at the end of senarii. *interduim* and *creduis*, again, figure only at the end of the longer measures. *antidhac* occurs nine times in all in Plautus and always at the end of the verse. Such restrictions on the archaic phenomena would suggest that the language of the comedies is, at least to some extent, stylized and artificial; and this would belie our provisional judgement that it is a reflection of contemporary spoken idiom.

H. Haffter, in a careful study of a few selected phenomena, has shown that there is, in fact, a clear distinction between the language of the senarii and that of the longer measures. Thus the *figura etymologica*, which even in Cicero's correspondence is used in certain passages of emotional intensity ('cura ut valeas meque ames amore illo tuo singulari', *ad fam.* 15. 20. 3) appears more frequently in the long measures than the iambic senarii. Even where it is employed in the senarii, it is clearly a studied stylistic device indicative of strong emotion; of abuse in 'pulmoneum . . . velim vomitum vomas' (*Rud.* 511), mockery in 'calidum prandisti prandium' (*Poen.* 759), glee in 'opsonabo opsonium' (*Stich.* 440), pathos in 'aequo mendicus atque ille opulentissimus censetur censu ad Accheruntem mortuos' (*Trin.* 493 f.). The device subserves, of course, the essential purposes of Plautus' manifold comic effects and so almost invariably occurs in the speeches of the chief comic characters—a slave, a parasite, and the like. The senarii and the other measures differ likewise in their employment of other stylistic devices characteristic of early Latin literature. These will be discussed in the course of the following chapter. For our present purpose a few illustrative examples will suffice.

Of first importance is the inflated or padded style which is achieved by a number of means. Most obvious among such devices is the accumulation of synonyms: 'spes opes auxiliaque a me segregant spernuntque se' (Capt. 517); 'ut celem patrem, Pistoclere, tua flagitia aut damna aut desidiabula?' (Bacch. 375); 'vos amo, vos volo, vos peto atque obsecro' (Curc. 148);[1] 'stulti stolidi, fatui fungi, bardi blenni, buccones' (Bacch. 1088). The same difference of styles between senarii and the long measures is found in Terence. In Phormio 458 we find the formal phrase used in taking farewell: 'numquid nos vis?' But in the trochaic septenarius v. 563 this appears in the inflated form 'num quid est quod opera mea vobis opu' sit?' Plautus, too, is rich in such padded expressions. Thus a variation on the simple opportune advenis is 'optuma opportunitate ambo advenistis' (Merc. 964), with which we may compare 'te expecto: oppido opportune te obtulisti mi obviam' (Terence, Ad. 322). The polite formula di dent quae velis is inflated to 'di tibi omnes omnia optata offerant' (Capt. 355). These examples illustrate yet another favourite stylistic device—assonance of various kinds. Alliterative phrases were, of course, a feature of the most ancient latinity as we can see from proverbial phrases (e.g. plaustrum perculi 'I've upset the apple-cart', Ep. 592; iam ipse cautor captust, Ep. 359), and from examples in the other Italic dialects (see next chapter). Examples of this may be amassed from almost any page of Plautus. Particularly frequent are alliterative word pairs, often in asyndeton: 'cibatus commeatusque', 'victu et vita', 'nec vola nec vestigium', 'oleum et operam perdere', 'vivus videns', 'impetritum inauguratumst', 'vivit valet', 'obliga obsigna', 'se adplicant adglutinant', 'complicandis componendis', 'labitur liquitur', etc. Extremely com-

---

[1] Even more elaborate is the 'pro deum popularium omnium adulescentium clamo postulo obsecro oro ploro atque imploro fidem' (Caecilius, com. 21).

mon, too, is the occurrence of tricola with alliteration (type *veni vidi vici*): 'exitium, excidium, exlecebra' (*Bacch.* 944); 'screanti, siccae, semisomnae' (*Curc.* 115); 'retines, revocas, rogitas' (*Men.* 114); 'compellare et complecti et contrectare' (*Mil.* 1052); 'supersit, suppetat, superstitet' (*Pers.* 331). As an example of a tricolon exhibiting the 'law of increasing magnitude' (see next chapter) we may quote 'fac fidele, sis fidelis, cave fidem fluxam geras' (*Capt.* 439). Rhyme effects are not infrequent: e.g.

> neque ut hinc abeam, neque ut hunc adeam scio, timore torpeo.
> (*Truc.* 824)

> pol magi' metuo ne defuerit mihi in monendo oratio.::
> pol quoque metuo lusciniolae ne defuerit cantio.
> (*Bacch.* 37 f.)

> teneris labellis molles morsiunculae,
> nostrorum orgiorum . . . —iunculae,
> papillarum horridularum oppressiunculae. (*Pseud.* 67 ff.)

> nemo illum quaerit qui optumus et carissumust:
> illum conducunt potius qui vilissumust. (*Pseud.* 805 f.)

The elaborate stylization of Plautus' language clearly emerges from a perusal of almost any page opened at random:

> liber captivos avi' ferae consimilis est:
> semel fugiendi si data est occasio
> satis est, numquam postilla possis prendere.::
> omnes profecto liberi lubentius
> sumu' quam servimus. (*Capt.* 116 ff.)

> nunc ego omnino occidi,
> nunc ego inter sacrum saxumque sto. (*Capt.* 616 f.)

> inicite huic manicas* mastigiae.::
> quid hoc est negoti? quid ego deliqui?:: rogas,
> sator sartorque scelerum et messor maxume?
> (*Capt.* 659 ff.)

For the elaborate stylization of the long measures and the cantica we may quote:

> haec est. estne ita ut tibi dixi? aspecta et contempla Epidice:
> usque ab unguiculo ad capillum summumst festivissuma.
> estne consimilis quasi quom signum pictum pulchre aspexeris?
> e tuis verbis meum futurum corium pulchrum praedicas,
> quem Apelles ac Zeuxis duo pingent pigmentis ulmeis.
> (*Ep.* 622 ff.)

illic hinc abiit, mihi rem summam credidit cibariam.
di immortales, iam ut ego collos praetruncabo tegoribus!
quanta pernis pestis veniet, quanta labes larido,
quanta sumini apsumedo, quanta callo calamitas,
quanta laniis lassitudo, quanta porcinariis.   (*Capt.* 901 ff.)

We can now see how profoundly we must modify our first conclusion. The language of Plautus indubitably contains numerous colloquial elements, but they are merely among the many ingredients from which Plautus compounded a highly elaborate and artificial language. Drawing no less freely on the language of law, religion, and contemporary tragedy, by the colloquial features listed above he achieved a note of raciness appropriate to the comic genre. But the language of Plautus even in his senarii is far removed from the everyday speech of the Hannibalic age. How inextricably the colloquial and the stylized are compounded we may observe from a few final examples. In the phrase *lepida memoratui* (*Bacch.* 62) the colloquial adjective *lepidus* is used with a dative of the supine, a construction of great rarity and antiquity. In 'magistron quemquam discipulum minitarier' ('to think that any pupil should threaten his master!', *Bacch.* 152), the construction and the frequentative verb are colloquial, the ending of the passive infinitive archaic. In *Poen.* 308: 'eho tu, vin tu facinus facere lepidum et festivom?' the colloquial tone is unmistakable (note the exclamation, the repeated *tu*, the adjectives *lepidus* and *festivus*), and yet the line contains a *figura etymologica*. As a final illustration, we may quote the amusing passage from the opening scene[1] of the Casina in which Olympio threatens Chalinus:

quid facies? :: concludere in fenstram firmiter,
unde auscultare possis quom ego illam ausculer:
quom mihi illa dicet 'mi animule, mi Olympio,
mea vita, mea mellilla, mea festivitas,
sine tuos oculos deosculer, voluptas mea,
sine amabo ted amari, meu' festus dies,

---

[1] Haffter points out that in opening scenes the language is often more highly stylized than in other passages of iambic senarii, e.g.

saepe ego res multas tibi mandavi, Milphio,
dubias, egenas, inopiosas consili,
quas tu sapienter docte et cordate et cate
mihi reddidisti opiparas opera tua.   (*Poen.* 129 ff.)

meu' pullus passer, mea columba, mi lepus'.
quom mihi haec dicentur dicta, tum tu, furcifer,
quasi mus in medio parieti vorsabere.
nunc ne tu te mihi respondere postules
abeo intro. taedet tui sermonis.   (*Cas.* 132 ff.)

The comedies of Terence, whose literary life falls some two generations after Plautus, usher us into a quieter and more subdued linguistic world. Gone are the exuberance, the verve, and vigour of Plautus' uproarious picaresque comedies. Terence's effects are subtler: reserve, reticence, and restraint characterize his style. These differences have been given a social interpretation. According to some scholars they correspond to class distinctions. Plautus reflects the idiom of the lower strata of the population whereas Terence uses the language of refined society—the cultured Scipionic circle. How far from true this judgement is of Plautus we have already seen. It now remains to discover what emerges from an application of the same criteria and methods of analysis to the language of Terence.

In pronunciation and grammar, as we should expect, the language has made some progress towards the classical norm. The phonetic change exemplified in *votare* > *vetare*, *vortere* > *vertere* has taken place (see above). Terence avoids, or employs more rarely, certain grammatical forms which appear freely in Plautus: e.g. metaplastic forms like *fervĕre*, *olĕre*, etc., are rarer; he never uses *dice* or *duce*; while *tetuli*, which is regular in Plautus, appears only twice in Terence. The optative forms in *-ssim*, so frequent in Plautus, are employed by Terence as a deliberate archaistic device in passages reminiscent of the language of law. *faxim* and *faxo*, of course, survive in stereotyped phrases. In one respect Terence is more archaic than Plautus: in the second singular passive he regularly uses the shorter forms in *-re*, whereas Plautus has nine examples of *-ris*, which Cicero prefers in the present indicative to avoid confusion with the imperative. Among the non-classical forms of Terence's language we may briefly note *ipsus* (also *ipse*), *hisce* (also *hi*), the dative singular feminine *solae*, certain active forms like *luctare*, *altercare*, imperfects of the type *insanibat*, and finally certain archaisms restricted to the end of metrical units (verse or half-verse): *-ier*, *siem*, *attigo*, *face*, *duint*, etc.

That Terence used a language of greater restraint and refinement is evident from a consideration of certain categories of words which above were taken as typical of colloquial speech. Terms of abuse and invective are used with greater economy and as pointers of character. There are fewer frequentative verbs, fewer diminutives, fewer compounds in *ad-*, *con- de-* (see above), and most of those which he introduced were later incorporated in the literary language. In his dialogue passages, too, Terence is at pains to achieve a closer approximation to natural speech. It has been shown, for instance by Haffter, that Terence prefers primary interjections like *hem*, *au*, *vah*, etc., to the secondary interjections *hercle*, *age*, etc., and far more often than in Plautus they constitute by themselves a complete utterance, e.g.

> ecquid spei porrost? :: nescio :: ah! (*Phorm.* 474)
> Geta! :: hem! :: quid egisti? (Ibid. 682)
> una omnis nos aut scire aut nescire hoc volo :: ah! :: quid est?
> (Ibid. 809)

> di obsecro vos, estne hic Stilpo? :: non :: negas?
> concede hinc a foribus paulum istorsum, sodes, Sophrona.
> ne me istoc posthac nomine appellassis :: Quid, non, obsecro, es
> quem semper te esse dictitasti? :: st! (Ibid. 740 ff.)

This exclamation in Plautus is invariably followed by an imperative, e.g. *st! tace*; *st! abi*. This passage illustrates yet another peculiarity of Terence's fidelity to colloquial usage: far more frequently than Plautus he allows an isolated *non* to stand in a negative answer, the supporting verb being supplied from the preceding question. This is merely one instance of the closer dovetailing in Terence of the speeches of the dialogue partners, who content themselves, as in natural speech, with the minimum of words, the sense finding its completion in the context of situation. The rapidity thus achieved will best emerge from a few examples:

> quid ago? dic, Hegio :: ego? Cratinum censeo
> si tibi videtur :: dic, Cratine :: mene vis? ::
> te.   (Ibid. 447 ff.)
>   salve, Geta! ::
> venire salvom volup est :: credo :: quid agitur?
> multa advenienti, ut fit, nova hic? :: compluria.::
> ita. De Antiphone audistin quae facta? :: omnia.
>   (Ibid. 609 ff.)

quid istuc negotist? :: iamne operuit ostium? :: iam.

(Phorm. 816)

Finally

quaeso quid narras? :: quin tu mi argentum cedo.
:: immo vero uxorem tu cedo :: in ius ambula.
:: enim vero si porro esse odiosi pergitis . . .
:: quid facies? :: egone? vos me indotatis modo
patrocinari fortasse arbitramini:
etiam dotatis soleo :: quid id nostra? :: nihil.
hic quandam noram quoius vir uxorem . . . :: hem :: quid est?
Lemni habuit aliam, :: nullu' sum :: ex qua filiam
suscepit.   (Ibid. 935 ff.)

Here we also find exemplified the naturalistic use of interruption
which again distinguishes Terence from Plautus, who makes surprisingly little use of it. Plautus, in fact, tends to make each
utterance an independent entity. In this respect, too, Terence re-
produces more faithfully the conditions of actual speech: e.g.

si quis me quaeret rufu' . . . :: praestost, desine.   (Ibid. 51)
cedo, quid portas, obsecro? atque id, si potes, verbo expedi.
:: faciam :: eloquere :: modo apud portum . . . :: meumne? :: intel-
lexti :: occidi :: hem!   (Ibid. 197 ff.)

Finally Terence, though less coarse and vigorous than Plautus,
still makes abundant use of colloquial words and turns of expression. Thus from a single play, the *Phormio*, we pick out *conraditur*
(40), *ibi continuo* (101), *non sum apud me* (204), *garris* (210), *de-
putare* (246); the affirmative replies *admodum, sic, oppido* (315 ff.);
tennitur (330), *atque adeo quid mea?* 'Well, for all I care' (389), *cedo*
'tell me' (398), *dicam . . . impingam* (439), *numquid patri subolet?*
'Has my father smelt a rat?' (474); the synonyms for 'rubbish!'
hariolare, fabulae, logi (492 f.); *commodum* = 'just now' (614), *faces-
sat* 'make off' (635), *effuttiretis* 'blurt out' (746), *dilapidat* 'makes
a hole (in our funds)' (897), *quid id nostra?* 'What has that to do
with us?' (940), *ogganniat* 'nags' (1030). There is thus no doubt
that Terence contains a strong colloquial element which, we may
presume, reflects contemporary usage. Whether this was the mode
of speech current in 'the Scipionic circle' is, of course, not capable
of proof. At any rate, Terence's greater refinement and reticence
may be interpreted as characteristic of upper-class speech. But
equally well the differences between Plautus and the younger

playwright may reflect differences of literary technique. For the language of Terence, though less lavish and obtrusive in its use of ornamentation, is far removed from even the most educated and cultured speech of everyday life. The analysis of a few passages will make this evident.

Alliteration appears even in iambic passages of colloquial colouring:

abi sis, insciens:
quoius tu fidem in pecunia perspexeris,
verere verba ei credere?   (*Phorm.* 59 ff.)

persuasumst homini: factumst: ventumst: vincimur:
duxit. :: quid narras? :: hoc quod audis :: o Geta!
quid te futurumst? :: nescio hercle: unum hoc scio,
quod fors feret feremus aequo animo.   (Ibid. 135 ff.)

(Note the asyndeton and homoioteleuton of the first line.)

quin quod est
ferundum fers? tuis dignum factis feceris,
ut amici inter nos simus?   (Ibid. 429 ff.)

neque mi in conspectum prodit ut saltem sciam
quid de ea re dicat quidve sit sententiae.   (Ibid. 443 ff.)

tum pluscula
supellectile opus est; opus est sumptu ad nuptias.
(Ibid. 665 ff.)

With this passage, elaborately figured with alliteration, anaphora, and chiasmus, we may compare:

qui saepe propter invidiam adimunt diviti
aut propter misericordiam addunt pauperi?
(Ibid. 276–7)

with clause parallelism, assonance, and homoioteleuton. The passages in the longer verses, as we should expect, show greater profusion of stylistic ornamentation. A few brief examples must suffice:

at non cotidiana cura haec angeret animum :: audio.
:: dum expecto quam mox veniat qui adimat hanc mihi consuetudinem.
:: aliis quia defit quod amant aegrest; tibi quia superest dolet:
amore abundas, Antipho.
nam tua quidem hercle certo vita haec expetenda optandaque est.
(Ibid. 160 ff.)

Here, besides the elaborate alliteration, we note the concluding 'congeries' with homoioteleuton.

'retinere amare amittcre' (175), 'deserta egens ignota' (751), 'orat confitetur purgat' (1035) may serve as examples of tricolon with asyndeton. Tricolon with anaphora, alliteration, and 'increasing magnitude' is exemplified in 'eius me miseret, ei nunc timeo, is nunc me retinet' (188). As a final illustration of studied and elaborate figuring we may quote:

di tibi omnes id quod es dignus duint!
:: ego te compluris advorsum ingenium meum mensis tuli
pollicitantem et nil ferentem, flentem; nunc contra omnia haec
repperi qui det neque lacrumet: da locum melioribus.

(Ibid. 519 ff.)

These examples suffice to show clearly that Terence employed the same conventional stylistic devices of the archaic literary language (see next chapter) which we have detected in Plautus. Though his effects are subtler, his art more concealed, Terence's idiom is far removed from the natural speech of any coterie however precious. Indeed doubt has been cast even on the statement in the *vita* that Terence was an intimate associate of Scipio Africanus and Laelius, while Jachmann has voiced the suspicion that the correct and pure speech attributed by Cicero to Scipio and Laelius may merely be an inference from the usage of Terence, who, it is suggested, himself created this urbane latinity in the effort to evolve a Latin equivalent for Menander's allusive and restrained ἀστειότης with its varied and subtle character effects. In Plautus, on the other hand, we have the language of musical comedy or *opéra bouffe*. On the qualities of Terence's style and the success of his endeavours to capture the effects of Greek new comedy, a foreign critic, far removed in time and place, can do no better than quote the ancient testimonies attributed by Suetonius (*Vita Ter.*) to those great masters of Latin—Cicero and Caesar:

Cicero in Limone hactenus laudat:
'tu quoque, qui solus lecto sermone, Terenti,
conversum expressumque latina voce Menandrum
in medium nobis sedatis vocibus effers
quiddam come loquens atque omnia dulcia dicens.'
item C. Caesar:
'tu quoque, tu in summis, o dimidiate Menander,

poneris, et merito, puri sermonis amator.
lenibus atque utinam scriptis adiuncta foret vis
comica ut aequato virtus polleret honore
cum Graecis neve hac despectus parte iaceres.
unum hoc maceror ac doleo tibi deesse, Terenti.'

That certain of his contemporaries also censured this want of force
and vigour is apparent from the prologue to the *Phormio* (4 f.):

qui ita dictitat, quas antehac fecit fabulas,
tenui esse oratione et scriptura levi.

CHAPTER V

THE DEVELOPMENT OF THE LITERARY LANGUAGE

A. POETRY

LANGUAGE, the instrument of man's communication with his fellows, is created, adapted, and refined in response to the manifold and ever-changing demands of society and the environment in which it is set. Thus the history of a language is nothing less than the history of a culture. Of the significance of the Greeks for the development of early Roman civilization and language much has been said in earlier chapters. When we now turn to study the growth of literary Latin this influence becomes overwhelming. From the crucible of history had emerged a nation of farmer-soldiers, tough and disciplined, the destined masters of Italy and the Mediterranean world. One by one the Hellenic and Hellenized cities and states went down before a force whose strength lay not in numbers or physique, not in wealth or cunning, but in disciplined cohesion and the practice of the *ius armorum*. But Vegetius, who thus diagnosed the causes of Rome's greatness, acknowledged Greek supremacy in the arts of civilization: 'Graecorum artibus prudentiaque nos vinci nemo dubitavit' (*de re militari* I. I).

It was no more than the blunt truth: at the time of Rome's triumph over the flourishing cities of Magna Graecia in the first part of the third century, for all her advance in wealth and power, there was still no native Roman literature worthy of the name. The revelation of the cultural treasures amassed by the world's most gifted people over a long and eventful history had an overwhelming effect. The Roman conqueror submitted to the defeated. Anxious that Rome should rank in culture with the Greeks, the victorious generals, along with statues and paintings, brought back from their campaigns philosophers and rhetors to educate their children. Typical of the philhellenic zeal among the Roman aristocracy is Aemilius Paullus, who in 168 crushed Perseus of Macedonia at Pydna: as the spoils of victory he demanded nothing but the king's library. Nor is Latin literature, at least in its beginning, any less a tale of plunder, and a Roman author's proudest boast was that he was the first to lay his hand to the pillage. It is true that the central fire of essential Roman genius burned steadily beneath this imposed mass of alien material and in the course of time was to burst into a flame which matched in splendour the brightest of the Greeks. Yet the historian of the language who is also a lover of Virgil must stress the fact that all Latin literary genres with the exception of satire ('satira tota nostra est' is all that Quintilian can claim) owed their form and much of their content to Greek practice and theory. So it is first to Greek literature that we must turn to reach an understanding of the progress of literary Latin.

The student of Greek literature soon discovers that he must learn not one language but many dialects. This is a consequence of the formalism of Greek literature, the unquestioned convention which established that to each genre there is appropriate a peculiar form of language. Thus the Homeric epics were the ultimate product of a tradition of poetry which, originating among speakers of the Aeolic dialect, had in the course of time passed over to bards whose native dialect was Ionic. Thus, in the poetical diction of the Homeric poems there is embedded a fund of words and turns of phrase of different chronological periods and different dialects. The epic dialect is an artificial product, remote from the normal speech of its creators. Yet the convention once established, every writer of epic down to the end of the Greek world composed in that dialect. Choral lyric again evolved among the Dorians, and so Doric became the dialect proper to this genre whatever the native dialect of the writer. This is why the Athenian drama abruptly changes its dialect when it passes from dialogue in iambics to choral lyric. The same principle holds good to some extent for prose. It was by Ionians that history, science, and medicine were first written: henceforth Ionic is the accepted language of scientific prose, as for instance the Hippocratean corpus, while the Athenian Thucydides gives the language of his history at least an Ionic colouring.

Such in brief were the linguistic conventions of Greek literature. But before we turn to the study of the Roman authors and their emulation of Greek models we must recall another fact. At the time when the Romans began their literary apprenticeship, Greek literature had passed its zenith. It was on the Hellenistic world of Alexander's successors that the Romans impinged and Hellenistic poetry was the creation of highly cultivated coteries of scholar-poets, with an overriding interest in literary techniques, taking pride in obscure, learned allusion, embellishing their works with outlandish words, the 'glossae', those bizarre jewels cut from ancient robes. The *doctus poeta* holds the stage, untiring in his researches to unearth new material for poetry. In language his foible is the rare antique.

It was at this period in the development of Greek literature that Rome began its apprenticeship in the art of writing.

> initium quoque eius (scil. grammaticae) mediocre extitit, siquidem antiquissimi doctorum, qui idem et poetae et semigraeci erant (Livium et Ennium dico, quos utraque lingua domi forisque docuisse adnotatum est) nihil amplius quam Graecos interpretabantur, aut siquid ipsi Latine composuissent praelegebant (Suet. *gram.* 1).

The Greek sensitivity to language in the various literary genres is apparent in the earliest Roman literature, which begins with the translation of the *Odyssey* into saturnians by Livius Andronicus, a native of Tarentum who was brought as a slave in 242 to Rome and there adopted into the *gens Livia*. Few fragments of his work survive, but an acute analysis by E. Fraenkel[1] has made it clear that the conventions of Hellenistic poetry with its distinction of genres prevailed. Thus the phrase *diva Monetas filia* (fr. 30) 'the Muse' contains the archaic genitive in -*as* which in Classical Latin survived only in *pater familias*. This was an archaism even in Andronicus' time, for elsewhere he uses -*ai*, as does even the archaizing *Senatus Consultum de Bacchanalibus*. What is significant is that of the genitives in -*as* quoted by Priscian (1. 198 f.) three come from the *Odyssey* of Andronicus, two from the *Bellum Poeni-cum* of Naevius, and one from the *Annales* of Ennius. Now all these belong to the genre of epic: Priscian quotes none from the trage-dies of these three poets although he was familiar with them. Other features foreign to tragic diction which may be detected in the fragments of Andronicus are *filie* (vocative), *dextrabus*, *dusmo*

---

[1] *R.-E.*, Suppl. V. 603 f.

(= *dumo*), *homōnem, fitum est*, third-person plurals of the type *nequinont*, and the adverb *quamde*. Fraenkel concludes

> again and again it may be shown how Livius is at pains by means of highly archaic forms of speech to lend dignity and remoteness to his epic, remoteness not only from every-day language but also from the style of less august poetical genres. . . . All his successors adhered to the same principle. To the language of Roman epic from its beginnings there was reserved the privilege of a solemnity greater even than that of tragedy, to say nothing of other poetica lgenres.

It should be emphasized, however, that all Roman poetical genres, tragedy and even satire, make use of archaisms as an ingredient of their diction. Epic is different in degree, not in kind.

In their search for archaic colouring the poets availed themselves of disused forms of declension and conjugation besides the obsolete words for which they drew largely on the language of religion and law. The material may be conveniently arranged under the two headings of morphology and vocabulary. In drawing up such lists we should, of course, bear in mind that archaism is a relative term. Many of the forms in early poetry which appeared ancient to the writers of the classical period were contemporary forms for the poets who used them. Among these are difference of gender such as *caelus* (m.) or *lapides* (f.), points of declension, like *exerciti*, *speres*, or of conjugation, like *fodantes*, *horĭtur*, *resonunt*, etc., which were eliminated in the process of normalization which we shall discuss below. Nor should we forget that imitation of predecessors which ancient theory enjoined on the poet. Thus poets later than Ennius may use a form or a word not *qua* archaism but because it had occurred in Ennius. This question of 'Ennianisms' will occupy us later in our discussion of the language of Virgil. With these provisos made, we may list among the most important morphological archaisms of early Latin poetical diction: in the noun declension the genitive singular in -*āī*, genitive plurals in -*um* (e.g. *factum*); among the pronouns and demonstratives, *ipsus*, *olli*, and the dative-ablative *quīs*; adverbs of the type *superbiter, aequiter, rarenter, concorditer* and *contemptim, iuxtim, visceratim*, etc. In the verbal system the most important phenomena are the infinitive passives in -*ier*, the imperfects of the fourth conjugation in -*ibat*, desiderative stems in -ss- such as in *prohibessis*, the perfects in *-ĕrunt* (a persistent colloquial form which was an archaism in poetry)[1] and *-ēre* for *-ērunt*. Finally we may mention forms like *fuas*, *superescit*. But it was not merely by sounds and forms that the appropriate colouring was achieved. The poetical genres were distinguished also in their permitted vocabulary. Greek practice in this matter had been analysed and formulated by Aristotle. Making a fundamental distinction between words in current usage (κύρια ὀνόματα) and those foreign to it (τὰ ξενικά) he had laid it down that elevated literary expression depends on the moderate use of such ξενικά, which raise the diction above the commonplace (ταπεινόν). Among the uncommon modes of expression he particularly singled out the *glossae* (strange or rare words) as particularly appropriate to the epic genre, although he allowed it also to make use of compound words, which were primarily the province of dithyramb, and of metaphor, which is especially a mark of iambic verse. The gloss was indeed especially characteristic of Greek epic in the mature form which appears in the Homeric poems. This was, as we have seen, a consequence of the history of epic poetry, for Homer is the culmination of a centuries-old bardic tradition which had preserved forms and words no longer current in the contemporary spoken idiom of the poet. Homer imposed his authority on all subsequent Greek poetry and provided an inexhaustible quarry of poetical materials. No source of comparable richness was available to the pioneers of Roman literature, and in any case few traces survive of the sources on which the early poets drew for their words of antique flavour. The historian of Latin must lament no less than Cicero the loss of the ancient *carmina*:

> atque utinam exstarent illa carmina, quae multis saeculis ante suam aetatem in epulis esse cantitata a singulis conviviis de clarorum virorum laudibus in Originibus scriptum reliquit Cato (*Brutus* 75).

Ennius, too, refers to his predecessors who wrote in the Saturnian measure. It was doubtless such traditional poetry which provided Andronicus and his successors with the numerous words characteristic of poetical diction such as *Camena*, *celsus*, *amnis* (an ancient 'Italo-Celtic' word related to our 'Avon'), *aerumna* (possibly of

---

[1] On the terms 'archaic', 'poetical', and 'colloquial', see c. VI.

Etruscan origin), *anguis* (= *serpens*), *artus* (= *membrum*), *letum* (= *mors*), *tellus* (= *terra*), *umeo* and *umor*, and further archaic verbs such as *defit, infit, claret, clueo*; and the numerous religious terms, such as the verbs *adolere, parentare, mactare, opitulari, libare*, the nouns *nemus, flamen, vates, epulo, polubrum, eclutrum, sagmen, lituus, libum, tesca*, and the adjectives *almus, castus, dirus* (possibly of Sabine origin), *augustus, obscenus, tutulatus, solemnis*. The majestic formulae of the law were, no less than religion, a source of unusual words. A passage of Varro (*L.L.* 7. 42) is enlightening in this respect. Commenting on Ennius' 'Olli respondit suavis sonus Egeriai' he writes:

> 'Olli' valet dictum 'illi' ab 'olla' et 'ollo', quod alterum comitiis cum recitatur a praecone dicitur 'olla centuria' non 'illa'; alterum apparet in funeribus indictivis quo dicitur: 'Ollus leto datus est'.

Here we have a clear indication of the formulae of law and religion as twin sources of poetic diction.

Dialect words, too, were received into the poetical language in accordance with Greek theory and practice. Apropos of the verse *veteres Casmenas cascam rem volo profarier* Varro (7. 28) comments, 'primum *cascum* significat *vetus*; secundo eius origo Sabina, quae usque radices in Oscam linguam egit'. Similar is his comment on *catus* in Ennius' *iam cata signa ferae sonitum dare voce parabant*: '*cata* acuta: hoc enim verbo dicunt Sabini'. It is possible, too, that *cohum*, which the poets are said to have used for *caelum*, is a dialect doublet of *cavum*. Other foreign 'glosses' are *meddix* and *famul* (both Oscan), *ambactus* (Gaulish), *sibyna* (Illyrian), and *rumpia* (Thracian).

Greek inevitably supplied the largest contingent under this heading, but serious Latin poetry was much more reserved than comedy and the popular language in admitting Greek words. Thus even *Musa* was refused entry by Livius Andronicus, who substituted *Camena*, the native word for 'a goddess of the springs and waters' (though it was ultimately of Etruscan origin, if we may believe Macrobius). Naevius for his part had recourse to a periphrasis to render Μοῦσαι: 'novem Iovis concordes filiae sorores' (*B.P.* fr. 1). Only Ennius boldly allows the foreign muses to stamp the ground of a Latin Olympus: 'Musae quae pedibus magnum pulsatis Olympum' (A. 1 W.). Ennius admitted other Greek words such as *bradys*, *charta, coma, lychnus,* but a feeling of uneasiness about such a procedure is made evident in his use of *aer*: 'vento quem perhibent Graium genus aera lingua' (*A.* 152 W.), and his successors showed themselves sparing in their use of Greek, as indeed of all foreign glosses. In this, too, they were obedient pupils of the Greeks who were aware that excessive use of this stylistic device would result in βαρβαρισμός.

Ennius' devotion to his Greek models led him to commit a few errors of taste which, however, had no effect on subsequent poetry. Aristotle included in 'glossae' certain word distortions, among them apocopized forms. In part this theory rested on a misunderstanding. Homer had preserved an ancient word δῶ, which to eyes of later generations looked like a shortened form of δῶμα. On the apparent authority of Homer Euphorion had ventured ἦλ for ἦλος. With such models before him Ennius was emboldened to write *cael* for *caelum* (*Spur.* 34 W.), *do* for *domus* (ibid. 35), and *gau* for *gaudium* (ibid. 33). Similar is the false use of 'tmesis'. This, too, was an archaic feature of Homeric diction which Ennius could legitimately echo with his *de me hortatur.* But such monstrosities as *cere . . . brum* ('saxo cere-comminuit-brum', *Spur.* 13 W.) did violence to the language. Eminent advocates have, however, protested Ennius' innocence of this particular offence. Another shortlived aberration was Ennius' use of the epic case-ending *-oeo* in *Mettoeoque Fufetioeo* (*A.* 139 W.). On this Quintilian (1. 5. 12) remarks 'Ennius poetico iure defenditur'. As we have seen, there is some evidence that this case form may have existed in dialect Latin.

It was not only in general matters of literary theory and conventions that Greek exerted its influence in the formation of the Latin literary language. The fact that so much of early Latin poetry is not merely imitation but even close translation of Greek meant that the Greek stood constantly at the elbow of his pupil. This may be exemplified in the line with which Latin poetry may be said to begin,

> virum mihi, Camena, insece versutum. (*Od.* 1)

a translation of ἄνδρα μοι ἔννεπε, Μοῦσα, πολύτροπον *Od.* 1. 1, where Andronicus has rendered the archaic ἔννεπε by a corresponding 'gloss' derived from we know not what source (he could hardly have anticipated the findings of modern philology which regards these two words as etymologically identical (< *en-seqᵂe)). The last word of the Greek original typifies a problem which taxed the resources of the Latin translator and imitator. Greek still retained in full vigour the power to create compound words which it used freely in poetry, especially as ornamental epithets. Latin, however, had largely lost this inherited facility. Thus Andronicus' *versutus* represents an idiomatic way of rendering the Greek compound πολύτροπος. Occasionally a native derivational type proved adequate to sustain the burden of the Greek. This is true, for instance, of the adjectives in -*ōsus*, which provided happy equivalents for the many Greek ornamental epithets in πολυ- and -όεις. Examples are: *frondosus* (Enn.), *fragosus, labeosus* (Lucr.), *piscosus, lacrimosus, squamosus, spumosus*, etc. The equivalence of such words to compounds is pointed by Cicero's coinage of *squamiger* and *spumifer* for the last two examples, just as he found in *aestifer* an equivalent for the metrically impossible *aestuosus. aestifer* is accepted by Lucretius and Virgil. Besides *squamosus* Virgil coined another substitute *squameus*, which may serve to typify yet another native Latin suffix stimulated by the pressure of the Greek and especially favoured by the hexameter poets because of its convenient metrical shape (see below). But on the whole the resources of Latin were inadequate to render the immense variety of Greek compounds. Andronicus himself, when at a loss, is content with the most make-shift substitutes: thus χαλκήρει (δουρί) simply appears as *celeris* (*hasta*), which imitates the sound while not rendering the meaning. But later poets, recognizing that the ornamental compound is an essential feature of the epic style, were driven to a procedure which was alien to the genius of their language. Andronicus' *quinquertio* for πένταθλος was still-born, but the most tasteless audacity was shown by the tragic poets. Nothing in epic can rival Pacuvius' (fr. 352 W.) notorious 'Nerei repandirostrum incurvicervicum pecus' (cf. ἀγκυλοχείλης κυρταύχην). Andronicus had contented himself with *simum pecus*. In general compound words were limited to a few well-defined types. For Naevius' *silvicola* there was ample precedent in words like *agricola*. But his creation *arquitenens* was the prototype of a class which was destined to play an important part in the diction of Roman epic—

suaviloquens, altitonans, omnipotens, sapientipotens, velivolans, etc.
Similar to these is the type exemplified by *suavisonus,* which
appears in a tragic fragment of Naevius, although perhaps Livius
may claim priority in this class with *odorisequus* which is attributed to him. There is in subsequent poetry a number of such
compounds in which the second part consists of a verbal stem:
e.g. *altisonus* (Ennius, etc.), *laetificus* (Ennius, etc.), *largificus*
(Lucr.), *velivolus* (Enn., etc.), *horrisonus* (Lucr., etc.), *montivagus*
(Lucr.), *frugiparus* (Lucr.), etc. In the works of Naevius we find
three other prototypes which account for much of subsequent
creation of poetical compounds:

1. *frondifer,* cf. *dulcifer, frugifer, flammifer,* etc. (Ennius), *aestifer,
   florifer, glandifer,* etc. (Lucretius).
2. *tyrsiger:* cf. *armiger* (Acc.), *barbiger, corniger* (Lucr.), *laniger,
   naviger, saetiger, squamiger* (Lucr.), etc.
3. *bicorpor:* cf. *bipes* (Naevius, *trag.*), *bilinguis* (Enn.), *trifax* (Enn.),
   biiugus (Lucr.), *tripectorus* (Lucr.), etc.

Apart from these there are few productive types. Compounds consisting of two noun stems such as *dentefabres, levisomnus, mult-
angulus, omnimodus,* etc., were much rarer. Prominent among these
are compounds in *-pes, alipes* (Lucr.), *sonipes* (Acc.), *capripes*
(Lucr.), *levipes* (Cic.), *mollipes* (Cic.). Of those which found general
acceptance we may mention *magnanimus, grandaevus, primaevus.*

Thus while the Roman poets dutifully wrestled with a recalci-
trant language to produce the poetical compounds rendered obligatory by the laws of the genre, in many cases they had to admit
defeat and either ignored Greek compounds or rendered them by
periphrases: thus τανύφυλλος appears as (*cupressi stant*) *rectis foliis*
(Enn.) πολύμοχθος as *magni* (*formica*) *laboris* (Hor.), εὔρροος as *late
fusa* (Cic.), θεοπροπέων as *fidenti voce* (Cic.).

Greek exerted yet another decisive influence on the form of the
literary language of Latin when Ennius broke with the custom of
his predecessors and instead of the native Saturnian measure composed his *Annales* in a Greek metre, the hexameter. Latin is poor
in the dactylic words which this measure requires and Ennius had
recourse to a variety of devices to avoid words of impossible
rhythmical pattern. Thus for *imperare, intuetur, involans* he used

H

‾ ⏑ ⏑   ‾ ⏑ ⏑   ‾ ⏑ ⏑
induperare, indotuetur, induvolans with a prefix *indo*, which occurs
in the Twelve Tables but was already obsolete in the time of
Plautus. This device was considered too bizarre by later poets who
solved the problem posed by words like *imperare* by using the frequentative form *imperitare*. Such metrical compulsion also explains the use of poetical plurals such as *gaudia, otia* and the
phonetic doublets of the type *vincula* but *vinclis*. In other cases
recourse was had to morphological devices such as the preference
for 'archaic' genitive plurals *parentum, cadentum, agrestum*, etc.,
or the choice of the perfect infinitive for the present: *continuisse*
for *continere*, although this, too, had its roots in archaic syntax.
The search for dactylic patterns is evident also in the preference
given to certain types of derivation: for *magnitudo* and *differentia*
Lucretius substituted *maximitas* and *differitas*. Neuters in *-men*
provide a convenient dactyl in the plural (*fragmina*), and this may
explain the preference of the poets for this type of formation,
which was a feature of the archaic language (Ps.-Servius *A*. 10. 306:
fragmina: antique dictum). Yet when full justice has been done to
Greece's fostering of Latin literature, the citation of a few lines
from its period of vigorous adolescence proclaims the essential
latinity of the language. It is not merely that the vocabulary is
predominantly Latin except for the small percentage of 'glossae'
admitted in deference to poetic law. The devices of stylization are
patently un-Greek. This appears immediately if we contrast a passage of Ennius with the Greek which he has translated

> ὦ μοι πῆι δή τοι φρένες οἴχονθ' ἧις τὸ πάρος περ
> ἔκλε' ἐπ' ἀνθρώπους;
>
> Quo vobis mentes rectae quae stare solebant
> ante hac dementes sese flexere viai?   (*A*. 194–5 W.)

Here we see exemplified that love of word-play (*mentes–dementes*)
and assonance, especially alliteration, which was deeply rooted in
Latin soil, if we may judge from proverbs like *mense Maio malae
nubunt*, and from religious *carmina* such as 'utique tu fruges frumenta vineta virgultaque grandire beneque evenire siris pastores
pecuaque salva servassis' (see above). Indeed the occurrence of
similar alliterative word pairs among the Italic peoples (e.g. the
Umbrian prayer: 'iovie hostatu anhostatu tursitu tremitu hondu

holtu ninctu nepitu sonitu savitu preplotatu previlatu ') shows that alliteration and assonance were endemic among the Italic peoples. Examples of this abound in Ennius, e.g.

> Haec ecfatus pater, germana, repente recessit
> nec sese dedit in conspectum corde cupitus
> quamquam multa manus ad caeli caerula templa
> tendebam lacrumans et blanda voce vocabam.
>
> (*A.* 44–47 W.)

where the *figura etymologica* should also be noted. Occasionally alliteration is pushed to excess as in the notorious

> O Tite tute Tati tibi tanta, tyranne, tulisti! (*A.* 108 W.)

In Ennius, too, we find fully developed the rhetorical devices of homoioteleuton (*Romani . . . Campani*), paronomasia (*explebant . . . replebant*), antithesis and isocolia (see section on prose), which henceforward set their stamp on the poetical language of the Romans. The following passages may be left to provide their own commentary.

> nec mi aurum posco nec mi pretium dederitis
> nec cauponantes bellum sed belligerantes
> ferro non auro, vitam cernamus utrique;
> vosne velit an me regnare era, quidve ferat Fors
> virtute experiamur. et hoc simul accipe dictum.
> quorum virtuti belli fortuna pepercit,
> eorundem libertati me parcere certum est.
> dono, ducite, doque volentibus cum magnis dis.
>
> (*A.* 186 ff. W.)

> pellitur e medio sapientia, vi geritur res,
> spernitur orator bonus, horridus miles amatur;
> haud doctis dictis certantes, sed maledictis
> miscent inter sese inimicitiam agitantes;
> non ex iure manum consertum, sed magis ferro
> rem repetunt regnumque petunt, vadunt solida vi.
>
> (*A.* 263 ff. W.)

Passages such as these reveal Ennius as the creator of the language of Roman epic. Of Virgil's debt to Ennius we shall speak later. Ennius' influence on Lucretius was so profound that F. Skutsch wrote: 'We may venture to say that apart from divergences in the construction of periods and the difference in the theme nothing can give a better idea of the Ennian style than a careful linguistic analysis of Lucretius.'

In its language the *de rerum natura* is largely unaffected by the reform movement of the 'urbanizers' whose work of purification and standardization is revealed in the rigid grammatical canons of the classical authors. In the imprecision of his grammar, Lucretius, for all the difference in time, is closer to Ennius and Plautus than to the Augustan purists. In him we find much the same variations of gender (*finis*, m. and f.), declension (*sanguen, sanguis*, etc.), conjugation (*sonere*), syntax (e.g. *cum* causal with the indicative), which are characteristic of archaic Latin literature. But this grammatical uncertainty we should scarcely label 'archaism'. Lucretius was no Alexandrian poet searching diligently for verbal effects to win the plaudits of salon preciosity. A rationalist zealot burning to save souls from religion, he used as the most effective instrument of clear exposition the language of his own time, not scorning an occasional colloquialism (e.g. *belle, lepidus*). But the Latin poet must bow to the laws of the genre. Hexameter forms, of course, he must create (e.g. *indugredi, discrepitant, inopi, disposta, disque supatis, seque gregari*). Even in his neologisms (and his theme obliged him to much invention—'nec me animi fallit Graiorum obscura reperta difficile inlustrare Latinis versibus esse, multa novis verbis praesertim cum sit agendum propter egestatem linguae et rerum novitatem', 1. 136 ff.) Lucretius uses the traditional moulds: e.g. adverbs like *moderatim*, and compounds like *falcifer*. In his devices of stylization, too, Lucretius ranges himself among the archaic poets. Of that 'congeries', the accumulation of synonyms which Ennius had reduced to absurdity with his 'maerentes flentes lacrumantes commiserantes' (*Spur.* 40 W.), Lucretius offers innumerable examples: 'inane vacansque' (1. 334), 'officere atque obstare' (337), 'saepta et clausa' (354), 'seiunctum secretumque' (431), 'levis exiguusque' (435), 'seiungi seque gregari' (452), 'speciem ac formam' (4. 52), 'duplici geminoque' (274), 'monstra ac portenta' (590). For sustained alliteration we may refer to 1. 250–64, a passage which also exemplifies the use of the constant ornamental epithet, balanced clauses marked by homoioteleuton and anaphora. The verb *virescunt*, which is first attested here, may serve to illustrate the fondness of the poets for verbs in -*esco*.

It was in his use of archaisms and 'glossae' that Lucretius, while conforming to convention and poetical propriety, revealed what effects could be achieved by an artist of genius. A bare list of these elements of his diction would range Lucretius with the gifted amateur poet Cicero, who was his contemporary—genitives in -*āī* in -*um*, infinitives in -*ier*, simple verbs for compound, and the rest. But it is especially in his use of such conventional devices of traditional poetic diction that Lucretius reveals the poet of genius. When his fire bursts through the superincumbent material of natural philosophy, the archaism and the gloss blaze with a light not of this world. Of the many passages of superb poetry we must content ourselves with the one (1. 80 ff.) in which Lucretius rendered the exquisite pathos of one of the most moving passages of Greek poetry—the Iphigenia chorus of the *Agamemnon*. Analysis will damage less if it precedes. *scelerosa* is an archaic formation in -*osus* (see above) for the more usual *sceleratus*, and it is combined in 'congeries' with *impia*. Further archaisms are the genitives in -*āī*, the anastrophe of *propter*, the adjective *tremibundus*. As 'glossae' we may consider the forms *Iphianassai, Danaum, Hymenaeo*. The theme itself makes inevitable the presence of ancient ritual terms: *infula, ministros, casta, hostia, mactatu, ʃelix faustusque*. Finally we may note a syntactical Grecism, the 'calque' *prima virorum*. Yet the presence of these ornaments of the genre in a passage which owes much of its magnificent pictorial qualities to Greek inspiration does not impair its essential latinity. It may serve to exemplify in all its phases the progress which the Romans had made towards the creation of an effective poetical language.

> Illud in his rebus vereor, ne forte rearis
> impia te rationis inire elementa viamque
> indugredi sceleris. quod contra saepius illa
> religio peperit scelerosa atque impia facta.
> Aulide quo pacto Triviai virginis aram
> Iphianassai turparunt sanguine foede
> ductores Danaum delecti, prima virorum.
> cui simul infula virgineos circumdata comptus
> ex utraque pari malarum parte profusast,
> et maestum simul ante aras adstare parentem

sensit, et hunc propter ferrum celare ministros,
aspectuque suo lacrimas effundere civis,
muta metu terram genibus summissa petebat:
nec miserae prodesse in tali tempore quibat
quod patrio princeps donarat nomine regem:
nam sublata virum manibus tremibundaque ad aras
deductast, non ut sollemni more sacrorum
perfecto posset claro comitari Hymenaeo,
sed casta inceste, nubendi tempore in ipso,
hostia concideret mactatu maesta parentis,
exitus ut classi felix faustusque daretur.
tantum relligio potuit suadere malorum.

We have now traced out some of the main lines in the development of the language of Roman epic. Before turning to the greatest master of this genre we must briefly survey the efforts made to create a style appropriate to tragedy. We have already seen that Andronicus and Naevius admitted certain archaisms to epic which were too remote from ordinary speech for use in tragedy. But in general it may be said that the linguistic and stylistic differences between epic and tragedy are merely of degree and not of kind, and that one uniform stylized language of serious poetry was evolved in opposition to that of comedy and prose. Archaisms, 'poetical' and compound words distinguish the language of tragedy no less than of epic. Tragedy made perhaps more sparing use of such material, but the fragmentary tradition of drama and early epic makes it impossible to establish reliable statistics. Yet the most audacious compounds are attested for tragedy (see above). The tragedians, too, provide a rich material to exemplify those devices of stylization which abound in epic: alliteration, assonance, asyndeton, tricola, and finally the 'congeries', the heaping of synonyms, which was so characteristic a mark of the ancient *carmina* and legal formulae of the Romans. A few examples will suffice:

1. Alliteration (often with word-play and *figura etymologica*):

quin ut quisque est meritus praesens pretium pro factis ferat.
(Naevius, *trag.* 13 W.)

laetus sum laudari me abs te, pater, a laudato viro.   (Id. *trag.* 17 W.)

Salmacida spolia sine sudore et sanguine.   (Ennius, *trag.* 22 W.)

constitit credo Scamander, arbores vento vacant.   (Ibid. 197 W.)

(In the last example note the prominent place given to the verbs, a favourite device of Virgil);

> Interea loci
> flucti flacciscunt, silescunt venti, mollitur mare. (Pacuvius 82–83 W.)
> cui manus materno sordet sparsa sanguine. (Accius 12 W.)

2. Tricolon in asyndeton:

With Naevius'

> Urit populatur vastat   (*carm*. 32 W.)

we may compare

> ibid quid agat secum cogitat curat putat.   (Ennius, *trag*. 349 W.)
> constitit cognovit sensit, conlocat sese in locum
> celsum; hinc manibus rapere raudus saxeum grande et grave.
> > (Accius, *trag*. 424–5 W.)
> miseret lacrimarum luctuum orbitudinis.   (Ibid. 54 W.)

3. The 'padded style':

> ne illa mei feri ingeni atque animi acrem acrimoniam.
> > (Naevius, *trag*. 49 W.)
> more antiquo audibo atque auris tibi contra utendas dabo.
> > (Ennius, *trag*. 324 W.)
> id ego aecum ac ius fecisse expedibo atque eloquar.   (Ibid. 154 W.)
> pacem inter se conciliant, conferunt concordiam.   (Ibid. 372 W.)
> > . . . ne horum dividae et discordiae
> dissipent et disturbent tantas et tam opimas civium
> divitias.   (Accius, 590–2 W.)

Such were the general characteristics of pre-Augustan poetical language. But before Virgil was to raise Roman poetry to supreme heights, a reaction set in against the archaizing habits and ideals professed by the Ennian school. The 'modern school', the *poetae novi*, transplanted to Rome that quarrel of the ancients and moderns which had once divided the literati of Alexandria when Callimachus rejected the long epic as practised by Apollonius Rhodius and pronounced a big book to be a μέγα κακόν. Of this new school, headed by the grammarian and critic P. Valerius Cato, Catullus was the most gifted representative. These poets, too, would hear nothing of the lengthy epic (Cicero writes apropos of Ennius, 'O poetam egregium! quamquam ab his cantoribus Euphorionis contemnitur') and devoted themselves to genres of smaller compass which allowed time for the most exquisite refinements of form, language, and metre. It was in this last matter, which lies outside the scope of the present book, that their reforms were most effective. One point of prosody deserves mention as having a linguistic interest. The *novi* banned the neglect of the final -*s* which earlier poetry had allowed (Cic. *Or.* 161: 'eorum verborum quorum eaedem erant postremae duae litterae quae sunt in "optimus", postremam litteram detrahebant, nisi vocalis insequebatur. ita non erat ea offensio in versibus quam nunc fugiunt poetae novi'). This was merely one instance of their distaste for archaisms in general which, identified with *rusticitas*, the antithesis of modern elegance and *urbanitas*, the *novi* wished to banish from the language of poetry. Yet this endeavour was to a great extent thwarted by the laws which a professed Alexandrian poet must acknowledge. The obligatory mimesis of the predecessors meant that much of what they might reject as archaism was welcomed as poetic tradition. Thus even Catullus does not shun morphological archaisms such as *alis, alid, Troiugenum, amantum, tetuli, face, citarier, deposivit, lavit, recepso, quīs, quīcum, ubertim, miseritus,* or the archaic words *autumant, grates ago, oppido, nasse, illa tempestate = illo tempore, cupiens = cupidus, apisci, auctare* (this in a prayer, 67. 2), *postilla.* In his use of compounds, too, Catullus is faithful to the practice of his predecessors. In the poem *Peleus and Thetis*, which belonged to the epic genre, we find, for instance, *letifer, corniger, caelicola,* and *raucisonus, veridicus,* etc. But in his other poems he coins compounds which go outside these well-established types and vies with his Alexandrian models in venturing *pinnipes, plumipes,* and *silvicultrix.* The ornaments of style, too, are of the traditional type, although he is more discriminating in his use of alliteration, which he reserves in the main for special effects:

> Thesea cedentem celeri cum classe tuetur.   (64. 53)
>
> plangebant aliae proceris tympana palmis
> aut tereti tenuis tinnitus aere ciebant.   (Ibid. 261-2)

Other examples ('frigoraque et famem', 28. 5; 'libenter . . . laetus', 31. 4; 'satur supinus' (note the asyndeton) 32. 10) are presumably old-established word-pairs of ordinary speech. One trick of style deserves particular mention in view of its importance for the practice of Virgil: if two nouns occur in a verse and one must be qualified by an adjective, then to achieve balance an epithet is provided for the other noun. Further, in such word-groups a highly artificial word order is adopted in which the adjectives are either in parallel or form a chiasmus: e.g.

>   a b A B
>   inrita ventosae linquens promissa procellae.   (64. 59)

But

>   non flavo retinens subtilem vertice mitram,
>   non contecta levi velatum pectus amictu
>   non tereti strophio lactentis vincta papillas.

> (Ibid. 63 ff.)

where the arrangement is different in three successive lines: (1) abAB, (2) abBA, (3) aAbB. Finally an example of the chiastic arrangement: 'ausi sunt vada salsa cita decurrere puppi' (64. 6) = AabB.

Now that we have traced out the main lines in the gradual development of the instrument of poetry which the Romans under Greek guidance had built from native materials, it is time to turn to Virgil. A Roman poet schooled in the Alexandrian tradition, he paid to his predecessors the due of imitation. The majesty of his theme and the laws of the genre prescribed a language of Ennian colouring and ornamentation. Virgil's fund of basic 'poetical' words is that of his predecessors (*ales, almus, aequor, amnis, arbusta, caelestes, coma, ensis, genetrix, letum, mortales, proles,* etc.) with their marked preference for simple verbs (*linquo, temno, sido, suesco*). His innovations, too, are cast in the traditional mould: e.g. adjectives in *-eus* (*arboreus, frondeus, fumeus, funereus*); in *-alis, -ilis* (*armentalis, crinalis, flexilis, glacialis, sutilis*); in *-bilis* (*enarrabilis, immedicabilis, ineluctabilis*); in *-osus* (*onerosus, nimbosus, undosus, montosus*); inchoative verbs in *-esco* (*abolesco, crebresco, inardesco*); frequentatives (*convecto, domito, hebeto, inserto*); agent nouns in *-tor, -trix* (*fundator, latrator, pugnator*); neuters in *-men* (*gestamen, libamen, luctamen*). Yet Virgil's exquisite sensibility could not ignore the indubitable refinements of taste and technique which had been achieved through the research and experimentation of the *novi*. On the other hand, a poet of intense earnestness was bound to reject an oppressive and self-conscious erudition destructive of moral and emotional effect. Virgil, therefore, while remaining true to the language of his predecessors in the epic genre, does not depart too far from contemporary forms of speech. He does not, for instance, use archaisms such as *duona, sos, endo, danunt, escit*, nor ancient metaplastic forms such as *caelus, sanguen, flucti, lavere*, though perhaps certain of these were rejected as 'vulgar' rather than archaic (see Chapter VI); nor again adverbs of the type *rarenter, disertim*, and *contemptim*. Banned, too, are the dialect 'glossae' *cascus, baeto, perbito*, which perhaps he regarded as 'ex ultimis tenebris repetita' (cf. Quintilian 8. 3. 27). It is true that examples occur of the genitive in *-āī*, of *olle* and *quīs*, of verbal forms *-ier, faxo, fuat*, of the particles *ast, ceu*, and of *pone*. But these archaisms are not laid on indiscriminately, as vague poetical colour. Some, of course, were dictated by metrical necessity (*lenibat, nutribant, maerentum*) or convenience (e.g. the occurrence of infinitives in *-ier* in the fifth foot such as *accingier artes*). Others again occur in deliberate echoes of predecessors, as for instance the Lucretian passage *Aen.* 6. 724 ff. with its careful pointing of the logical structure by the particles *principio . . . hinc . . . ergo*, the archaism *ollis* (used only in this form by Lucretius), the elaborate alliteration (e.g. 'mens agitat molem et magno se corpore miscet'), which is particularly frequent at the end of the verse (e.g. 'vitaeque volantum, moribundaque membra, carcere caeco'). We may note further the pleonasm *revisant rursus*, and the numerous echoes of Lucretian (Ennian) phraseology (e.g. *globum lunae, modis miris, volantum* for *avium*).

But, *imitatio* apart, Virgil's archaisms are used with delicate and deliberate artistry. As with Lucretius, they are dictated by the theme. It is noteworthy, for instance, that the form *fuat* occurs in Virgil only in a speech of Jupiter (*A.* 10. 108), a passage worth examining in the present context. The words of the *pater omnipotens* are introduced by the archaism *infit*. The scene is sketched with alliteration of Ennian intensity:

> . . . eo dicente deum domus alta silescit
> et tremefacta solo tellus, silet arduus aether,
> tum Zephyri posuere, premit placida aequora pontus.

The speech itself opens with an impressive 'dicolon abundans':

accipite ergo animis atque haec mea figite dicta.

His judgement, which begins with the majestic polysyllable *quando-quidem* 'in as much as' (never used by Cicero in his speeches nor by Caesar), has the balanced binary structure rooted in the language of religion and law:

quandoquidem Ausonios coniungi foedere Teucris
haud licitum, nec vestra capit discordia finem:
quae cuique est fortuna hodie, quam quisque secat spem,
Tros Rutulusne fuat, nullo discrimine habebo,
seu fatis Italum castra obsidione tenentur
sive errore malo Troiae monitisque sinistris.

In the last line we sense the *dolo malo* of the *leges sacrae* and the *sinister* of the language of augury. Thus the archaism *fuat* finds its setting in a majestic context where the father of gods and men sits in the judgement seat. Marouzeau has pointed out a number of instances where such archaisms colour the language spoken by the gods: *quianam* is used by Jupiter (10. 6), *moerorum* by Venus (10. 24), *ast* by Juno (1. 46). No better illustration could be found of Quintilian's dictum 'verba a vetustate repetita . . . adferunt orationi maiestatem aliquam' (1. 6. 39).

The Sibyl, too, speaks a language not of this world:

olli sic breviter fata est longaeva sacerdos:
Anchisa generate, deum certissima proles.

This whole passage (6. 317–36), describing Aeneas' arrival at the Styx, is particularly rich in archaic colouring: *enim* 'indeed', the assonance *inops inhumataque*, the anastrophe *haec litora circum*, the archaic significance of *putans*, the locative *animi*, and finally the phrase *ductorem classis*, where an antique gem in a modern setting of 'glossae' forms the splendid line

Leucaspim et Lyciae ductorem classis Oronten.   (334)

In this passage we may note, further, the Ennian reminiscence *vada verrunt* and *vestigia pressit*; the patronymic expressions *Anchisa generate*, *Anchisa satus*, which were a feature of Latin epic style from Livius Andronicus on; the syntactical Grecism (this a 'gloss') *iurare numen*, and finally the unlatin *-que . . . -que* which is a 'calque' coined by Ennius as a convenient hexameter ending on the lines of Homeric expressions such as ὀλίγον τε φίλον τε, πόλεμοί τε μάχαι τε, etc.

Virgil also has recourse to archaism when he is concerned to evoke the solemnity of prayer (e.g. *alma, nequiquam*):

> alma, precor, miserere, potes namque omnia nec te
> nequiquam lucis Hecate praefecit Avernis.   (6. 117–18.)

Here, too, lies the significance of an apparently insignificant detail —the archaic *atque* introducing a passage which evokes the pathos of the unburied dead:

> atque illi Misenum in litore sicco
> ut venere vident indigna morte peremptum.   (162 f.)

These lines, with their repetition of *Misenum* and the 'gloss' *Aeoliden*, mark the climax of a passage rich in Ennian colouring and phraseology (e.g. 'caecosque volutat eventus animo secum; vestigia figit; multa inter sese vario sermone serebant') on which Virgil has lavished all the resources of his verbal magic:

> quo non praestantior alter
> aere ciere viros Martemque accendere cantu.   (164 f.)

> .   .   .   .   .   .

> sed tum forte cava dum personat aequora concha,
> demens, et cantu vocat in certamina divos,
> aemulus exceptum Triton, si credere dignumst,
> inter saxa virum spumosa immerserat unda.   (171 ff.)

Finally,

> tum iussa Sibyllae,
> haud mora, festinant flentes aramque sepulcro
> congerere arboribus caeloque educere certant.
> itur in antiquam silvam, stabula alta ferarum:
> procumbunt piceae, sonat icta securibus ilex,
> fraxineaeque trabes cuneis et fissile robur
> scinditur, advolvunt ingentis montibus ornos.   (176 ff.)

The remainder of the Misenus episode will serve to exemplify another device of Virgilian art. The gloss, we have seen, was one of the traditional ornaments of the epic genre as practised by Virgil's predecessors after the manner of the Greeks, though Lucretius had been notably more sparing in his use of this ornament than Ennius, Cicero, or Catullus. Virgil, too, is economical of a device whose excessive use would lead to barbarism (see p. 101). As with archaisms the gloss is reserved for special effects. If we exclude from the definition of 'gloss', as we should, those words which belong to the common fund of poetical diction (*letum*, *amnis*, and the rest), we may note in the passage under discussion the augural terms (*ob*)*servare*, *agnoscere*, *optare*, *laetus*, and the elaborate ritual expressions of the burial scene with its 'glossae' *pyra* for the native word *rogus*, and *cadus* for *situla*, and finally the Greek scansion of the word *craterĕs*.

It would be vain to attempt a spectrograph of Virgil's verbal music with its complex harmonies and shifting patterns of assonance. Rhetorical structure and embellishment, however, are a matter of great importance for post-Augustan poetry and demand at least a brief treatment. During the last century of the Republic a thorough training in Greek rhetoric had become a normal part of a Roman's education. In this school the Romans learnt the writing of artistic prose and the construction of complicated balanced periods (see next section). The adaptation of the artistic period to hexameter poetry was not the least of Virgil's achievements wherein he outstripped his predecessors. The 'archaic' poet Lucretius and the 'neoteric' Catullus had both failed to solve this problem, such long sentences as they composed (see Skutsch, *Aus Vergils Frühzeit*, p. 65) being without inner harmony and balance but consisting for the most part of strings of subordinate clauses. But Virgil had learned from his masters of rhetoric that prose of higher emotional tension demands, not long elaborate periods with the subordinate parts carefully dovetailed into the central thought, not hypotaxis, but parataxis, with suppression of logical connecting particles. Rhetorical questions, exclamations, short rapid sentences mutually balancing, with the symmetry marked by devices such as antithesis, anaphora, homoioteleuton, chiasmus—such were the devices prescribed for the achievement of power and energy and intensity (δεινότης) in prose.[1] It was this style which Virgil introduced into Roman epic.

In the first place his periods rarely exceed the length of four hexameters, the optimum as prescribed by Cicero (see next section

[1] See W. Kroll, *N.J.* 1903, pp. 23 f.

and cf. Cicero, *Orator* 222). Thus the narrative opening of *Aeneid*, Book 6 begins with two periods each consisting of three co-ordinated 'cola' (see next section):

> sic fatur lacrimans, classique immittit habenas,
> et tandem Euboicis Cumarum adlabitur oris.
> obvertunt pelago proras; tum dente tenaci
> ancora fundabat navis et litora curvae
> praetexunt puppes.

Such simplicity is everywhere the mark of Virgil's narrative style. But in the 'Asianic' style of pathetic prose, simplicity of syntactical structure is compensated by elaborate rhetorical artifices of 'concinnitas' (see next section), antithesis, word-order, and assonance. So, too, in Virgil even simple sentences exhibit such rhetorical stylization. We may point out, for instance, the tricolon 'with increasing magnitude':

> bella, horrida bella
> et Thybrim multo spumantem sanguine.   (6. 86 f.)

The tricolon with anaphora:

> ante fores subito non voltus, non color unus,
> non comptae mansere comae.   (Ibid. 47 f.)

The κύκλος in

> cessas in vota precesque,
> Tros, ait, Aenea, cessas?   (Ibid. 51 f.)

Compare

> socer arma Latinus habeto
> imperium sollemne socer.   (12. 192 f.)

The 'dicolon abundans' in

> errantisque deos agitataque numina Troiae;   (6. 68)

and compare

> omnia praecepi atque animo mecum ante peregi.
> (Ibid. 105)

Such balanced binary structures are particularly characteristic:

> fataque fortunasque virum moresque manusque.   (Ibid. 683)

> quos dulcis vitae exsortis et ab ubere raptos
> abstulit atra dies et funere mersit acerbo.   (Ibid. 428-9)

compare

> qui sibi letum
> insontes peperere manu lucemque perosi
> proiecere animas. (Ibid. 434-6)

> sed revocare gradum superasque evadere ad auras,
> hoc opus, hic labor est. (Ibid. 128 f.)

> nunc animis opus, Aenea, nunc pectore firmo. (Ibid. 261)

> (Aeneas) maesto defixus lumina voltu
> ingreditur ⋮ linquens antrum ⋮ caecosque volutat
> eventus animo secum. (Ibid. 156-7)

where two co-ordinated principal clauses each of fourteen syllables
flank the central participial phrase. Often the symmetry is pointed
by carefully placed assonances. The following passages exemplify
one of Virgil's favourite devices—homoioteleuton in verbs placed
in the first and final position of the verse.

> talibus Aeneas ardentem et torva tuentem
> *lenibat* dictis animum lacrimasque *ciebat*.
> illa solo fixos oculos aversa tenebat. (6. 467-9)

> at regina, nova pugnae conterrita sorte
> *flebat*, et ardentem generum moritura *tenebat*. (12. 54 f.)

> nec minus interea Misenum in litore Teucri
> *flebant* et cineri ingrato suprema *ferebant*. (6. 212-13)

> pars calidos latices et aëna undantia flammis
> *expediunt* corpusque lavant frigentis et *unguunt*.
> (Ibid. 218-19)

> it tristis ad aethera clamor
> *bellantum* iuvenum et duro sub Marte *cadentum*.
> (12. 409-10)

It is, of course, in the speeches that we find the most complex
structural patterns. The speech of Palinurus (6. 347 ff.) may serve
as an example. It begins with a coordinated pair of cola of equal
length ('parison'), the balance marked by homoioteleuton:

> . . . neque te Phoebi cortina fefellit,
> dux Anchisiade, nec me deus aequore mersit.

The same 'isocolia' is preserved and carefully pointed throughout:
e.g.

> cui datus haerebam custos cursusque regebam. (6. 350)

> paulatim adnabam terrae, iam tuta tenebam.   (358)
> ferro invasisset praedamque ignara putasset.   (361)

In *spoliata armis, excussa magistro* (for *excusso magistro*) the construction is strained to preserve the parallelism. We note in passing the arrangement of adjectives and nouns (abBA) in:

> tris Notus hibernas immensa per aequora noctes.   (355)

Finally, as Norden has pointed out, the whole speech has an orderly rhetorical arrangement with a brief 'prooemium' (—*mersit*), 'narratio' (*namque—in litore venti*), and an epilogue which takes the form of a 'commiseratio' culminating in two lines of studied alliteration:

> da dextram misero et tecum me tolle per undas,
> sedibus ut saltem placidis in morte quiescam.   (370 f.)

In Virgil's hands the long process of the refinement of native resources under supervision by Greek technicians reached its acme, and the Latin language had finally been shaped into a potent and sensitive instrument of high poetry.

While it is no part of our task to trace Virgil's influence as a poet and thinker (and Roman poetry was not to remain long on these heights), his influence on the subsequent history of the literary language was immense. Suffering the fate of most great authors, he was turned into a school textbook, learnt by heart, recited, made the victim of 'explication des textes', parsed, and finally carved up to provide exemplifications for grammatical rules. In this way every schoolboy and every scribe became a Virgilian. But we anticipate, and it is time to trace the parallel growth of artistic Latin prose.

B. THE LANGUAGE OF LITERARY PROSE

The ultimate source of any literary language is the spoken language in its various forms and modes. From this raw material most human societies, especially after the invention of writing, have evolved particular forms of linguistic expression which, although difficult to define, we may classify as 'literary'. In tracing the main lines in the growth of literary Latin prose we must bear in mind the following considerations. It is commonly in the sphere of religion and law that the first steps are taken which distinguish formal literary expression from colloquial speech. For man's guidance in his conduct towards the gods and his fellow men rules are formulated. Such religious and legal formulae embodying the *mos maiorum* handed down from generation to generation preserve archaic forms of speech. Hence a literary language which evolves from them will be a blend of the colloquial and the archaic. Then we shall consider the forms of persuasive and effective utterance, the natural rhetoric which increasing experience and self-criticism will transform into a coherent body of doctrine. For this the Romans were mainly indebted to the Greeks, though certain of their stylistic devices were rooted in Italian soil. In particular the insistence on 'clarity' (σαφήνεια) as the main virtue of effective utterance means that the interrelations of the parts of a complex thought find explicit linguistic expression. Accordingly the naïve juxtaposition of simple sentences is gradually built up into the complex period with careful subordination of its constituent parts. Finally we shall be faced with another phenomenon of constant occurrence: the centralization of government in organized states, the domination of a certain class, the prestige enjoyed by its social habits, of which not the least important is its mode of speech, result in the growth and imposition of a standard language. In Latin this expression of class fastidiousness is summed up in the word *urbanitas*.

For the early stages in the development of Latin prose we are even less well situated than for poetry, since few specimens have survived. We have, of course, the fragments of the Twelve Tables quoted by later authors. But these consist in the main of bald, terse ordinances of the simplest structure: e.g. *si in ius vocat ito. ni it, antestamino. igitur em capito.* Most characteristic of this style is that there is no explicit expression of the subject of the verb, which must be understood from the context: 'If (a plaintiff) summons (a defendant) to court, (the defendant) shall go. If he does not go (the plaintiff) shall call a witness. Then he shall arrest him.' This syntactical peculiarity, like so much else in the Twelve Tables, finds its counterpart in the archaic Greek laws. Thus the all-pervading influence of Greek is revealed even in the earliest and seemingly most Roman documents in the Latin language (see above).

Literary prose, too, like poetry, begins with the translation of Greek; for the earliest surviving specimens of Latin prose literature are the passages quoted by Lactantius from Ennius' translation of the Ἱερὰ ἀναγραφή of Euhemerus. That Lactantius preserved the language of Ennius (in frags. I, III, IV, VI–VIII, XI) with no very serious verbal discrepancies has recently been cogently reaffirmed. Its main characteristics appear in the following quotation:

> exim Saturnus uxorem duxit Opem. Titan, qui maior natu erat, postulat ut ipse regnaret. ibi Vesta mater eorum et sorores Ceres atque Ops suadent Saturno, uti de regno ne concedat fratri. ibi Titan, qui facie deterior esset quam Saturnus, idcirco et quod videbat matrem atque sorores suas operam dare uti Saturnus regnaret, concessit ei ut is regnaret. itaque pactus est cum Saturno, uti si quid liberum virile secus ei natum esset, ne quid educaret. id eius rei causa fecit, uti ad suos gnatos regnum rediret. tum Saturno filius qui primus natus est, eum necaverunt. deinde posterius nati sunt gemini, Iuppiter atque Iuno. tum Iunonem Saturno in conspectum dedere atque Iovem clam abscondunt dantque eum Vestae educandum celantes Saturnum. item Neptunum clam Saturno Ops parit eumque clanculum abscondit. ad eundem modum tertio partu Ops parit geminos, Plutonem et Glaucam. Pluto Latine est Dis pater, alii Orcum vocant. ibi filiam Glaucam Saturno ostendunt, at filium Plutonem celant atque abscondunt. (Frag. III (Vahlen, p. 223) = Warmington, R.O.L. i. 418 f.)

Particularly noteworthy points in this passage are the simplicity of its syntactical structure, the *naïveté* of the sentence-connexions (*exim, ibi, tum, deinde posterius,* etc.), and the redundant use of the anaphoric pronoun *is*.[1]

While it is likely that Ennius is rendering faithfully the style of the corresponding passages of Euhemerus, who was affecting for his own purposes the manner of the early Greek folktale, such *naïvetés* are universal characteristics of unadorned folk-narrative. We find them no less in the example of the *sermo inliberalis* quoted by the author of the *ad Herennium* (4. 11. 16):

> 'hic tuus servus me pulsavit'. postea dicit hic illi: 'considerabo'. post ille convicium fecit et magis magisque praesente multis clamavit!

---

[1] See E. Laughton, *Eranos,* xlix, 1951, pp. 35 ff.; and E. Fraenkel, ibid., pp. 50 ff.

We may compare, too, a passage from the chronicler Calpurnius Piso (quoted by Gellius 7. 9):

> Cn. Flavius, patre libertino natus, scriptum faciebat, *isque* in eo tempore aedili curuli apparebat quo tempore aediles subrogantur, *eumque* pro tribu aedilem curulem renuntiaverunt;

the passage from a speech by C. Gracchus quoted by Aulus Gellius with the comment that it is in the tone of ordinary conversation (10. 3. 5):

> his annis paucis ex Asia missus est, qui per id tempus magistratum non ceperat, homo adulescens pro legato. *is* in lectica ferebatur. *ei* obviam bubulcus de plebe Venusina advenit . . .;

and finally a passage from Cato's practical handbook of husbandry:

> alvom si voles deicere superiorem, sumito brassicae quae levissima erit P. IIII. *inde* facito manipulos aequales tres conligatoque. *postea* ollam statuito cum aqua. *ubi* occipiet fervere, paulisper demittito unum manipulum. fervere desistet. *postea* ubi occipiet fervere, paulisper demittito ad modum dum quinque numeres; eximito. item facito alterum manipulum, item tertium. *Postea* conicito, contundito. . . .   (*de agr.* 156. 2)

Our study of the progress of prose from such simple forms of expression may well begin with Cato, who stands at the end of the archaic period. For all his anti-Hellenic venom and his pronouncement that those who study poetry and attend *convivia* were no better than loafers (*grassatores*), and despite his recipe for writers *rem tene verba sequentur*, he was himself not altogether innocent of the arts of the despised Greeks. The colloquial basis of his language is apparent in such features as *nemo homo*, the diminutives *pauculos homines*, *mediocriculum exercitum*, the adverbs *derepente*, *desubito*, *nimis* = 'very', *futare* = *saepius fuisse*, in the superfluous *is* and *ibi*, and the many syntactical dislocations. We must classify here, too, the numerous verbal compounds, especially those in *con-*, which above were found to be characteristic of the colloquial language. In one passage of Cato (*de agr.* 129) we find *confodere, conspargere, combibere, comminuere, coaequare*. Note, too, the 'hypercharacterized' *coaddo* and *dishiasco*. Among his archaisms we may mention the pronoun *quīs* (abl. plur.), the verbal forms *imposivi, experirus*, the infinitives in *-ier*. It is possible, of course, that some of these were, in fact, contemporary forms; but that Cato used archaisms as a deliberate device to lend dignity and solemnity to his style is apparent, to quote only one example from one fragment of the *de sumptu suo* which ends: 'vide sis quo loco res publica siet uti quod rei publicae bene fecissem, unde gratiam capiebam, nunc idem illud memorare non audeo, ne invidiae siet. ita inductum est male facere impoene, bene facere non impoene licere'. Here in company with the colloquialism *vide sis* we find the form *siet* which Plautus reserves for the end of the verse, that repository of archaisms. But *impoene* is even more archaizing than Plautus, who uses the form *impune*.

Among Cato's devices of stylization are those now familiar from our study of Plautus and the language of poetry. The primitive 'padded' style will be sufficiently exemplified by a passage from the speech 'For the Rhodians':

> scio solere plerisque hominibus rebus secundis atque prolixis atque prosperis animum excellere atque superbiam atque ferociam augescere atque crescere. (21. 8 f. J.)

The traditional alliterative dicola in asyndeton appear in the speech against Galba: 'multa me dehortata huc prodire: anni aetas vox vires senectus'. Nor are examples lacking of alliteration ('asperrimo atque arduissimo') and other forms of assonance such as homoioteleuton, to achieve which he did not hesitate to coin new words: e.g. 'aestate frigido, hieme formido' (87. 10 J.), and the word *optionatus* in 'maiores seorsum atque divorsum pretium paravere bonis atque strenuis: decurionatus, optionatus, hastas donaticas aliosque honores' (39.3 J.). *fugella*, too, in the *figura etymologica* 'fugit . . . fugella' (45.6 J.), is an instance of the word-play frequent in this somewhat primitive style: cf. 'cognobilior cognitio' (26.10 J.), 'honorem emptitavere, malefacta benefactis non redemptitavere' (69. 7 J.). Such devices of assonance, as we have seen, were endemic in Italy. To these we must add the influence on early prose of Ennius' poetry. We find much the same modes of word formation: e.g. the abstracts in -*tudo* such as Cato's *duritudo*; adjectives in -*bundus* ('neque enim tuburchinabundum et lurchinabundum iam in nobis quisquam ferat, licet Cato sit auctor', Quintilian 1. 6. 42); -*osus* (*disciplinosus, consiliosus, victoriosus* are attributed to Cato by Gellius 4. 9. 12); adverbs in -*im* and -*ter* (e.g. *pedetemptim, arenter*) and frequentative verbs in -*tare, -itare* (*emptitare*). Doubtless many of these words were the products of natural analogical procedures; and such coincidences of language need not be evidence of Cato's debt to the language of poetry. But the influence of Ennius is particularly apparent in 'deinde postquam Massiliam praeterimus, inde omnem classem ventus auster lenis fert, mare velis florere videres' (34. 4 ff. J.) and in phrases such as *dum se intempesta nox praecipitat*, *sub tela volantia*, and the *multi mortales* of the following passage from the speech against Quintus Minucius, from which it will be seen to what heights of pathos and power this archaic prose could rise:

> dixit a decem viris parum bene sibi cibaria curata esse. iussit vestimenta detrahi atque flagro caedi. decem viros Bruttiani verberavere, videre multi mortales. quis hanc contumeliam, quis hoc imperium, quis hanc servitutem ferre potest? nemo hoc rex ausus est facere: eane fieri bonis, bono genere gnatis, boni consulitis? ubi societas, ubi fides maiorum? insignitas iniurias, plagas, verbera, vibices, eos dolores atque carnificinas per dedecus atque maximam contumeliam inspectantibus popularibus suis atque multis mortalibus te facere ausum esse! set quantum luctum, quantum gemitum, quid lacrimarum, quantum fletum factum audivi? servi iniurias nimis aegre ferunt. quid illos bono genere natos, magna virtute praeditos opinamini animi habuisse atque habituros, dum viverent?
>
> (41 J.)

It was doubtless passages like this that Cicero had in mind when he wrote (*Brutus* 294): 'orationes autem eius ut illis temporibus valde laudo: significant enim formam quandam ingeni, sed admodum impolitam et plane rudem'. Such was the language of elevated Latin prose towards the middle of the second century B.C., a blend of colloquial speech with the archaic forms of the religious *carmina* and the formulae of the law, embellished with native cosmetics, with the *lumina* of Greek rhetoric, and the flowers of contemporary poetic diction. It was this curious amalgam which during the course of the next century was refined into the language of classical prose. The process was essentially one of selection and rejection, the pursuit of *latinitas* under the banner of *urbanitas*. How this exclusive and fastidious attitude to language developed among the Romans is difficult to trace. Doubtless the rapid growth of the urban proletariat, with immigrants speaking dialect or broken Latin, stimulated the disdain and class-consciousness of the ruling

aristocracy. Certainly Cicero in lamenting the decay of pure latinity since the age of Scipio ascribes it to the influx of new elements
of the population into the city:

> sed omnes tum fere, qui nec extra urbem hanc vixerant neque eos
> aliqua barbaries domestica infuscaverat, recte loquebantur. sed hanc
> certe rem deteriorem vetustas fecit et Romae et in Graecia. con-
> fluxerunt enim et Athenas et in hanc urbem multi inquinate loquentes
> ex diversis locis. quo magis expurgandus est sermo. . . . (*Brutus* 258)

While the mention of the same phenomenon in Greece, where the
Atticist movement had begun about 60 B.C., must rouse the suspicion that *urbanitas* is yet one more instance of the Greek domination over Roman literary life and theory, the effects of the purge
were powerful and salutary. The Roman intelligentsia, standing
in conscious superiority over the teeming life of the capital, began
a process of linguistic ξενηλασία: the expulsion of the rustic, the
provincial, and the foreign ('neque solum rusticam asperitatem sed
etiam peregrinam insolentiam fugere discamus' *de or.* 3. 44). Of the
many programmatic statements we may choose one by Cicero. In
one passage he confesses himself at a loss to define *urbanitas*, particularly in matters of pronunciation:

> qui est, inquit, iste tandem urbanitatis color? nescio, inquam; tantum
> esse quendam scio. id tu, Brute, iam intelleges cum in Galliam veneris;
> audies tum quidem etiam verba quaedam non trita Romae, sed haec
> mutari dediscique possunt. illud est maius, quod in vocibus nostrorum
> oratorum retinnit quiddam et resonat urbanius.   (*Brutus* 171)

Elsewhere he does give some guidance on matters of pronunciation, e.g. the pronunciation of final *-s*:

> quin etiam, quod iam subrusticum videtur, olim autem politius,
> eorum verborum, quorum eaedem erant postremae duae litterae quae
> sunt in 'optimus', postremam litteram detrahebant, nisi vocalis
> insequebatur.   (*Orator* 161)

On another point, the aspiration of consonants, he confesses that
his own obstinate pedantry had finally to yield to popular usage:

> quin ego ipse, cum scirem ita maiores locutos ut nusquam nisi in
> vocali aspiratione uterentur, loquebar sic ut 'pulcros', 'Cetegos', 'trium-
> pos', 'Cartaginem' dicerem; aliquando, idque sero, convicio aurium cum
> extorta mihi veritas esset, usum loquendi populo concessi, scientiam
> mihi reservavi. (*Orator* 160.)

But it is in the *de oratore* that he outlines the chief heads of pure latinity: correct vocabulary and forms with due regard for number and gender:

> ut Latine loquamur non solum videndum est ut et verba efferamus ea quae nemo iure reprehendat, et ea sic et casibus et temporibus et genere et numero conservemus ut ne quid perturbatum ac discrepans aut praeposterum sit, sed etiam lingua et spiritus et vocis sonus est ipse moderandus. (*de or.* 3. 40)

It will be convenient to trace the puristic purge and the emergence of the classical canon under these headings.

We have had occasion above to mention some of the morphological uncertainties of archaic Latin, the confusions of gender, the fluctuating forms of declension, conjugation, and word-formation. Cato could still allow himself the genitives *illi, alii, soli, nulli* and the dative feminines *unae, eae, illae*. We find, further, *clivum* for *clivus*, *sagus* for *sagum*. Other non-classical forms are the locatives *die proximi* and the extraordinary analogical genitive plural *bovĕrum* (elsewhere the forms *regerum, lapiderum, nucerum, naverum* occur). Among the verbal forms *solui* and *ausi* do duty for the classical 'semi-deponents', while his *fitur* and *fiebantur* can scarcely be quoted without repugnance in a book which may fall into the hands of the young. As for *iussitur* and *possitur* it may be urged as an extenuating circumstance that *potestur* was used by Ennius and Pacuvius.

In syntax, too, the purists restricted the much greater freedom of the earlier writers, who had at their disposal, for instance in oratio obliqua, not only the accusative and infinitive but also *quod* and *ut* (e.g. 'narrat ut virgo ab se integra etiam nunc siet', Terence, *Hec.* 145). The indicative in indirect questions had always been common. In this matter Caesar and Cicero show a curious divergence, for the former avoids the indicative altogether while the latter has no fewer than fifty-four examples, half of which occur in the letters. In case usage we may single out the temporary stifling by classical authors of the tendency to replace bare cases by prepositional phrases, e.g. *ad* with the accusative for the dative: *ad praetores . . . honorarium dabant* (Cato, 64. 1 J.), *de* with the ablative for the genitive ('si posset auctio fieri de artibus tuis', 60. 1 J.); *ab* with the ablative also occurs as a substitute for the genitive.

In all this process of pruning and weeding, the Roman purists were doubtless guided in the first place by sound linguistic common sense. Orators and advocates of the stamp of Crassus, whom Cicero praised for his 'Latine loquendi accurata et sine molestia diligens elegantia' (*Brutus* 143), doubtless rejected archaisms and artificialities of diction for the sound practical reason that they were ineffective. No less important was the influence of Greek rhetorical theory based on sound Greek practice, which insisted on clarity (σαφήνεια), logicality, and the avoidance of ambiguity as the prime rhetorical virtues. It was doubtless to achieve clarity that the Roman authors sifted the manifold resources of the pre-classical language in the effort to achieve the ideal of the *mot juste* for each notion and of one construction to express each syntactical relationship. Thus the bare ablative of time is alone used by Cicero and Caesar, although earlier authors had permitted themselves *in tempore*, etc. Classical, too, is the refinement that the instrumental ablative in phrases like *maximo clamore* can dispense with the support of *cum*, although the preposition is used by earlier authors. Likewise the use of *cum* with a bare modal ablative (*cum salute*) becomes canonical only in classical prose. Two more examples must suffice to illustrate the general tendency to eliminate syntactical doublets. The use of *si* in the sense of 'whether' in indirect questions, which is frequent in earlier Latin and doubtless also in the colloquial language of classical times (it occurs in Cicero's letters), is avoided in classical prose, presumably on the grounds that to this conjunction was reserved the meaning 'if'. Similarly the multi-functional conjunction *ut* in Cicero sheds the following meanings: 'since', 'where', 'how' (except in exclamations *vides ut*, etc.), 'as it were' = *quasi quidem*, nor does Cicero use a bare *ut* to introduce independent wishes.[1]

It is, however, in vocabulary that the *elegantia*, the fastidious selectivity of classicism, is most apparent. Cicero in praising Athenian taste had written:

> quorum semper fuit prudens sincerumque iudicium, nihil ut possent nisi incorruptum audire et elegans. eorum religioni cum serviret orator, nullum verbum insolens, nullum odiosum ponere audebat. (*Orator* 25.)

[1] See W. Kroll, *Glotta*, xxii, 1933, pp. 1 ff.

Such an out-of-the-way and offensive word was, for instance, the preposition *af*: 'insuavissima praepositio est "af", quae nunc tantum in accepti tabulis manet ac ne his quidem omnium' (*Or.* 158), or again the un-Latin compound words which Cicero rejects: 'asperitatemque fugiamus: ''habeo ego istam perterricrepam'' itemque ''versutiloquas malitias''' (*Or.* 164). Caesar, according to Gellius (I. 10. 4) had made a similar programmatic pronouncement: 'ut tamquam scopulum sic fugias inauditum atque insolens verbum'. Cicero, too, wrote in praise of Caesar's exquisite sense of language: 'sed tamen, Brute, inquit Atticus, de Caesare et ipse ita iudico . . . illum omnium fere oratorum Latine loqui elegantissime' (*Brutus* 252), a sensitivity which was a product not merely of *domestica consuetudo* but was based on extensive reading and diligent study even of recondite works. On such principles the classical authors set to work to thin out the tangled growth of their inherited literary language. The authors of religious and legal texts, in their anxious efforts to cover every possible manifestation of divine activity and human ingenuity and iniquity, had evolved formulae such as:

> neve post hac inter sed coniourase neve comvovise neve conspondise neve conpromesise velet neve quisquam fidem inter sed dedise velet. (*Senatus Consultum de Bacchanalibus* 12 f.)

Such accumulations of synonyms, the technical name for which is 'congeries', had become, as we have seen, a characteristic of high style and was much affected even by Cicero in his early works until Molo of Rhodes dammed his youthful redundance ('is dedit operam, si modo id consequi potuit, ut nimis redundantis nos et supra fluentis iuvenili quadam dicendi impunitate et licentia reprimeret et quasi extra ripas diffluentis coerceret', *Brutus* 316). In the event classical prose eliminated all the above verbal compounds for 'to conspire' except *coniurare*, although it added *conspirare*, not included in the above text. But while the theoretical principles pertaining to *elegantia* represented a body of common doctrine, their practical application has results which are puzzling to the modern reader. The avoidance of archaisms such as *topper, oppido, aerumna, autumo* presents no problems. They were all rejected by Virgil as unsuitable even for the archaizing language of poetry, presumably as *ex ultimis tenebris repetita*. On the other hand, the aversion of Cicero (after the early speeches) and Caesar for *donec* and their preference for *dum* were perhaps due to the fact that the former conjunction was a forceful upstart not yet free from the suspicion of vulgarism. Much the same may be true of *quia* as against the preferred *quod*. Archaism and vulgarity were the Scylla and Charybdis between which the classical purists sailed their anxious course.

Similar sensitivity to the tone of a word may explain why Caesar prefers *non modo, non solum* to the *non tantum* favoured by those who completed his work, *tantum* being ambiguous. It has been pointed out, too, that *quomodo* and *quamquam* are avoided by Caesar, although the latter occurs four times in Hirtius' Book 8 of the *de bello gallico*. Caesar, again, shows a preference for *priusquam* as against *antequam* and for *posteaquam* as against *postquam*. Differences of tone, vulgarism, and urbanity may account for many of these subtleties but, as Marouzeau suggests in his discussion of these facts, we should not ignore the factor of personal choice and sheer verbal habit. Why should Caesar never use *quando* or *mox*, and almost totally neglect *igitur* in favour of *quare* and *itaque*? Why his preference for *timeo* as against *vereor* and *metuo*? As for habit, the curious tendency for a word once activated to recur is illustrated by Caesar's use of the rare phrase *e regione* no fewer than seven times in the seventh book of the *Gallic War* although only one other example is found in the rest of that corpus.

For all their theoretical insistence on the avoidance of the *inauditum verbum*, the Roman writers never cease to lament the *patrii sermonis egestas* as compared with Greek. Much indeed remained to do before Latin could function as an instrument for the higher intellectual activities. Perhaps Cicero's greatest contribution to the Latin language came with his enforced retirement from politics when he devoted himself to the translation of Greek philosophical works. In so doing he largely created the vocabulary of abstract philosophical thinking. We shall see evidence of this activity in his various attempts to find a Latin equivalent for the rhetorical technical term περίοδος. A letter to Atticus (13. 21. 3) affords us another fascinating glimpse into Cicero's workshop. The problem under discussion was how to render the words ἐπέχειν, ἐποχή in their sense of philosophic suspension of judgement. Cicero had decided on *sustinere* (*Ac.* 2. 94), but Atticus suggested *inhibere,* which Cicero had at first accepted but subsequently repented of:

> Now to return to real business; your suggestion *inhibere,* which I had found very attractive, I am not at all pleased with. The term is wholly nautical. I was aware of this, of course, but I thought that rowers rested on their oars (*sustinere*), when they were given the order 'inhibere'. But that this is not so I learned yesterday when a ship was putting in to my villa. For they do not rest on their oars (*sustinent*) but row in a different way. That is far removed from ἐποχή. So please see that the former rendering is restored in my book. Pass this on to Varro if he happens to have changed it. Nothing is better than Lucilius'
>
> > *sustineas currum ut bonus saepe agitator equosque.*
>
> And Carneades always compares the guard (προβολή) of a boxer, and the reining in of a charioteer to ἐποχή. But the *inhibitio* of rowers involves action and indeed a fairly violent one of rowing to turn the ship astern.

By such prolonged experiment in the translation of Greek terms Cicero introduced into Latin many new words *cinctutis non exaudita Cethegis* and in so doing hammered out the fundamental vocabulary of abstract thought which has become the common possession of western European peoples: e.g. *qualitas* (ποιότης), *quantitas* (ποσότης), *essentia* (οὐσία), etc.

While the careful choice of words was a powerful factor in securing the clarity of expression on which classical purists insisted as the prime virtue, it was in their successful construction of complex periods that they showed the greatest virtuosity and made their most important contribution to the development of European prose. This involved in the first place the ironing out of the inconsistencies of constructions, the inevitable anacolutha, the 'contaminations', the 'sense constructions' and faults of congruence, the *nominativus pendens*—in a word, all those illogicalities inherent in rapid colloquial speech which were discussed above. In the second place came the organization of unconnected co-ordinated sentences into larger units with careful and explicit subordination of the various constituent parts to the main thought—the replacement of parataxis by hypotaxis which will be discussed in detail in Chapter X. The most important discovery in the search for clarity and balance in a long period was that the subject should be kept unchanged throughout. The clumsiness and unsteadiness of a sentence which was ignorant of this device will be apparent from the following passage of Cato's *Origines*:

> nam ita evenit, cum saucius multifariam ibi factus esset, tamen vulnus capiti nullum evenit, eumque inter mortuos defetigatum vulneribus atque quod sanguen eius defluxerat cognovere, eum sustulere, isque convaluit, saepeque postilla operam rei publicae fortem atque strenuam perhibuit illoque facto quod illos milites subduxit exercitum servavit.   (19. 9 ff. J.)

Here the constant change of subject requires the wearisome repetition of the anaphoric *is, eum*. Note, too, that the introductory *ita evenit* has no influence on the constructions, and would best be followed in our punctuation by a colon. The unity of the subject could not be achieved, however, until the emergence of the conjunct and absolute participial constructions. The verbal adjective in -*nt*- which we know as the present participle was already a feature of the IE. parent language. In the earliest Latin texts it was used almost exclusively in nominal functions. In Cato and the early annalists, for instance, the present participle does not possess the characteristic verbal function of governing an object in the accusative case, and much the same is true of Plautus' usage. Terence admits a direct object but, with two exceptions, only when the participle is in the nominative case. This is the predominant usage in Varro, although he has examples where the participle is in the accusative and one where it is in the dative. Gradually usage became more flexible with variation from author to author (Sallust is notably freer than Caesar), until Cicero with his great virtuosity uses the transitive participle in all possible cases. In the ablative absolute, too, few examples of the present participle occur in Plautus and Terence apart from those where they are adjectival in function (e.g. *me praesente, sciente*) and not until Sallust and Caesar is the construction freely used. It was this new syntactical device which rendered possible the organization of the periods, so complex and yet so coherent and lucid, in which the pages of Cicero abound.

The long complex period demanded not merely logical arrangement for ease of comprehension. It must always be borne in mind that Roman prose style was based on the spoken word and evolved in the practice of oratory. Cicero gives Marcus Aemilius Lepidus the credit for having been the first Latin orator to achieve the lightness of the Greeks and the artistic period:

hoc in oratore Latino primum mihi videtur et levitas apparuisse illa Graecorum et verborum comprensio et iam artifex, ut ita dicam, stilus. (*Brutus* 96)

It will be evident that the conditions of public speaking impose *inter alia* certain limitations on the length of the constituent parts of a sentence: there is a maximum breath-unit. It was doubtless such practical considerations which had led in Greece to the emergence of a style in which the sentence was broken up into 'limbs' (κῶλα) and 'pieces' (κόμματα), terms which Cicero rendered as *membra* and *incisa* (*Or.* 211). Ideally the full period consisted of four such *membra*, each approximately the length of an hexameter verse (*Or.* 222). But the long periodic style is more appropriate to historical writings and epideictic oratory (*Or.* 207) and should be used sparingly in court and in the forum, where if overdone, it will fail because it produces the impression of insincerity. In actual court practice the greater part of the speech will consist of sentences organized in *membra* and *incisa*. Cicero quotes (*Or.* 222 f.) an example of such a style from Crassus ('quin etiam comprehensio et ambitus ille verborum, si sic περίοδον appellari placet, erat apud illum contractus et brevis, et in membra quaedam, quae κῶλα Graeci vocant, dispertiebat orationem libentius', *Brutus* 162):

missos faciant patronos, ipsi prodeant . . .; cur clandestinis consiliis nos oppugnant? cur de perfugis nostris copias comparant contra nos?

On this passage he comments: 'the first two parts are what the Greeks call κόμματα and we *incisa*; then the third is a κῶλον or as we say, *membrum*, and finally there follows a period—not a long one but consisting only of two 'verses', that is to say *membra*'. Such a style is particularly effective, writes Cicero, in passages devoted to proof or refutation, and he quotes an example from his own 'Corneliana': 'o callidos homines, o rem excogitatam, o ingenia metuenda' (thus far in *membra*): then with an *incisum*: 'diximus'. Then again a *membrum*: 'testis dare volumus'. Finally there follows the shortest possible *comprehensio* (= period) consisting of

two *membra*: 'quem, quaeso, nostrum fefellit ita vos esse facturos?'
(*Or.* 225).

The ancient orators used elaborate devices to throw into relief
the constituent parts of an utterance constructed *incisim* and *mem-
bratim*. Here again we may with profit read from the master's
analysis (*Or.* 164 ff.) of his own practice in giving such 'definition'
to a period:

> et finiuntur aut compositione ipsa et quasi sua sponte aut quodam
> genere verborum in quibus ipsis concinnitas inest; quae sive casus
> habent in exitu similis, sive paribus paria redduntur, sive opponuntur
> contraria, suapte natura numerosa sunt, etiamsi nihil est factum de
> industria.

Cicero goes on to remark that Gorgias had been the first to pursue
concinnitas by such devices, and he quotes as an example from his
own work a passage from the *pro Milone* 10:

> est enim, iudices, haec non scripta sed nata lex, quam non didicimus,
> accepimus, legimus, verum ex natura ipsa arripuimus, hausimus,
> expressimus, ad quam non docti sed facti, non instituti sed imbuti
> sumus.

Another device productive of *concinnitas* favoured by Gorgias and
his successors is antithesis. Of this, too, Cicero remarks, he made
frequent use:

> nos etiam in hoc genere frequentes, ut illa sunt in quarto Accusa-
> tionis (= *in Verrem* 2. 4. 115): 'conferte hanc pacem cum illo bello,
> huius praetoris adventum cum illius imperatoris victoria, huius
> cohortem impuram cum illius exercitu invicto, huius libidines cum
> illius continentia: ab illo qui cepit conditas, ab hoc qui constitutas
> accepit captas dicetis Syracusas'. (*Or.* 167.)

While the self-conscious theorizing which lies behind the writing
of harmonious balanced Latin prose is one of Greece's many gifts
to literary Rome, the device itself was native on Italian soil.[1] Here,
too, we may see the influence of the *carmina* and the language of
the law. In prayer, curse, and magic the *concepta verba* naturally
assumed a balanced form in which the length of the units was
limited by the necessity for clear and majestic utterance and

---

[1] It is worth recalling here that 'Parallelismus membrorum' is said to be a distinctive feature of the most ancient Semitic poetry. J. D. Young (*Jb. f. Kleinas.
Forsch.*, 1953, pp. 231 ff.) writes, 'When you find parallelism as a regular feature
in a Semitic composition, you have poetry.'

breath pauses. Of the many examples of prayers I choose one preserved by Livy I. 10. 6 ff. (cf. the augural formula discussed in Chapter III).

Iuppiter Feretri	
haec tibi victor Romulus	8 syllables
rex regia arma fero	8 ,,
templumque his regionibus	9 ,,
quas modo animo metatus sum	10 ,,
dedico sedem opimis spoliis	11 ,,
quae regibus ducibusque hostium caesis	13 ,,
me auctorem sequentes posteri ferent	12 ,,

It is this style which is aped, for instance, by Plautus in *As.* 259 ff.

> impetratum inauguratumst
> quovis admittunt aves
> picus et cornix ab laeva
> corvos parra ab dextera
> consuadent.

The logically constructed period with inner harmony and balance of its constituent parts (*concinnitas*) received its ultimate refinement when the arrangement of the words was made to conform to a rhythmical pattern. Cicero had laid it down (*Or.* 201) that in the *collocatio verborum* consideration must be given to three things: *compositio, concinnitas,* and *numerus.* In our examination of *numerus* we may again take Cicero as our guide, even though he notoriously does not give a complete account even of his own rhythmical practice. Speech, he maintains (*Or.* 228), should not flow unchecked (*infinite*) like a river, nor come to a stop just for lack of breath. Like a blow delivered by a skilled boxer, a sentence which is rhythmically controlled has greater punch. This can be demonstrated by breaking up the arrangement of words in a sentence of good rhythmical structure:

> the whole thing would be ruined as, for instance, in the following passage from my *Pro Cornelio: neque me divitiae movent, quibus omnis Africanos et Laelios multi venalicii mercatoresque superarunt.* Make a trifling change: *multi superarunt mercatores venaliciique* and the whole effect is spoiled.... Or if you take a disorderly sentence of some unskilled speaker and square it up by a slight change in the order of

the words, what was loose and untidy becomes close-knit (*aptum*).
Take an instance from Gracchus' speech before the censors: *abesse*
non potest quin eiusdem hominis sit probos impro̅ba̅rĕ qui̅ impro̅bos
prŏbet̅. How much better knit it would have been if he had said:
quin eiusdem hominis sit qui improbos probet̅ prŏbo̅s i̅mprŏba̅rĕ.
(*Or.* 232 f.)

Here we have an example of the trochaic clausula which was among
those preferred by Cicero for the cadences of a period. This ditrochee
was a favourite cadence of the Asianic school. 'How the crowd
shouted its admiration when Gaius Carbo ended with *patris dictum*
sa̅pie̅ns̆ tĕme̅rĭtas̆ fili comprobavit̆' (*Or.* 214). But it is a mistake to
keep too much to one rhythm. There are other pleasing cadences.
The cretic (– ‿ –) and its equivalent, the paean, in two forms (– ‿ ‿ ‿
and ‿ ‿ ‿ –), the former appropriate to the beginning, and the
latter a favourite cadence of the ancients. 'I do not absolutely
reject it but prefer others' (*Or.* 215). In actual fact modern analysis
has shown that his preference was for cretic and trochee (– ‿ – |
– ‿) with its various resolutions and for the double cretic, whereas
the double trochee, the 'Asianic' clausula, lost some of its attraction as Cicero's art and taste developed.

The fully developed ornate style with its typical features of
concinnitas and rhythm was, of course, not to be used on every
occasion. The proprieties of the genre had to be observed:

> nam nec semper nec apud omnis nec contra omnis nec pro omnibus
> nec cum omnibus eodem modo dicendum arbitror. is erit ergo elo-
> quens qui ad id quodcumque decebit poterit accommodare orationem.
> (Cicero, *Or.* 123)

The prooemium, for instance, should be modest in tone, the *narratio* simple, and lucid almost in the tone of everyday speech. Caesar,
too, whom Cicero praises as the outstanding example of pure
latinity ('illum omnium fere oratorum Latine loqui elegantissime',
Brutus 252), affects different styles. His Commentaries are written
in an austere, matter-of-fact style, with certain peculiarities reminiscent of the official chancellery language ('nudi enim sunt, recti
et venusti, omni ornatu orationis tamquam veste detracta', *Brutus*

262). But in his speeches 'ad hanc elegantiam verborum Latino-
rum . . . adiungit illa oratoria ornamenta dicendi' (*Brutus* 261).
Thus Norden has pointed out the rhetorical devices in a quotation
from Caesar's *Anticato* (e.g. 'putares non ab illis Catonem sed illos
a Catone deprehensos' quoted by Pliny, *Ep.* 3. 12. 3), while
Löfstedt has detected rhythmical clausulae in the quotation from
the *de analogia* (Cic. *Brutus* 253): 'ac si, ut cogitata praeclare
eloqui possent (– ∪ – – –), nonnulli studio et usu elaboraverunt
(– – – –), cuius te paene principem copiae (– ∪ – – ∪ –) atque in-
ventorem (– – – ∪) bene de nomine ac dignitate populi Romani
meritum esse existumare debemus (– ∪ – – ∪): hunc facilem et
cotidianum novisse sermonem (– ∪ – – ∪) num pro relicto est
habendum?' (– ∪ – – ∪ – ∪); and further in the quotation 'tamquam scopulum sic fugias inauditum atque insolens verbum'
(– ∪ – – –). Note, too, the 'congeries' *inauditum atque insolens*.

Even with these limitations and concessions to the distinction of
genres, the stylistic ideals (*elegantia, concinnitas, numerus*) of which
Cicero was the master practitioner were not universally accepted.
There were the misguided Atticists who believed that a rough and
unpolished manner of speaking represented the only true Attic
style (*Or.* 28). Worse still were the Thucydideans, *novum quoddam
imperitorum et inauditum genus*, who think themselves regular
Thucydideses if they have pronounced a few scrappy disconnected
phrases: 'sed cum mutila quaedam et hiantia locuti sunt, quae vel
sine magistro facere potuerunt, germanos se putant esse Thucy-
didas' (*Or.* 32). The brevity and obscurity of the Athenian historian
were inappropriate for oratory. While Cicero does not deny Thucydides' excellence as an historian, the speeches of Alcibiades as they
appear in Thucydides he characterizes as 'grandes ... verbis, crebri
sententiis, compressione rerum breves et ob eam ipsam causam
interdum subobscuri' (*Brutus* 29). It was such a style, the polar
opposite of the Ciceronian, choosing archaic and poetical words,
compressed instead of full, deliberately cultivating *inconcinnitas*
and rejecting *numerus*, which was created by the historian Sallust.
The archaisms affected by him are those now familiar from previous
pages—parataxis, clumsily constructed periods with change of subject and superfluous use of the anaphoric *is*, alliterative combinations of words (*laetitia atque lascivia, mansuetudine atque misericordia*,

K

clades atque calamitas), asyndetic tricola often with alliteration, ('animus aetas virtus vostra me hortantur', *Cat.* 58. 19; 'pro pudore pro abstinentia pro virtute audacia largitio avaritia vigebant', *Cat.* 3. 3), the rarity of the conjunct participle, the supine with a direct object, etc. In vocabulary his lavish use of old words occasioned the reproach 'priscorum Catonis verborum ineptissimum furem'. Typical is the word *prosapia* (used in the phrase *homo veteris prosapiae*) which occurs in Cato, is characterized by Cicero as *vetus verbum*, and is condemned by Quintilian (1. 6. 40), who places it among the words 'iam oblitteratis repetita temporibus . . . et Saliorum carmina vix sacerdotibus suis satis intellecta'. To all this he added the standard rhetorical devices discussed above— isocolia, homoioteleuton, alliteration, chiasmus, antithesis, and the rest. But the genre of history imposed other requirements. Cicero (*Or.* 65) had classified it with the epideictic brand of oratory whose aim is to delight rather than convince so that it may allow itself far-fetched metaphors and arrange words as painters do their various colours. Quintilian (10. 1. 31) goes further: 'est enim proxima poetis et quodam modo carmen solutum; ad memoriam posteritatis et ingenii famam componitur; ideoque et verbis remotioribus et liberioribus figuris narrandi taedium evitat'. For such poetical effects appropriate to the genre, Caelius Antipater, Sallust's predecessor as a writer of historical monographs in the Hellenistic manner, had drawn on Ennius. The language of Sallust, too, was strongly influenced by old Roman poetry and in particular by the *Annals* of Ennius. This influence is evident in his syntax (e.g. the genitives *aevi brevis, nuda gignentium, frugum laetus ager*), his word-formation (*necessitudo, vitabundus, harenosus, imperitare, insolescere*), the use of simple for compound verbs, and above all in his vocabulary which draws abundantly on the standard 'gradus ad Parnassum' (*aequor, proles, suescere*, etc.). We may detect, too, Ennian alliterative phrases such as *mare magnum* ('a rough sea'), *multi mortales*, and *fortuna fatigat*, and even hexameter endings, e.g. *fortia facta canebat*. Finally we must add the Thucydidean compression and studied variation in the modes of expression: 'pars . . . alii'; 'spes amplior quippe victoribus et advorsum eos quos saepe vicerant'; 'in suppliciis deorum magnifici, domi parci, in amicos fideles erant' (*C.* 9. 2); 'audacia in bello, ubi pax evenerat aequitate' (*C.* 9. 3); 'quippe quas honeste habere licebat abuti per turpitudinem properabant' (*C.* 13. 2).

In this elaborate and highly artificial style, one of the most original creations of Latin literature, scholars long believed (and the belief persists) that they could detect many vulgarisms and so were inclined to regard it as a species of 'democratic Latin' affected by Sallust much in the spirit which induced a demagogue from the Claudian gens to call himself Clodius. This misapprehension about a style described by the ancients (Gellius 17. 18) as *seria et severa oratio*, where the dominant note is Thucydidean σεμνότης (i.e. aloofness, majesty), has been occasioned by an indiscriminate use of the terms 'vulgar', 'archaic', 'poetical' (*archaismes conservés par le peuple*) which will be discussed in the next chapter. For Sallust's importance in the history of the literary language it will suffice to recall the words of admiration used of him by Tacitus, himself perhaps the most original of Latin stylists: 'Sallustius . . . rerum Romanarum florentissimus auctor' (*Ann.* 3. 30).

Wholly different was the style of another great master of Latin historical writing. Livy explicitly rejected the stylistic principles and practice of Sallust and adhered to the Ciceronian school. Copious and abundant in expression (Quintilian 10. 1. 32 speaks of the *Livi lactea ubertas*), he avoids *illa Sallustiana brevitas* and constructs the most elaborate periods. But history is not oratory and Livy's sentences are not of the kind which will instruct the listener in the assembly or in the courts, who looks for credibility and not *species expositionis* (Quintilian, loc. cit.). Thus the lucidity of Livy's complicated periods is impaired by his fondness for participial constructions where Cicero preferred subordinate clauses with the logical relationship carefully marked by the conjunctions. In general, Livy's periods are slower in movement and more embarrassed in construction than those of the great master of classical prose. This is not to deny his genius as an original stylist. The difference between the two authors lies perhaps not in greater or lesser artistry but is one of function and genre: Cicero's sentences are directed to the enlightenment of a listener; Livy is composing a prose poem (*carmen solutum*) for the delectation of a reader.

The historical genre, as we saw, demands poetical colour. In Livy as in Sallust we find Ennian phraseology and reminiscences:

'scutis magis quam gladiis geritur res', 9. 41. 18, recalls 'vi geritur res', Ennius, *Ann.* 263 W. (cf. Sallust 'gladiis res geritur', *Cat.* 60. 2); Ennius' 'bellum aequis manibus nox intempesta diremit', *Ann.* 170 W., is mirrored in 'aequis manibus hesterno die diremistis pugnam', 27. 13. 5; for the alliterative phrase 'plenum sudoris ac sanguinis', 6. 17. 4, cf. 'sine sudore et sanguine', Ennius *trag.* 22 W. Many 'Virgilian' turns of phrase in Livy are to be explained by their common dependence on Ennius, e.g. 'vi viam faciunt', 4. 38. 4, cf. 'fit via vi', *Aen.* 2. 494; 'agmen . . . rapit', 3. 23. 3, cf. *Aen.* 12. 450; 'iam in partem praedae suae vocatos deos', 5. 21. 5, cf. *Aen.* 3. 222 'ipsumque vocamus in partem praedamque Iovem'.

Ennian origin may be suspected also for resemblance between Livy and Lucretius: 'in volnus moribunda cecidit', 1. 58. 11, cf. 'omnes plerumque cadunt in volnus', Lucr. 4. 1049. In general the vocabulary of Livy abounds in the standard poetical words (*proles, pubes, proceres,* etc.) and formations (e.g. *lacrimabundus*). We may remind ourselves that Hellenistic historiographers adorned their prose with poetical words like κλαυθμός, λαιμός, ἀδηρίτως, μῆνις, λαῖλαψ, etc., an affectation which excited the scorn of Lucian in his 'How to write History'. We may observe, too, the now familiar poeticisms of syntax: *incerti rerum, aeger animi, cetera egregius.*

It has long since been pointed out (by Stacey) that Livy's style is not uniform throughout his work. The first decade contains many archaic and poetical features 'whereas in the third and still more the fourth decade Livy returned to the stricter forms and norms of classicism'. Thus the word *regimen*, of a type familiar in the archaic language, occurs five times in Livy: of these four are found in the first decade while the fifth occurs in the third decade in an alliterative phrase *regimen rerum omnium* with which we may compare Ennius' 'id meis rebus regimen restitat' (*trag.* 231 W.). Similarly *somno revinctus* (cf. Ennius, *Ann.* 4 W. 'somno leni placidoque revinctus') is abandoned by Livy after two examples in the first decade. The change in style emerges sharply from the statistics of two other phenomena. In the third personal plural of the perfect indicative active the normal prose ending as preferred by Caesar and Cicero was -*ērunt*, -*ēre* being, as we have seen, archaic and poetical. It is the latter form which predominates in the first decade, particularly in the first six books (with 77 per cent. in Book 3 and 73 per cent. in Book 2). But in the following books there is a steady diminution until in Book 41 there are only two examples of -*ēre* as against 58 of -*ērunt*. Significant is the rise of the curve in Book 21 where 42 per cent. -*ēre* is a pointer to the greater poetical colouring of this whole book. As for the frequentative verbs the following statistical table speaks for itself:

	1 Dec.	*3 Dec.*	*4 Dec.*	*5 Dec.*
agito . .	47	25	17	4
clamito .	14	1	1	2
dictito . .	15	3	—	—
imperito .	6	4	—	—

What lies behind these indications of a gradual return to 'modern' usage is again that sense of linguistic decorum which above all characterizes the ancient writers. Just as Virgil makes more lavish use of archaisms when he turns to majestic and solemn themes, so Livy when describing the legendary beginnings of the great Roman state donned the mantle of poetry ('mihi vetustas res scribenti nescio quo pacto antiquus fit animus', 43. 13. 2).

Certain phenomena in Livy, as in Sallust, have been dubbed 'vulgar'. It is not without significance that these have been detected particularly in the first books (e.g. the frequentative verbs). Thus (*introducti*) *ad senatum* is later replaced by the more correct *in senatum*. The participial phrase introduced by *sine*, e.g. *sine praeparato commeatu* later gives way to *nusquam praeparatis commeatibus. qua . . . qua* in the sense *partim . . . partim* (which is found in Plautus and Cicero's letters but never in Caesar or Sallust) occurs nine times in the first decade and only there. But a different interpretation of the facts is suggested for instance by Servius' comment 'antique dictum est' on Virgil's *ne saevi, Aen.* 6. 544. Livy also used this non-classical form of a prohibition: e.g. 'erit copia pugnandi; ne timete' (3. 2. 9), and here, too, we must choose between 'vulgar' and 'antique dictum'. It would appear questionable whether a Roman author of genius, with his sensitivity to the laws of the genre and his elaborate schooling in the propriety of words, would have admitted vulgarisms precisely in those parts of his work where he is evidently and admittedly concerned to evoke the

atmosphere of a remote and legendary past. It is not Livy who is
at fault (whatever may be the *patavinitas* with which he was
reproached by Asinius Pollio—Quintilian 1. 5. 56) but our stylistic
classifications of the vocabulary (see next chapter on the complex
' archaic–vulgar–poetical ').

C. POST-CLASSICAL POETRY AND PROSE

We have now followed the progress of literary Latin along the
paths of prose and poetry, paths which reached their summits
of perfection in the mature oratory of Cicero and in Virgilian epic.
Each of these literary languages was distinct of its kind, the product of a tradition which insisted on scrupulous observance of
the proprieties of the genre. These were the peaks which dominated the literary landscape of Classical Latin. They are joined,
of course, by intermediate eminences—historical prose juts out
towards poetry while comedy scarcely rises above the level plain
of everyday Latin ('comicorum poetarum, apud quos, nisi quod
versiculi sunt, nihil est aliud cotidiani dissimile sermonis', Cicero,
Or. 67). But in general it is true to say that the classical ideal as
manifested in the oratory of Cicero and the Virgilian epic drew a
sharp line between the language of prose and that of poetry. It was
this sharp contrast which was blurred in post-classical literature.
Poetry invaded prose and rhetoric dominated poetry. The style of
Virgil with its sophisticated highly rhetorical technique contained
the seeds of its own decay. Macrobius later praised Virgil for this
very rhetorical quality 'facundia Mantuani multiplex et multi-
formis est et dicendi genus omne complectitur' (*Sat.* 5. 1. 4), but it
was dangerous in the hands of men of lesser genius. Poetry produced no great figure after Virgil, whose influence remained un-
challenged and overwhelming. Of Lucan, perhaps the most talented
of the post-classical epic poets, Quintilian writes (10. 1. 90): 'Luca-
nus ardens et concitatus et sententiis clarissimus et, ut dicam quod
sentio, magis oratoribus quam poetis imitandus'. Of Statius, too,
it has been said (W. Kroll) that 'his Silvae are occasional speeches
and ἐκφράσεις in poetical form, while Juvenal and Persius in some
of their satires discuss general θέσεις in the manner of the rhetorical
schools'. As for the vitiation of prose style we can hardly do better
than summarize the diagnosis of the one great literary genius the

post-Augustan age produced. In his *Dialogus de Oratoribus* Tacitus discusses the question why it is that, whereas former ages had been so prolific in orators of genius, his own generation was completely lacking in eloquence. Marcus Aper, one of the personages of the dialogue, in defending the modern style of oratory, makes the point (*Dial.* 19) that the public (of Ciceronian times), because it was untrained and unsophisticated, tolerated and admired the performance of a man who could speak for a whole day using all the tricks of the trade as laid down in the dry-as-dust treatises of Hermagoras and Apollodorus. But in his own generation, when practically everyone in the audience had at least a smattering of the art, the orator had to use new effects and beware of exciting the impatience of his hearers. 'Would anyone today sit out the five Verrine orations? Nowadays your juryman races ahead of the speaker and rejects him *nisi aut cursu argumentorum aut colore sententiarum aut nitore et cultu descriptionum invitatus et corruptus est.* Your restless casual listener demands *laetitiam et pulchritudinem orationis'.* And there were the young students of oratory, themselves 'placed on the anvil', who wanted something to take home and indeed to write home about: 'referre domum aliquid inlustre et dignum memoria volunt; traduntque in vicem ac saepe in colonias ac provincias suas scribunt, sive sensus aliquis arguta et brevi sententia effulsit, sive locus exquisito et poetico cultu enituit' (ibid. 20). Cicero, he admits, in the works of his later years had approximated to such a style, but his early speeches had many of the faults of antiquity, slow to begin, long in narration, and careless in digression. Above all, there was 'nothing to excerpt and take home with you' ('nihil excerpere, nihil referre possis', ibid. 22).

Poetical colour and rapid sentences exploding in epigram—such were the ideals of the new style. Seneca had been at once its prophet and its first great exponent. Rejecting the puerilities of the archaists who spoke the language of the Twelve Tables, he affected a sententious brevity—*plus significas quam loqueris*—in which antithesis was the chief effect. It is his influence on the young that the Ciceronian Quintilian laments ('si rerum pondera minutissimis sententiis non fregisset' (10. 1. 130), an influence all the more pernicious because his stylistic vices were so attractive (*abundant dulcibus vitiis).* Tacitus, too, had put into Messalla's mouth a eulogy of Cicero: 'ex multa eruditione et plurimis artibus et omnium rerum scientia exundat et exuberat illa admirabilis eloquentia' (*Dial.* 30), and he spoke with contempt of those who 'in paucissimos sensus et angustas sententias detrudunt eloquentiam' (ibid. 32). But it is evident that this Ciceronian ideal applied only to the oratorical genre. In his own historical works Tacitus brought to perfection the compressed, tortured, epigrammatic style enriched with archaic and poetical colour which his admired predecessor Sallust had elaborated. The intensity and agony of his thought finds expression in the deliberate avoidance of *concinnitas*, in the laboured 'variatio' of expression of which every page offers examples: *minantibus intrepidus, adverus blandientes incorruptus*; *quidam metu, alii per adulationem*; *crebris criminationibus, aliquando per facetias*; *Suetonio, cuius adversa pravitati ipsius, prospera ad fortunam referebat*; *palam laudares, secreta male audiebant*; *vir facundus et pacis artibus,* etc. In the interests of brevity he ruthlessly pruned every superfluous word, achieving a concentration of expression perhaps equalled only by Horace in his Odes. The majesty of his theme and the austerity of his personality are reflected in the σεμνότης which the ancients had found in the style of Thucydides. This is achieved by the use of archaic (e.g. *perduellis, bellum patrare*) and poetical expressions and constructions: e.g. the genitives *incertus animi, ambiguus consilii,* the plain ablatives of 'place where' (*campo aut litore*), the instrumental of the agent (*desertus suis*); and above all by the use of poetical words, among which we may cite as typical the use of simple verbs for compound: e.g. *apisci, ciere, firmare, flere, piare, quatere, rapere, temnere* and the inchoatives *ardescere, clarescere, gravescere, notescere, suescere, valescere,* etc. Reminiscences of the poets, especially of Virgil, abound: e.g. 'colles paulatim rarescunt', *Germ.* 30 (cf. 'angusti rarescent claustra Pelori', *Aen.* 3. 411), 'quibus cruda ac viridis senectus', *Agr.* 29 (cf. 'sed cruda deo viridisque senectus', *Aen.* 6. 304); 'vulnera dirigebant', *Hist.* 2. 35 (cf. *Aen.* 10. 140). Symptomatic is his avoidance of everyday terms destructive of σεμνότης: of this we may cite the almost comic anxiety to avoid calling a spade a spade: 'per quae egeritur humus aut exciditur caespes', *Ann.* 1. 65; while agriculture, building, and commerce are rendered 'ingemere agris, illaborare domibus, suas alienasque fortunas spe metuque versare', *Germ.* 46. Löfstedt draws attention to Tacitus' studied perversity in his choice between adjective and defining genitive. Thus he writes (*Ann.* 1. 7) 'per uxorium ambitum et senili adoptione' for the more usual *uxoris, senis*. But for the traditional *bellum civile* and *virgines Vestales* he substitutes *bellum civium* (*Hist.* 1. 3) and *virgines Vestae* (*Ann.* 1. 8). This use of forms distant from those of his own day reminds us of his own epigram *maior e longinquo reverentia*. The poetical quality of the style is well exemplified in the following description of the attack on the island of Mona and the destruction of the sacred groves (*Ann.* 14. 30):

> stabat pro litore diversa acies, densa armis virisque, intercursantibus feminis; in modum Furiarum veste ferali, crinibus deiectis faces praeferebant; Druidae circum, preces diras sublatis ad caelum manibus fundentes, novitate aspectus perculere militem, ut quasi haerentibus membris immobile corpus vulneribus praeberent. dein cohortationibus ducis et se ipsi stimulantes, ne muliebre et fanaticum agmen pavescerent, inferunt signa sternuntque obvios et igni suo involvunt. praesidium posthac impositum victis excisique luci saevis superstitionibus sacri; nam cruore captivo adolere aras et hominum fibris consulere deos fas habebant.

Among much else in this passage we may note the personification of *acies*, the poetical *fundentes, pavescerent, fibris* (for *extis*), the use of the adjective for the genitive (*muliebre agmen, cruore captivo*), the archaism *adolere aras*, and the elaborate alliteration in the last sentence.

It was observed long ago by Wölfflin that Tacitus' mature style was the product of a gradual growth. Thus the archaic formation *claritudo* (see above) does not appear in the minor works, it achieves equality with *claritas* in the *Histories* (3: 3), and in the *Annals* it is fifteen times more numerous (30: 2). In the same way *omnia* gradually yields to *cuncta, essem* to *forem, non possum* and *possum* to *nequeo* and *queo, cresco* to *glisco*, etc. Of the simple verbs quoted above *notesco* and *gravesco* are found only in the *Annals* (elsewhere *innotesco, ingravesco*). In syntax, too, *apisci* is constructed with the genitive first in the *Annals*, where again we find the only examples of *id aetatis, id temporis* against the earlier use of *eo, illo temporis*, etc. Another peculiarity of the *Annals* is the growing fondness for the ablative absolute without a subject: *intellecto, quaesito, properato, saepe apud se pensitato*, etc. No such example occurs in the minor works and only six in the whole of the *Histories*. Another indication is anastrophe of the preposition, of which only five examples occur in the *Histories* as against fifty in the *Annals*.

Löfstedt has shown that from Book 13 of the *Annals* onwards Tacitus in some respects retraced his steps and returned to more normal modes of expression. This emerges clearly from the statistics of a few selected phenomena. (In the table *Annals A* = Books 1–6, 11, 12, *Annals B* = Books 13–16.)

	Dial.	Agr.	Germ.	Hist.	Ann. A.	Ann. B.
{ forem	0	4	0	51	62	1
{ essem	10	8	2	17	31	29
{ quis	0	1	0	23	54	7
{ quibus	..	..	..	71	45	50
{ quamquam	..	..	..	..	44	6
{ quamvis	..	..	..	..	4	11

These observations do not imply any major change of style: they are merely minor modifications of detail. We may attribute them to a more mature literary taste which realized that an overmannered archaism impaired rather than promoted the desired σεμνότης.

The polar opposite of the compressed style of Seneca and the modern school is that which Tacitus attacks in the *Dialogus* 26: 'neque enim oratorius iste, immo hercle ne virilis quidem cultus est, quo plerique temporum nostrorum auctores ita utuntur, ut lascivia verborum et levitate sententiarum et licentia compositionis histrionales modos exprimant'. Quintilian, too, censures the modern *lascivia*: 'alios recens haec lascivia deliciaeque et omnia ad voluptatem multitudinis imperitae composita delectant' (10. 1. 43). Such stylists, of course, were carrying on the long tradition of Asianism, which was to be stimulated in Rome by the so-called Second Sophistic. Of this florid style, with its exuberance (*laetitia*) and *poeticus cultus*, its elaborate symmetry and effects of assonance, we may choose as the most distinguished representative Apuleius. A great virtuoso of language, who in accordance with ancient doctrine adapted his style to the genre, Apuleius ranges from the comparative simplicity and sobriety of the *Apology* to the suffocating luxuriance of the *Metamorphoses*. In this work he uses every device the language offers, archaic and modern, colloquial and grand. The tone of a highly ornamented artificiality is set right from the beginning where he describes his native country as 'glebae felices aeternum libris felicioribus conditae, mea vetus prosapia[1] est'. The details of his journey read almost like a parody of the poetical *strata viarum* construction: 'postquam ardua montium et lubrica vallium et roscida cespitum et glebosa camporum ⟨emensus⟩ emersi' (1. 2). His fondness for abstract types of expression, so wearisomely characteristic of the grand style, is exemplified in 'simul iugi quod insurgimus aspritudinem fabularum lepida iucunditas levigabit' (1. 2); or combined in an 'abundant' tricolon: 'Aristomene . . . ne tu fortunarum lubricas ambages et instabiles incursiones et reciprocas vicissitudines ignoras' (1. 6). The elaborate effects have their greatest piquancy in the description of trivial scenes. Thus 'I saw with my own eyes a juggler swallow a sword point first' is rendered as 'isto gemino obtutu circulatorem aspexi equestrem spatham praeacutam mucrone infesto devorasse' (1. 4). Socrates begins (1. 7) a recital of his woes 'imo de pectore cruciabilem suspiritum ducens', a phrase on a Virgilian pattern with an archaic *suspiritus* combined with an adjective *cruciabilis* apparently first coined by Apuleius. His words are introduced by the archaic-poetical *infit*; in the phrase 'dum voluptatem gladiatorii spectaculi satis famigerabilis consector in has aerumnas incidi', *aerumnas* is one of the stock archaic-poetical words, while *famigerabilis*, which he frequently uses (e.g. quite typically in conjunction with the playful and colloquial *uxorcula*, 9. 5), is known before Apuleius only from a citation in Varro's *De lingua latina*. Socrates gives to the *anus scitula* an account of his *domuitionis*, a word used previously by Accius and Pacuvius. His very modest *grabattulus* is placed *pone cardinem* (an archaic preposition), and when it shakes beneath his own trembling, another Pacuvian word *succussus* rises from the dead: 'grabattulus etiam succussu meo inquietus' (1. 13). The *grabattulus*, indeed, is a potent prompter of tragic 'tumor': 'iam iam grabattule, inquam, animo meo carissime, qui mecum tot aerumnas exanclasti, conscius et arbiter quae nocte gesta sunt' (1. 16), where *exanclare* is one of the words condemned

---

[1] On *prosapia*, see p. 136.

by Quintilian as *oblitteratis repetita temporibus*. The language of the prurient and provocative love scenes (e.g. 'ipsa linea tunica mundule amicta et russea fasceola praenitente altiuscule sub ipsas papillas succinctula illud cibarium vasculum floridis palmulis rotabat in circulum', 2. 7), dripping with diminutives, recalls the Plautine *papillarum horridularum oppressiunculae* (see p. 78). But what most characterizes the Asianic style is the steaming jungle of verbiage fetid with every rhetorical flower, *tumida et pusilla et praedulcia*, to quote from Quintilian's famous condemnation. One example must suffice—the advice of the wicked sister (5. 20):

> novaculam praeacutam, adpulsu etiam palmulae lenientis exasperatam, tori qua parte cubare consuesti, latenter absconde lucernamque concinnem, completam oleo, claro lumine praemicantem, subde aliquo claudentis aululae tegmine, omnique isto apparatu tenacissime dissimulato, postquam sulcatos intrahens gressus cubile solitum conscenderit iamque porrectus et exordio somni prementis implicitus altum soporem flare coeperit, toro delapsa nudoque vestigio pensilem gradum pullulatim minuens, caecae tenebrae custodia liberata lucerna, praeclari tui facinoris opportunitatem de luminis consilio mutuare et ancipiti telo illo audaciter, prius dextra sursum elata, nisu quam valido noxii serpentis nodum cervicis et capitis abscide.

Such *lascivia, levitas*, and *licentia* did not win universal approval. Against the men who, clad in dyed and meretricious trappings of style, made their commentaries dance and sing (Tacitus, *Dial.* 26) were ranged those who preferred even a 'hairy toga' (*hirta toga*). Rejecting the 'curling-irons of a Maecenas' (*calamistros Maecenatis*), like Messalla they did not cease 'vetera tantum et antiqua mirari' (Tacitus, *Dial.* 15). Rating Lucilius above Horace and Lucretius above Virgil, these men were addicted to words *velut rubigine infecta*. Among the archaists we may cite Fronto as a typical example—Fronto who could complain of Cicero 'in omnibus eius orationibus paucissima admodum reperias insperata atque inopinata verba, quae non nisi cum studio atque vigilia atque multa veterum carminum memoria indagantur'. Such was the spirit of his age, the slave once again of a Greek literary mode which induced the Emperor Hadrian himself to prefer Cato to Cicero and Ennius to Virgil.

In this warfare of the opposing schools of style which dominated the whole history of post-classical prose-writing there were the inevitable compromisers like the younger Pliny, who counted himself among the admirers of the ancients, emulated Cicero, but did not altogether despise the talents of his own time. At the same time he confesses a fondness for *verba quaesita et exculta* and can fashion a pointed *sententia*.

As the centuries went by the world grew old and dreamed of its past; and prose was, at least stylistically, the work of epigoni, emphasizing and exaggerating now the peculiarities of one model, now of the other. The use of Virgil as a textbook and the basis of grammatical teaching resulted even in prose in a dislocation of the normal order of words. To backward-straining, nostalgic eyes foreshortening confused the genres and the styles. All the chests and cupboards of Roman literature were ransacked to robe these literary posturings, and the ageing Muse found nothing incongruous in a cosmetic which sanctioned the simultaneous application of lipstick and woad. Typical of the complete corruption of taste is Sidonius Apollinaris, a man schooled in traditional grammar and rhetoric, who in the fifth-century Gaul of Goth and Burgundian paid a pathetic tribute of laboured imitation to the splendour of dying Rome. Apropos of the style of his letters W. B. Anderson has remarked on 'the ostentatious combination of stylistic elaboration with sesquipedalian verbiage, Frontonian archaisms, weird neologisms and verbal jingles which makes the correspondence such a nerve-wracking conglomeration. . . . The result is a *reductio ad absurdum* of all the resources of rhetoric and a travesty of the Latin language.' This poisonous crop had to be cleared and the stubble burnt in barbarian fire before the field could again be made fruitful.

Meanwhile the speech of everyday life, subject to the universal laws of linguistic change, adapting itself to the manifold demands of new situations and fresh experiences, had steadily drifted away from the artificial literary language, distorted as it was from its beginnings by the pull of a superior culture and an alien tongue. To the study of this underground stream of the living language we must now turn our attention.

CHAPTER VI

VULGAR LATIN

I N attempting to trace the further history of spoken Latin from
the point where we left it in Chapter III, we encounter the same
methodological difficulties. Classicism, in its fastidious search for
urbanitas and *elegantia*, had imposed upon national speech severe
restrictions of form, syntax, and vocabulary. Still more remote
from ordinary modes of expression were the 'modern' style of
Seneca and his imitators and the Asianism of Apuleius, tricked out
with archaisms and poeticisms. Straining his ears to catch the
small talk of everyday life, the philologist finds himself enclosed,
as it were, in a perpetual theatre where the language is frozen in
statuesque poses, or moves with the stylized gestures of ballet
against an ornate backcloth. Such is the nature of the vast bulk of
the evidence which presents itself to the historian of the Latin
language. Yet outside this theatre, in the home, the club, and
the street, the spoken language, that most delicate and adapt-
able instrument of man's co-operation with his fellows, changed
steadily until in the course of the centuries it emerged in the manifold forms of the modern Romance languages. Of this 'Vulgar
Latin', the postulated ancestor of the modern vernaculars, which
have in their turn evolved literary forms, we can have only indirect
knowledge. But before we proceed to discuss the sources from
which such information can be drawn, the term 'Vulgar Latin'
itself must be clarified.

Every spoken language appears in a variety of forms, even on
the lips of one and the same speaker. Speech, we have often said,
is a mode of social behaviour. Our linguistic gesturings and posings
assume adaptations appropriate to the given occasion, formal,
grave, and stiff in conference, informal, gay, and relaxed in the
company of our intimates. Add to this the differences of speech
between the social classes, the educated, the half-educated, and
the uneducated. Yet here, too, the boundary constantly shifts.
Even within a given social class the different generations affect
their own idioms. The vulgarisms of the street picked up by the

young and adopted by flighty grandmothers find their way into polite drawing-rooms. The 'guts' of today will become the 'pluck' of tomorrow. Demagogic Clodii court popularity, and evangelizing Christians gain converts, best in the language of the people. But of language it cannot be said that 'omnia fatis in peius ruere'. Snobbery is rife in speech as in other modes of social behaviour, and persons of prestige become objects of imitation to their inferiors. The progress of political life, too, changes the fabric of society, a new ruling class rises not wholly assimilated to accepted modes of polite speech. These were a few of the manifold universal forces at work in the gradual transformation of Latin. We cannot hope to seize so Protean a phenomenon in a firm terminological grip. Many attempts at definition have been made, but 'Vulgar Latin' remains a shimmering mirage. We may fix our attention on individual points of phonology, morphology, syntax, and vocabulary and detect in the documents available to us deviations from classical usage. Then, working backwards from the modern Romance languages, we postulate ancestral forms which will account for the points of resemblance. The coincidences between the reconstructions and the non-classical features of the documents will enable us to identify the latter as reflections of spoken Latin. In this way we may build up a composite picture of 'Vulgar Latin'. But the method is essentially atomic, dealing separately with individual points each of which has a more or less accidental first appearance in the documents (see below). We have no text which is a faithful record of even one mode of contemporary speech. The chisel of the stonemason, the pen of the loquacious nun, and the chalk that scribbles on the wall, disregard the tongue and move self-willed in traditional patterns. It is only through their occasional inadvertences, almost willy-nilly, that the writers give us hints that their natural speech deviates from the language of the schoolroom which they are at pains to use. There are, as it were, in the dead landscape of literary Latin, seismic areas where occasional eruptions reveal the intense subterranean activity which one day will make a new world of language.

Some of these areas we may now briefly survey. For the Republican period we first quote the interesting passage from the rhetorical treatise *ad Herennium* 4. 14, where the author in distinguishing the levels of style quotes an example of the *adtenuatum genus*—'id quod ad infimum et cottidianum sermonem demissum est'.

> nam ut forte hic in balneas venit, coepit, postquam perfusus est, defricari. deinde ubi visum est ut in alveum descenderet, ecce tibi iste de traverso 'heus', inquit, 'adolescens, pueri tui modo me pulsarunt. satis facias oportet'. hic qui id aetatis ab ignoto praeter consuetudinem appellatus esset, erubuit. iste clarius eadem et alia dicere coepit. hic 'vix tamen', inquit, 'sine me considerare'. tum vero iste clamare voce quae perfacile cuivis rubores eicere potest. . . . conturbatus est adolescens: nec mirum, cui etiam nunc pedagogi lites ad oriculas versarentur imperito huiusmodi conviciorum.

Noteworthy is the expression 'ecce tibi de traverso', with which we may compare Cicero's 'ecce autem de traverso' (*ad Att.* 15. 4 A 1), while the lively 'sympathetic' dative *tibi* recurs in 'ecce tibi e transverso' (*Acad.* 2. 121). *id aetatis* we already know as a feature of popular speech, while the periphrastic *dicere coepit* was to become a frequent substitute for the aoristic perfect in late Latin. Finally *oricula* for *auris* is the ancestral form of French *oreille*, Italian *orecchio*, while *eicere* in the weakened sense 'bring forth' anticipates later usage (see p. 171).

The Atellan farces of Pomponius and Novius provide us with further material. Varro (*L.L.* 7. 84) remarks: 'in Atellanis licet animadvertere rusticos dicere se adduxisse pro scorto pelliculam'. From the surviving fragments we may quote, further, the futures *vivebo* and *dicebo*, the nouns *particulo, manduco* 'glutton' (for *manducare* in the sense 'to eat', see below), and among the verbs the inchoatives *gallulascere* (from a diminutive **gallulus*) in the sense of *pubescere, roborascere*, and the denominatives *sublabrare, praelumbare, incoxare* 'squat'. Among the Greek words we note *rhetorissare*, while *dicteria* 'witticisms' is one of the many Greco-Roman hybrids of the vulgar tongue (see below). Finally the Atellans provide us with what is apparently the earliest example of the substitution of the accusative for the nominative in the plural of first declension nouns (see below), *quot laetitias insperatas modo mi inrepsere in sinum*. Löfstedt explains this example from the influence of the Italic dialects, but it is not wholly free from the suspicion of being a contaminated construction in which the first element is an accusative of exclamation.

Cicero's letters, especially those to his intimate friends such as Atticus, reflect the latinity of urbane conversation in late Republican times, although in a letter to Paetus he proposes to use the 'sermo plebeius; verum tamen quid tibi ego videor in epistulis? nonne plebeio sermone agere tecum?' (*Ep.* 9. 21. 1). The most pronounced characteristics of the style are ellipse and rapidity. The bonds between the friends are so close that the merest hint may suffice to convey the desired meaning. It is this which sometimes makes the correspondence as difficult to understand as one part of a telephone conversation: e.g. 'itane? nuntiat Brutus illum ad bonos viros? εὐαγγέλια! sed ubi eos? nisi forte se suspendit' 'Really? Does Brutus say that he (Caesar) (is joining) the patriots? Splendid news! But where (will he find) them? (He won't) unless he hangs himself' (*ad Att.* 13. 40. 1). The syntax shows mucḷ parataxis and parenthesis, with the usual interjection of formulae of politeness such as *amabo te*. Note further the colloquial use of adjectives for adverbs, e.g. 'ad M. Aelium nullus tu quidem domum sed sicubi inciderit' 'On no account should you call on him [broach the matter] only if you should happen to meet him'. The vocabulary is studded with forceful and picturesque words—diminutives (e.g. *aedificatiuncula, ambulatiuncula, diecula, vulticulus, bellus, integellus*), frequentative forms of the verb, and hybrids (*tocullio* 'a Shylock', from τόκος 'interest'). A tone of affectionate playfulness and racy slang speaks from passages such as 'hoc litterularum exaravi egrediens e villa. . . . de Atticae febricula scilicet valde dolui. . . . sed quod scribis "igniculum matutinum γεροντικόν" γεροντικώτερον est memoriola vacillare . . . quid ergo opus erat epistula? quid cum coram sumus et garrimus quicquid in buccam?' (*ad Att.* 12. 1), where we may note *inter alia* the ancestral form of the Romance word for 'mouth' (*bouche, bocca*, etc.).

Whereas Cicero reflects the *sermo cottidianus* of educated Romans, in the conversation of host and guests at Petronius' *Cena Trimalchionis* we catch a whiff of the gutter. There are vulgarisms of pronunciation (*copones*), the genders are confused (*fatus, vinus, caelus, librum*). We find many faults of declension (*stips, Iovis, bovis, lacte, schemam, diibus*). There is much confusion of active and deponent verbs (*exhortavit, loquis, loquere, ridentur, somniatur*), many 'regularized' verb forms (*fefellitus sum, vetuo, mavoluit, plovebat, faciatur*).

In syntax the 'where' and 'whither' constructions are confused (*videbo in publicum*), *fruniscor* is constructed with an accusative, the accusative and infinitive is replaced by noun-clauses introduced by *quia* (*dixi quia mustella comedit*, 'I said the cat had eaten it'). The vocabulary is forceful, coarse, often indecent, and studded with Greek words and Greco-Roman hybrids. The following passage will serve as an illustration.

> uxor, inquit, Trimalchionis, Fortuna appellatur, quae nummos modio metitur. et modo modo quid fuit? ignoscet mihi genius tuus, noluisses de manu illius panem accipere. nunc, nec quid nec quare, in caelum abiit et Trimalchionis topanta est. ad summam, mero meridie si dixerit illi tenebras esse, credet. ipse nescit quid habeat, adeo saplutus est. sed haec lupatria providet omnia et ubi non putes. . . . familia vero, babae babae, non mehercules puto decumam partem esse quae dominum suum noverit. ad summam quemvis ex istis babaecalis in rutae folium coniciet. (37. 2–10)

> '"Trimalchio's wife", he said, "is called Fortuna. She simply rakes in the cash. And what was she only the other day? Saving your honour you wouldn't have wanted to take a crust of bread from her. And now, God knows how, she's made the grade and is Trimalchio's one-and-only. The fact is that if she tells him in broad daylight that it is dark, he'll believe it. He doesn't know himself what he owns, he's simply rolling. But this old bag has her eyes in front and where you can't imagine. As for their servants, bless my soul, I believe that not one in ten knows his own master. The fact is that he could knock any of these yes-men into a cocked-hat."'

Note: *topanta* = τὰ πάντα, *saplutus* = ζάπλουτος. *lupatria* is a hybrid of *lupus* with the ending found in πορνεύτρια, etc., and *babaecalus* 'yes-man' is a noun coined from the Greek exclamation βαβαὶ καλῶς 'bravo!'.

The suggestion has been made that the table-talk of Trimalchio and his guests does not reflect the *sermo plebeius* of native Latin speakers. Salonius has pointed out that the dinner-party takes place in a Greek city, presumably of southern or central Italy, and that most of the speakers are of Greek extraction. Moreover, the remarks made by the educated Eumolpius contain no such mistakes of pronunciation, morphology, or syntax as the other speakers. Salonius inclines, therefore, to the belief that Petronius is satirizing the broken Latin of Greeks resident in central or southern Italy. Heraeus, however, has shown that a great number of the vulgar-

isms of the *Cena* recur in glosses and other sources of vulgar Latin:
e.g. *ipsimus* 'the master', a 'superlative' of *ipse*, is the basis of
Italian *medesimo* < *met ipsimus*; *expudoratus* is found in glosses
and is the ancestor of Italian *spudorato*; the form *vetuo* is paralleled
by similar analogical presents, *vacuo, consuo, conticuo*, etc. So while
it is not impossible that solecisms like *loquis* are not authentic
vulgarisms (but cf. *sequis* elsewhere), Petronius does in the conversation of Trimalchio and his guests reveal to us something of
the *sermo plebeius* of the first century A.D.

Less colourful but no less valuable as sources of vulgar Latin are
the writers on technical subjects whose main concern it is to convey information with few stylistic pretensions. Such are the works
of the elder Cato, Vitruvius, and in later times the *Mulomedicina
Chironis*, a fourth-century translation of a Greek veterinary work,
the *de observatione ciborum* of Anthimus (sixth century), the *Oribasius Latinus* in both versions (sixth century) and the agricultural
work of Palladius (fifth century). These works, besides their numerous vulgarisms of spelling and grammar, instruct us in matters of
vocabulary which in the nature of things lay outside the range of
subjects discussed in higher literature. A great number of the
topics are, of course, of narrow specialist interest, but they often
provide us with evidence of everyday words which survive in the
modern Romance languages. Thus the French *poulain* and its
other Romance equivalents are derived from *pullamen*, which is
attested three times in the *Mulomedicina Chironis*.[1]

We have already said that none of these texts, for all their
unpretentious nature, can claim to be a true and undistorting mir-
ror of the spoken language. The same holds good of the charming
Peregrinatio Aetheriae, an account of a pilgrimage to the Holy
Places undertaken about A.D. 400 by a nun (her name is a matter
of some doubt, Aetheria and Egeria being both urged with some
confidence) from Galicia or Aquitania. A lady of high social rank,
who was accorded great facilities by people of consequence, she yet
writes in a simple and unaffected style but not without some
anxious concessions to the grammarians. It has been pointed out,
for instance, that she never uses the analytical forms of the comparative with *magis* and *plus*, which were surely current in her day,

[1] Niedermann, *N.J.* xv, 1912, 313 f.

while on another occasion she lapses into a 'between you and I'
mode of expression in falsely using the moribund dative case for
the correct *ad* with the accusative; *ingressus est discipulis* (for *ad
discipulos*). A typical specimen of her style is:

> nos ergo sabbato sera ingressi sumus montem. . . . . ibi ergo mansimus
> in ea nocte et inde maturius die dominica cum ipso presbytero et
> monachis, qui ibi commorabantur, coepimus ascendere montes
> singulos. qui montes cum infinito labore ascenduntur quoniam non
> eos subis lente et lente per girum, ut dicimus in cochleas, sed totum
> ad directum subis ac si per parietem. . . . verum autem in ipsa sum-
> mitate nullus commanet; nichil enim est ibi aliud nisi sola ecclesia et
> spelunca, ubi fuit sanctus Moyses (3. 1 ff.).

Important as reflecting changes in spoken Latin are, further, the
numerous inscriptions written by uneducated persons, among
which we may single out for mention (1) the so-called *defixiones*, or
imprecatory texts inscribed on lead tablets, magic nails, and the
like whereby the authors hoped to bring about the undoing of their
enemies; (2) the *graffiti* of Pompeii; and (3) the epitaphs on the
tombs of humble folk. As an example we quote the heart-cry of a
would-be 'nobbler':

> adiuro te demon quicunque es et demando tibi ex anc ora ex anc die
> ex oc momento ut equos prasini et albi crucies occidas, et agitatore
> Clarum et Felice et Primulum et Romanum ocidas collida neque
> spiritum illis lerinquas. (= De 8753, DV 861.)
> 'I adjure thee demon, whosoever thou art, and demand of thee
> that from this hour, this day, this moment, thou afflict and kill the
> horses of the green and white (faction) and kill and batter the driver
> Clarus and Felix and Primulus and Romanus and leave no breath of
> life in them.'

Noteworthy are the change *ae* to *e* (*demon*), the accusative after *ex*,
while the last word *lerinquas* (for *relinquas*) has got its traces badly
tangled.[1]

Finally we may mention the explicit statements about 'incorrect' and 'vulgar' Latin made by grammarians and writers of
glossaries: e.g. in the *Appendix Probi*, so called because it is
appended to a manuscript of the *Instituta artium*, ascribed to
the grammarian Probus. These notes on current errors of speech
were probably drawn up in the third or fourth century A.D. Much

---

[1] Such 'metathesis' is a frequent phenomenon in Vulgar Latin: e.g. Italian
padule < *palude*, *sudicio* < *sucidus*, etc.

later are the glosses of Reichenau (eighth or ninth century) which explain earlier Latin words in the current idiom (e.g. *binas = duas et duas*; *pulcra = bella*; *oppidis = castellis vel civitatibus*; *semel = una vice*). The encyclopaedist Isidore of Seville (seventh century) also quotes terms which he labels *vulgo*: e.g. 'fimus, id est stercus quod vulgo laetamen vocatur' (17. 2. 3); 'caulis . . . qui vulgo thyrsus dicitur' (note *tursus* 'stalk', a Greek loan-word in Vulgar Latin, which still has descendants in Romance). Occasionally contemporary pronunciation is betrayed by a false etymology: e.g. 'tonica [i.e. tunica] vestis antiquissima appellata quia in motu incedentis sonum facit. tonus enim sonus est' (19. 22. 16).

From such sources scholars have been able to tabulate some of the changes undergone by Latin during the transition period before the emergence of the Romance languages.

PHONOLOGY

Accentuation

There is general agreement that Vulgar Latin had a stress accent which in the main fell on the same syllable as in Classical Latin. Apparent exceptions are cases involving falling diphthongs like *-ie-* in words of the type *pariĕtem*. Here the semivowel became consonantal and the accent was transferred to the following vowel *paryétem*. Penultimate vowels before consonant groups ending in an *-r* attracted the accent so that Classical Latin *ténebrae* was in Vulgar Latin pronounced *tenébrae*; similarly *integrum* became *intégru(m)*.

Vowels

The most important modification of the vowel system in Vulgar Latin was the elimination of the phonemic distinctions based on quantity, which were a fundamental feature of Classical Latin (e.g. *mīseram*: *mĭseram*). In Vulgar Latin all stressed vowels became long while unstressed vowels were short. That the original short accented vowels were lengthened is clear *inter alia* from their treatment in Romance: thus the French, Spanish, and Italian descendants of *fŏcum* show diphthongization (*feu, fuego, fuoco* < V.L. *fócum*). Similarly *pĕde(m)* appears as *pied, piede*. The first break in the ancient system of distinctions based essentially on quantity was made when the long vowels received a more closed pronunciation than their short equivalents: *fīdus* [fi·dus] but *fĭdes* [fɪdes]. Consequently when the system developed in such a way that all accented vowels became long and unaccented vowels short, it was the differences in vowel *quality* which were made the basis of the phonemic distinctions. The new system now comprised nine vowels of different timbre, [e], [ɛ], [i], [ɪ], [o], [ɔ], [u], [ʋ], and [a], there being no distinction of timbre between *ā* and *ă*. This full system was preserved, at least in accented syllables, in isolated parts of the Romance territory (Dacia and some dialects of Sardinia). Elsewhere a simplification was introduced through the convergence of [o] and [ʋ] and [e] and [ɪ] (see below). This simpler system formed the basis of the Continental West Romance. The three stages may be tabulated thus:

Cl. L.	ă	ĕ	ē	ĭ	ī	ŏ	ō	ŭ	ū
Early V.L.	a	ɛ	e		i	ɔ	o	ʋ	u
C.W.R.	a	ɛ	ẹ		i	ɔ	ọ		u

It is difficult to give a precise date to the emergence of the new system. It so happens that the dates of the first documentary evidence for the individual changes of vowel quality vary from detail to detail. But it is likely that the system changed as a whole and that the gradual shift simultaneously affected all the constituents of the phonemic system. The above changes are reflected in our texts and inscriptions by confusions of spelling which we interpret on the principle that sound symbols are not interchangeable unless they have the same or closely approximating values. In so doing we must bear in mind that the Latin alphabet did not in general distinguish between long and short vowels. Consequently the single letter *e* now had two values, [ẹ] from *ē* and [ɛ] from *ĕ*. Similarly *i* could represent [i] < *ī* and [ẹ] < *ĭ*. This meant that when the partially educated writer was faced with the task of rendering his own pronunciation [ẹ] he could use either *e* or *i*. Thus we find spellings like *sebe* for *sĭbĭ*, and *ficit* for *fēcit*. The following examples of non-traditional spelling reflecting changes of pronunciation will be conveniently listed under rubrics representing the Classical sounds (e.g. *e*×*i*) from which the development started.

ĕ×*ĭ*

>   *posuiru* (= *posuerunt*), *minsibus* (= *mēnsibus*), *filix*, *crudilitas*; *sene* (= *sine*), *menus* (= *minus*), *frecare*, *elud*, *elo*, *semul*, *enitio*, *trebuni.*

ĕ×*ae*

The open pronunciation of *ĕ* is indicated by the spelling *ae*, this diphthong having developed to [ɛ] (see below): *baene*, *maerenti*, *daeder* (= *deder(unt)*).

ō×*ŭ*

>   *annus* = *annos*, *cognusco*, *nubis*, *tonecas* = *tunicas.*
>   *norus* = *nurus*, *con* = *cum*, *alonnus* = *alumnus*; cf. *'coluber non colober'*, *Appendix Probi.*

A spelling like *frunte* for *fronte* cannot be accounted for on purely phonetic grounds. The form is presumably analogical, based on the nominative *frō(n)s* > *frūs.*

The diphthongs, too, were considerably modified. We have already seen above that in certain country dialects *ae* had been monophthongized to *e*. This process of monophthongization became general in Latin starting with the unaccented syllables in Republican times and spreading to the accented syllable in the first century A.D. The change is attested by spellings which interchange *ae* and *e*: e.g. *baene*, *daeder(unt)*, *braevis*, etc.; *que* = *quae*, *precepto*, etc. Similarly *oe* became *e*: e.g. *penam* for *poenam*, *amenus* for *amoenus*. *au*, on the other hand, despite the fact that it had early become monophthongized to *o* in certain country dialects of Latin and in the Italic dialects of north and central Italy, was retained in Vulgar Latin; and it survives to this day in Rumanian (*aur* < *aurum*). In Italian, too, the contrast between *luogo* and *oro* shows that the change of *ō* to *uo* must have been completed before the change of *au* < *ō*. The evidence of Spanish and French supports the conclusion that in Vulgar Latin *au* was preserved and that its monophthongization took place independently in the separate Romance languages.

In unaccented syllables vowels tended to be unstable or to disappear completely. Syncope was particularly frequent in syllables following the stress. Many of the entries in the *Appendix Probi* attest such syncope: *speculum non speclum*, *vetulus non veclus*, *tabula non tabla*, cf. inscriptional examples, *dulcisma*, *vetrani*,

Caesri. In final syllables, though there were uncertainties in quality
($o \times u$ and $e \times i$), the vowels were preserved until long after the
break-up of common Romance. It remains to mention the changes
of *i* and *u* in hiatus after a consonant. That such sounds occasionally had consonantal value even in earlier Latin is evident from the
scansion of words like *dormio, facias, abiete,* etc. This pronunciation became general in imperial times. The alphabet had no special
sign to distinguish this [j], but the sound change is implicit in
spellings such as *abalenare, quetus*. Initially and intervocalically
the consonantal [j] first became a spirant with the value of *j* and
then evolved to an affricate [dj] or [dʒ], a sound which is represented variously as *z* (e.g. *Zanuarius, Zoviano*), as *s* (*Sustus =
Iustus*), as *di* (*codiugi = coniugi*), *gi* (*congiugi*), or simply as *g*
(*Troge = Troiae*). This sound, too, was the end-product of the
complexes *de, di, ge, gi* (see below). Post-consonantal *u* also had a
non-syllabic value in Latin poetry (e.g. Ennius' dissyllabic *quattuor*) and this sporadic pronunciation anticipated its generalization
in Vulgar Latin. Here, too, the consonantal value is implicit in the
febrarius of the *Appendix Probi* and inscription *quattor, Ianarius,* etc.

Consonants

In the modification of the consonantal system the chief points
to be noted are:

1. The change of intervocalic *b* to a bilabial fricative [β], identical in
pronunciation with consonantal *v* (hence such spellings as *cuuiculo* for
cubiculo), and the reverse spellings of *b* for *u* (*unibersis, cibitatis, bixit*).

2. Palatalization (yodization). Before a vowel the combination *ti*
developed to *ty*, which from the second century A.D. became *ts* as is
evidenced by the spellings *Vincentza, sapiensie, tersiu,* etc.[1] The palatalization of *c* took place much later, there being no unequivocal
evidence until the sixth century. In Classical Latin this sound was
pronounced as a plosive [k] in all positions. Before *i̯*, and somewhat
later before *i* and *e*, the consonant was palatalized and a glide sound
developed [kj]. The next stage postulated is [tj], which developed as
above to *ts*, the convergence of *ci* and *ti* being apparent from the
confusion of orthography: *nuncius, amicicia, tercium, nacione* and *con-
ditio, solatium. intcitamento* seems to imply an affricate pronunciation
[ts] or [tʃ], but the treatment varies in different parts of the Romance

[1] A parallel phenomenon is the development of *di > dy > dz*, a sound which
was represented by the spelling *z* (cf. Isidore 'solent Itali dicere *ozie* pro *hodie*'):
zes = dies, oze = hodie, Ziomedes, etc.

territory. It is noteworthy that the more archaic dialects of Sardinian have remained immune from this palatalization.

g was likewise palatalized before a front vowel, yielding a sound which became identical with *i̯*, whence the reverse spellings *gi*, etc., listed above. In the intervocalic position preceding the accent the palatal fricative (evidenced by *septuazinta*) was dropped: *trienta, Agrientum, quarranta* (= *quadraginta*). Before -*m* this sound was labialized: *fraumenta, sauma*, cf. 'pegma non peuma' (*Appendix Probi*).

3. The intervocalic voiceless plosives were voiced in Western Romance: e.g. *logus, tridicum, fegit, quodannis*. This phenomenon is dated to the fifth century and later.

4. *b* intervocalically became a bilabial fricative, as is evidenced by the frequent interchange of *b* and *v*: e.g. 'plebes non plevis, tabes non tavis' (*App. Probi*).

5. Final *m* was weakly pronounced from the earliest times and there are innumerable inscriptional examples of its omission. On the evidence of Romance it was lost in all words except monosyllables (hence French *rien* < *rem*). Final *n* was more tenacious and its disappearance, which the Romance languages attest in all words except monosyllables, was presumably the result of independent developments after the break-up of common vulgar Latin. Final *t* had also been dropped at an early date in certain dialects of Latin (Ch. III). Vulgar Latin shows the same tendency with regional differences. Inscriptional examples are *ama, valia, fecerun*.

6. Of group phenomena the following deserve mention. Among the numerous instances of assimilation we may note that of -*nd*- > -*nn*- (e.g. 'grundio non grunnio'), which is ascribed by some to the influence of Oscan. *x* (i.e. *cs*) was assimilated to *s(s)* (e.g. *visit* = *vixit*). The phonetic equivalence of *x* and *s(s)* resulted in reverse spellings (e.g. 'miles non milex', *App. Probi*). The parallel assimilation of *ps* is found at Pompeii as early as the first century (*isse* for *ipse*). This, too, finds a parallel in Oscan and Umbrian. The change of -*rs* to -*s(s)* manifested itself early in Vulgar and local varieties of Latin (*susum, rusum, dossum*). In other consonant groups, where the second element was a liquid or nasal, pronunciation was facilitated by the insertion of an anaptyctic vowel: e.g. *ineritia, frateres, omines, nutirices*, etc. Here, too, we may classify the development of a prothetic vowel before *s* followed by a voiceless plosive: e.g. *ispose* = *sponsae, iscola* = *schola, ispeculator, istatuam*.

MORPHOLOGY

Gender

The hypothetical primitive Romance language reconstructed from analysis and comparison of the Romance languages shows a nominal system with only two genders. The process of eliminating the neuters started at an early date. Such confusions of gender have already been discussed above. In imperial times the process was accelerated through the removal of most of the phonetic distinctions between masculines and neuters of the second declension. So we find *fatus, caelus, monimentus*, etc. But, as is common in periods of transition, temporary gains were made by the category which was destined to disappear: e.g. *titulum*. Phonetic developments had left untouched, however, the most striking distinction between masculines and neuters of the second declension—masculine -*ī*, -*ōs*, and neuter -*a* in the nominative and accusative plural. In general -*ī* and -*ōs* prevailed in Romance, but there have been successful encroachments in the plural: e.g. *digita* (< *digitus*), where it was supported by the coherence of a group of nouns denoting parts of the body—*bracchia, cubita, genua*, etc. In other instances the plural in -*a* was treated as a collective singular and became the basis of new feminine first-declension nouns: *castra, gaudia, ligna, bracchia, armenta*.

Declension

The loss of final -*m* and the weak pronunciation in some regions of -*s* and the interchange of *u* and *o* and *i* and *e* in final syllables did much to destroy the phonetic basis of the classical inflexional system, as will be apparent from the following tables:

	C.L.	*V.L.*	*C.L.*	*V.L.*	*C.L.*	*V.L.*
N.	-ă	-a	-us	-ǫ(s)	-ĭs	-ę(s)
Ac.	-am	-a(m)	-um	-ǫ(m)	-em	-ę(m)
G.	-ae	-e	-ī	-i	-ĭs	-ę(s)
D.	-ae	-e	-ō	-o	-ī	-i
Ab.	-ā	-a	-ō	-o	-e	-e

To these disruptive forces we may add syntactical developments which since early times had created prepositional phrases as substitutes for the simple cases (e.g. *ad*+accusative for the dative, see below). The consequence of these developments was that by the eighth century the Latin declensions were reduced to a two-case system.

First declension

These nouns received recruitment from a general tendency towards a clearer characterization of gender. Thus feminines in -*us* divested themselves of their misleading garb: e.g. *nura, socra*. There were similar adherents from other types: *coniuga, sacerda* (for *sacerdos*), *nepta, tempesta*. The Greek neuter loan-words in -*ma* were also inscribed in this class, as were certain third-declension Greek nouns which the Roman adopted in the accusatival form: *hebdomada, lampada*.

Among the inflexions the genitive singular shows a variety of forms -*ae* or -*e*, -*as*, and -*aes* or -*es* (*villaes, Quintiliaes, Prisces, sues, secundes, liberates*), where the -*s* is due to either the influence of third-declension nouns or the Italic ending -*as* (also preserved in *paterfamilias*). Datives and ablatives like *feminabus, filiabus* follow the example of *deabus*, but these have been eliminated in Romance. A curious development, based apparently on Greek proper names like *Psyche, Psychenis*, was the declension *Anna: Annanis, mamma: mammanis*. Some masculines in -*a* were similarly declined *scriba *scribanis* (> Fr. *écrivain*).

Second declension

Here, too, we find a tendency towards a distinctive characterization of gender in the neuters: *vas* > *vasum, os* > *ossum*. Despite the elimination of the neuters (see above), the distinctive plural ending -*a* survived in southern and central Italy and Dacia and was even adopted by some masculine nouns: *fructa, digita*. In the inflexions we find temporary aberrations in the dative-ablative forms such as *diibus, filibus, alumnibus, amicibus*.

Third declension

Phonetic development obliterated the distinction between -*es* and -*is*. Hence the frequent confusions which the grammarians are at pains to correct: e.g. (*Appendix Probi*) 'tabes non tavis', 'suboles non subolis', 'lues non luis', 'fames non famis', etc.

The nominative singular was often transformed under analogical influence: early examples are *Iovis, bovis, lacte*. We find, further, *carnis* and *stirpis*. The *Appendix Probi* corrects a form *gruis*, while *suis* is used by Prudentius. Such nominatives established a parisyllabic system. The reverse process is seen in the forms *orbs* and *nubs* pilloried by the *Appendix Probi*.

In this declension, too, the neuters became masculine (e.g. *frigorem, pectorem, roborem*). But the neuters registered some gains: *cinus* for *cinis, cineris*, while a *pulvus* is suggested by Romance forms such as Span. *polvo*. Analogical levelling had early affected the declensional type *sanguis, sanguinis* and had created a nominative *sanguen*. Later the reverse process is apparent in the nominative *pollis* for *pollen*. A new nominative *glandis* was substituted for *glans* (see above) and then a new declensional stem *glandinis* was created, with which we may compare *lendis, lendinis*.

In the inflexions we may note that in the ablative singular *-ĕ* prevails over *-ī*, and in the accusative plural *-ēs* over *-īs*. The genitive plurals such as *omniorum, parentaliorum* are based on the nom. acc. *omnia, parentalia*, while *mensis* is fickle, showing *mensorum* or *menserum* according as it is more attracted by *annorum* or *dierum*.

The fourth and fifth declensions were absorbed respectively into the second and first. This process, too, had started early (e.g. *senati*): later inscriptions frequently exhibit forms such as *portico, mano, introito, sumptis, spirito*, etc. In the fifth declension the existing doublets like *materies, materia* facilitated the transformation of words like *glacia, facia, *rabia. spes* and *res* joined the third declension, but for *spes* there was also an *-n-* form of the oblique cases: *spes, spenem* (cf. above on first declension).

Adjectives

Here, too, the tendency to distinct character zation of gender is apparent. The *Appendix Probi*, for instance, pillories the forms *paupera, acrum, tristus, tetrus* (= *taeter*). Other forms of the same kind are *gracilus, sublimus, praecoca*.

For the degrees of comparison Romance uses the analytical forms with *magis* or *plus* according to region (see below). The beginning of the process of replacement can be traced far back in Latin, comparatives and superlatives being particularly subject to the popular tendency towards 'hypercharacterization': e.g. *magis maiores* in Plautus. Such pleonasms became increasingly frequent in the later vulgar language, where we also observe forms with double suffix such as *proximior, extremior, pessimissimus, minimissimus*, and even the combinations *plus magis* and *magis plus, magis magisque amplius*.

The type *miserrima* is regularized to *miserissima*, cf. *integrissima*. Note further *iuvenior* and *pientissimus*.

Pronouns

Noteworthy is the indiscriminate use of *hic, ille*, and *iste*, the use of *ipse* as an anaphoric pronoun replacing *is*, and the reduction of *ille* to the status of definite article and *unus* to that of indefinite article. *cuius, cui* continue to influence the declension of the other pronouns: e.g. *ipsuius* and *illui* (for earlier forms see pp. 254 f.). For the dative feminine singular forms like *illae* and *illaei* are found. Demonstratives are strengthened by a prefixed *ecce*: hence Fr. *cet* < *ecce istum*. For *ipsimus* the emphatic form of *ipse* see p. 153.

The pronouns provide an interesting example of the constant renewal of linguistic elements. Even in prehistoric times Latin had given strength to the demonstratives by compounding two different stems: **ol-se, is-te* (see pp. 254 f.). This tendency persists in the usage of late writers who combine two demonstratives: *is ipse, ipse ille.*

The adverbs and prepositions share in this tendency towards a fuller form. There are many compounds such as *abante, ab intus, de contra, in ante*, etc., and these were often used as prepositions. Compound prepositions are: *de post, de super, de inter*. Prepositional phrases, too, function as prepositions: e.g. 'per girum ipsius colliculi', 'in giro parietes ecclesiae', 'de latus montem', 'de latus casa' (*Per. Aeth.*).

Verbs

The confusion of deponent and active continues: *sequis* (cf. Petronius' *loquis*), *conarit, deprecebat, miraret*; but *doleatur, dubitamur, vetor, obitus sum, iuvantur* (modelled on *auxilior, opitulor*). The distinctive passive forms in *-r* have disappeared in Romance, where they have been replaced by periphrases of the perfect participle and the verb 'to be' (*amatur > amatus est*), or by reflexive expressions. Both substitutes are found in Vulgar Latin. The reflexives are particularly frequent in the third person where the subject is a thing, the process being rooted in personifications such as 'Myrina quae Sebastopolim se vocat' (Pliny *N.H.* 5. 121). Sometimes reflexive and passive constructions are contaminated, e.g. *se extinguitur*.

The tendency towards confusion in the conjugational classes of the present tense persists (see above on *sonĕre, tonĕre, fulgĕre, fervĕre*, etc.). But whereas earlier the third conjugation had suffered defections to the second, later this process was reversed and changes exemplified in *lugunt, pendunt, miscĕre*, and *ridĕre* resulted in the virtual elimination of the *-ēre* type in some branches of Romance although it triumphed in Spain. Note, however, that comparative Romance linguistics finds it necessary to postulate *sapēre* (based on the perfect *sapui*) and *cadēre*. The latter may be due to the influence of *iacēre*, but for this verb inscriptions attest *iacio* and *iacis*. These might, of course, be phonetic variants due to the confusion of *e* and *i* as in *iubis*, but passage to the fourth conjugation is evident in *doliens, libiens* and in *florivit, florire*, while *doleunt* is presumably a graphic rendering of *doliunt*. The fourth conjugation also wins over recruits from the third—*disciunt, serpio, *lucire, gemire*.

Originally the inflexions alone were sufficient to indicate the person and the pronouns *ego, tu,* etc., were used for emphasis. In the popular language their use became habitual and their force weakened so that they were ultimately reduced to the status of prefixes: *j'aime, tu aimes, il aime.*

In the personal endings phonetic developments caused the loss of *i* in hiatus (*-io* > *-o, -iunt* > *-unt*) and the obliteration of the distinction in pronunciation between unaccented *-ēs* and *-is*, or *-et* and *-it*. The *Peregrinatio Aetheriae* shows a fondness for the spelling *contiget, benedicet, colliget, prendet*. The corresponding plural forms *ponent, tendent, vadent, tollent, reponent* cannot, of course, be phonetic equivalents of the correct *-unt*. In view of the fact that the second conjugation was moribund in Vulgar Latin it might be thought that Aetheria's preference was the reaction of over-anxious ignorance to the schoolmaster's thundering '*pendent non pendunt*', but *-ent* has prevailed in Spain and there is strong evidence that Aetheria came from Galicia.

Of the tenses the imperfect suffered little change and has survived almost intact in Romance, except that *-iebam* > *-ebam*. But the *-ibam* forms also persisted throughout latinity.

The future indicatives in Latin were in origin either old subjunctive forms (*legam*) or forms compounded with the verb 'to be' (*-bo*) (see pp. 271 f.). Throughout the history of Latin this tense remained true to its modal ('voluntative') origin: on the one hand, the future indicative was used with imperatival force while, on the other, the subjunctive expressed futurity. In Romance too, where the old future forms have disappeared, their place has been taken by periphrases of modal force: (1) *facere volo*, (2) *facere debeo*, (3) *facere habeo*. In later Latin we find ample traces of these developments: (1) is preserved in Rumanian, (2) appears in Sardinian, and (3) in the other Romance languages. This last construction originally had the force of 'must', 'have to' (e.g. 'vallem nos traversare habebamus', *Per. Aeth.* 2. 1), but examples of the plain future significance are frequent enough in late Latin. The classical types of the different conjugations are occasionally confused: with the Atellan forms *dicebo, vivebo* (see above) we may compare, for instance, *inferevit* (= *inferebit*), while the second conjugation often makes its future in -*am*: e.g. *habeam, lugea(t)*.

In the perfect the irregular ('strong') forms of the stem tend to be replaced by regular ('weak') forms: thus *praestavi* appears for *praestiti* and *salivi* for *salui*. In the -*v*- perfect the contracted forms -*asti, -astis, -arunt* had always been preferred in popular speech. Originating in the purely phonetic loss of -*v*- between similar vowels (*delevero* > *delero*), the process was carried further by analogical influences. Thus we find -*āi* (*probai, calcai*) on the model of -*ii*. In the third person singular vulgar inscriptions attest the form *laborait* (preserved also in Old Sardinian). But most numerous are examples of -*aut* (*pedicaut, triumphaut, donaut*, etc.), which is the parent form of the Romance endings (Ital. *amó, amao*; for the phonetic development cf. *auca* < *avica*).

Of the strong perfects the reduplicated type still shows the power of expansion: *impendidi, edidit, prandiderit*. These analogical forms were confined to dental stems (model *credo, credidi*); elsewhere the reduplicated forms were weeded out, only *dedi* and *steti* surviving in Romance. The long-vowelled type also yields ground: e.g. *lexerit* for *lēgerit, capui* for *cēpi*. Most vigorous was the -*si* type which gained considerable ground in late Latin and Romance ('In Vulgar Latin there were perhaps some thirty or more new formations', Grandgent). The type in -*ui*, though it lost its footing in the first and fourth conjugation, where it was anomalous, encroached in the second and third conjugations: the process may be detected early (e.g. *parcuit* (Naevius), *serui* (Ennius)). Inscriptional examples are *reguit, coguit, convertuit*, and even *fecuit*, while Romance philology postulates **bibui, lēgui, vīdui*, etc.

Among the inflexions of the perfect there is no trace in Romance of the archaic -*ēre*, or of the form -*ērunt* which predominates in classical literature. Thus the short-vowelled form *-ĕrunt* found in the comic poets must have persisted in popular speech.

SYNTAX

Only a few of the most important features will be discussed.

The use of the cases

On the evolution of the two-case system see above.

The tendency observable from Plautus onwards to use prepositional phrases for simple cases receives new stimulus from the phonetic decay of the inflexions (see p. 160): thus *ad* with the accusative replaced the dative (*ad eum dicit, ad febricitantes prosunt*, etc.). The expressions for *where* and *whither* being confused (see below, p. 177), *ad* with the accusative also does duty for locative expressions ('fui ad ecclesiam', *Per. Aeth.*), but examples with names of towns and countries are found as early as Livy (see Syntax).

Similarly the pure ablative is replaced by periphrases with *ex, ab*, and *de*, preference being given in the popular language to the last (*de navibus egredi, de palatio exit, de marmore facta*). Even the causal and instrumental ablative is so substituted: *fatigati de vigiliis, de oculis tangentes crucem, ungeatur . . . de illo oleo* (*Per. Aeth.*). *In* with the locative ablative appears in expressions of time contrary to Classical usage (see Syntax).

For *de* with the ablative as a substitute for the genitive examples may be found from Plautus onwards (*dimidium de praeda*): later this usage developed so far that it could be used without a governing noun: 'ampullam in qua de oleo . . . continebatur' (*Vita Aridii*).

After prepositions there was great confusion between ablative and accusative (*ab hortu(m), con quen, cum libertos, ex donationem, pro salutem, pro hoc ipsud, sine lesionem, a monazontes, de hoc ipsud, de carnem; contra ipso loco, venit in civitate sua*). But many of these examples, of course, have merely orthographic significance in view of the loss of *-m*.

The verb

The Classical Latin perfect possessed two functions—aorist 'I said', and perfect 'I have said'. The creation of a periphrastic

form to express the 'present state' began early, e.g. 'multa bona
bene parta habemus' (Plautus), but its full development was not
reached until a late period: e.g. 'haec omnia probatum habemus'
(Oribasius), and 'episcopum invitatum habes' (Gregory of Tours).
Of the non-finite parts of the verb only the present active infinitive
and the present and perfect participles were left intact. The supine
was in general replaced by the infinitive but has survived in
Rumanian. It was most tenacious in certain fixed phrases, e.g.
dormitum ire, for which late authors often used the variant *dormito
vadit* (cf. Aetheria's 'reponent se dormito'). The gerund, too, was
replaced by the infinitive, but in the modal ablative it served as a
substitute for the present participle (e.g. Aetheria's 'redire . . .
dicendo psalmos'), a usage the beginnings of which may be traced
back to Plautus (see pp. 320 f.). The gerundive appears in Late Latin
as a substitute for the future passive participle. It was originally
indifferent as to voice (e.g. *secundus* = 'following') and Plautus
uses it in a sense which comes close to that of an active future
participle ('haecine ubi scibit senex, puppis pereundast probe',
Epid. 73, 74). In later Latin, too, examples occur where a gerundive
like *moriendi* is equivalent to *morituri*. Here again we find a
typical feature of an age of transition in that a dying form gives a
flicker of life: thus *recepturus* is used for *recipiendus*, and *scripturas*
for *scribendas*. Finally, the gerundive in the nominative also occurs
as a substitute for the present participle: *iubandi sunt* 'are helpful'
= *iuvant* (Oribasius). The future active participle is rare in Vulgar
Latin but is used in periphrastic substitutes for the future: e.g.
redditurus sit (*Per. Aeth.*). The present participle, too, occurs in
periphrases. In Romance it survives as an adjective, its participial
function having been usurped by the gerund. The present infinitive
passive and the perfect infinitive have disappeared in Romance.
That the perfect infinitive was moribund is shown by the fact that
late writers often use it as a substitute for the present.

The following are points of note in the syntax of the moods. The
subjunctive is replaced by the indicative in many constructions.
Since early times the indicative had been found in indirect questions. Later it occurs in many other constructions: in consecutive
clauses (e.g. 'ecclesia valde pulchra . . . ut vere digna est esse
domus Dei', *Per. Aeth.*); after causal *cum* ('cum his omnes tam

excelsi sunt'); after expressions of doubting ('procul dubium est quod . . . permansit', Greg. T.). The subjunctive, however, is found for the classical indicative, in various types of subordinate clause, and it tends to become a mere mark of subordination. We find it, for instance, after causal *quod* ('Iulia . . . fecit quod Ambibolus frater negligendus facere noluerit', DV. 1481); in temporal clauses introduced by *priusquam, dum*, etc. ('tu dum esses ad superos nemo mihi formonsior ulla', DV. 1373). Particularly characteristic of Late Latin is the subjunctive (though examples occur also of the indicative) in noun-clauses introduced by *quod, quoniam*, and *quia* after verbs of saying, etc., as a substitute for the classical accusative and the infinitive.

VOCABULARY

Before considering the relationship of the vocabulary of popular spoken Latin to that of literature it will be well to recall once more that in Latin there was no uniform literary vocabulary. The dictionary was as it were a chest of drawers each containing verbal garments appropriate to different occasions. Löfstedt has pointed out that the distinction made by the old-fashioned handbooks of synonyms between *portare* 'carry a heavy or irksome burden' and the more colourless *ferre* does not hold good. The distinction is rather one of style. The author of the *Bellum Africanum*, for instance, uses *sarcinas in acervum comportare* (69. 2) whereas the strict classicist Caesar uses *conferre*. The same relationship exists between *deportare* and *devehere, se reportare* and *se ferre*. Thus the Romance languages with their *portare, porter*, etc., have preserved the word which we may assign to the *genus demissum*. So, too, with the synonyms *grandis* and *magnus*: the *Bellum Africanum* uses *grande praesidium*, etc., where Caesar preferred *magnus*, and the Romance languages confirm the distinction (Fr. *grand*, It. *grande*). No less illuminating is the relationship of *occidere* and *interficere*. The former verb with its obvious etymological connexion with *caedo* had a more drastic meaning, 'cut down, slaughter', as against the colourless, euphemistic *interficere*, 'do away with'. It is *occidere* which predominates in Plautus and Terence, in Petronius, Aetheria, the *Mulomedicina*, Oribasius, and the *Defixiones*, where we also find the reinforced compound form *peroccidere* (see below). It remains to add that Romance has preserved *occidere* (It. *uccidere*), but not *interficere*.

With this essential distinction of style and genres in mind, we may assert that the basic fund of words in the early Empire popular speech hardly differed from that of literary Latin. The colloquial language is characterized, of course, by its preference for colourful and drastic expressions which with the change of generations lose their force and emphasis. A child who first and constantly hears 'mug' will in all innocence use it as the normal expression. It was by this universal process of linguistic attrition that the Latin frequentative and inchoative verbs gradually lost their original force and replaced the simple verbs from which they were derived. Thus *cantare, adiutare, iactare, pensare, saltare* alone survive in Romance: e.g. Fr. *chanter, aider, jeter, penser, sauter*.

Of great importance, too, for Romance are the inchoatives in -*ēscere* and -*īscere* (*canēscere, virīscere, florēscere, dormīscere*). Yet another manifestation of the constant striving after forceful expression in the popular language is its preference for words of fuller form. As was pointed out by Wackernagel, the imperative of *scire* in Latin is *scito* not *sci*. So, too, in the Latin Bible *esto* is used for *es*, and *vade* does duty for *i*, whereas in the plural *ite* appears and never *vadite*. In the indicative, too, *vadis, vadit* oust *is, it*, while in the subjunctive a grammar which registers only the forms of greatest frequency would conjugate *vadam, vadas, vadat, eamus, eatis, vadant*. Much the same observations have been made on the usage of the forms of the verb 'to go' in other 'Vulgar' authors: the monosyllabic forms are avoided and replaced by the corresponding forms from *vadere* and *ambulare*. So, too, *diu* yields to expressions such as *longo tempore, tot* and *quot* to *tanti* and *quanti, vir* to *homo*, etc. How strong this aversion to words of little bodily substance was is shown by an interesting observation which Löfstedt has made: the medical writer Theodorus Priscianus in describing the treatment of patients normally uses the present tense (*nutrio, concedo*, etc.), but where he has occasion to use the verb 'to give' he uses the future *dabo* in avoidance of the monosyllable *do*. One important result of this preference for more substantial words was the predominance established by compound verbs over the corresponding simple forms. A stock example is the suppression of *edo* (which in any case was further handicapped by its anomalous conjugation *edo, ēs, ēst*) in favour of *comedo* where originally the verbal prefix gave completive force, 'eat up'. The following are a few of the many examples of the preference for compound verbs in Vulgar Latin: *pertransire, perexire, perconfirmare, disseparare, perdiscoperire, conducere, expandere*. In the nouns and adjectives the preference of the popular language for the fuller and more expressive diminutive forms and its reflection in the vocabulary of the Romance languages have already been discussed. Examples are legion: *avicellus* (*oiseau*), *soliculus* (*soleil*), *genuculum* (*genou*), *agnellus* (*agneau*), *cultellus* (*couteau*), *vetulus*, reduced to *vetlus* and pronounced *veclus* (It. *vecchio*, Fr. *vieux*).

Vulgar Latin and Romance vocabulary provides many other instances of the elimination of usual commonplace and polite words by highly coloured slang equivalents. The word *testa*, for instance, 'earthenware pot' was used in a transferred sense 'shell' by Varro and Cicero. Later it occurs in the meaning 'skull' and finally it became the normal word for 'head' (Fr. *tête*, etc.). A passage from the Atellan writer Pomponius (179) gives a clue to the sort of context ('I'll knock your block off') in which this shift of meaning was effected: 'iam istam calvam colapis comminuissem testatim tibi', where *testatim* = 'to smithereens'. So, too, *bucca* '(distended) cheek' (cf. Pomponius' 'puls in buccam veniet') is eventually used for 'mouth' (cf. Cicero's 'quod in buccam venerit scribito', *ad Att.* I. 12. 4), while in various Romance dialects we find descendants of other forceful equivalents: *gula, gurges, gurga. spatula* 'shovel' was used for the 'shoulder-blade of a pig' and then became the usual word for 'shoulder' (cf. *épaule*, etc.). As parallels for this generalization of meaning in words referring strictly to animals (cf. the use in German slang of *fressen* for *essen*) we may quote *gamba* (from Gk. καμπή), which was the technical term for a joint in the back leg of a horse. The Romance meaning 'leg' (*jambe*) appears in a gloss: *crura* : *gambe, tibie* (*CGIL* v. 495). *perna*, too, strictly 'the ham of a pig', appears in Spanish *pierna*, Portuguese *perna* 'leg'. Forceful expressions are also found among the verbs referring to common activities; e.g. 'to talk' (*garrire, garrulare, fabulari, parabolare*); another expressive word of this group, *muttire*, is based on *muttum* (used in the expression *muttum nullum* 'mum's the word!'), which is the ancestor of Fr. *mot*; 'seek, look for' (*circare, chercher*); 'eat' (*manducare, pappare* cf. *CGL* v. 525. 15: 'ut dicamus infantibus papa', i.e. *manduca*); 'go, depart' (*salire*); 'arrive, approach' (*se plicare*, cf. Spanish *llegar*); 'hurry' (*addensare*). *mittere* and *conicere* do duty for *ponere* and *locare*, while *eicere*[1] comes to mean nothing more than 'to put out, draw out'. A midwife schooled in Classical Latin would be surprised at the advice given to her by Soranus; but his *foras eiciat* meant merely 'let her draw the baby out' and not 'throw it outside'.

The striving for forcefulness reflects itself also in pleonastic expressions (see above, p. 75): *par idem, omnes universi, ceteri alii, omne totum, ambo duo, singulis diebus cottidie, sursum ascendere, intus penetrare, ante praeparatus, amplius augmentare*, and even *muliebria feminarum*. The same tendency produces double adverbs, conjunctions, and prepositions, *tum deinde, itaque ergo, ergo igitur, deinde postea, paene vix, ita sic, sic taliter, ut quia, nec non etiam et.*

Certain characteristic features of later Latin mentioned in the preceding analysis, some of which have survived in Romance, are attested also in Early Latin, but are absent from the language of classical authors. This phenomenon of the 'classical gap' was discussed long ago by F. Marx. *fabulari*, for example, as we saw in Chapter IV, was constantly used by the writers of comedy as one of the colloquial words for *dicere*. It was avoided by Caesar and Cicero, yet that it remained in constant colloquial use is evident from the fact that it survives today in Spanish *hablar*. Yet another Spanish word *mozo* (Portuguese *moço*) 'lad' derives from *musteus*, *mustus* being a rustic word meaning 'new, fresh' which in Cato used of a young lamb and in Naevius of a girl (*virgo*). But classical literature knows only the substantivized *mustum*, 'new wine'. Among the early Greek words which entered the popular language was *campsare*, a nautical term meaning 'to round a cape', etc. (see p. 81). This appears in Ennius but is lost to view until it appears after many centuries in the *Peregrinatio Aetheriae*, with a slight change of meaning, 'turn off the road', the semantic progression being evidently 'round (a cape, etc.)' > 'change course' (cf. *CGL* iv. 227. 38, 'deverticulum, ubi camsatur'). The word survives in It.

[1] See above, p. 150.

cansare. Löfstedt, who has discussed the subject more recently, notes that the adjective *canutus* is found in a fragment of Plautus and then turns up again in the Late Latin *Acta Andreae et Matthiae* and survives in Italian *canuto*, etc. *Minaciae* again, which is Plautine, and reappears in the *Liber ad Gregoriam* (5th cent.), is the parent of Fr. *menace* and It. *minacci*. The absence of such words from classical texts (except in so far as it can be explained by the narrow range of subjects covered by classical literature so that no occasion arose to use certain words) may be put down to purist fastidiousness in linguistic matters, that *elegantia* and avoidance of *rusticitas* which was discussed in the previous chapter. In this way a selective screen is interposed between the modern observer and the living language. Later on gaps were torn in this screen, but it was never wholly removed, so that much of the spoken Latin was hidden from view until it emerged in the Romance languages.

More difficult to explain is the apparent paradox that many 'vulgarisms' appear in the language of the poets. The pleonastic *nec non et*, for instance, is frequent, especially in later Vulgar Latin. Examples occur in Varro, but it is significant that the expression occurs much oftener in the *de re rustica* than in the *de lingua latina*, with its greater stylistic pretensions. But examples also occur in Virgil, Lucan, Statius, and other poets. Collective singulars, again, like *miles*, are a frequent mode of expression in the Augustan and later poets and in the poetically coloured prose of Livy and Tacitus. At the other end of the scale examples can be quoted from the *Mulomedicina Chironis* and *Peregrinatio Aetheriae*, to name only two sources of vulgar latinity. In the use of the dative we may observe similar coincidences of the two spheres of usage. Adnominal datives of the type of Virgil's *miseris velamina nautis* and Tacitus' *ministros bello, seditioni duces* are paralleled by Cato's *satui semen*, and the evidence of Romance shows that the usage survived in the popular language. The so-called 'sympathetic dative', too, is a pronounced characteristic of popular Latin which may be observed in Plautus, the vulgar dialogue parts of Petronius, and in the later sources of Vulgar Latin. Yet it is also a favourite mode of expression with the Augustan poets. Of the adverbial use of the predicative adjective a colloquial example has already been quoted from Cicero's letters (*nullus tu quidem domum*) and it is attested throughout the history of colloquial Latin from Plautus (*is nullus venit, citus e cuneis exsilit*, etc.) to late examples like *festinus venit* (*Vitae Patrum*). But the poets provide no less impressive a series of examples: e.g. Livius Andronicus' *citi . . . venimus* and Virgil's *solvite vela citi*.

The explanation of the phenomenon is suggested by the observation that the 'sympathetic dative' is warmer and more intimate in character than the corresponding genitive construction—the explanation is, in brief, that the coincidences of usage at opposite stylistic poles have common psychological roots. Under the stimulus of the personal situation the speaker, impatient of logic, allusive and elliptical rather than explicit and precise, resorts to those vivid and warm, exciting and colourful modes of expression which are no less appropriate to poetry. Popular expressions were undoubtedly a conscious artifice in certain genres of poetry (e.g. Catullus' *uni, culus, verpa, futuere, nummi = pecunia*, and similar phenomena in the *Satires* of Horace), but poetry so self-conscious in technique as that of the Augustans must be acquitted of 'vulgarisms' no less than the prose of Tacitus with its unremitting search for σεμνότης. In our stylistic analyses the hyphen must be omitted from the designation 'vulgar-poetical'. The same is true of 'vulgar-archaic' (see above). Rustic dialects often preserve in common use many terms which have long disappeared from the standard language. A Cheshire gardener once advised me that my exhausted soil needed 'trench-delving', using a word previously familiar to me only from poetry ('the deep-delved earth'). It was doubtless such examples which prompted Cicero's observation: 'rustica vox et agrestis quosdam delectat, quo magis antiquitatem si ita sonet, eorum sermo retinere videatur' (*de or*. 3. 11. 42). Such features owe their inclusion in higher poetry and majestic prose to this quality of *antiquitas*. The laws of the genres would enforce rigid exclusion of all that is 'rustic' or 'vulgar'.

The Vulgar Latin briefly characterized in the preceding analysis was carried by Roman soldiers, administrators, settlers, and traders to the various parts of their growing Empire. Sicily, Sardinia, Corsica, Dalmatia, and the south and east coasts of Spain had been brought under Roman sway by the end of the third century B.C. and the expansion continued until with Trajan's conquest of Dacia the Roman Empire reached its greatest extent, including Britain in the far west and the Hellenistic kingdoms in the east, with the northern frontier on the Rhine and the Danube. The impact of Latin on the indigenous peoples of this vast area varied according to the degree of civilization which they had attained. Broadly speaking it may be said that in those regions where Greek civilization and language had taken firm root Latin made little headway (see below). In the west, however, the natives succumbed no less to the culture and organizing genius of their new masters than they had to their superior military technique. The consequence was that a common civilization was developed varying little from country to country. Latin, the language of the new ruling power, was adopted by the native aristocracies and ultimately by all elements of the population until the native languages, except for a few scattered pockets, became extinct. This process was doubtless gradual and affected the new romanized towns first, before spreading thence to the country-side. Moreover, rapid though the expansion of the Empire had been, more than 300 years had elapsed between the incorporation of Sardinia and the conquest of Dacia. During this period Latin, like all languages, had continued to evolve, and it is certain that the Latin of the settlers of the third century B.C. differed from that of the legionaries of Caesar in the first century B.C. and of Trajan in the second century A.D. If we add to this the immense variety in race, language, and culture among the subjugated peoples and the notable differences in Roman policy towards them, the philologist would confidently expect to observe considerable differences of dialect in a language spread over so vast an area and acquired as a foreign language by peoples of such differing backgrounds. Yet despite the most painstaking analysis of the available documents from the different parts of the Empire, the regional peculiarities established amount to no more than a few trivialities. Thus H. F. Muller (*A Chronology of Vulgar Latin*) observes that even in the Merovingian period the barbarisms which increasingly disfigure written documents are 'practically the same over the whole western Romania'. Entwistle also notes that 'what vulgarisms occur in the inscriptions of Spain are typically those of all Romania rather than Spain in particular and not infrequently run contrary to later Peninsular speech habits'

(*Spanish Language*, 51). In vocabulary, it is true, the pre-Roman inhabitants made certain limited contributions to the Latin spoken in their respective territories. These refer in the main, as we should expect, to objects and activities peculiar to the particular regions. Thus certain words of Gaulish religion survive in the Gallo-Romance dialects: the Walloon *dûhin* 'gnome' is traced back to *dusius* 'a sort of demon', while the name for the sacred oak of the Druids, *cassanus*, lives on in Fr. *chêne*. To these may be added certain carpenter's terms such as *charpente, copeau, tonneau*; topographical words like *arpent, borne*; the 'women's words' *pièce* and *bercer*. Von Wartburg (*Les origines des peuples romains*, 50) notes, further, apropos of rural words, that 'that part of the terminology which is common to town and country is Latin, but the part which belongs exclusively to the cultivator is Gaulish'. He quotes as examples *champ, pré, pierre, sable*, on the one hand, and *raie, sillon, caillou, grève, boue*, on the other. On the few pre-Roman words in Spanish which include mining terms and topographical features such as *nava* 'plain' (Basque *naba*), *vega* 'wooded ground by a river' (Basque *ibaiko*) see Entwistle, *Spanish Language*, 33 ff. The Germanic contribution was more considerable, as is natural in view of the important part played by the Germanic peoples in the later history of the Empire. The common possession of many of these words by several Romance languages indicates that they must have been borrowed during the 'Vulgar Latin' period. It is not surprising to find that many of these are words relating to warfare—*werra, helm, wardan* (= *observare*), *sporo*, 'spur'—and the names denoting the colour of horses *blank, brun, grisi, falwa*. But though it has been estimated that some hundred Germanic words had been borrowed into Vulgar Latin before 400 B.C., surprisingly few are attested in Roman authors: *burgus* (defined as *castellum parvulum* by Vegetius), *bandum* 'a flag', *uargus* 'a vagabond', a latinized *deraubare* 'to rob', a few zoological terms like *ganta* 'white goose', *bison, carpa, urus, taxo* (adj. *taxinus* > Fr. *taisson*), and a miscellaneous group containing *brado* 'ham', *canna* 'sort of vessel', *flasca* 'drinking-vessel', *harpa* 'harp', *hosa* 'trousers', etc.

H. F. Muller argues that the written texts reflect a real uniformity of speech in western Romania, and he ascribes this absence of dialectalization to the 'colossal work of colonization and social transformation' wrought by the Christian Church between the fifth and the eighth centuries. 'At no time was there a more thorough interpenetration among the people of these regions.' On this we must comment that the evidence warrants a conclusion only about literate people. It is, in fact, difficult to reconcile the uniformity of language evidenced by the texts over so great an area with the dialectal differentiations of living languages which field-work has everywhere demonstrated even in the most highly organized and centralized states. We are thus forced to the conclusion that the language of the available Vulgar Latin documents is a written κοινή, a lingua franca used for administrative and other purposes of communication and written everywhere with but minor modifications and concessions to popular usage by all literate persons. Thus our sole direct sources for Vulgar Latin of the later Empire effectively conceal from observation the dialectal differentiations which must always have existed and will continue to exist. It is symptomatic that the inscriptional evidence of Spain contradicts later Peninsular developments. Significant, too, is the fact that we find an analogous phenomenon in the Greek half of the Roman Empire where it has also proved impossible to detect regional differences in the κοινή which on the written evidence had supplanted the numerous local dialects (with one exception).

In preceding chapters we have seen ample evidence of the overpowering influence of Greek on the language and literature of the Romans. From earliest times the Greeks had penetrated and moulded Italic civilization. Greek craftsmen and purveyors of culture, high and low, had settled in Rome supplying words from their various callings. Roman nobles had brought Greek pedagogues to instruct their children, who in later years made the grand tour of Greece to be educated to gentlemanliness. The upper classes had become bilingual, receiving formal instruction in Greek even before their own language. With the expansion and consolidation of the Empire the bonds were drawn tighter and we reach a period of full symbiosis when Rome gave as well as received. The result is an impressive series of parallel developments in the Latin and Greek of this period. We should perhaps exclude phenomena which are the products of universal linguistic forces such as the analogical levellings of the morphology, the replacement of simple cases by prepositional constructions, hypercharacterization, and pleonasms such as *postremissimus, extremior*, and the constant renewal of the vocabulary by the preference given to colourful and forceful modes of expression. More doubtful is the intransitive use of transitive verbs which may be observed in both languages (e.g. *avertere* and ἀποστρέφω), while in both Latin and Greek dying deponents affect the health of active verbs (see p. 163 and compare ἐλπίζεσθαι). In Greek, too, we find the effacement of the distinction between the expressions for 'where' and 'whither' (*ubi, quo, ποῦ* and *ποῖ*). Parallel, too, is the increasing preference for compounded forms of adverbs and prepositions (ἔκπαλαι, ὑπεράνω, ἀπέναντι, κατέναντι, ἕνεκεν χάριν; for Latin see p. 163). We may count here, too, the growing preference for abstract and substantive, over concrete and verbal, modes of expression. Among common syntactical developments are the creation of a periphrastic future, and the use of *ab* and ἀπό after the comparative. There is a traffic even in suffixes: Gk. -ισσα, of Macedonian origin, appears in *abbatissa, prophetissa, ducissa* and became richly productive in the Romance languages. A Greek preposition κατά, used in distributive phrases ('cata singulos ymnos . . . orationes dicunt', *Per. Aeth.*), appears also in *catunus*, a 'calque' of Gk. καθείς (late for ἕκαστος), and is fused with the native Latin expression *quisque unus* to form *cascunus*, the ancestor of It. *ciascuno* and Fr. *chacun*. παρά, too, was combined with a Celtic word *veredus* to form the Low Latin parent of German *Pferd*. In vocabulary similar phenomena are to be observed. Latin literature continued to depend largely on translation and imitation of the Greek. Words differ, however, from language to language in the range of their semantic field. Thus the English word *way* though etymologically identical with *Weg* has applications not found in the German word: in English we may say 'a way of life' but not *Lebensweg* in German. But in a translation literature the word of the recipient language may acquire part of the semantic field of the translated foreign word. Instances often quoted are the technical words of the grammarians. Thus πτῶσις 'a fall' from the particular sense of the 'fall of the dice' had come in Greek to designate a grammatical 'case'. The Latin word *casus*, which is a literal translation, acquired the same technical meaning in Roman grammatical terminology. In the same way *punctum* acquired a new meaning from στιγμή, *conquirere* 'to dispute' from συζητεῖν, *idoneus* 'right and proper' from χρηστός, *advocare* 'console' from παρακαλεῖν, *crepare* 'to die' from ψοφίζειν, while *sera* 'evening' corresponds to ὀψία. In syntax, closeness of translation prompts the use of quite un-Latin constructions, e.g. *si percutimus in gladio?* (22. 49) for Luke's εἰ πατάξομεν ἐν μαχαίρῃ; That this instrumental use of *in* with the dative is not Latin is expressly stated by Augustine in his discussion of the 'Itala' version of Exodus xvii. 5: '"in qua percussisti" dixit pro eo quod dicimus "de qua percussisti"'. This latter expression is an interesting testimony for the current usage in Vulgar Latin which is continued in the instrumental use of *de* in French. It remains to add that the popularity of the construction in later Greek owes something to Hebrew influence.

The uniformity of Late Latin as it appears in the available sources, we have said, can hardly reflect the modes of actual speech in the various localities of Rumania. Yet the postulation by scholars of a more or less uniform primitive Romance, the parent language of the modern Romance languages, must prompt the question at what date the 'break-up' occurred. Before we attempt an answer, it will be well to reflect on the methods used in historical linguistics. To establish such a chronological boundary we must first decide which characteristics stamp a given form of language as 'French' and not 'Latin'. Such a definition can take the form only of a list of details from phonology, morphology, syntax, and vocabulary. In fact a dialect or language can hardly be defined satisfactorily except *in extenso* as the sum of its characteristics. Such generic features once decided upon, a chronological series of texts is ransacked to establish the first emergence of these phenomena, which will give us a series of *termini post quos*. Our method is in fact atomic, and the dates of first emergence vary from detail to detail. This is evident from a recent discussion of the date of proto-Romance by R. A. Hall:

> It is perfectly true that without Latin it is impossible to date proto-Romance. But as it is we must place it far enough forward in time to include the simplification of *ei* to *i* (*ca.* 150 B.C.), of *ae* to *ē* (first century A.D.) and of the nasalizing of *n* before *s* (first century B.C.) and the loss of *h* (Catullus or earlier). On the other hand we

must place it far enough back in time to precede the merger of *ẹ* and *i* and *ọ* and *u* (first–second century A.D.) and the establishment of a new series of palatal phonemes through the merger of the palatal allophones of *k* and *g* before front vowels with the developments of *ki* and *i* respectively. On the whole the period of the late Republic and the Early Empire (Augustan age) is indicated as the best time at which to set Proto-Romance. Certain probable survivals of features attested in earlier Latin (e.g. Plautine *cuius, -a, -um* 'whose', as an adjective in Ibero-Romance; Plautine *-nunt*, 3 pl. of verbs in Italian *-no*) would indicate that the beginning of our period should perhaps be put as far back as 250–200 B.C. (*Language*, xxvi, 1950, 19)

While certain of the facts enumerated may be open to doubt (it is quite improbable that the Old Latin forms like *danunt* have anything to do with the Italian 3 pl. ending), Hall's statement may serve to typify the sort of conclusion to which the essentially atomic method of linguistic research must inevitably lead. Failure to comprehend this has entailed so many barren disputes, for instance about degrees of relationship between languages, about the existence and position of dialect boundaries, and, what concerns us here, about the dating of the 'break-up' of proto-Romance into the various Romance dialects. It is not surprising that estimates vary between the fifth and the ninth century A.D., since the various phenomena chosen as definitive of 'French' as distinct from Latin have different dates of first emergence. The problem is not unlike that of the distinction of dialect and language. There a rough-and-ready solution is reached by using the criterion of intelligibility (see pp. 6 f.). If we use the same criterion to draw a line between 'Latin' and 'the Romance vernaculars', the answer to the question 'When did Latin cease to be intelligible to the uneducated masses?' is perhaps supplied by the experience of Charlemagne. In the belief that God would be pleased no less by right speech than by right conduct and that the study of literature would enable the clergy to penetrate more deeply into the mysteries of the sacred books, Charlemagne decreed a revival of learning. It was soon borne in on him that you cannot communicate with a people in a language they have long ceased to understand nor thereby save their souls. In 813 the legitimization of the *sermo rusticus* gave formal recognition to the fact of unintelligibility. This date may serve as a convenient chronological boundary-mark between Latin and the Gallo-Romance vernaculars. The student will hardly need a reminder that the process of change which had steadily widened the gap between the spoken and the written language had taken many centuries. Finally, the statement that 'Vulgar and medieval Latin are an outgrowth of Classic Latin brought about by different social conditions'[1] is true only if we understand by 'Vulgar Latin' the vulgarized written κοινή which appears with few variations in the sources enumerated above. He will bear in mind that from its beginning to its end written Latin in all its forms is an artificial language.

[1] Muller and Taylor, *Chrestomathy of Vulgar Latin*, Preface, p. iii.

CHAPTER VII

SPECIAL LANGUAGES—CHRISTIAN LATIN

SPEECH, we have said, is a social activity, and language an instrument whereby a speaker co-ordinates his behaviour with that of his fellow men. This instrument and its use a speaker learns by imitation from the society into which he is born; primarily, of course, within the circle of his own family, then from his playmates and schoolfellows, and finally from the associates of his adult life. Though the fundamental habits of speech are established early in life, the process of adaptation to the manifold and changing demands of social intercourse never ceases. In this way a man's habits of speech, his language, faithfully reflect the influences to which he has been exposed throughout his life. It is a product of group activity. Linguistic behaviour varies, of course, from individual to individual. This is partly a reflection of the unique personality of each speaker and partly the result of a failure to achieve perfection of imitation, for it may be recalled that speech is fundamentally a mimetic process. Such personal idiosyncrasies do not prevent the functioning of speech as a means of communication. They merely overlie a fundamental identity of habits which is the indispensable prerequisite for mutual understanding. This common constituent in the speech habits among the individuals of a linguistic community is the language of that community. A 'language' is thus an abstraction, a sort of multiple photograph achieved by the superimposition of countless individual prints. The picture will vary according to the individuals who are chosen as representing the 'associates' of the first speaker. For every person enters into social relations of infinite complexity varying from the intimacy of his own family to the most formal and distant acquaintanceship. His social behaviour is adapted accordingly, and as a consequence his individual acts of speech form part of a number of differing 'languages' which reflect differences in the degree of intimacy, local differences, dialects, differences of social position, and so on. But despite all these differences we may compile a fund of words and expressions together with the necessary grammatical machinery which is in general use among the majority of the members of a given community. This we call the 'common language'. However, even in the most primitive societies individuals form members of narrower, more exclusive groups—priests, soothsayers, magicians, doctors, metal-workers, and so on. Such groups have their own esoteric interests, a special world of objects and notions, and they develop the necessary linguistic machinery to communicate and co-ordinate their peculiar activities. Such a language of a community within a community we call a 'special language'. It will in the main consist of a special vocabulary, but peculiarities of pronunciation, word-forms, and syntax are also sometimes found (see below on Christian Latin). As specialist and technical, such a language is marked by greater precision and exclusiveness, which may become self-conscious and deliberate. There is, of course, no hard-and-fast dividing line between a special language and the general language of which it is an offshoot. A lawyer may be a father of a family and spend his evenings in the pub. There he will not wholly divest himself of his peculiar legal habits of speech, while a lay litigant among his cronies will be tempted to air his knowledge of the law and its language. In this way there is a constant interchange between general and special languages to the enrichment of both.

To designate its peculiar objects, processes, and notions a group of specialists may coin new words and expressions (neologisms) or, more frequently, give a twist to words already existing in the general language (semantic shift). Thus the Roman soldier[1] designated the various types of battle formation with the words *cuneus* 'wedge', *globus* 'troop', *forfex* 'pincers', *serra* 'saw', *turris* 'tower', *caput porci* 'hog's head'. A variety of animal names were applied to siege operations; *testudo* 'tortoise', *musculus* 'mantlet', *aries* 'ram', *scorpius*, kind of catapult, *cuniculus*, etc. Here we may mention *papilio* 'tent'. The colourful and picturesque quality universally characteristic of soldiers' language appears in *noverca* 'stepmother', 'rough ground in a camp', *muli Mariani* 'forked sticks used for carrying packs', *turturilla* 'dicitur locus in castris extra vallum in quo scorta prostant' (*CGL* v. 524. 30), *tenebrio* 'shirker', *litterio* 'penpusher', *muger* 'cheat', 'is qui talis male ludit', *murcus*

---

[1] See W. Heraeus, *A.L.L.* 12. 255 ff.

'a man who has cut off his thumb to avoid military service', *focaria* 'soldier's wife'. The specialist in killing will need a variety of expressions to distinguish the different types of blow. Thus Servius, on *Aen.* 10. 314, tells us that *haurire aliquem* is to 'stab from the flank': 'cum a latere quis aliquem adortus gladio occidit'. The euphemism *allevare* is expressly stated to be a soldiers' word by St. Augustine (see below, pp. 191 f.). Military or gladiatorial exercises were called *battualia*, from the Vulgar verb *battuere* discussed above. From the Vulgar noun-form of this word, *battalia*, have come Fr. *bataille*, Engl. *battle*.

Of vastly greater importance for the history of Latin and indeed of Western civilization was the language evolved by another exclusive group. The early Christian communities lived their lives in conditions eminently those which are creative of a special language. With a new outlook which penetrated and transformed their whole world, living an intense and highly organized community life with its ritual and common meals, rejecting the traditional paganism and all its works, driven in on themselves by persecutions, the early Christians became almost a secret society, evolving a species of Latin which was largely incomprehensible to outsiders. Since, with the triumph of Christianity, this special Latin came to colour the language of the Western world, we must attempt to ascertain the conditions in which it evolved. The life of the earliest Christian communities is, however, shrouded in obscurity, and all we can do is to analyse the peculiarities of the language as they appear in the earliest documents of Christian Latin and endeavour to reconstruct the social conditions which would account for them.

It has been said that the Latin language was brought twice to the Western world, and on both occasions it transmitted a message from the Greeks. Cicero had absorbed and found Latin expression for Hellenistic pagan humanism which is still largely the framework of our mental world. This language was imposed on western Europe by the conquering legions and the military governors, administrators, and traders who came with and after them. It is of no less prime importance to grasp that Christian Latin, too, is even more the language of translation from the Greek. It was in the Greek language that the Christian message was brought to the Gentiles from its cradle in Palestine. The infinitely flexible Greek proved adequate not only to tell in simple language the moving story of the Saviour and His Passion; it had also rapidly furnished a rich technical language for the organization and the doctrinal formulation of the Church. The character of this Biblical Greek lies outside the scope of the present volume. Let it suffice to say that in the main it was the 'Vulgar' Greek of the common language evolved in the Empire of Alexander and his successors, not without the peculiarities of vocabulary inevitable in a special language and bearing some traces of its Hebraic origins. In its new hellenized form Christianity gradually penetrated the Western world, making its first converts among the Greek-speaking residents of the great cities. Thus Mark wrote for the Roman community in Greek, and Paul, too, composed his Epistle to the Romans in Greek. Of the character of the Greek population in Rome we have written in previous chapters. 'The Greek κοινή was the current language of all the déracinés, prisoners of war, freedmen, small traders, sailors, and many others who of oriental origin but driven from their homes by wars or economic or social causes had established themselves in the big cities and especially the big ports of the West.'[1] It was among such humble folk that Christianity gained its first converts. The Kingdom of Heaven was promised to the poor. These two facts are of prime importance for the understanding of Christian Latin: the new religion came in Greek guise and to the simple folk of the back streets. There was, of course, a great deal of bilingualism in the Rome of this period. The Good News must soon have been passed on to speakers of Latin. Doubtless there was between friends of different mother tongues much stumbling and confused translation and exposition. The language would have been vulgar, studded with Greek technical terms, and distorted by the pull of the original; for accurate and idiomatic translation is a skilled business. This process is reflected in the earliest Latin versions of the Bible, which were doubtless necessitated by the growing number of converts who had no Greek. Such versions were probably made piecemeal and without any central direction or organization: St. Augustine writes (De doctrina christiana 2. 11. 16): 'ut enim cuique primis fidei temporibus in manus venit codex graecus, et aliquan-

[1] Chr. Mohrmann, Vigiliae Christianae, iii, 1949, pp. 67 f.

tulum facultatis sibi utriusque linguae habere videbatur, ausus est interpretari.' A few examples chosen from the surviving parts of these early versions (the so-called *Itala* or better *Vetus Latina*) will demonstrate their fundamental characters: vulgarity of speech form, literalness, and the use of Greek loan-words or 'calques'. How small the *aliquantulum* of Greek could be is evident from one translation ιδου ει καλη 'behold thou art beautiful' as *vide si speciosa*, where a word-for-word transposer has confused εἰ 'if' with εἶ 'thou art'.[1] The Latin version of the Epistle of Barnabas quotes from the Old Testament (Is. lviii. 8a) in the words *vestimenta tua cito orientur*, which is puzzling until a glance at the Gk. τὰ ἰάματά σου ταχὺ ἀνατελεῖ solves the riddle: ἰάματα 'healing' has been taken for ἱμάτια 'clothes'. The same author translates χειροτονία as *suadela malorum*, evidently connecting the Greek word falsely with χείρων 'worse'. Extreme literalness was doubtless prompted by piety towards the inspired sacred Scriptures, not one syllable of which should be lost. An example of this is the rendering of ὑπεράνω by *super summum*. But compound prepositions and adverbs were a feature of both Latin and Greek during this period (see previous chapter). ὑπεράνω, therefore, was merely a strengthened form of ἄνω. A Latin equivalent has to be found even for ἆρα, the interrogative particle of Greek; this is rendered *putas* while ἆράγε appears as *putasne*, e.g. *putasne intelligis?* (Act. 8. 30). Stummer quotes examples even of false gender. In Amos vi. 2 τὰς κρατίστας ἐκ πασῶν τῶν βασιλειῶν τούτων appears in an early version as 'quae sunt optimae ex omnibus regnis eorum', where *optimae* appears in the feminine as in the Greek despite the fact that it refers to a neuter noun *regnum*. Other examples of extreme literalism in early Latin translations are quoted by C. Mohrmann in a recent article on the origins of Christian Latin in Rome.[2] The Latin version of St. Clement's epistle to the Corinthians keeps faithfully to the order of words, and fidelity to the Greek even prompts the choice of case forms alien to Latin syntax. Thus μᾶλλον ἀνθρώποις ἄφροσι . . . προσκόψωμεν ἢ τῷ θεῷ is rendered 'magis hominibus dementibus . . . offendamus quam Deum'. In syntax, too, there are

---

[1] See F. Stummer, *Einführung in die lateinische Bibel*, to which I am much indebted in this paragraph.

[2] *Virgil. Christ.* iii, 1949, pp. 67 ff.

numerous Grecisms: *dignari* is constructed with the genitive like καταξιοῦσθαι; *ut* with the infinitive parallels ὥστε; *qualiter* does duty as a conjunction as a stand-in for ὅπως ('obsecrationem facientes qualiter . . . custodiat' = ὅπως . . . διαφυλάξῃ); while even the substantival use of the Greek participle, which in Latin is normally translated by a relative clause, does not daunt the author of the Clemens Latinus: for τοὺς . . . δουλεύοντας he ventures 'eos qui . . . servientes'.

Many of the Greek technical terms denoting things and notions foreign to the pagan world naturally had no Latin equivalents. They were, therefore, simply transliterated and established themselves ineradicably in the language of Latin Christianity: *anathema, anathematizo, angelus, apostata, apostolus, baptisma (baptismum), baptizo, catechumenus, charisma, clerus, diaconus, ecclesia, episcopus, presbyter,* etc. Even where it would have been possible to find an equivalent, undesirable pagan associations often ruled it out of court. *vates* or *fatidicus* could not do service for *propheta* nor *templum* or *fanum* for *ecclesia*. But it was not merely such technical words which were embodied by the authors of the early versions of the Bible. Whether it was out of anxious piety or sheer incompetence, many Greek words like ἀκηδία were simply transliterated *acedia* and a denominative *acediari* was coined as an equivalent of ἀκηδεῖν. ἀγγαρεύειν, too, appears as *angariare*. Some of these transliterated forms are sometimes given the non-technical senses of the Greek equivalents. Thus *presbyter* is found for *senior, paradisus* for *hortus, diabolus* for *accusator*. But these were aberrations. We have seen how Greek flooded the language of everyday life, both in its cultivated and vulgar forms. But national pride had largely debarred Greek intruders from the official language and that of serious prose literature. C. Mohrmann, in a recent study of the Greek words in Christian Latin, has pointed out that in their borrowings the Christians remained true to this tradition of literary Latin. 'Most of the Christian Greek loan-words are very old and they are almost always the result of vulgar or rather "pre-literary" borrowing. . . . They are residues of the bilingualism of the early Christian communities and most of them have so to speak been sanctified by the memory of oral preaching.' Thus firmly rooted in popular affection these Greek technical terms resisted all puristic onslaughts and were eventually accepted as part of artistic Christian Latin prose. The poets remained longer under the ban of traditional pagan poetry (see Mohrmann, *R.E.L.* xxv, 1947, pp. 285 f.): *martyr, angelus, apostolus, episcopus, propheta*, etc., would have produced that excess of 'glossae' which, in Aristotle's judgement, led to barbarism. The first Christian poets often substitute for the above words *testis, nuntius* or *minister, missus, antistes*, and *vates* (or *praeco*) *dei*. But gradually even the poets' resistance broke down and Prudentius provides instances of most of the usual Christian loan-words from Greek.

Apart from these technical words Christian Latin discarded the transliterations of some of the early versions and had recourse to the much subtler process we have already studied in the creation of philosophical vocabulary by Cicero—the phenomenon of loan-translation or calque whereby a native word acquires certain meanings attached to its literal equivalent in the creditor language. Thus *virtutes* as an equivalent of ἀρεταί sometimes means 'miracles'; *cogitans, cogitatus* in rendering μεριμνῶν, μέριμνα, and φροντίς come to mean '*anxious* thought, care'; *conspersio* takes over from φύραμα the sense 'dough'; *dominicum* like κυριακόν means 'the Lord's (House)'; *magnalia* 'great deeds' = μεγαλεῖα; *mediator* 'Christ as the mediator between God and man' = μεσίτης; *mundus* acquires the double meaning of κόσμος; and *verbum* or *sermo* the force of the untranslatable λόγος with its two facets of 'reason' and 'word'.

While such phenomena of Christian Latin would suffice in the absence of any further evidence to establish the fact that the Christian message came to Italy in the Greek language, it is no less apparent that it was delivered first to the poor and the lowly. The missionaries who first preached the Gospel in the Latin West like the prophets of old spoke to their hearers in the language of the people (cf. 'prophetae communi ac simplici sermone ut ad populum sunt locuti', Lactantius, *div. inst.* 5. 1. 15). The literary language with its artificial character, an instrument of salon epideixis needing long training and study for its correct manipulation, was destructive of sincerity. To bring hope and comfort, to banish evil and dispel darkness, the missionaries used the homely speech of everyday life. The consequence is that a grammatical survey of the *Vetus Latina* and Vulgate would be in the main a repetition of what has been written in the previous chapter. We find in word-formation the same preference for words of greater body (*aeramentum, coronamentum, factitamentum, gaudimonium, aegrimonium*), abstracts in *-tudo* (*grossitudo, rectitudo, poenitudo*), diminutives (*oviculus, agniculus, umerulus, leunculus, auricula, domuncula* (translating οἶκος!), *iuvencula*), etc. Among the adjectives, popular formations are those in *-bilis* (*acceptabilis, odibilis, reprehensibilis*), *-osus* (*linguosus, meticulosus, staturosus*), and *-bundus* (*biliabundus, famulabundus*). We find, further, the adverbs in *-im* and *-ter* (*commixtim, particulatim, duriter, granditer, sinceriter*), the denominative verbs of the first declension (*aeruginare, cibare, custodiare, potionare, nutricare, minorare, amaricare, manicare* = ὀρθρίζειν), intensive-frequentative formations (*applotare, febricitare*). In morphology the now familiar phenomena appear: nom. sing. *lampada, retia* for *rete, ossum, ossuum* for *os, ossis*, the tendency towards the elimination of the neuters (*signus, verbus, vinus*, etc.) ; *famis, nubis* for *fames, nubes*, etc. 'Hypercharacterization' in the degrees of comparison (*pluriora*), and the use of superlative for the positive (hence the comparatives *infimior, proximior*). The verbal system is subject to the same processes of analogical levelling (*odio, odibo, odibam, odivi*; note, too, the perfect forms *accēdi, collexi, avertui, sinui, salivi, silevi*). The verbs change their conjugational class (*exercĕre, lugĕre, florīre, fugīre, serpīre*). The vulgar uncertainty in the forms of the future manifests itself (*augeam, doceam, diligebit, metuebitis, sepelibo*). Active and deponent forms interchange (*admirare, exhortare, certari, paeniteri, taederi*, and, inevitably, the horror, ancient and modern, *fieretur*). In syntax the expressions for 'where' and 'whither' are confused, *ad* and *apud* are interchanged, the instrumental is expressed by *de* and *in*, the demonstrative approximates to the definite, and *unus* to the indefinite article. Noun clauses introduced by *quod, quia*, and *quoniam* do duty for the classical accusative and infinitive, the indicative is used in indirect questions, and the ablative of the gerund does duty for the present participle. In a word we have reproduced here the whole physiognomy of Vulgar Latin.

The vulgar stamp of Biblical Latin, we have said, reflects the speech habits of the early Latin-speaking converts to whom the Gospel was preached. But the constant use of this language in divine worship gave a new dignity and sanctity to these humble forms of speech, and the language of the Bible and liturgy was destined to have a profound effect on the language of even the most highly educated and cultivated Roman Christians throughout the centuries. This is expressly attested by Augustine in the *De doctrina christiana* 2. 14. 21:

quamquam tanta est vis consuetudinis etiam ad discendum, ut qui in Scripturis sanctis quodam modo nutriti educatique sunt, magis alias locutiones mirentur, easque minus latinas putent quam illas quas in Scripturis didicerunt neque in latinae linguae auctoribus reperiuntur.

The vulgar usages were firmly implanted by constant hearing and speaking and, indeed, singing. Thus Augustine, apropos of the vulgar future form *floriet*, writes (*De doct. christ.* 2. 13. 20):

illud etiam quod iam auferre non possumus de ore cantantium populorum: 'super ipsum autem floriet sanctificatio mea' nihil profecto sententiae detrahit. auditor tamen peritior mallet hoc corrigi, ut non 'floriet' sed 'florebit' diceretur. nec quidquam impedit correctionem nisi consuetudo cantantium.

The same reverence for the language of the sacred Scriptures is evinced by all the writers of Christian Latin. Dr. C. Mohrmann notes that even educated and cultured authors like Cyprian do not reject the traditional 'vulgarisms' (thus earning the scorn of the pagans, who dubbed him 'Coprianus'). Minucius Felix, who endeavoured to influence educated circles, was at pains to avoid hurting their linguistic sensibilities and so shunned the special Christian words and turns of phrase except for a few indispensable terms like *carnalis*, *vivificare*, and *resurrectio*. Of greater significance is the attitude of Lactantius, the 'Christian Cicero'. Even he, despite the vaunted classical quality of his language and style, did not avoid the now traditional peculiarities of Christian Latin. As for Augustine we must, writes Dr. Mohrmann, make a clear distinction between his different styles. In his *City of God* he was concerned to defend the Christians against pagan reproaches that the new religion was responsible for the catastrophes which had afflicted the Empire. Addressed to pagan circles obsessed with the ancient humanism, this work shows greater literary polish and refinement than his more popular sermons. Yet what has been said of Lactantius holds good also of the *De civitate Dei*. Augustine draws freely on the special Christian lexicon, and even in syntax, where he shows a more anxious respect for correct literary usage, the typical Christianisms are not lacking. Finally we may recall Jerome's procedure in his revision of the existing Latin versions of the Bible, when he was concerned to make the minimum of alterations. In preparing himself for this work he did not disguise from himself the storm of protests which was likely to burst on the man who ventured to interfere with the well-known and beloved text:

> quis enim doctus pariter vel indoctus, cum in manus volumen assumpserit et a saliva quam semel imbibit viderit discrepare quod lectitat, non statim erumpat in vocem me falsarium me clamans esse sacrilegum, qui audeam aliquid in veteribus libris addere, mutare, corrigere? (*Praefatio in evangelistas ad Damasum.*)

In general Jerome remained true to the principles laid down, and, for all his efforts towards greater linguistic refinement, his pious hand wisely left many of the 'vulgarisms' of the ancient texts untouched. Hallowed by centuries of Church usage, they had been stripped of all suggestion of 'vulgarity' even for the most refined and cultivated of Christian authors. It was this feeling which inspired the proud defiance of an Augustine in the face of pagan scorn for the solecisms and barbarisms in the sacred Scriptures and the speech of the faithful. 'A man who is asking God to forgive his sins does not much care whether the third syllable of *ignoscere* is pronounced long or short. . . . What is correctness of speech except the observance of the usage of others, confirmed by the authority of speakers of old?' (*De doct christ.* 2. 13. 19); 'melius in barbarismo nostro vos intellegitis quam in nostra disertitudine vos deserti eritis', he exclaims in another passage (*serm.* 3. 6). Much the same consciousness and defence of linguistic barbarisms had already been expressed by Arnobius (*Adv. gent.* 1. 59) and even by the Ciceronian Lactantius; and this encomium of vulgarism became something of a *topos* among Christian writers (cf. Gregory the Great, *ep.* 5. 53a, p. 357. 33 E.–H.). For our present purposes it is important to note that certain vulgarisms had become almost obligatory constituents of a *special Christian idiom.* Augustine's conversion entailed a linguistic conversion.

That the Latin of the Christians was a special language (*Sonder-*

sprache) is a thesis first put forward by Mgr. J. Schrijnen and vigorously maintained in a series of studies by his pupils, especially Dr. Mohrmann. This school of thought lays great stress on the sociological fact that the early Christians were a closely knit social group with special interests and a tightly drawn discipline affecting every aspect of their lives, setting themselves apart from the body of pagan society. The result was a coherent system of linguistic differentiations affecting not only vocabulary but morphology and syntax and even certain metrical phenomena. That new technical terms for Christian ideas, objects, and institutions should have been created is entirely expected. These Schrijnen designates 'direct Christianisms'. What is more striking is that special Christian terms were created for things not specifically Christian ('indirect Christianisms'). Schrijnen and his pupils have listed a number of usages in this category which occur exclusively in Christian authors: *veraciter, subsequenter, transgressor, exspoliatio, aporiari, indeficiens, confortare, supplantatio, honorificare, subintrare, degradare, cohabitare, mortificare, retributio, fornicari, prostitutio, operator, negator,* etc. Augustine himself refers to a distinctive *ecclesiastica loquendi consuetudo* which is binding on Christians: 'hos [that is 'the martyrs'] multo elegantius, si ecclesiastica loquendi consuetudo pateretur, nostros "heroas" vocaremus' (*De civ. Dei* 10. 21). In another passage he refers to the special idiom of the Scriptures apropos of the meaning 'cunning' which *sapiens* bears in Gen. iii. 1 and he proudly sets Christian usage against secular idiom: 'nam quemadmodum loquantur auctores mundi quid ad nos?' That such special words occurred also in everyday speech of the Christians seems to be implied by another passage of St. Augustine. Augustine is commenting (*Quaest. hept.* 7. 56) on the use of *occurrere* in the sense 'to kill' in Judges and Kings (e.g. *vade, occurre illi*):

> quod ideo non intellegitur, quia non est consuetudinis apud nos ita dici. sic enim quod militares potestates dicunt: vade, alleva illum, et significat 'occide illum', quis intellegat, nisi qui illius locutionis consuetudinem novit?

The context, then, is the peculiar meanings words may have in specialist circles (here the language of soldiers), which are unintelligible to those not familiar with this usage (*consuetudo*). He then goes on to give another instance. 'Solet vulgo apud nos dici: "compendiavit illi", quod est "occidit illum"; et hoc nemo intellegit, nisi qui audire consuevit.' If *vulgo apud nos* means 'commonly among us Christians' (and it is difficult to interpret it in any other way), then we have in this passage a direct testimony to the existence of a special Christian word not referring to a thing specifically Christian—in Schrijnen's terminology an 'indirect Christianism'. The main modes of procedure in the creation of these new specifically Christian terms have already been touched upon—loan-words (*apostatas*, etc.), loan-translations (*lavacrum* 'baptism'), neologisms (*trinitas, incarnatio, tribulatio, salvatio, univira*), and, most important, the use of existing Latin words in new Christian meanings. In this the translators and expositors often showed great sensitivity to subtle shades of meaning in Latin. Thus Löfstedt has pointed out that of the numerous synonyms in Latin for 'to beg, ask' *orare* was gradually ousted by *rogare, petere, precari*, etc., and survived only in a few stereotyped phrases. Thus *orare* had acquired an aura of remoteness and archaism, a 'glossic' quality which made it appropriate to express the humble petitioning of God. Hence the Christian meaning of *orare* 'to pray'. The pejorative meaning of *saeculum* 'the pagan, profane world' also had its roots in 'secular' Latin: early in Latin we find contexts in which this word is used in despairing and contemptuous contexts rather like 'the modern world', 'the present generation': e.g. 'novi hoc saeculum moribus quibus siet' (Plautus, *Trin.* 284) and Tacitus' famous passage 'nemo illic vitia ridet, nec corrumpere et corrumpi saeculum ['modern'] vocatur' (*Germania* 19. 1). The Romans experienced some difficulty in translating the important word σωτήρ 'saviour'.[1] Cicero had defined this term (*in Verrem* 2. 2. 154) 'is est nimirum "soter" qui salutem dedit'. Elsewhere he coined the word *servator*, while in imperial times we find the compound *conservator* as one of the titles of Jupiter. It was doubtless this pagan flavour which made the early translators of the Bible reject *conservator*. They sometimes used the rare *salutaris* which in Cicero (*de fin.* 3. 20. 66) is applied to Jupiter, but a new term was coined from *salvare* (itself a neologism)—*salvator*. Tertullian ventured *salutificator*, but this was still-born. *salvator* did not immediately

---

[1] See C. Mohrmann, *Vigiliae Christianae*, iv, 1950, 193 ff.

win approval. Arnobius speaks of Christ as *sospitator*. Augustine brushed aside puristic scruples with his characteristic common sense:

> Christus, inquit, Jesus, id est Christus Salvator. hoc est enim latine Iesus. nec quaerant grammatici quam sit latinum, sed christiani quam verum. salus enim latinum nomen est. salvare et salvator non fuerunt haec latina antequam veniret salvator: quando ad latinos venit et haec latina fecit. (*serm.* 299. 6)

Χάρισμα, too, occasioned verbal experiment in the effort to grasp the manifold meanings of this central Christian word: *donum*, *donatio*, *munus* were tried but the choice finally fell on *gratia*. The special languages were drawn on and their terms filled with Christian content. In particular the Christians, considering themselves as the soldiers of Christ, made much use of military terminology,[1] 'vocati sumus ad militiam dei vivi iam tunc cum in sacramenti verba respondemus' (Tertullian, *mart.* 30. 1. 9). The *sacramentum* is the soldiers' oath, the *catechumeni* are the recruits (*tirocinium, novicioli*). The clergy are the *duces* and their flock the *gregarius numerus*. The martyr, after his exercises in prison, when he has put off the *animae impedimenta*, dies a true and brave soldier's death: 'huic sacramento militans ab hostibus provocor. par sum illis, nisi illis manus dedero. hoc defendendo depugno in acie, vulneror, concidor, occidor' (*Scorp.* 4: RW. p. 153. 14). The reward which he receives from the *Imperator Christus* is the *donativum vitae aeternae*. Finally we may mention that *paganus* was the soldier's contemptuous term for a 'civilian'. Used by the Christians to denote all those not enrolled in the army of Christ, it acquired its modern sense of *pagan*.

One final example from Teeuwen's list must suffice to illustrate this fascinating emergence of a new mental and spiritual world. In the first troubled centuries *pax* meant for Christians not so much the end of war as the 'cessation of persecution'. But it had another and deeper sense, the *pax* which Christ gave to His followers, the peace between man and his God which Christ the mediator had brought about. The faithful were *filii pacis*, Christ Himself is the *pax*, and those who die in the faith *in pace dormiunt*—an expression which gave rise to the semantic divisions of *pax* (1) 'state of

[1] On this see W. J. Teeuwen, *Sprachlicher Bedeutungswandel bei Tertullian*, 1926.

soul after death', (2) 'the place of eternal peace'. Such *peace* was only vouchsafed to those who died 'in the faith'. So *pax* also implies 'belief in Christ'. But such faith is confirmed in baptism which brings *pax* and enrols its recipient in the community of the Church, the *familia Christi*. Thus *pax* comes to mean 'the community of the Church'. Membership of the Church implied the acceptance of orthodox beliefs so that *litterae pacis* could mean 'certificate of orthodoxy'. Membership of the Church also involves common worship and in the Early Church during the Mass the members of the congregation gave one another an *osculum sanctum* in token of their fraternity. This was also known as the *osculum pacis* and finally as the *pax*. This term came to be used outside the ritual for 'a kiss' exchanged by relatives or fellow Christians. This usage survived in the OIr. *póc* 'a kiss' and M.Sc. Gael. *pòg*.

The existence of a special Christian vocabulary is thus established beyond reasonable doubt. The attempts to isolate corresponding facts of morphology and syntax have been less convincing: the separate phenomena adduced such as the *quia* and *quod* constructions for the accusative and infinitive, the indicative in indirect questions, the infinitive of purpose, the nominativus pendens, etc., can all be paralleled from contemporary secular texts (see previous chapter). The occurrence of a *limited group* of 'vulgarisms', a peculiar constellation of 'sub-standard' syntactical constructions, in other words a 'Gestalt' occurring in this precise form only in Christian documents, might be accepted as positive evidence of a special Christian idiom. But this has so far not been established, and it would appear that no important differences of syntax can be detected between secular and Christian Latin prose.

'Christian Latin' no less than 'Vulgar Latin' has been the occasion of terminological disputes. We are dealing with a particular adaptation of the Latin language to express new 'things'—objects, acts, notions, forms of organization—and in particular to translate the Greek terms already evolved to designate these things. It need hardly be said that Christian concern with these specifically Christian things and their linguistic references to them vary in intensity and concentration from occasion to occasion. The 'Christianisms' will naturally be at their greatest density in the sacred Scriptures and the liturgical texts. Then familiarized by constant use in divine worship, Bible readings, sermons, and pastoral epistles, many of these special terms and turns of phrase passed into the common speech of the Christian communities. It would be vain to attempt to assess the various degrees of concentration and dilution, still more to affix distinctive labels. Schrijnen, however, has been at some pains to insist on a distinction between (1) the early Christian vernacular, (2) ecclesiastical Latin (as used in the Itala and Vulgata, *acta martyrum*, conciliar records, pastoral epistles), and (3) liturgical Latin. It is difficult to see what useful purpose is served by this terminological hair-splitting. Nor need we linger over the problem whether the 'Christianisms' established form merely an 'agglomération' or constitute a system 'sensiblement une'. It is one more of the pseudo-problems created by de Saussure's fatal dichotomy between 'la parole' and 'la langue'. Research establishes by the separate study of individual details that such-and-such facts are peculiar or not peculiar to the Latin of Christians. The sum total of such facts constitutes Christian Latin; their systematic presentation by the grammarian is the Christian Latin 'language'. That organizational terms should occur in the administrative records might be expected, nor need it occasion surprise that liturgical terms occur in liturgy, nor again that the dilution of Christian terms should be greatest in the everyday speech of the early Christians. But this last, of course, we have no opportunity of studying.

The existence of a special Christian idiom, even if we confine this provisionally to certain facts of vocabulary, prompts the question of how and when it came into being. Because of the predominance of Africans among the first great Christian authors and the fact that the oldest of the official acts of the martyrs, the *acta sanctorum Scillitanorum* (A.D. 180) relating to the Christians of the town of Scilli, was written first in Latin, the opinion has long been held that the cradle of Christian Latin was in the Roman province of Africa and that it spread thence to Italy and the other Latin-speaking provinces. This view was challenged by Schrijnen and it has recently been the subject of an informative article by Dr. Mohrmann, who addresses herself to the question of the growth of Christian Latin *in Rome*. Its first phase, the emergence of a Christian spoken idiom is concealed from our observation, but this is what determined the subsequent evolution. It must have come into being—on the lines sketched above (see pp. 184 f.)—through the gradual increase in Latin-speaking converts among what was in the beginnings a community of Greek and bilingual Christians. Their growing numbers created an irresistible demand for Latin versions of the sacred Scriptures and pastoral works. This came about during the second century. The second phase of the latinization of the Roman Church, the use of Latin in the official correspondence of the Church, may be dated from the middle of the third century, while the third and final phase was reached when Latin invaded the conservative stronghold of the liturgy, an event which took place during the pontificate of Pope Damasus between 360 and 382.[1] Of the first and decisive phase, as we have said, we have no first-hand evidence, but there are some texts among the Latin versions written in Rome which throw light on the second phase. The translation of St. Clement's epistle to the Corinthians is confidently dated to the second century A.D.; this makes it earlier probably even than the most ancient *dated* document of Christian latinity —the *passio martyrum Scillitanorum*. In the *Clemens latinus* there are numerous citations from the Old Testament in a Latin notably different from the text of the epistle itself. These specimens from a Latin Bible show the extreme literalism and 'vulgarity' of the most ancient versions. What is most important is that this version diverges considerably from the Old Testament used by the African Cyprian. The version of the epistle itself exhibits the now familiar vulgarisms. But though extremely close it is sensitive to subtleties in the Greek and as a whole testifies to the existence of a mature and rich Christian idiom with many of the 'direct Christianisms' listed above—*apostolus, angelus, baptizare, ecclesia, episcopus*, etc.; *caritas, confiteri* in the double meaning 'to praise' and 'to confess', *gratia, orare, passio, pax, saeculum*, etc. There are certain experiments which were not adopted into the language of Christianity, e.g. *minister* 'deacon', *honorati* 'office-holders, clergy', *scissura* 'schism'. Nor is *scripturae* definitely established for 'the holy scriptures'. Dr. Mohrmann concludes that in this document from the Roman community of the second century we find the same process of linguistic differentiation as has

---

[1] Th. Klauser, *Miscellanea Mercati*, i. 467 ff.

been observed in Christian documents of African provenance. The differences between the two idioms are unimportant. The 'Sondersprache' of which it is a rudimentary specimen is already oecumenical in character. The *Pastor Hermae*, too, the author of which was probably a Latin speaker living in Rome, provides evidence for the existence of Roman Latin technical terms relating to the Christian life. For instance, he uses the expression στατίωνα ἔχω and himself explains this phrase by the Gk. νηστεύω 'I am fasting'. Now *statio* as a technical term for *ieiunium* is known from Tertullian and designates a particular type of fast on Wednesdays and Fridays. Thus the *Pastor Hermae* attests the existence of a highly technical term relating to the organization of Christian life, a purely Latin 'direct Christianism' fifty years before Tertullian and perhaps thirty years before the composition of the *passio martyrum Scillitanorum*. That he wrote in Greek is no less significant—a Christian Latin idiom was emerging even while the official language of the Church remained Greek.

It was not until the middle of the third century that we find Roman Christian texts which are not translations but were originally composed in Latin. The works of the schismatic Novatian, a writer of considerable literary gifts and inclined to purism, exhibit the normal elements of Christian Latin. In a comparison of Novatian with Tertullian Dr. Mohrmann points out the former's independence of his predecessor. Thus he prefers the more popular *incorruptio* to Tertullian's *incorruptibilitas*. In the translation of the important word λόγος in the Bible African idiom preferred the rendering *sermo* while the ancient European versions used *verbum*. This latter word appears in Novatian's citations from the Scriptures, but in his own text he rings the changes on both words. Certain contributions to theological vocabulary are apparently to be credited to Novatian; *praedestinatio*, for instance, is first found in his works.

The letters of Pope Cornelius, the contemporary of Novatian, to Cyprian are more conservative in syntactical structure, but in them, too, writes Dr. Mohrmann, 'we find the whole technical vocabulary relating to the organisation and life of the Christian communities': e.g. *populus* and *plebs*, *fraternitas*, *pax* (in the sense of harmony and unity within the Church), *schisma* (replacing the earlier *scissura*), *catholicus*, and the whole set of terms for the ecclesiastical hierarchy.

Finally we have some specimens of a more popular type of Christian idiom. *Epistle* 8 among the correspondence of Cyprian emanates from the Christian community of Rome and lays stress on the necessity of helping and redeeming those who have been vanquished in that contest with the Adversary, the persecution. The vulgarisms are of an extreme kind (e.g. 'discere poteritis a plures a nobis . . . quoniam ea omnia . . . et fecimus et facimus ; excubat pro omnes ; omnis periculus', etc.) and the syntax is clumsy and slipshod in the extreme. The text, therefore, we may suppose, comes close to the spoken idiom current among the more uneducated members of the Roman community. It is interesting to note the technical terms *papas* (accusative *papatem*), a title bestowed on all bishops at that time, *subdiaconus, ecclesia, fraternitas, caticumeni* (Vulgar for *catechumeni*), *presbyter, communio, saeculum, saecularis*. The persecution has evoked its own special terminology : it is an *agon*, a *certamen*, conceived as a wrestling-match with the *adversarius*, one of the popular euphemisms for the Devil. Those who win (*vincere, stare in fide(m)*) receive the martyr's crown. But others are seized with weakness (*adprehendi infirmitate*) and fall (*cadere, ruere*) and make the pagan sacrifice (*ascendere*). Yet they may repent and mend their ways and desire to be restored to the bosom of the Church (*communionem desiderare*). In previous chapters it has been pointed out that the popular language of the Romans was larded with Greek words. It is interesting to note that in this Roman Christian text of vulgar character we find a Greek loan-word which does not occur elsewhere—*thlibomeni* 'the distressed', and, further, the expression *zelus dei*. Brief though this text is, it affords us a fascinating glimpse of the language current among uneducated Christians in the Rome of the third century A.D., an idiom rich in technical terms and largely incomprehensible to the uninitiated ; in a word, a special language.

We may now briefly resume the conclusions which Dr. Mohrmann has drawn from the study of these texts from Christian Rome. The *Clemens latinus*, with a language already characteristically Christian. challenges the belief in the priority of the Christian Latin of north Africa. One hundred years later, the works of Novatian, the epistles of Cornelius, and the epistle from the Roman clergy reveal a highly developed special language already far advanced towards the maturity it reaches in Augustine and Jerome. What is interesting is the stability of this special idiom. Despite their widely differing stylistic levels the three groups of texts from third-century Rome have a common core: for instance, it is symptomatic that even Novatian with all his literary culture uses the construction *quoniam* to introduce noun clauses. Moreover, this idiom is oecumenical, for the differences between Africa and Rome are insignificant. This same idiom, which was later to appear in Spain and Gaul, we may confidently assume, was gradually hammered out as the story of the Gospel and the fundamentals of the Christian faith began to be communicated by bilingual speakers to monoglot Latin converts. It was doubtless the product of a long process, much of it hidden from our eyes, of great intricacy involving many people of greater and lesser ability and education, proceeding by trial and error, each word and turn of phrase having to win popular acceptance. In this sense it is true to say that the new Christian language was a creation of the people (Mohrmann). Its oecumenical character, the comparative uniformity which underlies the insignificant differences in the versions and writings of the different provinces, was produced, as linguistic uniformity always is, by intense intercommunication. We should not ignore, of course, that fundamental uniformity of culture and language throughout the Latin-speaking part of the Roman Empire. This milieu favoured uniformity in the reaction of the Latin language to the new Christian ideas. But the development and maintenance of a universal Christian Latin idiom was largely due to the constant coming and going of representatives of the different churches and the exchange of ideas through personal contacts and not least by correspondence. The epistle, it has been said, is a characteristic form of Christian literature.

It will now be amply clear that the Latin spoken by the Christian community in Rome was not received as a gift from north Africa. This thesis had in any case little *a priori* probability. It is hardly conceivable that the Latin-speaking Christians of Rome had been deprived of the normal human mechanism of speech-exchange, with its adaptability to new ideas and new situations, and had

o

remained in dumb helplessness to learn, to discuss, and to hand on the Good News in the Latin tongue until north Africa took the seal from their lips. Tertullian, in particular, has been dethroned by Schrijnen and his pupils and stripped of his honorific title as 'The Father of Christian Latin': 'Tertullian was neither the father of ecclesiastical Latin nor of early Christian Latin' (Schrijnen).

Norden's judgement on Tertullian is well known.[1] He was the child of his own age, a representative of the Asianic movement which had now lasted for half a millennium. Yet his passionate and impetuous spirit did violence to the Latin language. In particular this bilingual author imported so many Grecisms of vocabulary and structure that he is scarcely intelligible without a knowledge of Greek. A closer study of Tertullian's work has shown that this judgement was distorted by Norden's reliance on too narrow a selection of texts. In particular the density of Grecisms is exaggerated. But the characterization of his style as a brand of Asianism still holds good. We find in Tertullian all those tricks of the 'modern' style which were analysed in Chapter V, conciseness, point, antithesis, asyndeton, symmetry, and, above all, the effects of assonance which will assume great importance in studied Christian Latin prose. A few examples will provide their own commentary. 'sordent silent stupent cuncta'; 'mulorum et milvorum carnes et corpora'; 'corrupti tam vitio valetudinis quam senio sepulturae'; 'iustitia rarescit, iniquitas increbrescit, bonarum omnium disciplinarum cura torpescit' (tricolon with 'increasing magnitude' and homoioteleuton); and finally a magnificent example of the Asianic sentence structure with *parison, anaphora, homoioteleuton*, etc. (see Hoppe,[2] p. 141):

> omnia iam pervia
> omnia nota
> omnia negotiosa
> solitudines famosas retro fundi amoenissimi oblitteraverunt,
> silvas arva domuerunt
> feras pecora fugaverunt
> harenae seruntur
> saxa panduntur
> paludes eliquantur

---

[1] *Die antike Kunstprosa*, ii. 608 f.
[2] *Syntax und Stil des Tertullian* (Leipzig, 1903).

tantae urbes quantae non casae quondam.

> iam nec insulae horrent
> nec scopuli terrent
> ubique domus
> ubique populus
> ubique respublica
> ubique vita.
>
> (*de An.* 30 (p. 350. 2 R.))

It was in the handling of the vocabulary that Tertullian showed his greatest genius and indeed capriciousness. 'It is and remains a riddle difficult to solve', writes Hoppe, 'how Tertullian could completely alter the ordinary and common meaning of many words.' Schrijnen contested Tertullian's priority and held that his language presupposes the existence of a considerable linguistic activity which had already hammered out the distinctive vocabulary of Christian Latin. That words appear for the first time in Tertullian does not prove that he invented them. However, there is no denying the bold virtuosity of Tertullian in subduing and distorting words to express the tempestuous and almost demoniac intensity of his will to dominate. If, with Schrijnen, we must deny him any part in the creation of the Christian *vernacular*, it still remains true that Tertullian was the first to use the Christianized Latin in large-scale literary works. His decisive contribution to Christian polemics and theology lies beyond the scope of the present work. But there is no denying his outstanding influence on Christian Latin as a language of literature. For the historian of the language he is and remains the prime and chief source of our knowledge of Christian Latin (Teeuwen). The 'father of Christian Latin', in Schrijnen's sense, he may not have been. Shall we say rather that he took a promising child, fostered it, and endowed it with riches which made it master of a new mental and spiritual world?

As the centuries went by, the organization of the Church and the Christian way of life proceeded apace. Christian thought matured and deepened. Its instrument of expression and communication was made more subtle and sensitive by a series of gifted writers (Cyprian, Arnobius, Lactantius, Ambrose). In Jerome and Augustine the language of Latin Christianity reached its fullest flowering. Of Jerome's work as reviser and translator we have already spoken. In dealing with 'the language' of Augustine we are faced with a situation more complex than with Cicero. For he not only wrote in genres of different stylistic levels: an added complication is that after a thorough training in the traditional rhetoric of the pagan schools he was, after his conversion, obliged to learn the new Latin idiom which it was incumbent on Christians to use: 'nec illa sane praetereo quae catechumenus iam, licet relicta spe quam terrenam gerebam, sed adhuc saecularium litterarum inflatus consuetudine scripsi', *Retract.* prol. 3. This secular *consuetudo* still dominates the early dialogues, which are thoroughly Ciceronian in sentence structure, vocabulary, and even in the clausulae. But after his conversion and baptism a change took place. It is not without significance for the development of his style that in *ep.* 24, after his ordination, he asked Bishop Valerius for leave in order to study the Bible. This incident perhaps marks the turning-point in his stylistic development or rather conversion. Henceforward Augustine turned away from the *inlecebra suaviloquentiae* and gradually acquired the *ecclesiastica consuetudo* (this is already apparent in the very different language and style of the *De vera religione* written in 389), reaching full mastery in the works written after his enthronement. But even in these works we may almost speak of 'a law of the genres', for Augustine adapted his style according to the nature of his recipients. The more pagan and literary character of the *De civitate Dei* we have already discussed. His *Confessions* though still stylized are looser in structure and remarkably different in the devices for marking the cadences of the periods (see below). But it is in his *sermones* that he comes nearest to popular speech, for they are in essence friendly conversations. The popular sermons of Augustine breathe a close intimacy between a congregation and a preacher who is sensitive to every reaction and anxious to make himself understood even by the duller (*tardiores*) of the brethren. Of the general characteristics of this language we may now briefly say that it embodies and exemplifies all the marks of Christian Latin with its direct and indirect Christianisms. What new contributions Augustine made conformed to the general tendencies of Christian and Late Latin.

There are, however, also stylistic aspects of his linguistic conversion which merit a discussion. It was noted above that the early Ciceronian works remained true to the cadential devices of pagan rhetoric. Augustine's new Christian style is marked not only by the abandonment of classical canons in vocabulary, syntax, and periodic structure; it also eschews the Ciceronian clausulae and instead makes use of those more popular stylistic devices which we saw were endemic in Italy and appeared in the infancy of Latin prose—short balancing phrases, in parallel or in antithesis, with the primitive adornments of assonance, alliteration, and rhyme. Such we find in the more popular of Augustine's works, his letters and his sermons (Glaser, *Wiener Studien*, xlvi. 193 ff.) and to a lesser extent in the *De civitate Dei*. From the *epistulae* Glaser quotes *inter alia* (137. 10):

> 'quid autem non mirum Deus facit in omnibus creaturae motibus, nisi consuetudine cotidiana viluissent? denique quam multa usitata calcantur, quae considerata stupentur! sicut ipsa vis seminum, quos numeros habet, quam vivaces quam efficaces, quam latenter potentes, quam in parvo magna molientes, quis adeat animo, quis promat eloquio?'

Cf. 173. 2. 3, ll. 5 ff.:

> 'nam si ea in me reprehenderis, quae reprehendenda non sunt, te laedis magis quam me, quod absit a moribus et sancto proposito tuo, ut hoc facias voluntate laedendi, culpans in me aliquid dente maledico quod mente veridica scis non esse culpandum. ac per hoc aut benivolo corde argues, etiam si caret delicto quod arguendum putas, aut paterno affectu mulceas quem adicere nequeas. potest enim fieri ut tibi aliud videatur quam veritas habet, dum tamen abs te aliud non fiat quam caritas habet.'

Examples abound in the *sermones*, e.g. 316. 1. 1:

> 'quidquid videtis quia fit per memoriam Stephani,
> in nomine Christi fit,
> ut Christus commendetur,
>   Christus adoretur,
>   Christus expectetur,
> iudex vivorum et mortuorum,
> et ab eis qui illum diligunt
> ad dexteram stetur.
> quando enim venerit,
> stabunt ad dexteram,
> stabunt ad sinistram.
> beati qui ad dexteram,
> miseri qui ad sinistram.'

But it is in the more formal sermons on the great occasions of the Christian year that these devices of popular rhetoric are raised to a new art-form. As an example we may quote from *Sermo* 199 *in epiphania domini*:

> 'ipse enim natus ex matre,
> de coelo terrae novum sidus ostendit,
> qui natus ex Patre
> coelum terramque formavit.
> eo nascente lux nova est in stella revelata,
> quo moriente lux antiqua est in sole velata.
> eo nascente superi novo honore claruerunt,
> quo moriente inferi novo timore tremuerunt,
> quo resurgente discipuli novo amore exarserunt,
> quo ascendente coeli novo obsequio patuerunt.
> celebremus ergo devota solemnitate et hunc diem,
> quo cognitum Christum Magi ex gentibus adoraverunt,
> sicut celebravimus illum diem,
> quo natum Christum pastores ex Iudaea viderunt.
> ipse enim Dominus Deus noster elegit Apostolos ex Iudaea pastores,
> per quos congregaret salvandos etiam ex gentibus peccatores.'

How deeply rooted in ancient Roman tradition such stylistic effects were many be seen from a single quotation from Ennius:[1]

> haec omnia vidi inflammari
> Priamo vi vitam evitari
> Iovis aram sanguine turpari. (*trag.* 106–8 W.)

We have now followed the adaptation and 'conversion' of popular Latin into an instrument of expression for the new Christian world. It was at first a special language of small closely organized and secluded groups. Such groups, however, have their contacts with the outside world and through such contacts words pass from the special languages into common usage. The Christians, for all their exclusiveness, could not wholly withdraw from the pagan world. Tertullian wrote in his *Apology*:

> non sine foro, non sine macello, non sine balneis, tabernis, officinis, stabulis, nundinis vestris ceterisque commerciis cohabitamus hoc

---

[1] Cf. also the charm for sore feet quoted by Varro, *R.R.* 1. 2. 27:
> ego tui memini
> medere meis pedibus
> terra pestem teneto
> salus hic maneto
> in meis pedibus.

saeculum. navigamus et nos vobiscum et militamus et rusticamur et mercatus proinde miscemus, artes, operas nostras publicamus usui vestro. (ch. 42)

Through this commerce, these contacts with the pagan world, one might confidently expect to find Christian words and turns of phrase becoming the common property of the whole linguistic community. Augustine is perhaps exaggerating when he says that the whole world uses the word *natales* in its Christian sense 'pretiosae martyrum mortes':

> quis enim hodie, non dicam in hac nostra civitate, sed plane per Africam totam transmarinasque regiones, non christianus solum, sed paganus aut Iudaeus aut etiam haereticus poterit inveniri qui non nobiscum dicat natalem martyris Cypriani? (*Serm.* 310. 1. 2)

But such borrowings are exceedingly rare. A study of the language of a non-Christian author such as Ammianus Marcellinus has shown that while he knows Christian expressions, few, if any, of them belong to his normal vocabulary. Where he has occasion to use such terms in dealing with Christian matters he usually adds a comment of the type *ut christiani appellant*. It was not by such processes that the common Latin became christianized. It was not that a closely knit group with special interests passed its linguistic coin into general circulation. The group constantly admitted new adherents and its converts were instructed in the special language. The grain of mustard seed grew into a mighty tree. Even Tertullian could already proudly proclaim (*Apol.* 37. 4):
'hesterni sumus et orbem iam et vestra omnia implevimus, urbes, insulas, castella, municipia, conciliabula, castra ipsa, tribus, decurias, palatium, senatum, forum. sola vobis reliquimus templa'. In the end not even the temples were left. The group absorbed the whole community, and its special language became the κοινή of the Western world. It is medieval Latin.

PART II

COMPARATIVE-HISTORICAL GRAMMAR

CHAPTER VIII

PHONOLOGY

In the following chapters we shall constantly make use of such formulae as 'Indo-European *p becomes f in Germanic'. As a preliminary it will be well to make clear what is implied by such formulations.

In tracing the history of the sounds of a language the philologist employs two methods. In the first place he studies the varying forms assumed by a word as recorded in a series of texts arranged in chronological order. Thus he may trace the Fr. *père* back to Lat. *patrem*. But when he has reached the earliest available texts, the historical method gives way to the comparative method. The comparative method is based on the primary axiom of linguistics that the relationship between sound and meaning is arbitrary. By this we mean that there is nothing in the psycho-physiological nature of man which results, for instance, in his spontaneously uttering the sound-complex 'grass' on observing this botanical growth. We Englishmen use this sound signal with this reference because we have imitated the older members of the speech community into which we are born, speech being essentially a mimetic process. If, then, we observe that in another speech community, say German, the sound signal *Gras* is used in the same meaning, we conclude that it is highly improbable that such an arbitrary allocation of sense to sound was arrived at independently by these communities. The greater the number of such coincidences the greater the improbability becomes. When we observe Engl. *grass, cow, milk, calf, ox, field,* etc., corresponding to German *Gras, Kuh, Milch, Kalb, Ochs, Feld,* etc., we must conclude that there must be some historical connexion between the two systems. In other words, if we could trace the chains of mimetic processes back through successive generations, we should eventually arrive at some form of speech community between the linguistic ancestors of the English and Germans which accounts for the resemblances observed between these two languages. So, too, Lat. *pater* is equated with a series of words in the related languages, Osc. *patír*, Gk. πατήρ, Skt. *pitár-*,

Goth. *fadar*. In a whole series of such self-evident equations it will be observed that *p* in Latin corresponds to a *p* in many other languages, e.g. in Greek, Sanskrit, Balto-Slavonic, etc., whereas an *f* appears in the corresponding words of Germanic languages. Since such parallelism in the sound-structure of words with similar meaning could not be accidental any more than would absolute identity, we must conclude that these Germanic words are likewise descended by various mimetic processes from the same common parent language. The reconstruction of the words and forms of this parent language is again a matter of probability. The consonants of the word for 'father' appear in the majority of languages as *p-t-r*, and so we may with some plausibility ascribe them to the parent language. The vowels are more difficult to assess, but scholars agree in representing the IE. form as **pətēr*. It should be borne in mind that this is nothing more than a convenient formula for expressing the cumbrous equation

Lat. *pater* = Gk. πατήρ = Skt. *pitár-* = Goth. *fadar* = OIr. *athir*, etc.

Similarly the parallelism observed in the constituent sounds of the series of correspondences may be conveniently summed up for the historian of the Latin language by such formulae as 'IE. **p* > Lat. *p*', rather than by the cumbrous Lat. *p* = Gk. *p* = Skt. *p* = Germ. *f* = Celtic *zero*. It should be stressed that the reconstructed IE. forms have no reality except as convenient formulae for observed parallelisms. They are mere summaries of relationships. Thus it will not be a valid objection to a reconstructed form such as **stə'wHró-* to say that no human vocal organs ever pronounced such a series of sounds. No such real phonetic existence is claimed for the formula. Nevertheless there are sounds which, with varying degrees of probability, we may ascribe to the parent Indo-European, and it is convenient for purposes of exposition and cross-reference to use a formula **IE. p* > Lat. *p* rather than on each occasion to use the full equation of which the formula is a summary.

VOWELS

Accent

The treatment of the IE. vowels in Latin varies according to the type of syllable in which they occur. They are particularly influenced by the accent.

Accent is the prominence given by various means to one syllable of a word over others of the same word or utterance. Such prominence may be achieved by pronouncing at a higher pitch (the pitch or musical accent) or by a stronger expulsion of breath (the stress or expiratory accent). In some languages accent may fall on any syllable of the word and the accent is said to be 'free'. In others it regularly falls on one particular syllable and is then said to be 'bound'. The primitive IE. accent was a free pitch accent, but this system was abandoned in Classical Latin, where the accent falls on the penultimate syllable if this is long and on the antepenultimate if the penultimate is short. Thus we should pronounce *dúcǐmus* but *ducámus*. (For exceptions see p. 221.) Scholars are, however, divided in their views of the nature of the Latin accent and we must briefly review the evidence. We have first the direct testimony of the Latin grammarians who, in describing the accent of their language, use a terminology which suggests distinctions of pitch rather than stress. Thus Varro contrasts the pitch of a sound, its *altitudo*, with its length, *longitudo*: e.g. 'cum pars verbi aut in grave deprimitur aut sublimatur in acutum' (*L.L.* 210. 10–16, GS.). Such testimony would appear to put it beyond doubt that Classical Latin possessed a pitch accent. The practice of the Classical poets who based their rhythms on the quantity of the syllables while neglecting the accent is regarded as an indirect corroboration. Such is the view held by most French linguists, who believe that the pitch accent persisted down to the fourth century A.D.

Outside France, however, scholars are inclined to question the reliability of the Roman grammarians. In grammatical studies as in much else, the Romans were slavish imitators of the Greeks. The very words *accentus*, *gravis*, and *acutus* are 'calques' of the Greek terms προσῳδία, βαρεῖα, and ὀξεῖα. So, it is suggested, we should be chary of accepting such descriptions of the Latin accent which are forced into a scientific terminology devised to describe a language of a different type. It is worth noting, too, that even the Greek grammarians continue to speak of ὀξεῖα and βαρεῖα long after the Greek accent had changed from pitch to stress. It may be safer, then, to ignore such tainted testimony and to rely on deductions from facts which we can observe for ourselves. Most important is the phenomenon of syncope, the elimination of unaccented vowels, for this is commonly an accompaniment of a strong stress accent. Crass examples are provided by English place-names such as *Gódmanchester* and *Wávendon*, which are pronounced [gʌmstə] and [wɔndən]. In Old Irish, too, Latin loan-words like *philosophus* and *apostolus* appear in the shrunken form *felsub* and *apstal*.[1] Such syncope occurred at all periods of Latin (see below): e.g. *auceps* < **avicaps*, *officina* < **opificina* (cf. *opifex*), *undecim* < **unodecem*, etc. Even when the vowels of the non-initial syllable were not wholly lost by syncope, they suffered weakening in various ways: e.g. *afficio* < **ad-facio*. These changes will be discussed in detail below. For the present it suffices to note that such syncope or weakening never affects the vowel of the first syllable in full words. These facts suggest the conclusion that Latin once possessed a stress accent on the initial syllable and it was this which produced syncope such as *aetas* < **aevitas* and weakening such as *occĭdo* < **obcado*. The penultimate law of Classical Latin reflects a subsequent change of habits which restricted the accent according to the conditions stated above. Note that a secondary accent occurred in words of four syllables or more: *aèdificávit*, *tèmpestátem*. This is revealed (1) by the fact that in Italian it causes doubling of the following consonant (e.g. *scellerato* < *scèlerátus*), and (2) by the fact that it counts as a full stress in versification (e.g. in the Saturnian[2] *dédet tèmpestatibus* || *aíde méretod* and in the fourth foot of a pentameter *dìlănĭ* | *ăntŭr ŏ|pēs*—see below). An enclitic draws the accent on to the last syllable of the word to which it is attached: *vidés-ne*, *egón*. With syncope of the final vowel we have the pronunciation *vidén*, *egón*. That the accent of early Latin fell on the first syllable is supported by the evidence of Osco-Umbrian, where

---

[1] Lindsay, *Latin Language*, p. 170
[2] There is, however, much uncertainty about the metrical basis of the Saturnian measure.

syncope is more violent than in Latin and there, too, affects all syllables except the first. Plautine versification also implies that the earlier accentuation still persisted in some words: those having the rhythmical structure ◡ ◡ ◡ ◡̆ (e.g. *fắcĭlĭŭs, mŭlĭĕrĕm, sĕquĭmĭnī*) are accented on the first syllable. In other respects Plautine prosody shows that the penultimate law was already operating in his time. That the accent was still one of stress is suggested by the continuance of syncope in the syllable immediately following the accent, e.g. *audācter* < *audáciter, sinistra* < **sinistera*. A stress accent is also evidenced by the law of iambic shortening (*brevis brevians*) according to which the long syllable in an iambic succession is shortened if the accent immediately precedes or follows: e.g. *mŏdō̆* > *mŏdŏ̆, mĭhī* > *mĭhĭ̆, bĕnē* > *bĕnĕ̆*, etc.

That the Latin accent differed in the classical period from the pitch accent of Classical Greek is indicated by the different metrical practices introduced by Roman poets in the metres they imitated from Greek models. Plautus and Terence tend to harmonize the ictus of the verse with the accent of the word, whereas in Greek the word accent plays no part whatsoever. The same is true of the hexameter as composed by Plautus' contemporary Ennius. Here we must interpose a remark on rhythm in general. Rhythm arises from the regular recurrence of sense impressions. Too great a rigidity in the recurrent pattern, however, soon produces weariness, and we derive delight from variations in the basic rhythm. But the peculiar tension between variations and the basic pattern is destroyed if such variations are so frequent or so complicated that the sense of the fundamental rhythm is lost. Consequently the hearer must be reminded at intervals of this basic rhythm and such reminders come most appropriately at the end of the complicated rhythmical patterns, the cadences. Thus the hexameter nearly always ended in – ◡ ◡ | – –. Now it has been pointed out that while the Roman poets did not secure the coincidence of ictus and accent in the first four feet of the hexameter, such harmony does occur in the last two feet, the proportion of 'successes' rising from 92·8 per cent. in Ennius to over 99 per cent. in Virgil. Similar facts have been observed for the pentameter, for it has been recently maintained that 'the rhythm sought by Tibullus, Propertius, Ovid, and Martial for the second half of the pentameter contains a strong ictus-accent concord in the fourth foot and an ictus-accent conflict in the second half of the fifth foot':[1] e.g.

únde mo|vétur á|mór, where the obvious intention is to set the dactylic rhythm firmly at the beginning of the second half of the pentameter but to avoid jingle by arranging a clash in the next foot. From all this it is apparent that at least one principle of rhythmical variation used by the Roman poets was the interplay of verse ictus and word accent, with a return to concord in the cadential part of the line where it was desirable to mark out clearly the basic rhythm. We meet nothing similar in Greek until the choliambics of Babrius (who always places an accent on the penultimate syllable), and by then the Greek accent had changed from pitch to stress. It is difficult, then, to resist the conclusion that this difference of metrical practice implies a Latin accent different from the Greek pitch accent, despite the common use of technical terms implying pitch. This does not preclude the possibility that the Latin accented syllable was pronounced at a higher pitch than the unstressed, but this is a secondary feature of stress as it is in English.

For the period after A.D. 300 there is general agreement among scholars that a stress accent characterized Latin. For this we have the testimony of grammarians like Pompeius (fifth century A.D.): 'ergo illa syllaba quae accentum habet plus sonat' (V. 126 K.). Syncope, too, continues to supply unmistakable evidence: *domina* > *domna* (hence It. *donna*), *oculum* > *oclu* (It. *occhio*).

VOWELS

The IE. phonological system included the vowels *a, e, o, i, u*, which could be either long or short, and the diphthongal combinations of the first three with the semivowels or sonants *i, u, r, l, m, n*. The treatment of these inherited sounds in Latin varies according to the type of syllable in which they occur. We shall discuss them under the three headings (1) initial syllable, (2) medial syllable, (3) final syllable.

Initial syllables

In the earliest Latin, as we have seen, these vowels were accented, and so persist with fair tenacity.

[1] G. A. Wilkinson, *Class. Qu.* xlii, 1948, p. 74.

a   *aciēs* = Gk. ἀκρός.[1]

    ago = Gk. ἄγω.

    ager = Gk. ἀγρός, Skt. *ájras*, Engl. *acre*.

    alius = Gk. ἄλλος.

ā   *māter* = Dor. Gk. μάτηρ, Skt. *mātár-*.

    frāter = Gk. φράτηρ.

    fāma = Doric Gk. φάμα.

e   *ego* = Gk. ἐγώ.

    genus = Gk. γένος.

    est = Gk. ἐστί.

1. Before a velar nasal [ŋ] *e* > *i*: *tinguo* = τέγγω, *quīnque* < **penqʷe* (with lengthened vowel on the analogy of *quīntus*). Note that *gn* was pronounced [ŋn]: hence *dignus* from **dec-nos*, cf. *dec-et*.

2. A neighbouring *u*-sound effected the change of *e* to *o*: e.g. *novos* = νέ(ϝ)ος, *novem* = (ἐν)νέϝα; *socer* = (σ)ϝεκυρός, cf. Skt. *çvá-çuras, soror* < **swesōr*, cf. German *Schwester*; *somnus* < **swepnos*, cf. Skt. *svápnas*, O.Norse *svefn*; *coquo* < **quequo* (see below, p. 225), *bonus* < OL. *duenos*. This tendency must have persisted until the time of Rome's first contacts with Greece if *ovare* is derived, as seems probable, from the Greek ritual cry of the Bacchantes εὔοι.

3. *e* became *o* before velar [ɫ] (see below). This explains the vowel of *volo*, etc., as opposed to *velim, velle*: note further *solvo* < **se-luo*, *olīva* < **elaiwā*. This change was inhibited by a preceding palatal consonant: thus we have *scelus, gelu*, etc., but *holus* < earlier *helus*.

ē   *fēmina* = Gk. θη-λή, etc.

    fēcit = Gk. ἔ-θη-κε.

    plēnus = Gk. πλή-ρης.

o   *octō* = Gk. ὀκτώ.

    ovis = Gk. ὄ(ϝ)ις.

    potis = Gk. πόσις, Skt. *pátis*.

1. *o* > *u* before a velar nasal [ŋ] and before [m]: *uncus* = ὄγκος; *unguis*, cf. ὄνυξ; *umbo*, cf. ὀμφαλός; *hunc*, OL. *honc* < **hom-ce* (but note *longus*, Goth. *laggs*).

2. *o* > *u* before a velar [ɫ]+consonant: *sulcus* = ὅλκος, *vult*, but *volo* (see above), *culpa*, OL. *colpa, multa*, OL. *molta*.

3. *ov* > *av* in the syllable preceding the accent: *cavére*, cf. κο(ϝ)έω, *favíssae*, but *fóvea, laváre*, cf. λό(ϝ)ω.

---

[1] Greek retains the IE. vowels to a high degree of fidelity; so it will suffice to quote corresponding Greek words. Note that '=' means 'is cognate with' *not* 'identical with'.

4. *vo-* > *ve-* before *r*, *s*, and *t*, the change taking place about the middle of the second century B.C.: *vorsus, voster, vortex, voto* > *versus, vester, vertex, veto.*

5. *u* for *o* occurs before *r* in a closed syllable in some words possibly of dialect origin (cf. *i* for *e*, above, p. 60): *ursus* for **orsos* (cf. ἄρκτος, Skt. *f̥kṣas*); *furnus* but *fornax.*

ō   *dōnum* = Gk. δῶ-ρον.
     ōcior = Gk. ὠκύς.
     (g)nōtus = Gk. γνωτός.

1. Here, too, we find the vowel closed to *ū* before an *r*, in *fūr* cf. Gk. φώρ and *cūr*, OL. *quōr*. This may be due to the influence of the preceding labial or labio-velar consonant, but it has been suggested that *fūr* is an early loan-word from Greek via the intermediacy of Etruscan (see p. 51).

2. *ōv* > *āv* in *octāvus*, parallel to the change of *ŏv* > *ăv*; but this is an isolated example listed conveniently here.

ə   This IE. sound is postulated to account for such equations as *păter* = Gk. πατήρ = Skt. *pitắ*; *status* = Gk. στατός = Skt. *sthitás*. From this it emerges that the Latin representation is *ă*, as in all IE. languages except Indo-Iranian.

i > *i*   *video* = Gk. (ϝ)ιδεῖν, Engl. *wit*, Skt. *vidmá* 'we know'.
     *dix, dĭcis, dĭcare = Gk. δίκ-η.

1. *i* > *e* before the *r* which developed from intervocalic *s* (see p. 230): **si-sō* > *sero*; *cinis, cineris* < **cinises.*

ī > ī   *vīs* = Gk. (ϝ)ίς.
     vīvus = Skt. *jīvás* < **gʷīv-* (see p. 227).
     vīrus = Gk. < (ϝ)ιός (**uīsos*).

u > *u*   *iuvenis* = Skt. *yúvan-*.
     iugum = Gk. ζυγόν, Skt. *yugám*, Goth. *juk* (Engl. *yoke*).
     ruber = Gk. ἐ-ρυθρός, Skt. *rudhirás*.

1. Between *l* and a labial *u* was unrounded to *i* presumably via [ü]: *lubet* > *libet* (cf. below on *oi*).

ū > ū   *mūs* = Gk. μῦς, OHG. *mūs*, 'mouse'.
     sūs = Gk. ὗς, OHG. *sū*, 'sow'.
     fūmus = Gk. θῡμός, Skt. *dhūmás*.

Diphthongs

ai > *ai* in Old Latin, > *ae* early in the second century B.C.
aedes (OL. *aidilis*) = Gk. αἴθω, Skt. *édhas*.
laevus = Gk. λαι(ϝ)ός; *scaevus* = Gk. σκαι(ϝ)ός.

ei This sound is clearly distinguished from inherited *ī* in early inscriptions, but it changed to *ī* by the middle of the second century B.C. The intermediate stage closed *ē* appears in such spellings as *devos, vecos*, and this pronunciation apparently persisted in certain country dialects. Thus *vella* for *villa* is attributed to *rustici* by Varro, *R.R.* 1. 2. 14.
OL. *deico* = Gk. δείκνυμι, etc.
 fīdo = Gk. πείθω (*φείθω), etc.
 īt = Gk. εἶ-σι, Skt. *éti*, Lith. *eīti*.

oi was preserved in Old Latin, but by the time of Plautus, if we may judge by his pun on *Lydus* and *ludus* (< *loidos*), it had become monophthongized to *ū*. There was apparently an intermediate stage *oe* which persisted in archaic spellings as are found, for example, in Cicero's *Laws* (*coerari*, etc).
OL. *oino*, Cl.L. *ūnus* = Gk. οἰνή 'one on a dice', Goth. *ains*, etc.
OL. *comoinem*, Cl.L. *commūnis* = OIr. *māin, mōin* < *moini-*.
OL. *coiravit*, Pael. *coisatens* = *cūrāvērunt*.
OL. *sūdor* = Skt. *svédas*, OHG. *sweiz* 'sweat' < *swoid*.

  1. In initial syllables after *v* a process of dissimilation changed *oi* to *ei* in Old Latin, which later became *ī* (see *ei*):
   vīdi = (ϝ)οῖδα, Skt. *véda*, etc.
   vīcus = (ϝ)οῖκος, etc.; *vīnum* = (ϝ)οῖνος, etc.
  2. The same change occurs after *l* before a labial consonant in *līquit*, if this form is derived from *leloiqᵘet*, which is uncertain. The *ī* might be imported from the compound *relīquit*, where *ī* is regularly a product of *oi* in a medial syllable (see below).
  3. The old spelling was preserved in certain words belonging to the conservative spheres of law and religion: *poena* (Gk. ποινή) but *pūnio, foedus* (OL. *foidere*), *moenia* (but *mūrus*, OL. *moiros, moerus* (related to our *mere* in *mere-stone*)); *Poeni* but *Pūnicus* (Gk. Φοίνικες).

au persists unchanged.
auris, aus-culto = Lith. *ausìs*, Goth. *ausō*.
augeo, augur, etc. = Gk. αὔξω, Goth. *aukan*.
paucus = Gk. παῦρος.

1. *au* in Latin also represents syncopated *avi-*: *auceps* < **avicaps*; *naufragus* < **nāvifragos*.

2. In dialect and vulgar speech *au* > *ō*: e.g. *olla, plostrum*, etc. Publius Clodius for political reasons adopted the vulgar pronunciation of his gentile name Claudius. Reaction against *ō* as a mark of vulgarity produced the hyperurbanism *plaudo*, as is evident from the compound *explōdo*, for *explaudo* should have developed to *explūdo* (see p. 220). Vespasian when chided for his vulgar pronunciation *plōstra* is said to have addressed his instructor as *Flaurus* instead of *Flōrus*.

eu   > *ou* in many languages of ancient Italy including Latin (p. 9). *ou* persisted in Old Latin but passed to *ū* in Classical Latin (earliest example in third century B.C.).

OL. *abdoucit*, Cl.L. *dūcit* = Goth. *tiuhan* < **deuk*.

OL. *Loucilios*, Cl.L. *Lūcius*, *lūcem* = Gk. λευκός, Goth. *liuhaþ* < **leuk*.

ūro = Gk. εὕω < **euso*.

1. In Latin-Faliscan between *l* and a labial consonant *ou* was dissimilated to *oi*. For instance **leudhro-* 'free' (cf. Gk. ἐ-λευθ-ερός) > **loufro-* (p. 228 on *-dh-* > *f*) in primitive Latin. This was then dissimilated to **loifro-* (cf. Faliscan *loifirtato*). In Old Latin this sound became *ei* (*leiber*) and thence passed to *ī* (*līber* see p. 217). This change is a species of dissimilation analogous to that of *u* between *l* and a labial consonant (see above, p. 216).

ou   > *ou* in Old Latin, thence > *ū*.

OL. *loucom*, *lūcus* = OHG. *lōh* 'clearing', Engl. *lea*, Lith. *laũkas*.

noutrīx, *nūtrīx* < old fem. **noutrī* < root **sneu*.

In general we may say that the tendency of Latin is to assimilate the first element of diphthongs to the second, although in special environments the first element dominates (e.g. *oi* > *ei*).

Besides the short diphthongs Indo-European possessed a series of long diphthongs, which are relatively best preserved in Indo-Iranian. Even in primitive Indo-European, however, the second element was lost in certain positions: e.g. before an *-m* (**gʷōus* but accusative **gʷōm*). In Latin these sounds are distinguishable from the corresponding short diphthongs only in a final position: before consonants they are shortened,

but before vowels the *i* series shed this sound, so that *ăi* > ā,
ōi > ō.

ēi   *rēs* = Skt. *rā́s* gen. sg. *rayás* < **rēis.*
ōu   *duō* = Skt. *dvā̆, dvāu* < **d(u)wōu.*
       octō = Skt. *aṣṭā́u*, Goth. *ahtau* < **oktōu.*

Non-initial syllables

In non-initial syllables, as we saw above, the short vowels and
diphthongs underwent a process of raising which varied according
as the syllable ended in a vowel or consonant: e.g. **ád-fa-cio,*
*ád-fac-tos > *af-fi-cio, af-fec-tus.* The facts may therefore be sum-
marized under the headings of (1) open and (2) closed syllables.

Open syllables. All short vowels proceed to *i*.

a *facio: conficio; cado: occido; ratus: irritus; mācina* < **mācănă*
   (Dor. Gk. μᾱχανά).

e *sedeo: obsideo; medius: dīmidius; lego: colligo*, etc.

o *(st)locus: īlico* < *in stlocō* (see p. 232); *novitās*, cf. Gk. νε(ϝ)ότᾱς;
   hospitem < **hostipotem.*

i *video: invideo; cito: incito; rigo: irrigo.*

u *caput: capitis; cornu: corniger; manus: manica.*

1. Before *l* the treatment varies according as this sound has a
palatal (*l* exilis) or velar (*l* pinguis) timbre. Before palatal *l* (i.e.
followed by *i*) the short vowel appears as *i*, before velar *l̄* (i.e. followed by *e, a, o, u*) as *u*: e.g. *sēdulo* < *sēdŏlo; exilium: exulans*s
familia: famulus; similis: simulare. So, too, the Greek loan-word;
scutula < σκυτάλᾱ; *crāpula* < κραιπάλᾱ; *paenula* < φαινόλης. Note
that *o* appears after *v* or a vowel: *parvolus, filiolus, viola.*
2. The progressive raising to *i* stopped at the intermediate stage
e before *r*, a consonant which in many languages has the effect of
lowering neighbouring vowels: *cinis: cineris; genus: generis;*
Falisci: Falerii; dare: reddere; camera < καμάρα. *o* persisted before
an *r: memoria, pectoris, temporis,* etc.
3. Before labials the vowel appears variously as *i* or *u*, the actual
pronunciation being apparently [y]: 'medius est quidam u et i
litterae sonus. non enim *optimum* dicimus aut *optumum*' (Quintilian 1. 4. 8). It is difficult to ignore this testimony from a trained
grammarian, but it is possible that persistent spellings such as
incipio but *occupo, regimentum* but *documentum,* reflect real differences of pronunciation, i.e. *i* after *i, e,* and *a,* but *u* after *o* and *u* in
the preceding syllable.

Closed syllables

a > *e*, and *o* > *u* ; *e*, *i*, and *u* remain unchanged.

a *aptus*: *ineptus*; *castus*: *incestus*; *annus*: *biennis*; *arma*: *inermis*;
parco: *peperci*; *damno*: *condemno*; Gk. τάλαντον: *talentum*.

    1. Before [ŋ] this *e*, like accented *e*, proceeds to *i*: *frango*: *confringo*; *tango*: *contingo*.
    2. Before velar [ɫ] (see above) this **e* > *u*: *calco*: *inculco*; *salsus*: *insulsus*.

e *sessus*: *obsessus*.

    1. Before velar *l*, *e* > *u*: *percello*: *perculsus* < **per-celsos*.

o *onustus* < **onostos*; *euntis* < **eyontes*; *alumnus* < **alomnos*;
secundus < **seqʷondos*; *industrius* < **endostruos*; Gk. ἀμόργη
> *amurca* (but this loan-word came via Etruscan).

    1. After *u*, *o* persisted until the first century A.D. The classical
spellings were thus *fruontur*, *sequontur*, etc.

u **dŭctos*: *adductus*, etc.

Diphthongs

ei and *ou* underwent the same changes as in initial syllables, i.e.
they were preserved in Old Latin and thence > *ī* and *ū*: e.g. *feido*:
confīdo; *douco*: *addūco*.

ai > *ei* in Old Latin and then > *ī*: *inceideretis* < **encaid-*;
aestimo: *exīstimo*; *aequos*: *inīquos*; Gk. ἐλαίρᾱ: *olīva*.

au > *ū*, presumably via *ou*: *fraudo*: OL. *defrūdo* ; *claudo*: *inclūdo*.
audio: *oboedio* has not been satisfactorily explained. It may
be merely an archaizing pronunciation of **obūdio* in the
language of the law.

oi The only example is *pōmērium* < **postmoiriom*.

Vowels and diphthongs in final syllables

Open syllables

a is apparently preserved in *ita*, *aliuta* (cf. *itidem*). These forms
were, in the opinion of some scholars, produced by iambic
shortening of **itā*, **utā* (see, however, p. 282).

e persists: *age*, *domine*.

o > *e*: *sequere* < *sequeso, cf. Gk. ἕπεο. On *ille* see under 'Pronouns' p. 256.

i > *e*: *mare, mari-a*; *anti (Gk. ἀντί) > *ante*. The ablatives *pede*, etc., are in origin locatives corresponding to ποδί, etc., in Greek.

In certain particles and forms of rapid speech the short vowel is sometimes lost: *quīn* < *quī-ne*, *sīn* < *sīne*, *vidēn* < *vidēsne*, *ain* < *ais-ne*. It is this which gave rise to apparent exceptions of the rules of accentuation: *vidés-ne* > *vidén*.

Final *i* was lost in the primary endings of the verb: *tremonti* > *tremunt*, *sonti > *sunt*, *es-ti > *est* (but on *ess* see p. 263).

Closed syllables

a > *e*: *artifex* < **-fax*, *rēmex* < **-ags*, *cornicen* < **-can*, *princeps*, *auceps* < **-caps*.

e persists: *auspex, senex, nōmen* (with *en* < *ņ*), *decem* (with *em* < *ṃ*).

    1. Before *-s* and *-t, e* > *i* in the third century B.C.: hence *agis* < **ages(i)*, *agit* < **aget(i)*; cf. the OL. genitives, *Cereres*, etc., and the perfect *dedet*.

i is kept in *ovis, lapis* < **lapid-s, salix*, etc. The divergent treatment seen in *iūdex* < **youz-diks, cŏmes* < *comit-s is probably due to the analogy of forms like *auspicem*: *auspex*; *artificem*: *artifex*.

u is unchanged: *manus, manum*, etc.

o > *u* in *aliud, istud*. Before *-s* and *-m* it persisted in Old Latin: *manios, Luciom*, etc., but > *u* by Classical times, except when it was preceded by *v, u*: hence *dominus* but *parvos, exiguos* etc.

    1. The divergent development, of *hospes* < *hostipots is again due to analogy of *artificem*: *artifex*, etc.

Diphthongs

For long diphthongs see p. 218. The short diphthongs underwent the same changes as in medial syllables.

-ai, -ei, and *-oi* all > OL. *-ei* > ClL. *-ī*. For examples see the case endings under 'Morphology'. The long vowels in final syllables were generally preserved, but shortening took place in Classical Latin before *-m, -t*, and *-nt*, and in polysyllables also before *-r* and

-l. Hence we have *dūcās, dūcēs,* etc., but *dūcăm, dūcăr, dūcăt, dūcĕm, dūcĕr, dūcĕt.* To these we must add the numerous examples of iambic shortening such as *ĕquă, bŏnă, ĕgŏ,* etc. But this process was both extended and restricted by analogical influences. Thus Plautus has the expected *rŏgă, căvĕ* although we later find *rŏgā, cavē.* Regular shortenings are seen in *mŏdŏ, bĕnĕ,* but *ergŏ* and *contră* cannot, of course, be due to the operation of this law. On vowel lengthening before certain groups of consonants see p. 231.

THE SONANTS

Certain types of sounds, according to the phonetic environment in which they occur, function as vowels or consonants, that is as syllabic or non-syllabic. Such were the IE. sonants *y(i), w(u), r(ṛ), l(ḷ), m(ṃ), n(ṇ).*

y (on *i* see above) initially was preserved in Latin: *e.g. iugum*: Gk. ζυγόν, Skt. *yugám,* Engl. *yoke; iecur*: Gk. ἧπαρ, Skt. *yakṛt.* Between vowels *y* was lost: e.g. *trēs < *treyes,* cf. Skt. *tráyas; moneo < *mone-yō.*
After consonants *y* was vocalized to *i.*
medius = Osc. *mefiai,* Gk. μέσ(σ)ος, Skt. *mádhyas < *medhyos.*
alius = Osc. *allo-,* Gk. ἄλλος *< *alyos.*
venio < gʷṃ-yō (see p. 227).

    1. *-dy-, -gy-, -sy- > -iy-* which was written *i,* e.g. *maius* (pronounced *maiyus*) *< *mag-yos; peius* (pronounced *peiyus*) *< *pedyos.* For *quoius < quosyo-s* see p. 255. Cicero is said to have preferred spellings with *ii* in such words (Quintilian I. 4. 11).
    2. *Iovis < *dyewes* is still spelt *Diovis* in Old Latin.

w was preserved initially before vowels and intervocalically:
vīdi = Gk. (ϝ)οῖδα, Skt. *véda,* etc.
vīcus = Gk. (ϝ)οῖκος, etc.
novem = Skt. *náva,* etc.
novos = Gk. νέ(ϝ)ος, Skt. *návas,* Engl. *new.*
ovis = Gk. ὄ(ϝ)ις, etc.

    1. Between similar vowels *w* disappeared and the vowels contracted: *sīs < sīvīs, lātrina < lavātrina, dītias < dīvitias.* But the *vi* was often restored by analogy.

2. *w* was preserved after *k*, *s*: *equos* = Skt. *áçvas* etc. < **ekwos*; *suāvis* = Skt. *svādús*, Engl. *sweet* etc. < **swādwi-s*.

3. *w* was vocalized after medial *t*: *quattuor* = Skt. *catváras*, Welsh *pedwar* < **qʷetwōres* (see p. 259).

4. *w* was lost after the labials *p* and *f*: *aperio* < **ap-weriō*; *forēs* = OSl. *dviri*, Engl. *door* < **dhwer-/dhwor-*.

5. *w* entered into combination with *d* (p. 225), *gh* (p. 229), and *gʷh* (p. 229).

6. *w* was lost before *u* and, except initially, before *o*: *somnus* < **swopnos *swepnos* (p. 231); *parum* < *parvom*; *deorsum* < *devorsum*; *soror* < **swesōṛ-* (see below).

On *colo, cum, cur* see p. 226.

r Consonantal *r* is preserved.

ruber = Gk. *ἐ-ρυθρός*, Engl. *red* (p. 228).

fero = Gk. *φέρω*, Engl. *bear* (p. 227).

1. When a following vowel was lost by syncope the *r* became syllabic and is represented in Latin by -*er*: e.g. *ter* = *τρίς* (*tris* > *tṛs* > *ters* > *ter*); cf. *certus* < **kritos*, *testis* < **terstis* < **tri-stis* (cf. Osc. *tristaamentud* = *testamento*); *ager* < **agros* (Gk. *ἀγρός*); *ācer* < **ācris*; *agellus* < **agṛlos* < **agrolos*.

r The IE. sonant *ṛ* (to be distinguished from the *r* which became sonant secondarily in Latin) is represented in Latin as *or*: *fors* = Skt. *bhṛtis* < **bhṛtis*.

mors = Skt. *mṛtis* < **mṛtis*.

posco = Skt. *pṛcchámi* 'I ask', Germ. *forschen* < **porc-scō* < **pṛk-skō*.

In a final syllable -*or* > -*ur*: *iecur*: Skt. *yakṛt* < **yeqʷṛ-t* (p. 226).

l is preserved in Latin.

linquo = Gk. *λείπω*, Engl. *leave* < **leiqʷ* (p. 226).

lego = Gk. *λέγω*, etc. < **leg*.

in-clutus = Gk. *κλυτός*, Skt. *çrutás*, < **klutós*.

ḷ is represented in Latin as *ol*:

mollis = Gk. *ἁ-μαλδ-ύνω*, Skt. *mṛdús* < **moldwis* < **mḷdu-*.

m is retained.

māter = Gk. *μάτηρ*, Engl. *mother*, etc.

nōmen = Gk. *ὄνομα*, Skt. *nắma*, Engl. *name*.

domus = Gk. *δόμος*, etc.

m̥ > Lat. *em*.

decem = Gk. δέκα, Skt. *dáça* < **dekm̥*.

septem = Gk. ἑπτά, Skt. *saptá* < **sept-m̥*.

centum (*en* for *em* by assimilation to the following *t*) = Gk. ἑ-κατόν, Skt. *çatám* < **(d)km̥tom*.

Final *m* was weakly pronounced and was little more than a nazalization of the preceding vowel: hence the spellings in OL. *oino, aide, duonoro*, etc.

n is retained:

novem, novus (p. 215).

genus = Gk. γένος, Engl. *kin*, etc. < **genos*

n̥ > Lat. *en*:

tentus = Gk. τατός, Skt. *tatás* < **tn̥tós*.

On *novem* for **noven* < **newn̥*, see p. 260.

Before *s*, Lat. *n* disappeared in final syllables with lengthening of the preceding vowel: e.g. *servōs, mensās, rēgēs* < **servons, *mensāns, *reg-n̥s*. In medial syllables the *n* was preserved longer (*mēnsis, ānser*, etc.), but the same tendency towards loss persisted throughout the history of Latin, so that the Romance languages show no reflection of *n* before *s*. Spellings like *cosol, cesor*, etc., occur at an early date, and this 'silent *n*' was often mistakenly introduced as in *thensaurus, formonsus*, etc.

When a following vowel was lost by syncope, *n* like *r* became syllabic and this *n̥* is represented by *en* or *in*: e.g. *Sabellus* < **Safn(o)los; sigillum* (< *sign̥lom* < **signolom*); cf. *pugillus* < **pugno-los, pastillus* < **pastn̥los* (*pānis* is from **pastnis*).

THE CONSONANTS

The IE. consonantal phonemes comprised a rich variety of plosives—voiceless (*p, t, k, q*, and *qʷ*), voiced (*b, d, g, g*, and *gʷ*), with the corresponding aspirated sounds (*ph*, etc. and *bh*, etc.). The only fricative was *s* (voiced *z* in certain environments).

Latin does not distinguish between the palatal and velar series nor between voiceless and voiced aspirates. Of the above system, Latin preserved in the main *p, t, k, (q), qʷ*, and *b, d, g, (g)*, the main changes affecting the voiced labio-velars and the aspirated plosives.

	Voiceless	Voiced	Voiceless aspirate	Voiced aspirate
Labial . .	p	b	ph	bh
Dental . .	t	d	th	dh
Palatal . .	k	g	kh	gh
Velar . .	q	g	qh	gh
Labiovelar .	q^w	g^w	q^{w}h	g^{w}h
Fricative . .	s	z	..	..

p *pater* = Gk. πατήρ, etc.
potis = Gk. πόσις, Skt. *pátis.*
septem = Gk. ἑπτά, etc.
clepere = Gk. κλέπτω, etc.

1. Initially the *p* is assimilated when the following syllable begins with a labio-velar: **peq^{w}ō > *quequō > *quoquō > coquō; *penq^{w}e > *quenque > quīnque* (lengthened *ī* after *quīntus*).

b Few equations have been established exhibiting this sound. *trabs* = Osc. *triibúm* 'domum', Lith. *trobà* 'house', Engl. *thorp*. *dē-bilis* = Skt. *balám* 'strength'.
See *tres, pater, est, septem, tego*, etc.

1. *tl > cl*: e.g. *pōclom < *pōtlom; saeclom < *saitlom; ex-anclare < ἀντλεῖν*. By-forms with an anaptyctic vowel also appear: *pōculum, saeculum*, etc.
2. After a consonant final *t* is lost: *lac < *lact*.
3. After a vowel final *-t > -d*: e.g. *feced*, etc. (see p. 263).

d *domus* = Gk. δόμος, etc.
dōnum, dare = Gk. δῶρον, etc.
edo = Gk. ἔδω, Engl. *eat*, etc.
cord-is = Gk. καρδ-ία, κραδ-ίη, Engl. *heart < *kerd/k̥d*.

1. In certain dialect forms an alternation of *d* and *l* is observed: *lingua × dingua; lacruma × dacruma; oleo × odor; sedeo × solium* (see p. 38).
2. *dw > b-* : e.g. *bonus, bellum*, OL *duenos, duellum*.
3. After long vowels final *d* is lost: *sē* for *sēd*, ablative *-ō* for *ōd* (p. 243).
4. After a consonant final *d* is lost: e.g. *cor < *cord*.

k See *centum, decem, vīcus, dīco* (OL. *deico* = Gk. δείκ-νυμι), etc.
q This IE. velar plosive is postulated to account for equations in which *satem* languages (p. 31) show a guttural plosive *k* as

distinct from a fricative s, etc., which in other equations corresponds to non-*satem* k: e.g. *cruor* = Gk. κρέας, Skt. *kravís* < **qrewəs*. The non-*satem* languages do not distinguish between the palatal (k, etc.) and the velar (q, etc.) series.

g   (g)*nōsco* = Gk. γι-γνώσκω, Skt. *jñā-*, etc., < **gnō*.
    genus = Gk. γένος, Engl. *kin*, Skt. *jánas* < **genos*.
    ago = Gk. ἄγω, Skt. *ájāmi* < **agō*.
    augeo = Gk. αὔξω, Goth. *auka*, Skt. *ójas-* 'strength' < **aug*.

g   This velar plosive is postulated like q to account for equations such as the following where *satem* g corresponds to non-*satem* g.
    tego = Gk. στέγος, Lith. *stógas*, 'roof' < **steg*.

The labio-velar plosives

These sounds which are postulated for Indo-European were probably velar plosives articulated with a simultaneous pouting of the lips ('lip-rounding'). In Greek they appear according to environment as dentals (τ, δ, θ), labials (π, β, φ), and palatals (κ, γ, χ). In the *satem* languages they are indistinguishable from the plain velars. In the 'Italic dialects' these sounds are represented by labials (for intrusions into Latin see p. 37).

q^w is retained in Latin:
    quis = Osc. *pis*, Gk. τίς, Skt. *kás* < **q^wi-*.
    quod = Osc. *po*, Gk. ποῦ, πόθεν, ποδ-απός, etc. < *q^wo-*.
    quattuor = Osc. *petora*, Dor. Gk. τέτορες, Skt. *catvā́ras* (see p. 259).
    sequor = Gk. ἕπομαι, Skt. *sácate* < **seq^w*.
    linquo, līqui, Gk. λείπω, Skt. *ri-ṇá-kti* < **leiq^w*.

    1. The labial element is lost:
    (a) Before u and o: *secundus* < **sequondos*; *iecur* < **iequor* < **yeq^wr̥-t* (p. 223); *colo* < **quolo* < **quelo* (p. 215) < **q^wel*. Note the contrast of *incola* with *inquilīnus*.
    (b) Before IE. y: *socius* < **soquios*: *lacio* < **laq^wyō* (cf. *laqueus*).
    (c) Before another consonant: *coctus* (cf. *coquo*); *relictus* (cf. *linquo*); cf. *nec* and *ac* which are the preconsonantal forms of *neque* and *atque*.
    (d) Before s: *vōx* < **wōq^ws* (cf. Gk. (ϝ)έπος).
    2. In certain complicated consonant groups -*qu*- is lost: *quīntus* < **quinqutos* (with lengthening of the vowel before -ηkt as in *sānctus, iūnctus*, etc.), *tormentum* < **torqumentum.*

g^w Initially before a vowel and intervocalically > v:

venio = Umbr. *benust* 'venerit', Osc. *kumbened* = 'convenit', Gk. βαίνω, Skt. *gam-*, Goth. *qiman* < *$g^w m̥yō$.

vīvus = Osc. *bivus* 'vivi', Skt. *jīvás* < *$g^w īwo$-.

veru = Umbr. *berus* 'veribus', Goth. *qairu*, OIr. *bir* < *$g^w eru$.

fīvo (OL. for *fīgo*) = Lith. *dýgti* < *$dhīg^w$. Cl.L. *fīgo* has been made from the perfect *fīxī*.

nūdus = Goth. *naqaþs*, Engl. *naked*, Ir. *nocht*. The Latin word has the root *nog^w* with a suffix -*edo*: *nog^w-edos* > *novedos* > *nūdus*.

1. After a velar nasal [ŋ] g^w is retained: *inguen* = Gk. ἀδήν < *$n̥g^w ēn$; *unguen*, *unguo* = Umbr. *umtu*, 'unguito', Skt. *anákti*, OIr. *imb*, 'butter' < *e/ong^w-.

2. Before *r* and *l*, g^w lost the labial element: *gravis* = Gk. βαρύς, Goth. *kaurus*, 'heavy', Skt. *gurús* < *$g^w r̥əw$-.
Cf. *grātus* = Osc. *brateis* 'gratiae', Skt. *gūrtás*, Lith. *gìrtas* < *$g^w r̥ətós$. *glāns*, *glandis* and Gk. βάλανος are from the same root with a different suffix; the *d* of the Latin word is found in Slavonic *želǫdĭ*: < *$g^w elə/g^w leə$.

The aspirated stops

In the prehistoric period in Latin and the 'Italic dialects' the voiced aspirated stops became voiceless and then changed to voiceless spirants, except after *s* when they lost the aspiration and became voiceless plosives: *bh* > *f*, *dh* > *$θ$* > *f*, *gh* > *$χ$* > *h*. These sounds were preserved in the main in the Italic dialects, but in urban Latin the treatment varied according to the phonetic environment.

bh   Initially > *f*:

fero = Gk. φέρω, Skt. *bhárāmi*, Engl. *bear* < *bher*.

flōs = Sabine *Flusare* 'Florali', Engl. *blossom* < *bhlō-s*.

fāma: Dor. Gk. φάμᾱ < *bhā*.

fuī = Gk. φῦ-ναι, Skt. *a-bhūt* 'he was', W. *bum* *i* 'I was' < *bhŭ*.

frāter = Gk. φράτηρ, Skt. *bhrātar-*, Engl. *brother* < *bhrātēr*.

1. Dialectal forms are found with *h* for *f*: *haba* (*faba*), *horda* = 'pregnant cow' (cf. *fordus* < *fero*).

Medially the spirant was voiced and then became the voiced plosive *b*:

nebula = Gk. νέφος, νεφέλη, Skt. *nábhas*, Germ. *Nebel* < **nebh*.

orbus = Gk. ὀρφανός < **orbh*.

ambo = Gk. ἄμφω.

dh   (> **θ*) > *f* which is retained initially:

fēci = Gk. ἔ-θη-κα, Skt. *adhāt* < **dhē*.

fēmina, fēcundus = Gk. τιθήνη, θῆλυς, Skt. *dhātrī* 'nurse' < **dhē* 'suckle'.

fūmus = Gk. θῡμός, Skt. *dhūmás* < **dhūmos*.

fingo, figulus = Osc. *feihúss* 'muros', Gk. τεῖχος, Skt. *dehas* < **dheigh* (cf. p. 229).

Note that in Greek and Sanskrit the first of two aspirates which begin adjacent syllables loses the aspiration (Grassmann's law).

Medially this spirant, too, was voiced and became the voiced plosive *d*:

aedes = Gk. αἴθω, Skt. *edhas* < **aidh*.

medius = Osc. *mefiaí* 'mediae', Gk. μέσ(σ)ος (for **μεθyος*), Skt. *mádhyas* < **medhyos*.

fīdo = Gk. πείθω (for **φείθω*, another example of Grassmann's law) < **bheidh*.

1. Internal *p* from *dh* became *b* in certain conditions:

(*a*) Before and after *r*: e.g. *glaber* = Engl. *glad*, Germ. *glatt*, 'smooth', but originally 'clear, bright', Lith. *glodùs* 'smooth' < **ghladh-ro-*. *verbum* = Umbr. *verfale*, Engl. *word* < **werdh-*. *barba* = Engl. *beard*, OSl. *brada* < **bhardhā*, which would normally give Lat. *farba*, but the first consonant has been assimilated to the following *b*. For *līber* see p. 218.

(*b*) Before *-l-*. Thus the instrument suffix *-dhlo* (Gk. *-θλο-*) appears as *-blo-(-bulo-)* in Latin: *stabulum* < **stə-dhlom*, cf. Germ. *Stadel*; *fābula* < **bhā-dhlā*.

(*c*) After *u*: *ūber* = Gk. οὖθαρ, Skt. *ūdhar*, Engl. *udder* < **ūdh*. *rūber* = Gk. ἐ-ρυθρός Skt. *rudhirás*, Engl. *red* < **rudhro-*. (Note that dialect *rūfus* is from **roudho-*: cf. Germ. *rot*, Goth. *raups*, Lith. *raũdas. rōbus* is yet another dialect variant.) *iubeo*: = Gk. ὑσ-μίνη, Skt. *yudh-*, 'fight' < **yeudh/yudh*. The original meaning of the root appears to have been 'move, shake, tremble', etc. *iubeo* is a causative = 'set in motion'.

gh > *χ, and then before and between vowels > h:
(h)anser: = Gk. χήν, Skt. haṃsás, Engl. gander, goose < *ghans-.
hiems: (him- in bīmus < *dwi-himo-s) = Gk. χίμαρος, χιών, Skt. himás < *ghi-em, *ghi-m. Another ablaut grade appears in hībernus < *gheimrinos, cf. Gk. χειμερινός.
humus, homo = Gk. χαμαί, Goth. guma < *ghem-, ghom-.
hostis = Engl. guest, Germ. Gast, OSl. gostĭ < *ghosti-.
veho = Gk. (ϝ)οχέομαι, Skt. váhati, Engl. wagon < *wegh-.

1. Initial gh before u > f (cf. gʷh):
fundo = Gk. χέϝω, χύ-το, Goth. giutan < *gheu-, ghu-; ferus = Gk. θήρ, OSl. zvěrĭ < *ghwer-.
2. Internally the combination -ghu- > -gw- > -v- (cf. the treatment of the labio-velar gʷ): brevis = Gk. βραχύς < *mreghw-i (the m is postulated because of other members of the equation not quoted here).
3. After a velar nasal [ŋ] gh > g:
fingo = Gk. τεῖχος, Engl. dike < *dheigh, *dhi-n-gh; lingo = Gk. λείχω, Engl. lick < *leigh, li-n-gh; ango, angustus = Gk. ἄγχω, Goth. aggwus, Germ. eng < *angh-.

gʷh Initially > f:
formus = Gk. θερμός, Skt. gharmás < *gʷhe/orm-.
de-fendo = Gk. θείνω, φόνος, Skt. han-ti 'he strikes', < *gʷhen-.
Internally
(a) between vowels > v: nix, nivem = Gk. νίφα, νείφει, OSl. sněgŭ, Engl. snow < *sneigʷh-, snigʷh-; voveo = Umbr. vufetes 'votis', Gk. εὔχομαι < *wogʷh-eyō; levis < legʷhu-i-s.
(b) after [ŋ] > g: ninguit 'it snows' < *sni-n-gʷh; anguis = Lith. angìs (cf. Gk. ὄφις, Skt. áhis).
(c) Before r we find a trace of the treatment of f in 'ancient' nefrundines (Festus), Praenestine nefrōnes, which in Lanuvine appears as b, nebrundines: Gk. νεφρός, Germ. Niere < *negʷhro-.

The glottal aspirate [h] of Latin was inherently an unstable sound and was progressively eliminated. Intervocalically it had disappeared by the third century B.C. (e.g. nēmo < *nehemo, bīmus < *dwi-himos). As a consequence this letter

was available as a mere orthographical device to mark syllabi-
fication, as in the spelling *ahēnus* where it was etymologically unjustified (< *ayes-nos*). The aspirate was lost in certain country dialects (e.g. *arena, edus, ircus, olus,* etc.).
Ignorant reaction against this mark of *rusticitas* produced
hyperurbanisms which prompted Catullus' mockery of Arrius'
hinsidias; cf. the comment of Nigidius (Aulus Gellius 13. 6. 3)
'rusticus fit sermo si aspires perperam'. An unetymological *h*
also appears in *humerus, hūmor,* and *haurio* (Gk. αὔω, etc.).

s   This sound remained unchanged initially and finally (see
septem, sus, genus, etc.) and also internally before and after
voiceless plosives (*sisto, est, vesper, axis*) and after *n* (*mēnsis,
ānser*). Intervocalically *s* was voiced to *z* and then became
r: *generis* < **genes-es, arborem* < **arbos-em, maiōrem* <
*magyōs-em, flōrem < **flōs-em* (cf. *flōs, flōsculus*). This change
was completed about the middle of the fourth century B.C.,
but a number of archaic forms such as *arbosem, pignosa,
lasibus* are attested. Where *s* appears in pure Latin words (on
borrowed and dialect words like *rosa, casa,* see pp. 37, 57), it
has resulted from the reduction of *ss* after long vowels and
diphthongs: e.g. *vīsus* < **vīssos* < **vid-tos, causa* < *caussa,
quaeso* < *quaesso.*

Before the voiced sounds *y, w, l, m, n, d, g,* and after *r* and *l,*
s was voiced to *z,* which became *r* before *g* (e.g. *mergo,* cf. Lith.
mazgóti), but elsewhere before the other sounds just listed the
z disappeared with compensatory lengthening of the preceding
vowel: *nīdus* < **nizdos* (Engl. *nest*), *quīdam* < *quis-dam, prīmus* < **pris-mos, aēnus* < **ayes-nos, prēlum* < **pres-lom.*

sr- initially > *fr-* (*frīgus,* cf. Gk. ῥῖγος < **srīgos*) ; and internally > *-br-* (*fūnebris* < **dhoines-ris,* (*con*)*sobrīnus* < **-swesr-
īnos*; on *soror* < **swesōr,* see p. 215).

Group phenomena

Latin exhibits the common phonetic phenomena such as
assimilation, dissimilation, glide sounds, and the simplification of
complex groups—which contribute to economy of effort and ease of
pronunciation. It will suffice to quote a few examples in which
these processes have clouded etymological transparency.

Assimilation. Consonants in juxtaposition are often assimilated. Most frequently the first is assimilated to the second ('regressive assimilation'). This is most obvious in the behaviour of the verbal prefixes: *occīdo* < **ob-caedo*, *attineo* < *ad-teneo*, *sufficio* < **sub-facio*, *differo* < *dis-fero*, etc. Note further *quippe* < **quid-pe*, *topper* < **tod-per*, *annus* < **at-nos* (Goth. *apn*); *somnus* < **swep-nos*, *summus* < **sup-mos*, *sella* < **sed-lā*, *grallae* < **grad-s-lae*, *corōlla* < **corōn-lā*. In the passive participles when the final voiced consonant of the root becomes voiceless by assimilation to the -*t*- of the suffix, the preceding vowel is lengthened: *āctus* < **ag-tos*, *lēctus* < **leg-tos*, *rēctus* < **reg-tos*. For 'progressive assimilation', where the first consonant of the group dominates, we may quote *velle* < **vel-se*, *collum* < **col-som* (cf. Germ. *Hals*), *torreo* < **torseo*, *ferre* < **fer-se*, *tollo* < **tol-no*. Assimilation may also affect vowels in adjacent syllables. Thus *homo* is from *hemō* (cf. *nēmo* < **ne-hemo*). Note, too, the vowel of the reduplication in *pupugi* (OL. *pepugi*), *momordi* (OL. *memordi*).

Dissimilation. The difficulty of pronouncing two similar sounds in rapid succession may be eased by changing one of them. This is particularly frequent in Latin with the combinations *r-r, l-l*: e.g. *peregrinus* became in VL. *pelegrinus* (Fr. *pélerin*), while *caeruleus* < **caeluleus* is an adjective formed from *caelum*. The effect of such dissimilation may be seen in the change of the common adjectival suffix -*ālis* (*navalis*, *mortalis*) to -*āris* when it is attached to nouns containing an *l*: *militaris*, *consularis*, *lunaris*. In the same way the instrument suffix -*lo*- appears as -*ro*: *speculum*, but *fulcrum*, *flagrum*. Other examples of dissimilation are *carmen* < **can-men*, *germen* < **gen-men*, *merīdiē* < *medī-diē* (a form still surviving on a sun-dial in Praeneste according to Varro, *L.L.* 6. 4.). Dissimilation may sometimes lead to the loss of one of the conflicting sounds: *agrestis* < **agrestris* (cf. *silvestris*). In some cases a whole syllable may be lost: e.g. *nūtrīx* < **nūtrī-trīx*.

Glide sounds. Ease of pronunciation may be effected by the insertion of sounds between the members of certain groups. Such is the anaptyctic vowel in *dracuma* < **dracmā*, *poculum* < *poclom*, *mina* < *mna* (Gk. μνᾶ). In other cases a consonant may appear as in Engl. *Thom-p-son*: cf. *sum-p-si*, *dem-p-si*, *sum-p-tus*, *exemplum* < **exem-lom*. Note further the vulgar pronunciation *autum-p-nus*, *som-p-nus*, etc. A glide consonant appears to have developed perhaps already in Indo-European between two adjacent dental plosives: **t-t*, **d-t* > *-tˢt-*, *-dˢt-*, etc., a combination of sounds which appears in Latin (and Germanic) as *ss*: e.g. *messis* < **metˢtis* (cf. *meto*), *passus* < **patˢtos* (*patior*), *quassus* < **quatˢtos* (*quatio*). This *ss* was simplified after a long vowel or diphthong: *vīsus* < **vīssos* < **vĭd-tos, cāsus* < *cāssus* < *căd-tus*. A glide *-t-* developed between *ss* and a following *r* (cf. *sister*) in *rāstrum* < **rāssrom* < **rād-trom*.

Finally we may quote some examples of the simplification of complex groups. *arsi* < **ard-si*; *fulsi* < **fulg-si*; *testis* < **terstis* < *tristis* (p. 223); *tostus* < **tors-tos*; *ultus* < **ulctos* (*ulciscor*); *tormentum* < **torqʷmentum*; *iūmentum* < OL. *iouxmentum*; *sēviri* < **sexviri*; *lūna* < **loucsna*; *cēna* (OL. *cesna*) < **cersna* (cf. Osc. *kerssnais* 'cenis'); *īlico* < *in stloco*; *posco* < **porc-scō* < **prk-skō*; *pruīna* < **pruswīna* (cf. Skt. *pruṣvā* 'hoar frost', OHG. *riosan*, Engl. *freeze*).

CHAPTER IX

MORPHOLOGY

SOME PRELIMINARY NOTIONS

Inflexion, stem, and root

THE analysis of a Latin word like *dēditīcius* reveals the following components. In the first place we note that the end of the word appears in different forms (*-m, -ī, -ō*, etc.) according to the part played by the word in the construction of the sentence. Such word-components having syntactical function are called inflexions: a complete tabulation is known as the declension of a noun. The rump of the word left over when the inflexions are removed is called the stem: *dediticio-*. Comparison with other words like *empticius, missicius*, etc., reveals a further component, which has been added to the passive participle stems, *dedit-, empt-, miss-*. This element *-icio* is known as a suffix. The analysis may proceed further. The residue *dēdit-* when compared with *dēdo, dēdere*, on the one hand, and with the series *dict-, duct-*, etc., on the other, yields another significant element, *-t-*, the suffix which characterizes the perfect participles passive in Latin. If this is removed we are now left with *dēdi-*, which is the constant element of a group of forms referring in various ways to the fact of 'giving up'. But still our analysis is not at an end: the verb *dēdo* on the evidence of *dē-pono, dē-duco, dē-doceo*, etc., yields a prefix *dē-*. Thus we are finally left with *dō*, which is the constant element in a whole constellation of words all connected with the fact of 'giving': *dō-no-m, dōnare, dōnatus, dōnatīvos, dōs, dăre, dătos*, etc. This, the ultimate functional unit of the Latin (and the IE.) word, is called the root. Thus the Latin word may contain three kinds of morphological units or 'morphemes': the root, one or more affixes (prefixes and suffixes), which are attached to a root to form a stem, and finally the inflexion which indicates the syntactical function of the completed word.

Vowel gradation, or ablaut

It will not have escaped the reader's attention that the root itself shows modifications: e.g. *dō* and *dă*. This is a complicated example of a widespread phenomenon known as vowel gradation or ablaut, that is the alternation of the vowel of a root (on ablaut in suffixes and inflexions see below) as a morphological device. Examples from English are the so-called strong verbs, *sing, sang, sung*; *drive, drove, driven*. Greek, which presents most clearly the original IE. system which our English examples reflect, shows that we must distinguish three ablaut grades: (1) showing the vowel *e*, (2) showing the vowel *o*, and (3) showing no vowel. These are known as the *e*-grade, the *o*-grade, and the zero grade respectively. A typical example showing the three grades is (1) γένος, (2) γόνος, (3) γί-γν-ομαι. If the root contains a diphthong, that is if the *e* is followed by one of the sonants *i, u, r, l, m, n*, then in the zero grade, on the disappearance of the vowel, the sonant assumes syllabic function if a consonant follows: e.g. (1) λείπω, (2) λέλοιπα, (3) λιπ-εῖν; (1) μένος, (2) μέ-μον-α, (3) μέ-μα-μεν (**me-mn̥-men*).

dō: dă exemplifies a more difficult series of ablaut gradations in which the full root does not contain a short vowel or a diphthong but a long vowel which shows merely a reduced form but does not altogether disappear in the 'zero grade'. This, of course, is no different in principle from the behaviour of the diphthong, which also leaves its sonant as a residue in the zero grade. Now we have noted that the diphthong *en* in the root *men* leaves a residue -*n̥*- in the zero grade (on the representation of this IE. sound in Latin and elsewhere, see p. 224). If we now turn our attention to a root with a long vowel, e.g. *stā* 'stand', we find in the verbal adjective in *-to*, which usually exhibits the zero grade (see below), the following series of forms in Latin, Greek, and Sanskrit respectively: *stătus*, στατός, *sthitás*. Here we observe the equation $a = a = i$ which is traced to an **IE. ə (see p. 216). Thus the gradation of the root may be represented as **stā: *stə*. In the same way the Lat. *dō: dă* leads us to postulate **dō: *də* and *fēci: făcio* leads us to postulate **dhē: *dhə*.

But this is an untidy symbolism. Let us assume that the ə of the zero grade is the residue of a diphthong just as *i, u, r, l, m, n* are residues respectively of *ei, eu, er, el, em, en*. In other words, let us symbolize the unknown IE. sound which yields *ē* in Latin and other related languages not as **ē* but as **eə*. Then the zero grade with loss of the main vowel will be ə and the relationship of *fēci* to *făcio* will be traceable to IE. **dheə: *dhə*. So, too, for *stā: sta* we may postulate *staə: *stə and for dō: dǎ, *doə: *də. If we wish, however, for a complete alinement with λείπω: λιπεῖν, etc., and show an e in the first grade, then all we have to do is to substitute *eə₁, *eə₂, *eə₃, for *eə, *aə, *oə respectively. These three IE. diphthongs are defined as the unknown sounds which account for the presence of ē, ā, and ō respectively in the words under examination. This purely theoretical analysis leading to the postulation of a new series of sonants, ə₁, ə₂, ə₃ ('laryngeals'), has been partially confirmed by the evidence of Hittite, where a phoneme transcribed as ḫ sometimes corresponds to the postulated IE. laryngeals. Note, too, that the ə₂ in *stəə₂tos, the zero grade of *steə₂ (= stā), provides an explanation of the aspirate which appears in Skt. sthitas. This example suggests that the postulated IE. laryngeal ə₂ was of such a phonetic nature as to cause the aspiration of a preceding voiceless dental plosive in Sanskrit.

Through this analysis of the apparently aberrant long-vowelled roots as one-time diphthongs it is now possible to make a simple general statement about the ablaut gradations of the IE. root. The root may exhibit three grades: an e-grade, an o-grade, and a zero grade. In roots containing a diphthong the second element (the sonant) is left as a residue in the zero grade.

In Latin the original ablaut has been much obscured by phonetic and analogical changes. Examples are *pendo: pondus*; *tego: toga* (*e* and *o* grades); *es-t: s-unt*; *ed-o: d-ens*; *genus: gi-gn-o* (*e* grade and zero grade). Further examples will be given in the analysis of the nouns and verbs.

Having established the chief morphological devices of Indo-European we may examine the processes of suffixation whereby noun stems are made from roots and from other stems. In this the convenient functional classification suggested by M. Leumann[1] will be adopted.

FORMATION OF NOUNS

The suffix may be 'zero': these are the so-called root nouns of the types *dux* (*dŭc-s*), *lūx*, *pāx* (*pāc-s*), *pēs*, *vōx*, *ōs*, etc. Such root nouns often form the second element of compound nouns: *iūdex* < *ious-dic-s, opifex, < *opi-fac-s, auceps, < *avi-cap-s*, etc.

[1] *Museum Helveticum*, i, 1944. pp. 129 ff.

A. *Substantives derived from substantives*

1. Diminutives in *-lo, -lā (-ulus, -culus, -ellus, -cellus,* etc.): *filiolus, foculus, homunculus; diecula; asellus, gemellus; ocellus, agellus, puella; corōlla,* etc.

2. Pejoratives in *-astro-: filiaster.*

3. Feminines:
   (a) *-(tr)-īc-*: e.g. *genetrix, victrix.*
   (b) *-īnā: regina, gallina, libertina.*

4. Collectives:
   (a) *-to-,* e.g. *arbustum, arboretum.*
   (b) *-ēlā,* e.g. *clientela, parentela.*
   (c) *-ātu-,* e.g. *senatus, equitatus.*

5. Abstract nouns:
   (a) *-ia,* e.g. *militia.*
   (b) *-īna,* e.g. *medicina, doctrina.*
   (c) *-tūt-,* e.g. *virtus, iuventus.*
   (d) *-ātu-,* e.g. *principatus.*

6. Names of persons derived from things:
   (a) *-ō* and *-iō,* e.g. *praedo, restio* (also from abstracts, e.g. *ludio, lucrio*).
   (b) *-no-,* e.g. *dominus.*
   (c) *-ārio-,* e.g. *balnearius.*
   (d) *-tōr-,* e.g. *vinitor.*

7. Locality names:
   (a) *-īnā,* e.g. *figlina.*
   (b) *-ārio-,* e.g. *granarium.*

B. *Nouns derived from verbs*

1. Verbal abstracts:
   (a) *-ti-,* e.g. *morti-s* (for the form of the nominative singular, see below).
   (b) *-ti-ōn-,* e.g. *actio.*
   (c) *-tu-,* e.g. *cantus.*
   (d) *-tūrā,* e.g. *cultura, pictura.*
   (e) *-io-,* e.g. *imperium.*
   (f) *-iē,* e.g. *species.*
   (g) *-ōr-,* e.g. *timor.*

2. Instruments:
   (a) -tro-, e.g. aratrum, feretrum.
   (b) -culo-, e.g. gubernaculum.
   (c) -cro-, e.g. sepulcrum.
   (d) -bulo-, e.g. stabulum.
   (e) -bro-, -brā, e.g. lavabrum; dolabra, latebra.
3. The product or result of the action:
   (a) -men, -mento-, e.g. semen, carmen; fundamentum, vestimentum.
   (b) -no-, e.g. donum, lignum, signum.
4. Agents: -tōr-, e.g. victor (on the feminine derivatives in -trīc- see above).
5. Localities: -tōrio-, e.g. dormitorium, conditorium.

C. *Nouns derived from adjectives*
   1. Abstracts:
      (a) -iā, e.g. superbia, audacia.
      (b) -tāt-, e.g. dignitas.
      (c) -itiā, -itiēs, e.g. laetitia, malitia; planities.
      (d) -tūdin-, e.g. magnitudo, turpitudo.
      (e) -mōnia, e.g. acrimonia.

D. *Adjectives derived from adjectives*
   1. Diminutives (see above): aureolus; tenellus; minusculus.
   2. Pejoratives (see above): calvaster, surdaster.
   3. Elatives (comparatives and superlatives: see below).
   4. Derivatives from the participle in -to-:
      (a) -īvo-, e.g. captivus, emptivus.
      (b) -īcio-, e.g. dediticius, empticius.
      (c) -ĭli-, e.g. textilis, fictilis.

E. *Adjectives derived from substantives*
   1. From nouns referring to persons and animals:
      (a) -io-, e.g. patrius.
      (b) -ĭcio-, e.g. patricius, aedilicius, tribunicius.
      (c) -īno-, e.g. divinus, bovinus, equinus.
      (d) -ĭco-, e.g. civicus, hosticus, poplicus.

2. From nouns referring to things:
   (a) *-āli-*, e.g. *annalis, navalis* (but also *regalis*).
   (b) *-ārio-*, e.g. *argentarius, ferrarius.*

3. Adjectives of locality:
   (a) *-āno-*, e.g. *urbanus, paganus, oppidanus.*
   (b) *-tico-*, e.g. *rusticus, aquaticus.*
   (c) *-tili-*, e.g. *aquatilis.*
   (d) *-stri-*, e.g. *campestris, palustris* ; *agrestis* (with dissimilation of the *-r*).
   (e) *-ēnsi-*, e.g. *forensis, atriensis.*
   (f) *-timo-*, e.g. *maritimus, finitimus.*
   (g) *-āti-*, e.g. *cuias* (cf. *optimates, nostrates*).

4. Temporal adjectives:
   (a) *-tīvo-*, e.g. *tempestivus, primitivus.*
   (b) We may conveniently list here the adjectives derived from temporal adverbs, *cras-tinus* and *hodie-rnus, noctu-rnus.*

5. Material adjectives:
   (a) *e-yo-*, e.g. *aureus, argenteus, aëneus.*
   (b) *-īcio-*, e.g. *caementicius.*
   (c) *-no-*, e.g. *salignus, ilignus.*
   (d) the Greek suffix *-ino-*, e.g. *prasinus.*

6. Adjectives meaning 'provided with', 'possessing':
   (a) *-ōso-*, e.g. *aquosus, herbosus, morbosus.*
   (b) *-ulento-*, e.g. *lutulentus, virulentus.*
   (c) *-to-*, e.g. *barbatus, hastatus.*
   (d) *-ido-*, e.g. *herbidus, fumidus.*

F *Adjectives derived from verbs*

1. The active participles and verbal adjectives:
   (a) *-nt-*, e.g. *-amant-, regent-,* etc.
   (b) *-tūro-*, e.g. *amaturus,* etc.
   (c) *-āc-*, e.g. *edax, bibax, rapax.*
   (d) *-ulo-*, e.g. *credulus, pendulus, bibulus.*
   (e) *-bundo-*, e.g. *ridibundus, vagabundus.*
   (f) *-ido-*, from verbs in *-ēre,* e.g. *calidus, aridus, nitidus, timidus.*

2. The passive participles and verbal adjectives:
   (a) -to-, e.g. amatus, etc.
   (b) -ndo-, e.g. amandus, etc.
   (c) -bili-, -lis, e.g. amabilis ; facilis, habilis.
   (d) -uo-, e.g. arvos, pascuus, caeduus, praecipuus, exiguus, irriguus.
   (e) -no-, e.g. plenus.
   (f) -āneo-, e.g. praeliganeus, supervacaneus, consentaneus.
3. Instrumental and local adjectives in -tōrio-, e.g. deversorius, cubitorius, sudatorius.

The foregoing systematic functional description says nothing about the origin and history of the suffixes. Many of them were inherited from the parent language: among these are the diminutives in -lo- ; the agents in -tōr- ; the verbal abstracts in -ti- and -tu- ; the masculine deverbatives in -ōs (-ōr-) ; the instruments in *-tro-, *-tlo-, *-dhro-, and *-dhlo- ; the adjectives with the widespread -yo-suffix, the verbal participles in -to-, -no-, -nt-, etc. Others again are combinations of or extended forms of inherited suffixes: e.g. -tōr-io-, -tū-din-, -tū-t-, -tā-t-, -tū-rā, -ti-ōn-; and -culo- which combines an ancient diminutive suffix *-qo- with -lo-.

Other extended forms of the inherited suffixes have arisen through false analysis which detached a part of the noun-stem with the suffix: thus farrāgin-eus (< farrāgo) is falsely divided as farr-āgineus, and this form of the suffix appears in ole-āgineus. So, too, -no- appears variously as -āno-, -īno-, and -ūno-, where the first vowels were originally the vowels of the noun stems. Similarly nocturnus is derived from a r/n stem *noctur (cf. Gk. νύκτωρ, νύκτερος) by means of the suffix -no-. This word was falsely analysed as noctu-rnus, and the suffix -rno- was used in other temporal adjectives such as diurnus, hodiernus, and modernus (Cassiodorus) from modo 'just now'. Another common process which deserves comment is what may be called relational displacement in a group of words. Thus from iudex, a noun iudicium is made, this being a substantivization of an adjective in -ius. From iudex again a denominative verb is coined, iudicare. Historically there is no direct connexion between iudicium and iudicare, but the native speaker who learns this group is unaware of history and in his mind establishes a relationship between the noun and the verb. In this way *-ium* became a deverbative suffix: *desiderium, delirium, imperium.*

Finally it should be noted that a suffix gains ground through infection of word by word as a consequence of close association in speech contexts. To illustrate this principle we may return to the first example quoted, *dēditīcius.* This suffix *-īcio-* perhaps originated in the word *novīcius,* which may be interpreted as an *-io-* derivative from a form **novīx.* Thence it appeared in *emptīcius* and spread in the language of law to denote persons acquired in various ways, *adoptaticius, adscripticius, conducticius, dediticius.* Such adjectives were also applied to things acquired (e.g. *advecticius*) and in the language of commerce came to be used in adjectival descriptions of various types of goods, e.g. *panis depsticius.* In the last resort, then, the history of a suffix is the sum of the formal histories of all the words exhibiting it, a task which would far exceed the narrow limits of this chapter.

THE DECLENSIONAL CLASSES AND THE CASE INFLEXIONS

Indo-European distinguished eight cases: nominative, vocative, accusative, genitive, dative, ablative, locative, and sociative-instrumental (on their functions see next chapter). This system was simplified in the various descendant languages by different processes of merging which go under the name 'syncretism'. Thus Greek merged the genitive and ablative and again the dative, locative, and instrumental. The Latin ablative is burdened with the functions of the original ablative, sociative-instrumental, and locative, though isolated locative forms survived in their original function. The details are reserved for discussion in the framework of the declensional classes.

By a declensional class is meant a group of nouns which resemble one another in their mode of inflexion. Inflexional behaviour in Indo-European varied according to the type of stem: we may list stems in *-ā, -o* (ablauting with *-e*), *-ei/i, -eu/u, -ī, -ū, ēi, -ēu, -āu,* and the various stems ending in consonants. These manifold declensional classes were reorganized in Latin into the five declensions set forth in the standard grammars.

The -ā declension

Singular

The *nominative* *-ā:[1] e.g. χώρᾱ etc. In Latin the vowel was shortened first in iambic words, e.g. *rŏtā, tŏgā* > *rŏtă, tŏgă* ('brevis brevians'), whence it became general in all words of this class.

Accusative *-*m*: χώρᾱν, Skt. *açvām*, etc. In Latin, long vowels were regularly shortened before final -*m* (p. 221), hence *rēgīnăm*, etc.

Vocative -*ă*: e.g. νύμφᾰ. Apparently < *IE. *ə*.

Genitive *-*ās*: χώρᾱς, Umbr. *tutas*, etc. This ending survives in OL. *ēscās, viās*, etc., and in the phrase (*pater*)*familiās*. It was replaced, however, by a new ending -*āī* (so Virgil's *pictai*) modelled on the -*ī* genitive of the *o*-declension (see below). It is likely that the process began in phrases where an *o*-adjective was combined with a masculine of the *ā*-class: *bonī agricolās > *bonī agricolāī*. -*aes* (*Aquiliaes* etc.) is a combination of -*ae* and -*ās*.

Dative *-*ā*+-*ei* > *-*āi*: e.g. χώρᾱι. This form is preserved in OL. *Menervai, Fortunai*, etc. In Italic the final -*i* was dropped before a word beginning with a vowel: hence OL. *matuta*. The usual ending -*ae* (for phonetic development see p. 221) goes back to the anteconsonantal form which was generalized. Note the provincial forms *Fortune*, etc. (see p. 59).

Ablative. In Indo-European this was identical with the genitive, as in Gk. χώρᾱς. In Italic a new inflexion -*ād* was created on the analogy of -*ōd* (see below). The final -*d* was dropped about 200 B.C., hence the classical ending -*ā*. OL. examples are *sententiad, praidad*, etc.

Locative. *-*ĭ* added to the stem produced the OL. *Romāi*, etc., which regularly proceeded to *Romae*. Note that the identical classical endings of the genitive, dative, and locative in this declension were originally distinct: *-*ās*, *-*āei*, *-*āĭ*.

Plural

Nominative *-*ās* < *-*ā*+*es*: e.g. Skt. *açvās*, Osc. *scriftas, aasas* 'arae'. This ending may persist in Pomponius' *laetitias insperatas* (but see p. 150). The Pisaurian form *matrona* shows 'rustic' loss of final -*s* (p. 124). But elsewhere in Old Latin we find -*ai* (*tabelai*), which is due to the influence of -*oi* in the *o*-stems (see below).

---

[1] The asterisked forms represent the IE. case endings.

Accusative *-ās < *ā+ns: e.g. Skt. *açvās*. In Italic the -*ns* was restored by analogy and -*āns* in Latin regularly became -*ās*. On the evidence of Latin alone the intermediate stage could not be detected, but the -*ss* of Oscan (*viass*) and the -*f* of Umbrian (*vitlaf*) rest on -*ns*. Greek, too, shows a similar development: e.g. Cretan τιμανς.

Genitive *-ōm < *ā-ōm. Both Greek and Latin replaced this ending by -*sōm* drawn from the demonstrative pronoun (Skt. *tāsām*, Gk. τάων, Lat. *is-tārum*, with rhotacism of intervocalic -*s*-; cf. Osc. *egmazum*): hence *dearum*, etc.

Dative and ablative. The original endings -*bhos* (Gallic Ναμαυσικα-βο) or -*bhyos* (Skt. *açvābhyas*) were replaced in Italic by a new ending -*āis* (Osc. *kerssnais*) based on the -*ois* of the *o*-stems (see below). For the Latin phonetic development -*ais* > *eis* > -*īs* see p. 221). Old Latin examples of the intermediate stages are *soveis* = *suīs*, and *nuges* = *nugīs*. In certain nouns the distinction between masculine and feminine was re-created by using the -*bus* of the other declensions: *deabus*, *filiabus*. Such forms had some success in vulgar speech: *feminabus*, etc.

The masculines of the *ā*-class are declined in the same way, but an -*s* appears in certain compound nouns, *hosticapas*, *paricidas*.

O-declension

Singular

Nominative *-s. On -*os* > -*us* see p. 221: *dominus*.

Vocative. This case shows the bare stem with *e*-grade of ablaut: *domine*; cf. Gk. ἄδελφε.

Accusative *-m. On -*om* > -*um* see p. 221: *dominum*; cf. Gk. δοῦλον.

Genitive *-o-syo, e.g. Gk. ἵπποιο, Skt. *açvasya*. This ending in Celtic and Italic was replaced by an -*ī* of obscure origin. Note that it is not attached to the stem vowel -*o*-, for Old Latin still distinguishes clearly between an original -*ī* and the diphthong -*ei*: *Latinī* (genitive singular), but *virei* (nominative plural). The -*ī* is, therefore, not < -*oi* but is a derivative suffix of like status with the stem-forming *o*. It has been brought into connexion with an adverbial suffix -*ī* of Sanskrit (see p. 294) and also with the -*ī* used to form feminines (*rēg-ī-na*). It may originally have been an adjectival suffix with the general significance 'belonging to, connected with'. This would accord with the syntactical usage of the genitive as the adjectival case. The denominative masculines of the type *rathī* 'charioteer' and the feminines like *rājñī*, Latin *rēgī-na* represent other specializations of the same suffix.[1]

Dative *ōi < **o+ei, e.g. ἵππωι. The *o* was shortened in Italic if the next word began with a consonant. An Old Latin example is *Numasioi = Numeriō*. Before a vowel the -*i* was dropped and this form of the inflexion has been generalized in Lat. -*ō*.

Ablative *-ōd: Skt. *açvād*. This is still preserved in OL. *Gnaivod*, *poplicod*, etc. On loss of -*d* see p. 225.

Locative *-o+ĭ. Cf. οἴκοι. Oscan, however, shows -*ei*, e.g. *lúvkeí* 'in the grove'. The Lat. -*ei* (*Delei*) and -*ī* (*domi, belli*) are traceable either to -*oi* or -*ei*. This case form survives only sporadically in Latin, where it has been replaced by the ablative.

Plural

Nominative *-ōs < **o+es, e.g. Skt. *açvās*, Osc. *Núvlanús = *'Nolani'. In Latin this inflexion was replaced by -*oi* under the influence of the demonstratives, a development which is paralleled in Greek. On the phonetic development *oi > oe* (e.g. *poploe* in the hymn of the Salii) > *ei* (*servei*, etc.) > *e* (*ploirume*) > *ī* (*servi*, etc.) see p. 220. In provincial texts an extended form -*eis*, -*es*, -*is* occurs with -*s* from the third declension: e.g. *leibereis, magistres, duomvires, ministris*.

Accusative *-o-ns, e.g. Cretan ἐλεύθερονς. On the phonetic development in Latin of -*ons > ōs* see p. 224.

Genitive *-ōm < **o+ōm. This persists in Old Latin with regular shortening of *ō* before *m*, *Romanom*, etc. These forms were still frequent in Old Latin, e.g. Plautus' *verbum, inimicum*, and they persist in the conservative phraseology of religion and the law: e.g. *deum, triumvirum, nummum*, etc. The usual ending -*ōrum* was made on the analogy of the -*ārum* of the *ā*-stems (see above).

Dative and ablative. The Latin ending is traceable to the IE. instrumental in -*ōis*: Gk. ἵπποις, Skt. *açvāis*, etc. The original diphthong is still seen in Paelignian *suois cnatois*. Festus quotes an OL. *privicloes*. The other phonetic stages were -*eis* (*castreis*), -*ēs* (e.g. Praenestine *ueque = suisque*), and finally the -*īs* of Classical Latin.

The neuter nouns of the *o*-class exhibit the old nominative and

---

[1] See Professor T. Burrow, *The Sanskrit Language*.

accusative singular inflexion in -*m*. In the plural the ending -*a* is traced to a feminine collective singular in -*ā* (hence the Greek construction with a singular verb). In iambic words like *iŭgā* the regular shortening to *iŭgă* took place and this form of the inflexion was generalized.

Nouns in -*io*- (-*ius*) have dialect nominative singulars in -*is*: *Caecilis*, etc. The vocative singular appears as -*ī*: *fili* (note that *mī* goes back to an enclitic genitive **mei* or **moi*). Later forms, *filie*, etc., are analogical innovations. In the genitive -*iī* was contracted to -*ī*, but here, too, analogy restored the unity of the declension (the first example of -*iī* in a noun occurs in Propertius). The contraction in the locative singular and nominative and dative plural did not take place until -*ei* had progressed to -*ī*. Hence in Early Latin the locative -*iei* is clearly distinguished from the genitive -*ī*. The same is true of the nominative plural -*iei* and the dative and ablative plural -*ieis* where contraction could not take place until the change of *ei* > *ī*.

Phonetic developments were responsible for a series of doublets arising from the declension of the word **deiwos*. **deiwos* and **deiwom* regularly > **deios*, **deiom* > *deus*, *deum*: but where no -*o* followed, the *w* was preserved: e.g. *deiwī* > *dīvī*. From each of these phonetic variants a complete paradigm was created: *deus* and *dīvus*.

Nouns in -*ro*-*s* lose the -*o* by syncope and progress phonetically through the stages -*ŗs* > *ers* > *err* > *er*: whence *ager* < **agros*, *sacer* < **sacros*. The vocative **-ere* lost its final vowel but it was restored in vulgar speech: so Plautine, etc., *puere*.

The third declension

The endings of the third declension in Latin are the result of the pooling of the resources of the consonant stems on the one hand and the *i*-stems on the other. The following tabulation shows the original situation in IE:

	i-stems	consonant stems
Sing. N.	**owi-s*	*duc-s*
V.		
A.	**owi-m*	*dŭc-m̥*
G. ⎫ Abl. ⎬	**owei-s* or **owios*	*dŭc-es* or -*os*
Dat.	**owei-ei* or **owiei*	*dŭc-ei*

		i-stems	consonant stems
Plur.	N.	*owei-es*	duc-ĕs
	A.	*owi-ns*	duc-n̥s
	G.	*owi-ōm*	duc-ōm
	Dat. ⎫ Abl. ⎭	*owi-bhos*	duc-bhos

In the *i*-stems we must distinguish between the substantival declension with accented root, e.g. *ów-i-os*, and the adjectival declension with accented suffix, which assumes the full grade, *ow-ei-s*. The above declension incorporates forms from both series. Nouns with a suffixed -*i* play an important part in the derivational system of Indo-European.[1]

Consonant stems (for peculiarities of liquid stems see below).

Singular

Nominative *-s: *vōx, rēx, index*, etc. Note that the final dental plosive is assimilated: *pēs* < *pēd-s, ferēns* < *ferent-s*.

Accusative *-m̥ > -em*: *rēg-em, iūdicem*, etc.; cf. Gk. φύλακα.

Genitive *-es*, e.g. OL. *Apolones, Veneres*. -*es* > -*is* (p. 221). The ablaut grade *-os* (Gk. φύλακος, etc.) is found in provincial texts, especially in Praeneste and South Italy, until imperial times: e.g. *nominus, regus, Venerus, Diovos*.

Dative *-ei*. This still appears in Old Latin (e.g. *Apolonei, salutei, virtutei*); > Classical -*ī* according to p. 221 : *rēgī*, etc.

Ablative. There was no special ending for this case in Indo-European (except in the *o*-stems). The Lat. -*e* is traced to the locative in -*ĭ* (this survives as the Greek dative, e.g. φύλακι). In the *i*-stems a form -*īd* was developed on the model of -*ōd* (whence also -*ād*, see above). This ending -*īd* is also found occasionally in consonantal stems: e.g. *opid, coventionid*.

Locative. A few words have special locative forms characterized by an -*ī* drawn from the *o*-class: *rūrī, Carthāginī, temperī*.

Plural

Nominative. The original *-ĕs*, still preserved in Oscan, e.g. *humuns* (with loss of ĕ by syncope) = *hominēs*, was replaced in

---

[1] For further details see T. Burrow, *The Sanskrit Language*.

Latin by the -ēs which belonged properly to the *i*-stems (see below): *rēgēs*, etc.

Accusative *-n̥s (Gk. φύλακας with α < n̥) in Italic > *ens*, whence *ēs* according to p. 224: *vōcēs, rēgēs*, etc.

Genitive *-ōm (Gk. φυλάκων) proceeds regularly to *-ŏm* > *um*: e.g. *rēgum*, etc.

Dative and *ablative* *-bhos was originally added directly to the consonant of the stem, e.g. Skt. *vāg-bhyas*, from *vāc* = *vōx*. We should therefore expect *rēgbus. The *-i* of *rēg-i-bus*, etc., is borrowed from the *i*-nouns.

The nominative singular of the neuter nouns was the bare stem: e.g. *lac* < *lact. In the plural the evidence of Gk. φέροντα and Skt. *bharanti* suggests that the original ending was *-ə* (p. 216).[1] Latin, too, has *-ă* (e.g. *nomina*), but this cannot be directly equated with Skt. *nāmān-i* since there was an intermediate stage of this case ending of which some traces survived. Thus the word for 'thirty', *trīgintā* 'three sets of ten', shows the plural ending *-ā*, cf. Umbr. *trioper* 'thrice', and Osc. *petiro-pert* 'quater', where *-o* is traceable to Italic *-ā. We must conclude, therefore, that the IE. neuter plural ending *-ə* which would have yielded *-ă* in Latin was first replaced by the *-ā* of the *o*-stem neuters and that this was then shortened as described above.

Ablaut in the declension

The consonant stems in Indo-European often exhibit vowel gradation in the final syllable of the stem. We may distinguish the following types. Some plosive stems show a lengthened vowel in the nominative singular and the normal vowel in the other cases. Latin examples are *pēs*: *pĕdis, abiēs*: *abiĕtis, pariēs*: *pariĕtis*. In the main, however, Latin has carried through analogical levelling of the paradigms: e.g. *vōx, vōcis* (but note the denominative verb *vŏcare*).

Polysyllabic *s*-stems of masculine and feminine nouns show a similar alternation *Cerēs*: *Cerĕris, pubēs*: *pubĕris, arbōs*: *arbŏris*.

[1] This equation has been impugned by T. Burrow (*Trans. Phil. Soc.* 1949, p. 46). The neuter plurals vary considerably and may be comparatively recent. In Vedic and Hittite, forms with lengthened vowels occur (e.g. Hitt. *widār* 'waters') and such forms are sometimes extended by *-i*, seen in Hitt. *kururi*, (Skt. *nāmāni*). It may well be that *-i* is suffixal and parallels the laryngeal suffix *-H* which lies behind the collective *-ā* < *aH*. If this analysis is correct, *-ə* must disappear from the handbooks.

Here, too, analogical levelling is usual: *honōs, honōrem*, etc. Note that the intervocalic -*s* is rhotacized and the resulting -*r* form introduced into the nominative: *honor, arbor*, with regular shortening of *o* in a final syllable (pp. 221 f.). *Mulier*, too, seems to have arisen from **mulies*, for the derived adjective *muliebris* is traceable to **mulies-ris* (p. 230). The original *s*-stem of such nouns is frequently revealed in derivatives: e.g. *honestus* (with *e*-grade), *arbus-tum*.

Neuter *s*-stems show *o*-grade in the nominative singular and *e*-grade elsewhere: hence the type **genos*: **genes-es* > *genus*: *generis*. Here, too, analogical levelling takes place: e.g. *robur*, but note *robus* in Cato and further the derivative *robus-tus*; cf. *fulgur*, but *fulgus* in Old Latin (Festus).

Masculine and feminine *n*-stems, too, made the nominative singular by lengthening the stem vowel and in Indo-European the nasal then disappeared. The other cases show variously normal grade (e.g. Gk. φρήν, φρενός) or zero grade (Gk. ἀρήν, ἀρνός). Latin has only one example of the latter: *caro, carn-is*. Of the former *homo*: *hominis, ordo*: *ordinis* are typical examples. But in this type, too, analogical levelling has removed the ablaut alternations: *sermō*: *sermōnis, liēn*: *liēnis*. In the neuters Skt. *nāma*, *nāmnas* points to an original declension **nōm-n̥, *nōmn-e/os*, which in Latin would yield *nōmen, *nōmnis. nōmin-is*, etc., represent **nōmenis* with the -*en* carried throughout the declension.

In -*r* stems the nominative singular is formed by lengthening the stem vowel: e.g. Gk. πατήρ, but Lat. *patĕr* with regular shortening of the vowel. The normal grade originally occurred in the vocative and accusative singular and the nominative plural (Gk. πάτερ, πατέρα, ἀνέρες). In the other cases zero grade was the rule (Gk. πατρός, etc.). In Latin, however, the zero grade has been generalized everywhere except in the nominative case: *pater, patrem, patris*, etc. The nouns in -*tōr* also exhibited originally ablaut gradation, but the long vowel was generalized throughout the paradigm, with, of course, the regular shortening in the final syllable of the nominative singular.

i-stems

The ablaut variations of the stem vowel *ei*: *i* are shown in the above table.

R

Singular

Nominative *-s. The expected form appears in *hostis, ovis*, etc. In certain words, however, *monti-, parti-, morti, ponti-*, etc., the nominative appears as *mons, pars, mors, pons*, etc. Whether this is due to phonetic reasons (syncope) or to the influence of the consonant stems is difficult to decide. Syncope is certainly responsible for the change of *-ri-s* adjectives like *ācris* to *ācer*, which originally did duty for both masculine and feminine; but a distinct form for the feminine *ācris* was recreated. *pugil, vigil*, and *mugil* are regarded as *-i* stems despite the genitive plurals *pugilum, vigilum*, and *mugilum*. The loss of the final syllable is explained as an analogical formation after the genitive *pugil-is*, etc., or as a dialect phenomenon (cf. Osc. *aidil = aidilis*). Some *i*-stems have a nominative singular in *-ēs*: e.g. *aedēs, caedēs, famēs*, etc., where *ē* may represent the long grade *-ēi-s*.

Accusative. The old form *-im* is still preserved in certain words of a technical character, e.g. *sitim, tussim, puppim, restim* and in the adverbs *statim* and *partim*. But in general *i*-stems have adopted the *-em* of the consonant stems.

Genitive. *-eis would proceed to Lat. *-īs*. *-is* has been introduced from the consonant stems: *partis*, etc.

Dative. *-eiei proceeded regularly to *-eei > ēi*, the ante-consonantal form of which, *-ĕi*, forms the basis of the classical ending *-ī*: *partī, ovī*, etc.

Ablative. Here, too, Latin created a special case from *-īd* on the analogy of *-ōd, -ād*: e.g. OL. *loucarīd*, classical *partī*, etc. But in general the *-ĕ* of the consonant stems was substituted. On the introduction of this ending *-īd* into the consonant stems see above. Note that in the present participle *-ĕ* is used where the verbal function is predominant and *-ī* where it is adjectival.

Plural

Nominative. *-ei̯-ĕs regularly became *-ēs*: *partēs, ovēs*, etc.

Accusative *-i-ns > īs, which is the regular classical form: *partīs, civīs*, etc. The introduction of the *-ēs* of the consonant stems began at an early date but the change was not generally effected until imperial times.

Genitive *-i-ōm > -ium: *civium, partium*, etc.

Dative-Ablative *-*i-bhos* > -*ibus*: *civibus*, *partibus*.

The nominative-accusative of neuter *i*-stems was the bare stem, the final -*i* becoming -*e* (p. 221): *mari > *mare*; *dulci > *dulce*; *levi > *leve*. Certain substantivized adjectives in -*ri* and -*li* show loss of the final vowel: *animal*, *tribunal*, *exemplar*, *calcar*. The nominative-accusative plural ends in -*ia*, but in Indo-European this case was made by lengthening the stem vowel, perhaps from the contraction of *-*iə*-. This old ending survives in *trī-gintā*. Thus the -*ă* of Latin (and Greek) is presumably acquired from the -*ā* of the *o*-stems (see above). That this was of very early occurrence is shown by the isolated form *quiă* which is in origin the neuter plural accusative of the interrogative stem *qui-s*.

U-stems (the fourth declension)

The ablaut gradations of this class resemble those of the *i-stems*: *-*u-s*, *-*u-m*, *u-os* or *eu-s, *(*u*)*u-ei*, *[-*ūd*], *eu-es, *-*u-ns*, *-*u(u)ōm*, *-*u-bhos*. The following points call for comment. The genitive singular -*eu-s* proceeded regularly in Italic to -*ous* and thence to Lat. -*ūs*: *manūs*, etc. Certain sporadic analogical innovations appear: *domu-is*, *senatu-is* have the ending of the consonant class, while OL. *senatuos* shows the -*os* commented on above. We find, further, in vulgar speech the forms *senat-ī*, etc., with the ending of the *o*-stems. The dative in -*uī* (OL. *senatuei*) is traceable to *-(*u*)*u-ei* which was the IE. ending, or to *-*eu-ei*, a form of the dative case for which there are parallels in other languages. The dative in -*ū* was in origin a locative which in Indo-European had the bare stem in -*eu* (or perhaps -*ēu*). Latin created a separate form for the ablative singular in -*ū-d* (see above): *castūd*, *manū*, etc.

Plural

The nominative *-*eues* should have proceeded via *-*oues* (p. 215) to *-*uis*. The -*ūs* actually attested is traced by some scholars to a syncopated form *-*ou-s*, which has no parallels in the other noun classes. It is more likely that in the *u*-stems we have an interaction of the nominative and accusative plural ending, based on the accidental similarity of -*ēs* nominative and -*ēs* (accusative) of the consonant stems (see above). -*ūs* is, therefore, to be traced to the accusative plural ending where it was the regular product of

-*u-ns*. The genitive plural **manu̜-ŏm* > *manu̜-ŏm* > *manŏm* > *manum*: e.g. *passum, exercitum*. The disyllabic form -*uum* is due to the analogy of the *i*-stems: *civīs*: *civium*:: *manūs*: *manuum*. In the dative-ablative plural the expected -*u-bus* is occasionally found (*arcubus, quercubus*, etc.), but in general the -*i* of the *i*-stems has intruded: *manibus*, etc.

In the neuters the nominative-accusative singular -*ū* (*genū*) for the expected **genŭ* may be traced to old plural or dual forms. In the plural the IE. case form **-ū* has been replaced by -*ua*, with the -*a* of the *o*-stems which had now become the characteristic neuter plural case ending for the nominative and accusative cases.

The fifth declension

This inflexional class was organized by Latin out of a scratch collection of nouns. Some were verbal abstracts in -*iē* (alternating with -*ī*): *aciē-s, faciē-s, maciē-s*, etc.; others were denominative abstracts with by-forms in -*ia* (*luxuries*, etc.). Others again originated in stems ending in a long diphthong, **diēu-m* (see below on *Iuppiter*), **rēi-m* (Skt. *rā-m*, etc.). *spēs* was an old *s*-stem (cf. OL. *spēres* and the denominative verb *spērare*). *quiēs* is an old *i*-stem **qui-ei-*. There are, further, some nouns with divided loyalties, e.g. *famēs, lābēs*. In fact few nouns of this class have the full paradigm set out in the grammar books. We see the language in the process of creating by analogical processes a new declensional class of long vowel stems, but only *diēs* and *rēs* present the full paradigm.

The starting-point was the accusative **diēm* < **diēu-m* (see below), whence the nominative was formed, characterized by the usual -*s*: *diēs*.

The genitive singular of the -*iē*- stems was originally -*iē-s* and this appears occasionally in OL.: *rabiēs, diē-s*. But this ending was replaced by the -*ī* of the *o*-stems: *diē-ī* (note the various phonetic developments, *diei, diē, diī*). In the dative singular **rēi-ei* > **rēī* > *rēī* > *rei̯* > *re* (all the unstarred forms are attested). In the ablative we find the Italic -*d* form in Faliscan *foied* 'hodie'. Elsewhere it has disappeared: *diē*, etc.

Plural

rēs, nominative and accusative, proceeds regularly from **rēi̯es* and **rei̯-ns* respectively. The genitive has the -*rum* discussed above: *diē-rum*. The dative *-bus* is attached directly to the *ē*-stem: *diē-bus*.

Stems in *-ī* and *-ū*

All the nouns with original *ī*-stems joined the *i*-stems in Latin with the exception of *vī-s* which has a regular accusative and ablative *vǐ-m*, *vī* (the genitive *vī-s* occurs in Varro). In the plural it appears as an *s*-stem, *vīres*, on the analogy of other monosyllables like *mōs*: *mōres*; *spēs*: *spēres*.

sūs has its genitive *suis* by regular development from **suu̯es*. The rest of the declension has been recreated on a consonant stem *suv -*: *su-em* (for **sū-m*), etc. For *su-ibus* we also find *sǔ-bus*. Another form *sū-bus* is probably not a direct descendant of the IE. *sū-bhos*, but made under the influence of *bū-bus* (see below).

Diphthong stems

IE. **nāus* 'ship' was converted into an *i*-stem in Latin: *nāvis*. The word for 'cow', 'ox', **gʷōus* (Skt. *gāus*, Dor. Gk. βώς) had in Indo-European lost the second element of the diphthong in the accusative singular **gʷō-m*: Dor. Gk. βῶν, Skt. *gā-m*. From this a new nominative *bōs* was created in Osco-Umbrian whence the word was borrowed by the Romans (p. 37). In the other cases the stem appeared thus: **gʷow-es*, **gʷow-ei*, etc., whence *bovis*, *bovī*. The Latin declension was recreated around this form of the stem: *bovem*, *bovēs*, etc. In the dative and ablative plural *būbus* continues **gʷou-bhos*, *bōbus* has its vowel from the other cases or may be from a dialect in which *ou > ō*.

*dyēus has a similar history. The second element of the diphthong was lost in the accusative singular: **dyē-m* (Gk. Ζῆν, Skt. *dyām*). From this a new nominative was created *diēs* (see above). *Iu-piter* is an old vocative from **dyeu-pəter* = Gk. Ζεῦ πάτερ. In the oblique cases *dyew-es*, etc. > *Iovis* (p. 215 on *eu > ou*). This stem was generalized so that *Iovem* replaced the original *diem* which had been specialized in the meaning 'day'.

Some irregular nouns

A very ancient class of neuter nouns was characterized by *-r* in the nominative-accusative singular and by *-n* in the other cases.

Thus the word for *water* shows an *-r* generalized in English and German *Wasser* whereas an *-n* appears in Swedish *vatn*. In Gothic the declension is *wato, watins* (genitive singular). Greek has ὕδωρ like U. *utur*, while Sanskrit shows *-n* (e.g. genitive singular *ud-nás*). This type of declension appears strongly in Hittite paradigms, but elsewhere only scattered fragments survive. The clearest Latin example is *femur, feminis* 'thigh'. *iecur* 'liver' must similarly have had its genitive **iecines* (cf. Skt. *yaknás*), but a new analogical genitive was created, *iecoris*, and this blended with the older form to produce the classical form *iecinoris*. The same is true of *iter*, where the old **itinis* and the analogical **iteris* combined to produce *itineris*, whence in its turn a new nominative, *itiner*, was created.

iuvenis, despite its appearance, is not an *i*-stem as may be seen from the genitive plural *iuven-um* and the derived noun *iuven-cus*. It is, in fact, an *n*-stem: cf. Skt. *yúvā, yúvānam, yūnás*. The Latin nominative has been remade on the basis of the genitive *iuven-is*. The same is true of *canis*,[1] but here the facts of the declension are more complicated. From Gk. κύων, Skt. *çvā*, Lith. *šuõ* we can reconstruct the IE. nominative **ku(u)ō(n)*, the genitive being **kun-os* (Gk. κυνός, Skt. *çunás*). In Latin the stem would appear to have had a reduced grade **kuǝn*. Phonetic developments would have produced in Latin a declension of startling irregularity: **cō, *conem, *quanis*, etc. This was levelled out to *canem, canis*, etc., and a new nominative *canis* was created as in the case of *iuvenis*. The fact that it is not an *i*-stem appears clearly from the genitive plural *can-um*.

ADJECTIVES

The degrees of comparison

Comparative. Two suffixes are utilized in the IE. languages to form the adjective used in comparisons. One was *-ios* (with lengthened grade *-iōs* and zero grade *-is-*), to which may be added another suffix *e/o n* (as in Gk. *-ιων* < **-is-ōn-*). This form of the adjective did not originally mean 'more': the suffix denoted that the quality designated by the root was present in some undefined degree: **mag-ios* meant 'biggish', whence, according to the context, the meanings 'rather big', 'too big', etc., emerged.

---

[1] *canēs* in Old Latin (Varro, *L.L.* 7. 32).

With the case of comparison (see Syntax, p. 300) the meaning 'rather big judged from a particular standard' progressed to 'bigger than'. The suffix was not attached to the stem of the positive, which had 'absolutive' sense: *mag-nus* 'big' as opposed to *mag-ịos* 'biggish'; cf. *nequam*: *nequior*; *senex*: *senior*. In other words the comparative is formed from a different root: *bonus*: *mel-ịos*. *minus* is, properly speaking, not a comparative at all, but a neuter substantive **minụos* of which *minuere* is the denominative verb.

The nominative case has lengthened grade which, as with *honōs*, etc., was generalized through the declension, intervocalic -*s*- becoming regularly -*r*-, which was then extended to the nominative singular: **maiōs*, **maiōsem*, etc. > *maiŏr*, *maiōrem*. The neuter singular *maius* is the regular product of **maịos* < **mag-ios* (p. 222).

The other comparative suffix, -*tero*, was originally attached to the second of contrasting pairs (e.g. Gk. δεξιός: ἀρισ-τερός). It was contrastive and separative in function. This is still apparent in the adverb *inter*, which is the contrastive-separative form of *in*: e.g. *inter-ficio* 'set apart, do away with', *inter-dico* 'mark off, put in an excluded class', *inter-eo*, etc. This suffix, which appears in Engl. *other*, *further*, etc., was used in Latin to denote contrasting pairs, *dexter*, *alter*, *uter*, *mater-tera* (as opposed to *amita*). In a few words it is combined with the -*is*- just discussed: *sin-is-ter*, *mag-is-ter*, *min-is-ter*.

The superlative also exhibits two suffixes originally different in function. -*to*- appears in the ordinal numerals (see below), where it denoted the member which completes a given group: its function was completive (so Benveniste). This was combined with -*is*- to produce the suffix -*isto*- exemplified in the English *sweetest* (Gk. ἥδιστος). Latin, however, has preferred the suffix -*mo* (-*ẹmo*- in certain phonetic environments), the original function of which (so Benveniste has suggested) was to denote the extreme member of a group: that is, it had originally spatial reference as in *summus* (**sup-mo-s*) 'topmost', *dēmus*, *infimus*, *prīmus* (**prīs-mo-s*). In *suprēmus*, *extrēmus* the suffix has been added to old instrumental forms (see below on adverbs). The suffix -*mo*- was combined with -*to*- in *intimus*, *ultimus*, *extimus*, *optimus*.

Another extended form of the suffix is -*simus*, where the s has a variety of origins: (1) *-t-t̥mo-* > *-ssimo-* (e.g. *pessimos* < **ped-t̥mo-*); (2) possibly syncopated forms of the *-is-* suffix. The most characteristic form of the Latin superlative suffix, *-is-simo-*, arose from the combination of *-is-* with *-s̥mo-*. When attached to noun stems ending in *-r* and *-l*, this suffix was obscured by phonetic changes: **facil-s̥mo-s* > *facillimus* (p. 231 on *-ls-*), **acri-s̥mo-s* > **acr̥s-samos* > *acers-samos (p. 223) > *acerrimus*; similarly *pulcherrimus* < **pulchro-s̥mos*.

No completely satisfactory solution has been offered of *plūs*, *plūrimus*. It is evident that these forms are related to the adjectives meaning 'much' in other languages (e.g. Gk. πολύς) which are formed from the root *pel 'fill' (Lat. *plē-nus*). The comparative stem *plē-yes-*, *plē-is*, which appears in Gk. πλεῖν (accusative) and superlative πλεῖστος, provides a satisfactory basis **pleis-̥mo-* for the OL. *plīsima* preserved by Festus. On the other hand, we have a neuter substantive from the same root *plewes (Hom. πλέος), which may be the basis of the OL. *plous*, so that Classical Latin *plūs* is no more a comparative in origin than its opposite *minus*. The true comparative *plē-yōs may lie behind the *pleores* of the *Carmen Arv.*, though the rhotacization suggests that the traditional form has been partially modernized.[1] We may then tentatively restore the following state of affairs: **plēyōs- *plē-is-̥mo* which would have produced Latin *pleōr- plūrimo-*. In the event the neuter substantive *plous* (frequently pairing with *minus*) replaced the comparative and then affected the form of the superlative: hence *plūs*, *plūrimus*. The *ploirume* of *CIL* i.[2] 9 may be regarded merely as one more instance of a favourite method of archaizing simply by the substitution of *oi* for the classical *ū* (see p. 217).

PRONOUNS

We must distinguish two groups: (1) the demonstratives and the relative-interrogative-indefinite stems, and (2) the personal pronouns.

(1) have *e/o* and *ā* stems respectively for masculine and feminine genders while the neuter singular, nominative and accusative, ends

---

[1] Festus, too, has modernized *pleisima to *plīsima*.

in -*od* (> *ud*): e.g. *is-te*, *is-ta*, *is-tud*. In the genitive and dative singular they have forms common to all genders: -*īus*, -*ī*.[1]

In many languages demonstratives tend to assume strengthened forms either by the combination of different demonstrative stems or by the attachment of deictic elements (what we may term the 'that-there', 'this-here' phenomenon). Latin illustrates both these processes. *is-tud* is a compound of the anaphoric stem *i*- and the demonstrative **tod*. *ille* has replaced an older *olle* which unites *ol* (cf. *ul-tra*, *ōl-im*) and the stem -*se* (see below). The chief deictic particles attached to pronoun stems are -*ce* and -*i* (see below on *hic*, *istuc*, etc.).

The inflexion of the genitive singular -*īus* (Plautus often scans *ēius*, implying a pronunciation *eįius*, which is also indicated by inscriptional EIIVS, etc.) has no parallel in other languages. In Indo-European the form was *e-syo* (Skt. *asya*), and it has been suggested that to this form Latin added the -*s* of the usual genitives (see above), **esyos* proceeding regularly to *eiius*. So, too, *huius* < **gho-syo-s*, *cuius* < **quo-syo-s* (cf. Skt. *kásya*). Other scholars would trace the form to *cuius*, which is an adjective in -*ios* still surviving in Plautus' *quoius*. This was incorporated in the declension (on the genitive as the adjectival case see below, pp. 290 ff.). The other pronominal genitives were simply modelled on *quoius*. From *quoius* analysed as *quoi-us* a stem *quoi*- was extracted which, with the addition of the usual dative ending, produced *quoiei* (so Old Latin), Plautus' *quoiī* and *quoi*. This last is the classical form, the spelling *cui* making its first appearance in Augustan times. Of the other inflexions only the genitive plural requires comment. -*rum* is to be traced to the feminine forms which in Indo-European had **-ā-sōm* (e.g. Skt. *tāsām*). Masculine -*ōrum* is an analogical innovation since Indo-European had **-oi-sōm* (Skt. *tēṣām*, *kēṣām* = (*is*)-*tōrum*, *quōrum*).

hic

The stem is **ghe/o, ghā-* (p. 229), to which the particle -*ce* is added. The masculine singular shows -*i*- in Plautus' *hĭc*, and this was remade to *hicc* on the analogy of the neuter *hocc* < **hod+ce*. The *i*-stem also appears in inscriptional plural forms *heis*, *heisce*,

[1] On the vulgar feminine form *illae*, etc., see p. 163.

Plautus' *hīsce*. Elsewhere the stem appears as *ho-*, *hā-*, which with the attachment of *-ce* (often in Old Latin in the full form) provides the familiar classical declension of this pronoun: *hom-ce*, *hām-ce*, *hod-ce* > *hunc*, *hanc*, *hoc(c)*. Note that Old Latin had not yet introduced the artificial distinction between *hae* (feminine plural < *hā-ī*) and *haec* (neuter plural < *ha+ī+ce*). On the genitive and dative singular see above. The ablative singular forms *hōc*, *hāc* < *hōd+ce*, *hād+ce*.

ille

ille is a modification of OL. *olle* (cf. *ul-trā*, *ōl-im*) under the influence of *is*, *iste*, *ipse*. *olle* is a combination of *ol* and *se/o* (see below). Forms with adjectival inflexion are also attested: *ollus*, *olla*. The deictic particles are occasionally attached: *illaec*, *illuc*, *illunc*, etc. The nominative plural occurs in the form *illisce* in Plautus (cf. *heisce*, etc., above). On the genitive and dative singular see above.

iste

This is another compound demonstrative only the second part of which is declined. Here, too, the deictic particles may be added: nominative singular masculine *istic*, feminine *istaec*, neuter *istuc*, etc. The genitive normally has the ending *-īus* (see above), but there is a form *istī* (with the usual ending of an *o*-stem) which appears in *istimodi*. OL. *istīs* (Plt.) is probably not a syncopated form of *istius* but *isti* + the genitival *-s*.

is

This stem, used in Indo-European in correlation with the relative pronoun, appears in the ablaut grades *i/ei*. The weak grade appears in the nominative masculine and neuter, *i-s*, *i-d*, while the expected accusative *im* occurs in the Twelve Tables. In a by-form of the nominative a particle *-om* was attached to the full grade: *eᵢ-om* (Skt. *ayam*), and this was used in Latin as the masculine singular accusative, *eᵢom* > *eum*, whence a new stem *eᵢo-* was created with a corresponding feminine *eᵢā-*. In the nominative plural masculine *eioi* regularly > *eiei* > *ei* > *ī*. The dissyllabic *eī* was remade on the analogy of *eum*, etc. Here, too, we find nominatives in *-s*: *īs*, *eis*, *eeis*, and *īeis*. The dative and ablative plural forms attested are the expected products of *eiois, *eiais, i.e. eis, īs, with the dissyllabic restorations eeis, ieis, etc. OL. ībus appears to be the expected product of *ei-bhos (Skt. ebhyás). On the genitive and dative singular see above.

To this stem a particle -em was attached: the nominative neuter singular id-em, being falsely analysed, produced a particle dem. This was added to is, eā, etc., producing īdem, eādem, etc. On the adverbs ibi, etc., see below.

so-, to-

Indo-European possessed a demonstrative pronoun *so, *sā, *tod, which yielded inter alia Gk. ὅ ἡ τό(δ). Ennius has the accusative forms som, sam, sōs, sās, which may belong here, while to- appears in tum, topper (< *tod-per), etc. sī(c), too, belongs here: it is the locative form *sei(ce).

ipse

In the Old Latin forms eumpsum, eampsam we find a combination of the stem eio- with som, sam (the p is a glide consonant as in sumpsi < sum-si). This som, sam is probably distinct from the above and goes back to the reflexive *suos. From the accusative forms a stem -pso -psā was extracted which appears in nominative feminine eapsa, masculine ipsus, etc. The latter was assimilated to iste and ille and so gave rise to the normal declension ipse, ipsa, ipsum. Note that the assimilation of the neuter ipsud to illud, etc., does not occur until late in the history of Latin. On the vulgar isse, issa, see p. 159.

Interrogative—Indefinite—Relative

The interrogative-indefinite stem of Indo-European had the form qui- quei- which was the same for all three genders: quis, quid. The expected accusative *quim acquired the -em of the consonant stems (see above). The instrumental quī still persists as an adverb, while the nominative plural *quei-es gave rise to the quēs of the Senatus Consultum de Bacchanalibus. The neuter plural quia was preserved only as a conjunction. The dative-ablative plural quibus was retained as a feature of the regular declension.

A corresponding relative stem quo- qua- was made in Italic. The masculine (*quoi* > *quei* > *quī*) and the feminine (*quae*) exhibit the deictic particle -*i*. *quod* shows the usual -*d* of the neuters. In the accusative *quom* persists only as a conjunction and was replaced by *quem* (above). On the genitive (*quoius*, etc.) and dative singular see above. The plural forms are regular products of **quoi*, **quai*, *quāi*, etc. Nom. pl. -*quās* is dialectal for *quae* (see p. 241). A by-form *quīs* in the dative-ablative plural continues **quois*, **quais*.

THE PERSONAL PRONOUNS

ego, *tu* are inherited IE. forms (Gk. ἐγώ, τύ, σύ). An extended form in -*om* appears in Gk. ἐγών, Skt. *ahám*,[1] and this is the basis of Lat. *egom-et* from which, by false analysis, a suffix -*met* was extracted: e.g. *mihi-met*, etc. In the accusative *mē*, *tē* continue IE. accented forms (Greek has unaccented με, σε). In Indo-European enclitic forms **moi*, **mei*, **toi*, **tei* were used in the functions of genitive, dative, and locative. Extended by the addition of genitival -*s*, **mei-s*, **tei-s* were the basis of OL. *mīs*, *tīs*. The classical *meī* and *tuī* were drawn from the possessive adjectives. *mihī* and *tibī* go back to **meghei*, **tebhei* (Umbr. *mehe*, *tefe*). Sanskrit shows the same consonants in the inflexion *mahyam*, *tubhyam*, but these forms presuppose IE. **meghi*, **tubhi*, with an added particle possibly related to the -*om* of **eg-om*. In the ablative Indo-European had **měd* unaccented and **mēd* accented. Sanskrit preserves the former (*măt*); the latter appears in OL. *mēd* (cf. *tēd* < **tu̯ēd*). These forms are to be distinguished from the Old Latin accusative forms *měd*, *tēd* where the added particle -*d* is of obscure origin. It is difficult to believe that there was confusion between accusative and ablative, or that the -*d* comes from the neuter pronouns.

The forms of the reflexive pronoun closely resemble the above. *sē(d)* < **su̯ē* (Gk. ἕ continues the short unaccented form). The genitive *suī* is drawn from the possessive adjective. *sĭbĭ* < **sebhei* with assimilation of *e* to *i* and iambic shortening as with *mihĭ*, *tĭbĭ* above. Ablative *sē-d*, too, parallels *mēd* and *tēd*.

nōs and *vōs* are inherited accented forms corresponding to the unaccented Skt. *nas*, *vas*. *nostrum* and *vestrum* are genitive plurals of *noster* and *vester*. *nostri* and *vestri*, the corresponding singular

---

[1] The aspirated consonant suggests the analysis **egH-om*.

forms, were used specially as the 'objective' genitive and first appear in Terence. Latin remade the dative and ablative by attaching the inflexion *-bhei* to the stems *nō-, vō-* extracted from *nōs* and *vōs*. To **nōbhei* and **vōbhei* an *-s* was added on the analogy of the common inflexion in *-bus*.

The possessive adjectives were formed by the addition of thematic *-o-* to the pronominal stems, **mei̯-o-s* > *meus*; **teu̯-o-s* (Gk. τεϝός) > OL. *tovos* > *tuus*; **seu-os* (Gk. ἑϝός) > *sovos* (e.g. Old Latin dat.-abl. plur. *soveis*) > *suus*. In the plural the contrastive suffix *-ter(o)* was added to the short forms *nŏs, vŏs*. OL. *voster* changed to *vester* (p. 216). The vocative singular masculine *mī* is traceable to the enclitic genitive **mei* discussed above.

THE NUMERALS

Cardinals

On *ūnus* < **oino-* see p. 217. The root **sem* (whence Gk. εἷς, μία, ἕν) appears in *sem-el, sim-plex, sin-guli*, and *sem-per*.

duō (*duŏ* by iambic shortening) is an inherited form < **IE. duu̯ō(u)*. This numeral had originally the inflexions of the dual, of which the following have been preserved in Latin: accusative plural masculine *duo* (Plt.); neuter *duo*. The plural endings *duōs, duom*, and *duōrum* and dative-ablative *duōbus* and, further, the whole set of feminine forms *duae*, etc., are innovations, for originally *duō* was both masculine and feminine. *ambō* is another inherited form (Gk. ἄμφω).

trēs (masculine and feminine) is the regular product of **trei̯es* (Gk. τρεῖς, Skt. *trayas*).

The word for 'four' shows vowel gradation with generalization of different forms in different IE. dialects. Latin *quattuor* is traced to **qʷe̯tuores* with a reduced vowel in the first syllable and the *o*-grade characteristic of the nominative in the second syllable (cf. Dor. τέτορες). Latin has discarded the inflexions and made this numeral indeclinable. There is no convincing explanation of the form *quadru-* used in compounds.

On *quīnque* < Italic *qʷenqʷe* < IE. **penqʷe* see p. 225.

sex could continue either **seks* or **sweks*: Gk. ἕξ, ϝέξ.

On *septem* < **septm̥* (Gk. ἑπτά) see p. 224.

octō < **oktō(u)* is a dual form of a word meaning 'a set of four fingers' (preserved in Avestan *ašti* 'four fingers' breadth').

novem is from **new-ṇ* (cf. *nōnus*, Engl. *nine*). The expected **noven* was transformed under the influence of *septem* and *decem*.

The numerals from 20 to 90 are derived from a noun stem **(d)kṃti-* meaning 'a set of ten'. The dual is seen in *vī-gintī*, where *vī-* (cf. Dor. *ϝί-κατι*) may be a congener of the Skt. adverb *vi* 'apart'. The remaining numerals of the group preserve the neuter plural in *-ā* (see pp. 243 f.). *trī-* and *quadrā-*[1] are neuter plurals and the *-ā* was extended by analogy to *quinquāgintā, sexāgintā, septuāgintā, nonāgintā. octōginta* possibly replaced **octuāgintā* (cf. Gk. ὀγδο(ϝ)ήκοντα), which influenced the form of *septuāgintā*.

On *centum* < **(d)kṃtom* see p. 224.

The numerals 200 to 900 are simply compounds of the cardinal numerals 2 to 9 and *centum*. Originally indeclinable they were treated in Latin as numerical adjectives. *ducenti, trecenti, sescenti* preserved the *c* which was voiced in *nōngenti, (*novem-genti), quīngenti,* whence also the *-ingentī* of *quadringenti, septingenti, octingenti*.

Indo-European does not appear to have possessed a word for 'thousand' and Lat. *mille* has no congeners.

Ordinals

The ordinals exhibit the suffixes *-to-* and *-mo-* discussed under the comparison of adjectives.

prīmus < **prīs-mo-s*, the superlative of *prius*.

secundus is a verbal adjective (see gerundive), of the verb *sequor*: < **seqʷondo-s*.

tertius < **trityos*, via **tṛtyos* (p. 223).

quartus. The original form appears to have been **qʷtru-tós* with the zero grade of the numeral (cf. Osc. *trutum* = *quartum*). The Latin word may be based on **qʷatwor-tos*, in which the full form of the cardinal numeral had been restored, with loss by haplology of the first dental. Praenestine retains the expected contraction *quorta*, which Latin further transformed to *quartus* under the influence of the cardinal form.

---

[1] The *d* is unexplained.

quīntus (< **quinqᵘtos*) and *sextus* show the suffix *-to*.

septimus and *octāvus* (on *ōv* > *āv* see p. 216) and *decimus* are adjectives made by adding the thematic *-o-* to the cardinal. This same type of formation is seen in **novenos*, which would regularly have produced **nūnus*, but the vowel quality *ō* was preserved under the influence of *novem*.

The ordinal 'twentieth' is formed by the addition of the suffix *-tₑmo* (see superlatives): *vī-kṃt-tₑmo* > **vīcenssimos* (for *t-t* > *ss* see p. 232) > *vīcēsimus*.

The multiplicative numeral adjectives are compounds in which the second element is either (1) *plo-* from the root *plē-* 'fill' (*duplus*, *triplus*, etc.), or (2) *plek-* from the root meaning 'fold' (*simplex*, *duplex*, etc.). Of the corresponding adverbs *semel* contains the numeral *sem-* but the suffix is unexplained. *bis* (**dṵis*), *ter* (**tris*), *quater* (**qᵘatrus*) contain an adverbial *-s*. The ending *-iēns* appearing in other adverbs of this class probably originated in the pronominal derivatives *quotiens*, *totiens*, in which, on the evidence of Sanskrit equivalents, we may isolate a suffix **-iṇt-* > Latin **-ient-*. This, combined with the adverbial *-s* just discussed, would produce *-iēns*.

The distributive numeral adjectives, apart from the isolated *singulus* (< **sem-gₑlo*), are formed with the suffix *-n-* from the multiplicative adverbs: **dṵis-noi* > *bīnī*, **tris-noi* > *ternī* (with *ter* restored for the expected phonetic development **trīnī*).

THE VERB

Inflexions

Active

The inflexions of the IE. verb were primarily concerned with the indication of person, which includes the category of number (singular and plural). Thus *-m*, *-s*, *-t* represented the first, second, and third persons singular, and *-me/o*, *-te*, and *-(e/o)nt* the corresponding plural forms. At some stage in Indo-European a particle *-i* was added to indicate 'here and now'. Hence arose the distinction between primary and secondary endings with time references to present and past respectively: *-mi* : *-m*, *-ti* : *-t*, *-nti* : *-nt*. The particle *-i*, it may be presumed, was originally optional: it does not appear

in the 'we' and 'ye' forms of the verb and it is doubtful whether
-si of the second person singular can be attributed to Indo-
European.

A further distinction we have to make is between thematic and
athematic forms of the verb. In verbal paradigms like *bhero-mes,
*bhere-te, *bhero-nti, etc., the stem which appears when the in-
flexion is removed is found to end in a vowel -e/o. This stem-forming vowel is called the thematic vowel. Other verbs like *ei-mi,
*i-mes, where the stem lacks this vowel, are called athematic verbs.
This apparently trivial distinction is of fundamental importance
in IE. verbal morphology, for the two classes of verbs are distinct
inter alia in their ways of forming the different moods (see below).
In the inflexions, however, it is only in the first person singular
active that there is any distinction : -ō is primary thematic and -mi
primary athematic.

Middle

Indo-European distinguished two 'voices'. In the 'active' the
verbal action was directed outwards from the 'ergative' subject
(see Syntax, p. 285). In the 'middle' the action was conceived as
operating in or on the subject : the action takes place in the person
of the subject, to the interest of the subject, etc. Thus verto 'I turn'
(something) contrasts with vertor 'the turning takes place in me';
πορίζω 'I provide', πορίζομαι 'I provide for myself, procure'. Thus
the middle forms of the verb, as denoting inter alia those actions
which take place in the person of the subject, were used also to
express the passive, for which there was no separate morphological
expression in Indo-European. The inflexions of the middle were
created by the addition of various particles to the primitive personal endings and it is likely here, too, that the temporal distinction between primary and secondary was a later development in
the history of Indo-European. The only IE. middle endings relevant to a study of Latin inflexions are -so, -to, -nto, which appear in
Greek as the secondary middle endings of second and third persons
singular and third person plural respectively, contrasting with the
primary -sai -tai, -ntai. The perfect tense had in the singular a
set of endings distinct from the above: -a, -tha, -e. We may now
proceed to an examination of the Latin verbal inflexions.

First person singular

Primary. The athematic -*mi* is preserved only in *sum*, where the
-*i* has been lost. Elsewhere the originally thematic -*ō* has been
generalized: *eo, fero, amo, moneo*. The same ending is found in the
future *-bhō* (p. 271). Lat. *ero* is an old subjunctive *esō* (p. 271).
Secondary. Latin preserves -*m*: *amabam, ferebam, amaveram,*
etc. This ending also appears in the forms of the subjunctive and
optative: *amem, regam, siem*, etc.

Second person singular

Owing to the loss of final -*i* there is no distinction between primary and secondary forms in Latin: *ducis, amas, eras, amabas, sies,*
etc. Plautus' *ess* is often equated with Homeric ἐσσί. But there is
evidence of an older form in Homer, εἰς, which is merely a way of
indicating a long syllable ἐσ-ς. This more ancient form received an
-*i* under the influence of ἐστί: ἐσσί. Plautus' *ess* may, therefore, be
equated with the more archaic Homeric form. It is doubtful
whether, in fact, Indo-European had evolved a separate primary
form for the second person singular any more than it had for the
plural.

Third person singular

Old Latin still distinguished primary -*t* (< *-*ti*) from secondary
-*d* (< *-*t*, p. 225); e.g. *esed, feced, sied*. The same distinction appears
in Osco-Umbrian: *fust* 'erit', *fusíd* 'foret'. In classical Latin the
primary -*t* was generalized: *dedit, fecit, siet, esset*, etc.

First person plural

There is no trace of the secondary *-mo* in Latin, which has
generalized *-mos* > -*mus*: *ducimus, ducebamus, duximus*, etc. A
different ablaut grade *-me* appears in Dor. Gk. φέρομες, etc.

Second person plural

Latin -*tis* is from *-tes*, in which the -*s* of the corresponding singular form has been added to the *-te* seen in Gk. φέρετε, etc.

Third person plural

Osco-Umbrian distinguished between primary -*nt* < *-nti* (e.g.
sent = *sunt*) and secondary -*ns* < *-nt* (e.g. *deicans* = *dicant, sins*

s

= *sint*). Latin has only -*nt*, from the generalized primary *-*nti*, of which the only direct evidence is the doubtful *tremonti* of the *Carmen Saliare* (No. 53). The extended endings -*nont* seen in archaic *danunt, explēnunt, redīnunt, nequīnont* are unexplained. If the -*n* is a stem-forming suffix (p. 267), it is difficult to explain why it should appear only in this person. Possibly these inflexions arose from dialect forms in which the final -*t* was dropped (e.g. *dedron* = *dederont*). Then *dan*, *explen*, etc., lacking the characteristic -*nt*, were extended by the usual -*ont*.

Medio-passive voice

In Italic and Celtic the inflexions of the medio-passive voices are characterized by an -*r* which is lacking in Greek, Sanskrit, Germanic, etc. This -*r* may be equated in the first place with the ending which in Osco-Umbrian distinguishes the impersonal passive: e.g. *fera-r* = 'there must be a carrying, one should carry', a type which is also found in Old Irish. This corresponds to the impersonal passive use such as Lat. *pugnatur* 'a fight is going on'. Thus the Latin forms -*tur*, -*ntur*, etc. may be explained as the combination of the middle inflexions with the -*r* of the impersonal. The relationship of this formant to the -*r*- which appears in a variety of functions in the verbal paradigms of other IE. languages (Indo-Iranian, Phrygian and Armenian, Tocharian, and Hittite) is unclear. It is possible that the plain *r*-forms of Italic and Celtic are in origin verbal nouns which merely named the action.

First person singular. In -*or* (OL. -*ōr*) the -*r* has simply been added to the primary thematic ending -*ō*. Elsewhere it is added to the verbal stem: *amer, regar, amabar*, etc.

Second person singular. The earlier Latin form is -*re* which has developed regularly from the middle secondary ending -*so* (p. 221): thus *sequere* apparently = Gk. ἕπεο (*seqʷe-so*). In forms other than the imperative an -*s* was attached on the analogy of the active *-es*: *sequere-s* > *sequeris*. In the occasional dialect forms *spatiarus, utarus*, the -*s* must have been attached to -*so* before the development of final -*o* to -*e*.

Third person singular. -*tur* arose from the attachment of -*r* to the secondary middle -*to*.

First person plural. -*mur* < secondary -*mo*+*r*.

Second person plural. The forms in *-minī* are usually explained as nominatives of the middle present participle used in periphrases such as **feromenoi (este)* (Gk. φερόμενοί ἐστε). From this a suffix *-minī* was extracted and applied to the various verbal stems: *regebāminī*, etc. This is improbable, and other scholars would trace it to infinitives in *-menai* which were used imperatively. Since the form is identical with that of the imperative mood it will be more appropriately discussed below.

Third person plural. *-ntur* arose from the addition of *-r* to the secondary middle inflexion *-nto*.

On the inflexions of the perfect see pp. 274 f. For the imperative see pp. 276 f.

FORMATION OF THE VERBAL STEMS

The tense stems

The student of Greek soon finds that he must distinguish three tense stems: e.g. present λειπ-, aorist λιπ-, and perfect λε-λοιπ- (corresponding to our own *drive, drove, driven*, see pp. 233 ff.). He learns further that these stems, except in the indicative, have no temporal reference but relate to the type of action, the so-called present stem representing *continuing action* (the durative stem), the aorist stem (λιπ-) representing momentary action, and the perfect (λε-λοιπ-) representing the state resulting from an action. Thus the present stem θνῄσκειν means 'to be in the process of dying', θανεῖν 'to expire', and τεθνάναι 'to be dead'. This, the prevalent school grammar-book doctrine, needs modification only in one point— the *stem* as such has no temporal reference even in the indicative, the reference to the past being contained in the prefixed augment and the secondary inflexions. Thus from one and the same durative stem λεγε/ο we may form a present tense λέγω and a past ἔ-λεγο-ν. These different representations of verbal action, durative, aoristic, and perfect, by the different 'tense' stems are known as the 'aspects' of the verb. The situation in Greek reflects that of Indo-European. The description of the function of the 'present' stem as 'durative', however, as opposed to the aoristic as 'momentary' does not cover all the facts. In the *Phaedo* of Plato, for instance, Socrates' friends are waiting outside the prison after the sentence of death has been passed. The warder invites them to enter and 'we found Socrates just relieved of his shackles'. Here the verb translated 'found' is καταλαμβάνειν which means 'catch', 'overtake', 'surprise'. The action referred to is clearly momentary, yet Plato uses the durative form κατελαμβάνομεν. This is merely one of many examples which suggest that the essential difference between the 'present' and the 'aorist' aspects is not between continuing and momentary action but rather that the durative stem has greater directness and vividness: it brings the event before the eyes in progress as in a news-reel. We may call it the 'eyewitness aspect' or the 'aspect of presentation'. The aorist, on the other hand, contains a colourless reference to the event as a unit of history. One and the same event, however momentary, may be presented as taking place before our eyes, κατελαμβάνομεν 'there we were surprising Socrates', or κατελάβομεν 'we found Socrates'. In the same way θνῄσκειν brings us into the presence of the death agony, θανεῖν records the fact of death, and τεθνάναι the state of death.

In Latin the three aspects of the IE. verb were reduced to two, for the verbal system shows a contrast only between the *infectum* and the *perfectum*, the latter combining the functions of the original aorist and the perfect. For each of these two aspects a complete tense system, present, past, and future, was developed: *dico, dicam, dicebam: dixi, dixero, dixeram.* Our exposition of the Latin tense systems thus falls into two parts: the formation of the stems (1) of the infectum and (2) of the perfectum.

Stems of the infectum

It will be convenient to begin by exemplifying some of the main morphological devices whereby Indo-European formed the progressive ('eyewitness') aspect. We choose those chiefly relevant to Latin.

I. Root stems which may be either (a) athematic, e.g. *ei-mi*, or (b) thematic, *deik-ō*. The athematic type shows ablaut alternations, the full grade appearing in the singular and the weak grade in the plural: e.g. *ei-mi*, *i-mᵉ/ós*.

Latin still has some traces of the athematic type, e.g. *ī-s, ī-t* (< *ei-s, *ei-ti*); *volt, vult* < *uel-ti*; *vī-s*, from the root *uei* 'wish'; *ēs, ēst* < *ed-s, *ed-ti* 'eat'; *fer-s, fer-t*, < *bher-s*, *bher-ti; for *es 'to be' see p. 269. But most Latin root stems are of the thematic type dūco, dīco, etc.

II. Stems showing reduplication. These, too, are divided into (a) athematic and (b) thematic, where (a) again exhibit ablaut gradation as in Gk. τί-θη-μι: τί-θε-μεν, δί-δω-μι: δί-δο-μεν. In the thematic reduplicated type the root normally appears in the zero grade: e.g. gi-gn-o (root *gen), sīdo < *si-zd-ō (root *sed), sero < *si-s-ō (root* sē/sə cf. sē-vi, să-tus).

III. Stems with an infixed nasal: e.g. iu-n-go (root *yeug/yug), li-n-quo (root *leiqʷ/liqʷ), scindo, rumpo.

IV. Stems with a nasal suffix: e.g. Gk. κάμ-ν-ω, δάκ-ν-ω, Lat. cer-n-o (*krinō), ster-no, si-no (perfect sī-vī), pello < *pel-nō, tollo < *tḷ-nō (cf. perfect tuli).

V. Inchoative verbs in -skō: Gk. βάσκω, Lat. posco (< pṛk, zero grade of prek+sko). This type is also found with reduplication: γι-γνώ-σκω. The Lat. gnōsco may also come from a reduplicated form. Phonetic developments have obscured disco < *di-dk-sko, with the zero grade of the root found in dec-et, doc-eo.

VI. Of great importance is the suffix -ye/yo. (i) This may be attached to a verbal root: e.g. spec-io (root in the normal grade), venio (root in the zero grade *gʷm̥-yō: cf. βαίνω). The suffix may also be added to already characterized present stems: vinc-io. (ii) With the aid of this suffix verbs are formed from nouns ('denominative' verbs). When attached to a vowel stem, the intervocalic -y- is lost. Hence we get the following types:

(a) from ā-stems: fugo, fugāre < *fugā-yō; (b) from e/o stems: albeo, audeo (from avidus); (c) from i-stems: finio; (d) from u-stems, metuo; (e) from consonant stems, custodio. From the denominatives albeo, etc., we must distinguish (1) the causative verbs in -éyō attached to the o-grade of the root as in moneo, doceo, torreo, etc., and (2) the presents expressing a state made by the attachment of a suffix -ē (used to form Greek aorist passives like ἐ-μάνη-ν) to the verbal root: e.g. vĭdēre, tacēre, iacēre (as opposed to the transitive iac-io), etc.

These manifold stem-formations were organized by Latin into the four conjugations familiar from the school grammar-books.

The first conjugation consists largely of -yo denominatives modelled on the type *fuga, fugāre*. Apart from these we find a few athematic verbs from roots ending in a long *ā*: *fāri* (cf. *fātum*, Dor. Gk. *φā-μί*). *stāre*, too, may be of this type. The irregular verbs of this conjugation like *domāre, sonāre*, with the perfects *domui, sonui* are formed from dissyllabic roots, **domā, *sonā*, with the suffix -*ye/yo*. The weak grades of these roots **domə, *sonə* appear in the -*to* participle (p. 280): *domitus, sonitus*.

The second conjugation comprises (1) athematic verbs with roots ending in -*ē*, e.g. *plēre, flēre*; (2) the *ye/yo*-denominatives from *e/o* stems; (3) the causatives of the type *moneo*; and (4) the *ē*-formations, originally intransitive, exemplified by *vidē-re*.

The fourth conjugation contains (1) root stems (*scio, fīo*); (2) denominatives from *i*-stems (*finio, vestio*); and (3) a group of verbs in which the root has been extended by the suffix -*ī*, which alternates with -*ĭ* according to a curious rhythmical principle. Stems consisting of a long syllable or two shorts have *ī*: *audīre, sāgīre, vāgīre, farcīre, sarcīre, sĕpĕlīre, ŏpĕrīre, ăpĕrīre*. These contrast with *iăcio, iăcĕre, căpio, căpĕre, făcio, făcĕre, fŭgio, fŭgĕre, quătio, quătĕre* (all with *ĕ* for *ĭ* before -*r* according to p. 219). Note that in *ferīre, salīre, venīre* the short vowel is followed by a sonant. *pario, parere, morior, mori* are exceptions. The distribution according to a clear rhythmical principle might suggest that the -*i* of *capis*, etc., is due to iambic shortening of *capīs*. But the type is Indo-European: e.g. Goth. *hafja* 'I lift', Skt. *kupyati* (Latin *cupio*). We must therefore postulate two forms of this primary suffix: -*ĭ* and -*ī* (possibly a product of *ĭ*+laryngeal).

In the inflexion of these three conjugations the vowels *ā, ĕ, ī*, after the disappearance of intervocalic -*y*-, contracted with following vowels. Thus **amāye-s, *amāye-t > amās, amāt* (shortened to *amăt* in Classical Latin), and this form of the stem *amā*- was generalized except for *amō < *amāy-ō*. So, too, in the denominatives and causatives of the second conjugation, **moneye-s*, etc. > *monēs*, etc. The generalization of this form of the stem *monē*- to the other persons (except *moneo < *money-ō*) was aided by the occurrence of *vidē-s, vidē-mus, vident*, etc., where the inflexions were attached directly to the stem *vidē*-. In the fourth conjugation *audio* and *audiunt* are the regular products of *audī-ō, audī-ont*. In the other persons *audīs*, etc., parallel the development in the first and second conjugations.

The third conjugation comprises the remainder of the types listed in pp. 266 f.: (1) root thematic verbs, like *dico*, *ago*, etc.; (2) the reduplicated stems *gigno*, etc.; (3) stems with infixed nasal, *rumpo*, etc.; (4) stems with a nasal suffix; (5) inchoatives in *-sco*; (6) a number of less frequent suffixes not listed above, e.g. *-to* (*necto*), *-do* (*tendo*), *-so* (a desiderative suffix seen in *quaesso*, *vīso*; from *quaesso* a suffix *-sse/o* was extracted which is seen in *petesso*, *lacesso*, *capesso*).

In this conjugation the thematic vowel *e/o* shows the customary weakening to *-i* in unaccented syllables (p. 219): **-esi*, **-eti*, **-ete-s* > *-is*, *-it*, *-itis*, **-omos* > *-imus*, **-onti* > *-unt*.

Some anomalous verbs

sum. The root *es* 'to be' as an athematic verb originally had the full grade of the root in the singular **es-mi*, **es-s*, **es-ti* and the zero grade in the plural **s-mos*, **s-te*, **s-enti*. *es* and *est* are regular products of this system. The full grade was introduced into the second person plural, *estis*, on the analogy of the singular. *s-enti* was given the thematic ending *s-onti* (whence *sunt*), and this influenced the form of the first person plural, **somos* > *sumus*; from this a new first person singular, *sum*, was created replacing **esmi*.

possum embodies an adjective *pote* or *potis*+*sum*: e.g. OL. *potisit*, *potis est*. *potest* results from the contraction of the neuter form *pote* with *est*.

volo is an old athematic verb **wel*. The third person singular *volt* is the regular product of *uel-ti* (see p. 215 on *el* > *ol*). In the plural **vl̥-te-s*, with the zero grade, yielded *voltis*. In the third person plural the substitution of the thematic ending *-ont* was the starting-point for the development of the thematic forms *volumus*, *volo*. *vīs*, we may recall, is formed from a different root **wei*, seen also in *in-vī-tus*. *nōlo* and *mālo* are contractions of *ne-volo* and *mag(i)s-volo* respectively. Uncontracted forms *ne vis*, *ne volt*, *mā-volo*, *mā-velim* occur in Old Latin.

fero, too, shows athematic forms *fers*, *fert*, *fertis* (cf. Gk. φέρτε). We may surmise that the source of the thematic forms lies in the third person plural *ferunt*, but in Greek and Sanskrit this verb, apart from a few isolated forms, belongs to the thematic class.

edo has athematic forms *ēs, ēst, ēsse,* etc., but the verb was brought progressively into the thematic class: *edunt, edimus, edo* and eventually *edis, edit, edere.*

fio. The stem *fī* was made by the attachment of the suffix *-ī* to the zero grade of the root 'to be': **bhw-ī-.* It was originally athematic, but followed in the main the fourth conjugation. Note, however, the Old Latin infinitive *fiere* (see below).

The tenses of the infectum

Imperfect

In Indo-European a past tense was made from the durative stem merely by the attachment of the secondary endings and (in some dialects) by the prefixing of an adverbial particle, the augment, though this might be omitted. Latin lost this facility and utilized a new suffix with preterite function *-ā* (found also in Celtic and Lithuanian), which was added to the root: e.g. **es-ā-m > erām* (*erăm* with shortening according to pp. 221 f.). This suffix was added to the root *bhu* and it is this preterite **bhu̯ām* which appears in the new Latin durative preterites ('imperfect'), *amā-bā-m, monē-bā-m, regē-bā-m, audiē-bā-m.* The origin of the first element in this periphrastic combination is a matter of speculation. It is conceivably a participle, for **amans-bhwām,* etc., would produce by regular phonetic processes the attested forms of the singular, whence *amā-,* etc., were extended to the plural. Other scholars regard *amā-, regē-,* etc., as the case form (perhaps locative) of a verbal substantive in *-ā* or *-ē, legē-bām* = 'I was in the act of reading'.[1] It has also been suggested that the forms may be derived from the regular infinitive ending *-si* (p. 278): e.g. **regesi-bām > *regezbām* (with syncope of the unaccented vowel) *> regēbam.*

In the fourth conjugation the most frequent form of the imperfect is *audiēbam.* But the type *audībam,* though less common, occurs through the history of Latin. It is probably an analogical form made on the model *amāre: amābam, monēre: monēbam* ::

---

[1] Note that the same verbal form occurs in the compounds of *arē-facio, putrē-facio,* etc.

audī-re: *audībam*. Note that a corresponding future form *audībo* was created which is no less frequent than the imperfect *audībam*.

Future

Indo-European possessed no future indicative and the descendant languages have independently created special forms with this function from expressions of *will, wish, likelihood,* etc. Among these was the IE. subjunctive with its double function of expressing will and likelihood (the voluntative and prospective subjunctive: see Syntax, pp. 309 ff.). The morphology of the subjunctive will be discussed below. For the present let it suffice to say that Latin had evolved two subjunctive formants, (1) -*ā*, (2) -*ē*. The first of these was used in the inherited functions of the subjunctive (pp. 309 ff.) and the second was specialized to express futurity. Hence the division of work between the two sets of forms in the third and fourth conjugations: *regās, regăt,* etc., subjunctive; *regēs, regĕt,* etc., future. In the first person singular *regō* of the latter series was identical with the present indicative, so that *regam* from the other system took over the double duty in this form.

In the first and second conjugations, however, phonetic development neutralized one or other of the two subjunctives. Thus *amāyās* became identical with the indicative *amās*, while in the second declension this fate overtook the type in -*ē*: *money-ēs*. Thus in these two conjugations only the types *amēs* and *mone-ās*, respectively, were left to carry on the functions of the subjunctive. The gap was filled by the creation of a new periphrastic future on the lines of the imperfect: this is a combination of the verbal stems *amā-, monē-,* with a short-vowel subjunctive (p. 277) of the root **bhu*: **bhwō, *bhwĕs,* etc., which produced the attested *amā-bis, monē-bis.* On the analogical innovation *audībo* for *audiam* see the preceding paragraph.

ero, eris, etc., originate in a short-vowel subjunctive of the root **es*: **esō, ese-s, ese-ti.*

In a number of languages the future is made from desiderative forms of the verb made with the suffix -*s* (cf. *quaes-so* and the Greek futures λύ-σ-ω, etc.). Such may be the origin of Latin forms like *capso, faxo, dixo.* s-futures are also formed occasionally in Old

Latin from *ā*- and *ē*-stems. The -*s*- remained unrhotacized and was represented as -*ss*-: *amāsso, enicāsso, commonstrāsso*. With these we may compare the desiderative verbs of the type *quaesso, capesso, lacesso* (p. 271), and the 'optatives' *servassint*, etc. (p. 278). Note that Plautus sometimes uses the infinitives in -*assere* for the future in -*turum*: e.g. 'illum confido domum in his diebus me reconciliassere' (*Capt.* 168).

The perfectum

This part of the Latin verb, with its double function corresponding to the IE. aorist and perfect, comprises stems drawn from both these series of tense stems. The old perfect stems are most obvious in the type with reduplication exemplified in Greek λέ-λοιπ-α, etc.: e.g. *ce-cin-ī, pe-pul-ī, pe-per-ī*, etc. Here the vowel of the reduplication is -*e*-, as in Indo-European. In some verbs, however, the vowel is assimilated to the vowel of the root: *momordī* (OL. *memordī*), *poposcī* (OL. *peposcī*), *cucurrī* (OL. *cecurrī*), *tutudī* (< *tundo*). In compound verbs where the accent fell on the initial syllable the vowel of the reduplication might be lost by syncope: *cecīdī*, but *occīdī* (< **obcecaidī*), *tetigī*, but *contigī*, *spopondī*, but *respondī*. *rettulī* corresponds to OL. *tetulī*, which was replaced by *tulī* extracted from the compound forms. Distinct from the reduplicated perfect is the Latin type with a lengthened root vowel. These forms originated in various ways. Some like *līquī* and *fūgī* are regarded simply as perfects of the first type which have lost their reduplication. Others like *vēnī, sēdī, lēgī, ēdī* have correspondences in Germanic preterites:[1] *qēmum* 'we came', *sētum* 'we sat'. Others again are the descendants of original strong aorists: *fēcī* (Gk. ἔ-θηκ-α), *iēcī* (ἧκα), with which we may group *pēgī* (*pango*), *cēpī* (*capio*), and *frēgī* (*frango*), formed on the analogy of the first two. In roots beginning with a vowel the long vowel may be due to the action of a lost laryngeal sonant, and these forms are traceable to the reduplicated type: e.g. if *em* < **ə₁em* the reduplicated perfect **ə₁e ə₁ em-ai* would yield Lat. *ēmī*. Within the structure of the Latin system, however, the lengthened grade of the perfect in all these corresponds to the normal grade of the present. The

---

[1] Note, however, that the lengthened vowel characterizes only the plural in Germanic: *sat* (sg.): *sētum* (pl.).

similar relationship of *scābī*: *scăbo*, *fōdī*: *fŏdio* may also be inherited and then extended to other verbs, e.g. *cāvī*: *caveo*, *mōvī*: *moveo*, etc. Note that *ōdī* has no corresponding present but a short vowel is seen in *ŏdium*: *ōdī* also is perfect, traceable to a reduplicated form of the root *$*_3$ed* > *od*.

Finally *vīdī* is an isolated phenomenon, with correspondents in Gk. ϝοῖδα, Skt. *véda*; it is an unreduplicated perfect of the root *weid*. *vīdī*: *video* may have been the model for the analogical extensions *cāvī*: *caveo* just noted.

The sigmatic type *dīxī* corresponds to the sigmatic aorists in other languages such as Gk. ἔδειξα < *e-dĕik-s-m̥*. Such aorists in Indo-European had a lengthened grade of the root in the indicative singular active and the zero grade in the other forms of the indicative, but Latin generalized the form with the lengthened vowel. Such are *vēxī* (root *wegh*), *rēxī* (*rego*), *scrīpsī* (*scrībo*), *tēxī* (*tego*), *fīxī* (*fīgo*, OL. *fīvo*), *dūxī* (*dūco*), etc. Such stems belonged properly to roots ending in plosive consonants or an *-s*, e.g. *cēdo*: *cessī*, *claudo*: *clausī*, *rādo*: *rāsī*, *clēpo*: *clēpsī*, *repo*: *rēpsī*. The type was extended to roots of other forms: e.g. *maneo*, *mānsī*. Note that the *-p-* in *sūmpsī*, *dēmpsī* is a glide sound. There were some analogical extensions. Thus *vīvo* does not end in a plosive (< *g^wīv*) and owes its perfect *vīxī* to the example of OL. *fīvo*: *fīxī*, *fīvo* being the regular product of the root *dhīg^w* (see p. 227). The form of the perfect stem was sometimes influenced by the present stem: e.g *iunxī* has the infix nasal properly restricted to the present stem *iungo* (cf. *pingo*: *pinxī*, *vincio*: *vinxī*, etc.).

The shortened forms of the s-perfect (*dīxtī*, *dīxem*, *dīxe*, *mīstī*, *accestis*, etc.) are due to loss of a syllable by haplology.

The type of perfect most characteristic of Latin, that in *-vī*, is not found elsewhere. That it nevertheless is of ancient origin is suggested by the fact that it often exhibits a grade of ablaut different from that of the present: e.g. *sēvī* as opposed to *sero* (< *si-s-ō*). The most plausible theory of its origin is that to the strong root aorist *bhū* (cf. Greek ἔ-φῦν) the inflexion *-ai* of the perfect (see below) was attached: *bhū-ai* > *fu(v)-ei*. This being analysed as *fu-vei*, the *-vei* was extended first to other root aorists like *gnō-*, *plē-*: *gnōvī*, *plēvī*. Subsequently it was attached to other verbal stems ending in a long vowel and so produced the regular type of perfect *amāvī, finīvī*, etc. With the stems ending in a short vowel *-e-uei, -a-uei, -o-uei* > *-uī* (cf. *denuo* < **denovo*, etc.), giving rise the type *moneo, monuī*. Similarly in the dissyllabic bases *domā/domǝ*, etc., **domǝ-uei* > *domuī*.

Other scholars find the origin of the *-v-* perfect in the *-u* which appears in Sanskrit perfects such as *jajñāu* 'I knew', *paprāu* 'I filled'. This is less satisfactory than the above explanation since in Sanskrit the *-u* appears only in reduplicated perfects whereas in Latin the two types are mutually exclusive; nor does it explain the long root vowel of *gnōvī, plēvī*.

Between similar vowels *-v-* disappeared with subsequent contraction of the vowels: thus *consuēveram* > *consuēram, audīvistī* > *audīstī*. These shortened forms of the stem were then extended to forms where the loss of *-v-* was phonetically unjustified: *amāsti, amāsse*, etc., *dēlēsti, delēsse, nōram, nōrunt*.

The perfects in *-īvī* present a special case, for the contracted forms always represent *-īvi-* (e.g. *audīstis*) and we never find **audīro, *audīrunt, *audīram*, corresponding to *amāro, amārunt, amāram*. On the other hand, the *v* is lost especially before *-e* from the time of Terence onwards: *audieram*, etc., although we never find the corresponding *amaero*, etc. A different explanation must therefore be found. It might be supposed that such forms originated in *audii, audiit* which represent an intermediate stage in which the *-v-* was lost but the vowels still uncontracted. But in Plautus such forms are few in number and such as there are (*perierunt, sierint*) parallel the perfect forms of the verb *eo: iī, ieram*, etc. Now *iī* is the regular form in Plautus while *īvī* is a later creation. On the other hand, the *v* is regularly preserved in *scīvī, sīvī*, etc. These facts suggest that it is *iī, ieram*, etc., which are the source of the perfects in *-iī*. On the model of a series like *perit, periit, perieram* the series *audit, audiit, audieram* was created.

Inflexions of the perfect

The IE. perfect was an 'intransitive' tense expressing a state persisting in the person of the subject (see above). The inflexions of the Latin perfect are also traceable to all intransitive endings which are reflected in the middle voice of Greek and Indo-Iranian and also in the Hittite *ḫi-* conjugation.

First person singular. In Indo-European the ending was -*a* (Gk. ϝοῖδα, Skt. *véda*). Lat. -*ī* (OL. -*ei*) corresponds to the middle ending -*ē* found in Sanskrit and Slavonic. It represents IE. -*ai* or-*Hai*.

Second person singular. The IE. ending was -*tha* (Gk. ϝοῖσ-θα), with a possible by-form *-*thai* due to the influence of the first person singular. This proceeded regularly to -*tī*: e.g. *vīdis-tī* (on -*is* see below).

Third person singular. IE. -*e* (Gk. ϝοῖδε etc.). This was extended in Italic by the secondary ending -*t* which became *d*: so OL. *feced.* Subsequently the *d* was replaced by the primary -*t*.

But OL. forms like *fuveit, redieit* (Plautus *vīxīt*, etc.) go back to the old intransitive ending *-*ai* extended by the common 3rd p. sg. inflexion -*t*: *-*ai-t* > -*ei-t*, > -*īt*.

The endings of the first and second persons plural need no comment.

Third person plural. Three forms of the inflexion appear: (1) -*ĕrunt* < *-*is-ont*, where the -*ont* is the primary thematic inflexion (on -*is*- see below). (2) -*ēre* preserves a trace of the *r*-ending which is found in no fewer than six of the IE. language groups (see pp. 13 f.). For present purposes we may note that -*r* was the secondary active ending corresponding to the expected -*ri* of the primary. -*ri* would develop to -*re* in Latin, where the ending appears to have been attached to the verbal stem in -*ē* representing the state (p. 267). (3) -*ērunt* is presumably a contamination of -*ĕrunt* and -*ēre*.

In the second persons singular and plural and the third person plural an element -*is*- appears. This is also found in the other forms of the perfect *amāvis-se, amāvero* (*amāviso), *amāveram* (*amāvisam), etc. -*is*- is considered to have originated in *s*-aorists of dissyllabic roots: e.g. *weidi-s-, whence it was extended by analogy to verbs of different types.

The tenses of the perfectum

The future is in origin a short-vowel subjunctive of *s*-aorists of the type just discussed: *weidi-s-o, *weidi-s-es > *vīdero, vīderis*, etc. In the third person plural the ending of the perfect subjunctive (see below) was used to avoid confusion with the indicative *vīdĕrunt*.

In the preterite of the perfect (pluperfect) we find the same suffix -*ā*- as in the imperfect. It was conceivably added to the extended stem in -is, weidis-ā-m > vīderām, or the pluperfect may have been an analogical creation made to correspond with the future in *ero* on the model of *ero*: *erām*.

The moods

Imperative

In Latin an imperative is formed only from the present stem with the exception of *memento* (< *memn̥tōd*, cf. Gk. μεμάτω; on -*tōd* see below). It consists of the bare stem: *es, dā, plē* (athematic), *age, lege, rege*, etc. (thematic). Note that certain imperatives in very frequent use, *fac, dic, duc*, have lost the final vowel. In the plural the inflexion is -*te*.

The passive forms *amāre, monēre, sequĕre* are traced to the ending -*so* (see above, p. 264). The corresponding plural inflexion in -*minī* is equated either with -μενοι which appears in the middle participles of Greek, or with the infinitive ending -μεναι (δό-μεναι). There would appear to be little doubt that the -*min*- is identical with the widespread suffix -*men*- which forms verbal nouns and adjectives (e.g. the Greek infinitives like δό-μεν; see also pp. 278 f.). A thematic form with reduced grade -*mno*- distinguishes the middle participles of the type *alumnus* (see below). The suffix would thus appear to have had certain medio-passive functions. Now a particle -*ī/ĭ*, possibly identical with the deictic particle, appears in other IE. languages in forms of the imperative and infinitive. Thus an imperative of the type *agiminī* may be plausibly analysed as a verbal noun **age-men* reinforced with the particle -*ī* (see below on the passive infinitive).

The imperative in -*tō* (*agito*, etc.) is clearly distinguished in Old Latin from the present: e.g. *hanc a me accipe atque illi dato* (Plt.). Corresponding forms are found in other IE. languages (e.g. Gk. ἀγέ-τω), and it is clear that Indo-European had only one form of this imperative which was used in both second and third persons singular and plural. In Latin a separate plural form was created by the addition of the characteristic inflexion -*te*: *agito-te*, etc., *agito* being then reserved for the second and third persons singular. -*tōd* (OL. *statod, licetod, datod*, etc.) was in origin the ablative of the demonstrative *to*-; with the meaning 'from that (moment, etc.)'.

On the basis of *es-to* falsely analysed as *est-o* new third person plural forms were created: *sunt-od*, *ferunto*, etc. On the peculiar dialect forms in a Lucerian inscription *fundatid parentatid*, *proiecitad* see below, on the subjunctive. The passive forms of the future imperative are made by the addition of the characteristic *-r* to *-to*. The rare form in *-minō* (OL. *progredimino*) is evidently of the same origin as *-minī* with the substitution of *-ō* derived from the *-tō* forms.

Subjunctive

The Latin subjunctive has the functions of the IE. subjunctive and optative (see Syntax) and, morphologically considered, it contains forms derived from both the IE. moods. In Indo-European there were three ways of forming the subjunctive. In athematic tenses the subjunctive was made by adding the vowel *ĕ/ŏ*: e.g. Gk. *ἴ-μεν* (indicative), *ἴ-ο-μεν* (subjunctive). This short-vowel type lies behind the futures *erō*, *viderō*, etc. (see above).

The subjunctive of thematic tense stems was formed by lengthening the thematic vowel: *ē/ō*. In Latin the *-ē-* was generalized: e.g. *amē-m*, *amēs*, *amĕt*, *amēmus*, *amētis*, *ament*. As we have already seen, this type of subjunctive was pressed into service as the future indicative of the third and fourth conjugations. The *-ē* was also added to the s-aorist producing the *-sē-* characteristic of the so-called imperfect subjunctive (Syntax, p. 310): *es-sĕ-m*, *ama-rĕ-m*, etc. Note *forem* < **bhu-sē-m*. *-sē-* also appears in the pluperfect subjunctive *vidis-sē-m*, etc.

The third type of IE. subjunctive concerns athematic stems ending in a vowel; in these the mood was formed by lengthening the vowel (Gk. *δύνᾰται*: *δύνᾱται*). We may perhaps trace to this type the subjunctives in *-ā-* which are peculiar to Italic. Some scholars equate this suffix with the preterite *-ā* discussed above. But it is difficult to see how the sign of a mood which essentially expresses an attitude to the future can have acquired preterite functions. Note that in Old Latin examples occur in which the *-ā-* was added to the root and not to the present stem: *fuat*, *attigas* (from *tag-* not *tang-*), *abstulas*, *advenat*, *duas*.

The IE. optative was formed by the addition of *-ī* to thematic stems (Gk. *φέρο-ι-μι*, etc.). The optative suffix of athematic stems

showed ablaut alternation: -*yē*- in the singular and -*ī*- in the dual
and plural. The only trace of this latter type in Latin is the archaic
subjunctive of *esse*: *s-*iē*- in *siem, siēs, siet,* and *s-*ī*- in *sīmus, sītis,
sient*. But this paradigm was regularized by the generalization of
the stem *sī*-: *sim, sīs, sit.* The -*ī* is seen also in the subjunctive
forms *velim, edim, duim,*[1] *creduīs* and further in the optatives made
from the *s*-aorist such as *faxim, faxīs, faxit, ausim*; *curassīs, celas-
sīs, prohibessīs* (pp. 271 f.). Such formations lie behind the perfect
subjunctive: e.g. *viderim* < *weidis-ī-m. From *viderim* a suffix -*eri*-
was extracted which was added to all types of perfect subjunctive:
egerim, dixerim, amaverim, etc. Latin has no trace of the thematic
type in -*oi*-.

It remains to consider the curious imperatival forms *fundatid,
parentatid, proiecitad* found in a Lucerian inscription. It is evident
that the language of this inscription reflects a dialect influenced
by Oscan. In Oscan the subjunctive of the *ā*-stems appears as
-*āīd* (*ā-ē-d*) and that of the *iacio* type as -*iād*. *parentatid* and
proiecitad are thus plausibly explained as blends of -*tōd* imperatives with the corresponding jussive subjunctives **parentāīd,
*proieciād.

The verbal nouns and adjectives

The infinitive

The so-called infinitive mood is strictly speaking not a mood but
in all IE. languages consists of isolated case-forms (chiefly dative
and locative) of verbal nouns. Such verbal nouns may appear as
the plain root (*ag) or with a number of suffixes and enlargements.
Of particular importance are the neuter verbal nouns in -*i*, -*s*, -*r*,
-*n* and the complex forms -*wer/wen* -*mer/men* in which the suffixes
er/en are added to roots extended by -*w* and -*m*.

The present infinitive in Lat. -*se* (*es-se*, *vel-se > *velle*, *fer-se >
ferre) may be interpreted as the locative singular of an *s*-stem, final
-*i* regularly becoming -*e* (p. 221). When preceded by the thematic
vowel the -*s* was rhotacized: *age-se > *agere.* Old Latin presents
a few examples with loss of the final vowel: *biber, tanger.*

---

[1] This form is based on *dou, an extended form of the root *dō*, found also in
Greek.

-*se* was also added to the perfect stem in -*is*- producing the characteristic perfect infinitive -*isse* (*amavisse, dixisse*, etc.).

The passive infinitive ends in -*ī*. This is traced by some scholars to -*ei*, which may be regarded as the dative of a root noun **ag-ei*, or the locative of a thematic noun **ago-*, the accusative of which appears in the Oscan infinitive *acum* < **ago-m*. Against this is the evidence of the Duenos inscription where the form *pacari* suggests that the Lat. -*ī* is an original long vowel and not the product of a diphthong. The above explanation also offers no satisfactory account of the specialization of this case of a verbal noun to express the passive. Now a long -*ī*, as we have seen, also characterizes the passive of the second person plural in -*minī*. It would seem more satisfactory to equate the two particles with this medio-passive function. In the imperatives the -*ī* was added to a verbal noun in -*men*; in the case of the infinitives it was added to the root nouns *ag-, dūc-, dīc-*, etc. *ī* may be traced to **iH*; cf. the alternation of *i* and *ī* in the formation of the verbal stems *faci-* and *audī-*.

In the Old Latin forms of the present infinitive passive, such as *agier, vortier*, etc., which provided a 'gloss' of a convenient metrical shape for the poets, the ending -*ier* is currently explained as -*ī* extended by the ending of the active infinitive with loss of the final vowel as in *biber, tanger*. H. Pedersen has suggested, however, that we have here a compound suffix -*i-er* forming a verbal noun comparable to the Hittite verbal abstracts in -*š-ar, -tar, -mar, -war* (cf. *i-ter*).

The future infinitive

In considering the morphology of this infinitive we must be guided by the fact that in Old Latin it may appear as an invariable form -*tūrum* without regard for the gender, case, or number of the noun to which it refers (e.g. 'illi polliciti sese facturum omnia', Cato quoted by Priscian; cf. 'hanc sibi rem praesidio sperant futurum', Cic. *in Verr.* 2. 5. 65. 167). This infinitive is therefore, in the opinion of some scholars, not identical with the future participle active (see below) but is the product of the supine with an infinitive of the verb 'to be', **esom*, which appears in Osc. *ezum*: **factu-esom* > *facturum*. This invariable form when used with a masculine or neuter noun in the accusative was felt to be an

T

adjective agreeing with the noun, and then received the appropriate adjectival declension. The weakness of the explanation lies in the fact that no such infinitive is found in Latin. It could, of course, be attributed to the 'Italic' period, but in Chapter I we have ventured to doubt the existence of 'common Italic'. *fore*, which functions as a future infinitive, is the normal Latin infinitive of the root *bhu*: **bhu-s-i*. On the infinitives of desiderative verbs in *-āsso* see p. 272.

On the basis of the active periphrastic future infinitives like *cubitum ire*, Latin created a future infinitive passive of the type *factum irī*.

The supine

The supines in *-tum* and *-tū* are the accusatives and datives (or locatives or ablatives) respectively of verbal nouns in *-tus* (p. 236). Dative forms in *-uī* are also found occasionally: e.g. *memoratuī* (Plt.).

The participles

The present participle is a verbal adjective made with the suffix *-nt-*. When combined with the thematic vowel *-o-* this suffix appears as *-ont-*. The only Latin example of this is found in the declension of *iens: euntem*, etc. < **ei̯ontem* and in *sons, insons* which contains the present participle of the verb 'to be', *s-ont-*. Elsewhere Latin has *-ent-*, which may represent either **-ent-* or **-n̥t-*, the latter being the weak grade which appears in Indo-European in the declension of athematic stems ending in a consonant. Note that *dens* is the present participle containing the weak grade of the root *ed: d-ens*.

The perfect participle passive of Latin is in origin an adjective in *-to-* which was neutral as to voice. In Indo-European it bore the accent and the verbal root appeared in the weak grade: *dĭc-tós, dŭc-tós, ŭs-tós* (root **eus*, as in *ūro*), *stătós* (from *stə-tós*, root **stā*), *sătus* (**sē*). In verbal adjectives which end in *-itus* the *i*-represents the weak grade of dissyllabic roots of the type *domā/domə, tacē/tacə: domitus, tacitus*. When the root ended in a dental plosive, *-t-t-* and *-d-t-* produced *-ss-* (p. 232), which was simplified after a long vowel or diphthong: *claud-tos > claussus, > clausus, *fid-tos > fissus, *fod-tos > fossus, sed-tos > sessus.

Though the -to- was originally attached to the root and the adjective was independent of the tense stems, its incorporation in the verbal conjugation resulted in many analogical interferences: e.g. mansus (perfect mansi), flexus (flexi), sparsus (sparsi), fluxus (fluxi). In combination with the verb 'to be' this participle provided the periphrastic conjugation of the perfect passive: amatus est.

The future participle active is an adjective with the common suffix -ro- attached to the stem of the verbal noun in -tū : futū-ro-s.

The gerundive

No satisfactory explanation has been offered of the Latin verbal adjective in -ndus. The suffix -do- appears, however, in other verbal adjectives like timidus where it has been attached to a verbal noun in -i-. The meaning of the gerundives was 'involved in the fact of rising, following', etc. With intransitive verbs they had intransitive significance: oriundus, secundus. With transitive verbs, e.g. agnus caedundus, the meaning 'involved in killing' could easily develop into the various meanings appropriate to different contexts, 'fit to be killed', 'going to be killed', 'bound to be killed', etc. In the third and fourth conjugations the suffix appears in Old Latin in the form -undus. That the change to -endus was due to the influence of the present participle is evident from the fact that eundum, which never has the form in -endus, is paralleled by the present participle euntem.

The gerund consists of the different cases of the substantivized neuter gerundive (see, however, pp. 321 f. and p. 341).

Only a few traces survive in Latin of the middle participle in -meno-: fēmina, from *dhē 'suckle', alumnus from *al 'nurture'. We have seen reason to doubt the theory which would equate the middle imperative ending -minī with the plural form of the middle participle.

INDECLINABLES

Under this heading we classify the adverbs, prepositions, prefixes, and particles which mark or strengthen the syntactical relationships of words and give local, temporal, and eventually logical indications. Some of these are extremely ancient and defy analysis: e.g. *en (in), *anti (ante), *op(i) (ob, obs), *apo (ap, ab, abs), *pro (pro), *eks (ex, ē), etc. In others we may detect (1) demonstrative stems: to- e.g. in tum, tam, tan-dem, topper, etc.; i- in ita, item, iam, etc.; no- in nam, dō-ni-cum, dō-ni-que, etc.) and (2) the interrogative-relative stem qui/quo- (quid-em, quip-pe, quom, quōr, etc.).

Many of the formants are peculiar to adverbial formations. ut, for instance, on the evidence of aliuta, uti-nam, and the correlative i-ta contains a suffix -ta, which may go back to IE. *-tə (cf. Skt. iti). This suffix has been added to the root *qʷu. To uta the locative ending or deictic particle -i was added: hence utei, utī < *uta-i. *qʷut- could be extended by an adverbial -s (Osc. puz < *qʷut-s), a form which accounts for uspiam, usque, usquam. The same root *qʷu- lies behind (c)ubi (ali-cubi, nē-cubi). The evidence of Osco-Umbrian (U. pufe) and other IE. languages shows that the primitive form was *qʷu-dhe which was extended by the addition of a locative ending, *qʷu-dhei > regularly to (c)ubī (p. 228). ubi has influenced the form of the correlative ibi, for which on the evidence of Sanskrit (iha) we should expect *idī < *i-dhe-i. cūr, OL. quōr, contains an adverbial formant r seen also in Engl. where, Lith. ku-r̃.

The great majority of adverbs are fossilized case-forms of nouns. Nominatives are versus and secundus. Accusatives are (1) parum, primum, multum, nimium, magis, minus, plus, etc. (neuters); (2) quom, tum, dum, nunc < *num-ce, partim, statim, olim (masculine and feminine). The characteristic Latin adverbs iam, nam, tam, quam, clam, palam are possibly feminine accusative forms of i-, no-, to-, etc. Temporal genitives are nox and dius. Ablatives are the common types in -ō(d) and -ē(d) and -ā(d): primō, meritō(d), intrō, retrō; bene, facilumēd; extrād, infrā. The -tos of intus (Gk. ἐντός), penitus, funditus, subtus, etc., is also an old ablatival ending. Locatives are hīc, noctū, temere ('in the dark', temperī, and penes. Such case-forms may be combined with affixes such as -per in parumper, semper, topper (*tod-per) and -em in quidem (cf. idem, p. 257). The dō- of donec (OL. donicum, donique) is identical with Engl. to. Other adverbs again are fossilized phrases: quārē, intereā, h ctenus, interim, adfatim, scīlicet (= scire licet), dumtaxat (taxat being the subjunctive of an s-aorist or of a desiderative form of the root *tag, ta-n-go). The common adverbial type in -ter is thought to be identical with the contrastive suffix -ter (p. 253). The starting-point was aliter, whence it spread first to words of related meaning such as pariter, similiter, and thence to other words.

CHAPTER X

SYNTAX

THE syntax of a language like Latin deals with the functional side of morphology (see previous chapter). It is concerned in the first place with the interrelations of words in the sentence as expressed in the inflexions, that is primarily with the functions of cases, tenses, mood, etc. The student of Latin, however, soon becomes aware that there are no single clear-cut functions attaching, for instance, to the various case-endings. Instead he is confronted with a bewildering multiplicity, e.g. datives of interest, advantage, and disadvantage, ethic, sympathetic, and final datives. This is due to a simple linguistic fact which it is essential to grasp in analytical and historical syntax. Words do not exist in isolation in a speaker's mind but cluster in associational groups. All members of such a group will tend to uniformity of syntactical behaviour. Thus if *impero* takes a dative, then the synonymous *iubeo* is likely to do the same. In fact *iubeo* is so constructed by Catullus and even by Cicero in one of his letters (*ad Att.* 9. 13. 2). In the same way *laedere* follows the example of *nocere*, and *sinere*, *pati* that of *permitto*, and *impedire* (in the grammarian Varro!) that of *obstare*. Thus syntactical development may be compared to the gradual growth of a fairy ring which is formed by the clustering of fungi around an original parent fungus. Such syntactical 'fairy rings' may intersect: that is a word may belong to various associational groups and partake in different constructions. The syntactical field of a language thus presents to the eye of the investigator an elaborate pattern of such 'fairy rings'. His task is first to establish and define their area and then endeavour to trace their growth back to the original focus of development. In fact he will discover that such an 'Ur-fungus' was itself a member of yet another 'fairy ring', for associational grouping of words is common to all languages. This means that the investigator never arrives, for instance, at the primitive function of a case. Instead he finds an interconnected system of 'fairy rings'. For the purposes of description and classification the syntactician will devise a general formula which comprises the observed usages, e.g. 'the noun in the dative case designates the person (or thing) implicated in the event referred to by the verb'. This formula should not be confused with the 'primitive single function', which presumably never existed. At all periods a language syntactically considered consists of associational groups ('fairy rings') of concrete usages. In the course of generations the rings grow and diminish and the patterns change. To define such rings and to trace the history of their growth are the essential tasks of descriptive, historical, and comparative syntax.

THE NOUNS

Nominative

The nominative is the 'naming' case, in which the word is a mere label such as occurs in lists, inventories, and the like. In this function it may be used predicatively: 'they called him "Corvinus"', *cognomen habuit 'Corvinus'*; cf. 'per valle illa quam dixi ingens' (*Per. Aeth.*). The nominative as the naming case makes a preliminary announcement focusing attention on the temporary centre of interest, the 'subject' of the utterance. A primitive type of utterance consists of two such nominatives, one the 'subject', the other the 'predicate': *ille servus*. A number of verbs are used to make explicit the relationship between subject and predicate: *est, factus est, creatus est, adest (tu mi accusatrix ades)*, etc. Where the centre of interest is already established and needs no explicit reference such predicative nominatives function as exclamations: *nugae!, fabulae!*; with an introductory deictic expression 'em tibi anus lepida!' (Plt. *Curc.* 120).

In many statements referring to an event the person or thing 'named' as the centre of interest is conceived as the initiator of the action: hence the so-called 'ergative' function of the nominative, which may be represented thus: ⟨◆⟩.

In the preliminary 'naming' expression we sometimes find two nominatives in apposition: *homo adulescens, homo servus, mulier meretrix*. In such examples a vague general term is given percision, as it were, by an afterthought: cf. 'nos libertinae sumus, et ego et tua mater'.

In loose colloquial speech, the topic of discussion once named, the sentence often goes off into a different construction. On this *nominativus pendens* see p. 80.

Vocative

The vocative is the case of address which calls for the attention of the hearer. It resembles in function the imperative of the verb, with which it also has a morphological similarity, both consisting of the bare stem. In Latin it has a distinct morphological characterization only in the second declension (see previous chapter), and even here the nominative is sometimes found, especially in poetry. Syntactically the noun in the vocative is isolated from the rest of the utterance and even a qualifying adjective originally took the nominative form: 'salve, primus omnium' (Pliny, *N.H.* 7. 117). But early in Latin we find an example of attraction into the vocative, if *macte*, as appears probable, is the vocative of *mactus* (see pp. 66 f.). But in general this phenomenon is a Grecism of the Augustan poets: e.g. 'prima dicte mihi, summa dicende Camena . . . Maecenas' (Hor. *Ep.* 1. 1. 1–3). Such examples are in the main poetical, prose preferring expressions of the type *o tu qui.* . . . Similar attractions occur also in the predicative adjective: 'quo moriture ruis' (Virg. *Aen.* 10. 811); 'tu quoque . . . miserande iaceres' (ibid. 10. 324 ff.).

Accusative

The accusative exhibits clusters of usage which may be generally defined as the end or goal towards which the action tends or is directed. The relationship is conceived thus: ⇥ It is seen most clearly with verbs of motion, Latin preserving the bare accusative to express this relationship in *domum, rus*, with names of towns and small islands, and in certain other phrases such as *exsequias, infitias ire, pessum ire, venum ducere*, etc. Most frequently, however, the supporting adverb has become the indispensable 'preposition' 'governing' the case. The perfect tense of such verbs of motion expresses the state resulting from the action, but the prepositional phrase appropriate to the other 'aspects' (see pp. 265 f.) persists: *ad urbem venire* > *ad urbem venisse*, and thence by an easy analogical link *ad urbem adesse*. In this way the preposition *ad* with the accusative comes to assume a variety of *locative* func-

tions: 'ubi summus imperator non adest ad exercitum' (Plt. *Amph.*
504); 'esse ad sororem' (Ter. *H.T.* 979); 'totam hiemem ipse ad
exercitum manere decrevit' (Caesar, *B.G.* 5. 53. 3); 'habes hortos ad
Tiberim'(Cic. *pro Cael.* 36); 'mihi . . . est ad portum negotium' (Plt.
Merc. 328); 'ego ad forum illum conveniam' (id. *Mil.* 930). *ad* thus
becomes interchangeable with *apud.*

Compound verbs arose from the fusion with simple verbs of
adverbs which once had formed an independent unit of the utterance. Once such fusion has taken place, the accusatives of the goal
being preserved, the compound verb appears to govern a direct
object (see below): *aliquem ad+ire* > *aliquem adire.* Hence the
phenomenon called the transitivizing function of verbal prefixes:
e.g. *accedere, advenire, aggredi, antecedere, circumire, incurrere,
irrumpere, introire, percurrere, subire, transmittere, oppugnare,* etc.
The list was extended by analogical influences of various kinds:
thus after *egredi, exire* we should expect the ablative. The accusative may be due to linking with its opposite *inire* or with expressions of similar meaning such as *relinquere.*

With certain verbs the accusative of the goal or end towards
which the action is directed is some external thing or person:
'shoot deer', 'eat bread', 'plant corn'. Such are the 'external'
accusatives expressing the direct object of the verb. Scholars are
inclined to separate this set of usages from the 'lative' of the 'goal
or aim', but there is no great gulf between them. The range of
verbs governing such accusatives was steadily increased in Latin
by analogical influences. Thus *amare* draws into its orbit a whole
variety of synonymous expressions: 'hic te . . . deperit, ea demoritur te' (Plt. *Mil.* 970), and even 'amare eum haec perditast'
(*Cist.* 132). By similar processes a number of verbs expressing
emotional states became transitive: fear (*timeo, metuo, abhorrere*),
hope and expectation (*sperare, desperare, manere, expectare, morari*[1]),
joy and regret (*laetari, ridere, gaudere, flere, lugere, gemere, dolere,
maerere, plorare, fremere, tremere,* etc.). The impersonal verbs
denoting emotional states are also so constructed: *me miseret,
paenitet, pudet, taedet, piget.* Many verbs which were originally

---

[1] The accusative after *morari* is best grouped here with its synonym *manere*:
'id modo moratus ut consulem percontaretur' (Livy 23. 47. 1) is classified by Ernout
and Thomas as an adverbial 'internal' accusative (see below).

constructed with other cases (genitive, dative, or ablative) through analogical interferences came to be used with the accusative: *abutor, careo, fungor, supero, indulgeo, servio, curo, studeo, ausculto,* etc. By such manifold processes the accusative case gradually extended its scope until from its originally concrete-spatial meaning of the 'goal or aim' it developed into the general grammatical expression for the verbal complement.

External accusatives are also found in Old Latin after verbal nouns: 'quid ibi hanc aditio est' (Plt. *Truc.* 622); 'quid tibi hanc curatiost rem?' (id. *Amph.* 519). Old, too, is the accusative after middle verbs of dressing and undressing: 'quid erat induta?; aspexit virginem ibi stantem in capite ostrinum indutam riculam' (Turp. 73); cf. *loricam induitur.* Alternatively the part of the body concerned appeared in the accusative (*caput velati*) with the garment, etc., in the instrumental ablative: e.g. 'togae parte velati' (Cato), cf. 'succincti corda machaeris' (Ennius). This provided the native Latin 'frame' for grecizing poetical idioms such as 'exuta pedem' (Virg. *Aen.* 4. 518), 'suspensi loculos' (Hor. *Sat.* 1. 6. 74), 'concussa metu mentem'(Virg. *Aen.*12. 468), and the much-discussed 'saepes Hyblaeis apibus florem depasta salicti' (id. *Buc.* 1. 53–54). Finally the construction is extended to adjectives, *exuta pedem* leading on naturally to *nuda pedem.* With this we reach the accusatives of respect, a category on which other lines of development converge which we must now trace.

In certain expressions the accusative of the goal refers not to an external object but to the content of the verb, to the result towards which the verbal action proceeds. Such usages are classified by grammarians under the heading *internal accusative,* as opposed to the *external* uses treated in the previous paragraph. As so often in syntactical phenomena the two spheres of usage merge into each other: 'build a house', 'light a fire', 'forge a sword', 'tell a lie', 'strike a blow', etc. Latin examples are: *facinus audere, mendacium dicere, foedus ferire, verbum muttire, lapides loqui, propino tibi salutem* (this is linked also with the external accusative after *volo,* etc.). An ancient type going back to IE. times is the accusative of the content which names the action signified by the verb: *aetatem vivere.* A stylistic sub-variety is the 'cognate accusative' in which the noun is drawn from the same root as the verb: *vota vovere,*

Ionum dare, cenam cenare, dicta dicere, auspicium auspicare. This inherited type of accusative developed to some extent under Greek influence: the prototype is Ennius' 'vicit Olympia'.

Certain instances of the internal accusative fructified and produced 'fairy rings' of usage sufficiently important to deserve special labels. From expressions like *longam viam ire* and *noctem pernoctare* there developed the accusatives of extent with reference to space and time. From 'space traversed' as in *non pedem discedat* the transition is easy to 'distance from' with *abest, distat,* etc. Parallel temporal expressions are: 'abhinc ducentos annos mortuus est'; and, still freer, 'iam multos annos est quom possideo' (Plt.). Finally, such accusatives figure with adjectives of measurement: *panem tris pedes latum,* cf. *annos octingentos natus.* On the intrusion of the ablative of 'time how long', *tota vita,* etc., see below.

The neuter singulars of the pronouns were used with particular freedom as internal accusatives: *istuc pessume consulis*; *istuc crucior*; *si quid erro*; *si id fallo*; 'advorte ut quod ego ad te advenio ("the purpose for which I am here") intelligas' (Plt. *Epid.* 456). Examples like *id maeret* give rise to 'id misera maesta est' (id. *Rud.* 397), where the accusative is one of 'respect' (see above). In purely Latin expressions such accusatives of respect are confined to the neuter pronouns: e.g. *nescio quid tristis est.* Usage developed more freely in imitation of the Greeks first in Augustan poets: 'qui genus?' (Virg. *Aen.* 8. 114); 'maculosus alvum' (id. *G.* 3. 427); 'nigra pedes' (Ov. *M.* 7. 468). Tacitus was the first to venture this idiom in prose: 'clari genus' (*Ann.* 6. 9); 'manum aeger' (*Hist.* 4. 81).

In Old Latin the neuters of certain adjectives also function as internal accusatives. Plautus in the main confines himself to adjectives of quantity—*multum, nimium, magnum, maxumum.* Here, too, Greek stimulated a native Latin usage, Catullus being the first with his *dulce ridentem* to render γελαίσας ἰμέροεν (Sappho). Prose abstains from such licence until after the time of Livy.

The different types of accusative may appear in one and the same sentence: e.g. 'quid nunc te litteras doceam' (Cic.). With the verbs of instructing we may group their contraries, the verbs of concealing, which likewise take two accusatives: e.g. 'ut celem patrem tua flagitia' (Plt. *Bacch.* 375). Verbs of 'making', 'thinking', 'calling' take an accusative of the direct object and a predicative accusative: e.g. 'is me heredem fecit' (id. *Poen.* 1070). Here, too, in many instances the predicative accusative expresses the result of the action. In others the two accusatives are in apposition: 'malam fortunam in aedis te adduxi meas' (id. *Rud.* 501). Such, too, are the 'accusatives of the whole and the part': e.g. 'meretrices . . . maiorem partem videas valgis saviis' (id. *Mil.* 93), in which the second accusative is merely a corrective afterthought—'that is the greater part of them'.

Internal and appositional accusatives are often petrified as adverbs. Examples are *nimium, plus, multum*; the adverbs of the type *partim, statim*, etc. (see previous chapter); and the originally appositional *id genus, omne genus*: e.g. 'coronamenta—omne genus —facito ut serantur' (Cato); 'aliquid id genus solitum scribere' (Cic. *ad Att.* 13. 12. 3); 'in hoc genus praediis' (Varro, *R.R.* 1. 16. 4). We may classify here temporal expressions of the type *id aetatis*: e.g. 'ego istuc aetatis non amori operam dabam' (Ter. *H.T.* 110). Finally, we have the accusatives of exclamation which depend on an unexpressed verb: *nugas! hercle rem gestam bene! artificem probum!*

Genitive

It is difficult to find a formula to cover all uses of the genitive. We shall begin therefore with some of the best-established departments of usage the antiquity of which seems beyond doubt.

The possessive genitive

This term is self-explanatory: *aedes eri, filius eri, patris amicus,* etc. The derived adjectives compete to some extent with this genitive (*erilis filius, Campus Martius, virgo Vestalis*, etc.), and some scholars have held that this was the more ancient usage. But in the purely possessive sense the genitive is regular even in the earliest Latin texts, the adjective having the wider and vaguer sense 'connected with'. Its sphere of reference thus includes that of the genitive. As a substitute for the genitive it belongs to a higher stylistic level (e.g. in Plautine 'long measures'). Possessive genitives may be used predicatively: 'fratris igitur Thais tota est' (Plt.); 'agrum numquam siris fieri gnati tui' (id.). The ellipse of an easily supplied noun explains such phrases as *ad Dianae (fanum)*.

The partitive genitive

From 'belonging to' there is an easy transition to 'part of'. Here the genitive stands to the noun defined in the relationship of the whole to its part(s). This is clearest in expressions of quantity: *granum salis, vini gutta, panis pondo quattuor, cadus vini*, etc. Partitive genitives are particularly frequent after singular neuter pronouns and adjectives: e.g. *aliquid, quid, multum, plus (negoti, rei, aetatis, animi,* etc.). They are most commonly genitives of nouns, but certain substantivized neuter adjectives also occur: *mali* and *boni* predominate in Old Latin, but Cicero considerably increased the number of such substantivized adjectives used in the partitive case. This use of the genitive is also found to some extent after non-quantitative expressions. Colloquial are those after adverbs of place and time: e.g. *ubi terrarum, nusquam gentium* (whence also *minume gentium*). Other examples after non-quantitative neuter adjectives belong mainly to poetry and poetical prose: e.g. 'incerto noctis' (Sallust), 'sub obscurum noctis' (Virg.). Partitive genitives are rarer after substantivized neuter plurals: Cicero has 'summa pectoris' and 'interiora aedium', but the usage was extended under Greek influence: e.g. 'in infera noctis' (Ennius), 'per cava terrae' (Sallust), 'strata viarum' (Virg.), 'angusta viarum' (Tac.).

Originally the partitive could function freely in the sentence as subject, object, etc. (*'some of the enemy' were killed; I drank 'some wine'*). There are some traces of this in Old Latin (e.g. 'aquae . . . addito', Cato), but such constructions were suppressed by the classical purists. They reappear in Vulgar Latin, where, being replaced by *de*+ablative, they became the ancestors of Romance expressions like *de l'eau*.

The partitive is found with certain verbs of filling and others of associated meaning: *complere, abundare,* etc.; *egere, indigere, carere, levare* ('me omnium iam laborum levas', Plt. *Rud.* 247), etc. The corresponding adjectives take the same construction; *plenus, largus, refertus, onustus, particeps, expers, ieiunus,* etc. From the firm Latin ground of the genitive with expressions of 'lacking', 'depriving', etc., Horace leapt into the Grecism: 'desine mollium tandem querellarum' (*Carm.* 2. 9. 17–18). Originally, too, *potiri*

'make oneself master of' and the corresponding adjectives, *compos,*
impos, took this genitive. *impos animi, compos animi, expers con-*
sili, and the like lead on easily to other expressions of bewilder-
ment and uncertainty: *incertus consili* and even *falsus animi* (Ter.).
Adverbial genitives like *desipiebam mentis* (Plt.), *animi exruciari,*
animi pendere, and the like also range themselves naturally with
this semantic 'fairy ring' and it hardly seems necessary to separate
them as 'locatives'. The purely Latin construction *potiri* with the
genitive made it possible for Horace to venture *regnavit populorum*
in imitation of the Greek (*Carm.* 3. 30. 12).

The partitives were originally used also with verbs of eating and
drinking. This led on naturally to 'being hungry for', 'thirsting
for'. So we may perhaps classify as partitives the genitives used
with verbs of desiring and their opposites (*domi cupio, mein fasti-*
dis?, studeat tui), and even the genitives with verbs of remembering
and forgetting. See below, however, on the genitive of the sphere.

The defining genitive (genitive of quality)

Possessive genitives were not confined to expressions of physical
possession. In place-names possessive genitives of the name of the
presiding deity, etc. (*lacus Averni, urbs Patavi*), give rise to the
so-called epexegetic or appositional genitives, among which is that
bugbear of schoolmasters, *urbs Romae,* which appears at the end
of the Republic. But possessives were also extended to other relations where the notion of possession was progressively weakened:
corporis candor, adventus hostium, fides clientum, iniustitiam leno-
num, until with *supplicium virgarum* the genitive 'rods' merely
defines the sort of punishment. So, too, *Poenorum bellum* is a
'Carthaginians' war; whether it is waged by or against the Carthaginians must be gathered from the context. But we need not on
that account set up special grammatical categories 'subjective'
and 'objective' genitives. The partitives, too, similarly increased
their scope: *virga lauri* leads on eventually to the 'appositional'
arbor fici (Livy, etc.).

In certain modes of expression the partitive merged with the
possessive to form an important 'fairy ring', the genitive of quality.
The relation of whole to part is easily extended to that of genus to
species, class to individual, etc. Similarly possessives like *patris*

filius lead on to *Graeci generis homo*. Such was the origin of the genitives of quality, which in Old Latin are largely concentrated around expressions of origin and belonging, and those of price,[1] measurement, and the like: e.g. 'talentum rem . . . decem', 'vir minimi preti', 'trium litterarum homo' (Plt.). The only examples in early Latin which lie outside this narrow semantic range are 'homo iracundus, animi perditi' (Plt. *Men.* 269) and 'tam iners, tam nulli consili sum' (Ter. *And.* 608). Even in Cicero and Caesar such genitives of quality are practically confined to nouns qualified by the adjectives *magnus, tantus, summus, maximus*. Later, however, this construction gained the upper hand over its competitor, the sociative ablative (see below).

The defining genitives may be used predicatively: 'magni sunt oneris' (Plt.). Here we find an important offshoot the 'characteristic' genitives: e.g. 'est miserorum ut . . . invideant bonis' (Plt.); 'ea exquirere iniqui patris est' (Ter.). Here the contribution of the possessive is particularly apparent.

The genitive of sphere (genitive of respect, reference)

The partitive and possessive are merely two of a number of interlocking genitival functions which are labelled 'genitives of the sphere'. We have seen how the partitive could express class (*iuniorum est*, 'he is one of, belongs to, the *iuniores*') and also how the possessive was extended until it became the case whereby one noun defines another. In a sentence like *ei non fidem habui argenti*, the genitive is adnominal and defines *fidem*. But if the adnominal bond is weakened it becomes possible by 'relational displacement' to interpret the sentence 'I did not trust him in money matters, as regards money'. Perhaps the genitive of reference arose in some such ways. What is clear is that it is already firmly established in Old Latin, especially in legal and judicial contexts, with verbs of accusing, summoning, condemning: 'iniuriarum . . . induci'; 'quem mendaci prendit manifesto'; 'probri accusare'; 'quarum rerum, litium, causarum condixit pater patratus' (Livy 1. 32. 11), etc. The number of such verbs was gradually extended (*interrogare, postulare, arcessere, urgere*, etc.). A somewhat isolated satellite of this group is the genitive sometimes found with *credo*: 'quoii

---
[1] See below on the genitive of the rubric.

omnium rerum ipsus semper credit' (Plt. *Asin.* 459). Another well-known group to be classified here comprises the genitives used with the impersonals like *paenitet, pudet, piget,* etc.: e.g. *facti piget; taedet tui sermonis.* Genitives of exclamation like *mercimoni lepidi! o mercis malae!* also belong here.

The genitive of the rubric

Grammarians label thus a small group of genitives found in what we may call book-keeping contexts: e.g. *lucri facere* to put down under the heading 'profit', 'consider as profit' (cf. *compendi, dispendi, sumpti facere; aequi bonique facere*). Here, too, we should classify the well-known genitives in expressions of valuation: *flocci, nauci, nihili, tanti, quanti, pluris, minoris.* Most of these are genitives in -*ī*, and Wackernagel argued that this -*ī* case is a special adverbial case preserved also in similar usages in Sanskrit and that it originally had nothing to do with the genitive. This view has been challenged, and it seems more likely that such genitives have developed from genitival usages discussed above. *dotis dare* 'give by way of dowry', can hardly be separated from partitive expressions of the type 'et dotis quid promiseris' (Plt. *Poen.* 1279). Contributions were also made by the qualitative genitives like *vir minimi preti* which goes closely with *homo trium litterarum,* the so-called genitive of the price being no more than a special lexical sub-variety of the genitive of quality. Thus the genitive of the rubric 'to consider as, enter as', is to be included in the genitive of the sphere.

We may now attempt a general formulation of the function of the genitive: *a noun in the genitive defines and delimits the range of reference of another noun or a verb.* In its adnominal uses it may be represented thus: ⊙; in the adverbial uses thus: ⊖. In later times the genitive began to be replaced by prepositional phrases (*ex, de*). In its possessive function it was further imperilled by the warmer, more colourful, and intimate possessive dative (see below). It persisted longest in the possessive, partitive, and qualitative functions.

The dative

The dative indicates that the person named is implicated or concerned in the event or state of affairs to which the verb or verbal expression refers. This function was transferred secondarily to non-personal nouns, but it has been noted that in Old Latin only one-twelfth of the nouns (and pronouns) in the dative refer to things. The function of the dative may be represented thus: $\overset{\cdot}{\longrightarrow}$.

The relationships thus generally indicated by the dative case in which a person (or thing) may stand to an event or state of affairs are legion. The following are some of the semantic 'fairy rings' deemed by grammarians sufficiently clear-cut to deserve special labels. It should be borne in mind that, strictly speaking, they are not grammatical but lexical subdivisions.

The person is interested as beneficiary or loser (the dative of advantage or disadvantage): 'tibi aras, tibi occas, tibi seris' (Plt.); 'si quid peccat, mihi peccat' (Ter.); 'mihi ego video, mihi ego sapio' (Plt.); 'ego tibi comminuam caput' (Plt.); 'saluti vestrae providere' (Cic.); 'pacem exposcere Teucris' (Virg.); 'vobis arabitur ager' (Livy). Prominent among the verbs concerned are those of giving (*do, mando, praebeo, largiri, solvo, sacrifico(r), fero*, etc.) and taking away (*demo, adimo, eripio, defendo, deest*). It is to this important semantic group that the case owes its name—*dativus* 'the giving case' (Gk. δοτική). Such datives of advantage and disadvantage occur in Latin with a number of verbs the English equivalents of which are transitive: e.g. *parco, indulgeo, invideo, medicor* (these also transitive in Old Latin), *faveo, ignosco, servio, noceo, obsum, consulo, studeo, nubo*, etc. The range of these datives was much extended by the poets: e.g. 'hunc . . . arcebis gravido pecori' (Virg. *G*. 3. 154-5).

Latin often combines a dative of advantage with the verb 'to be' to express the fact of possession. In the bulk of the Old Latin and Ciceronian examples the subject is an abstract noun. Since this is regularly the case in Germanic it is possible that this restricted usage is an ancient inheritance. Even in Old Latin, however, these datives of possession had been extended to concrete things: 'est ager . . . nobis'; 'quot digiti tibi sunt?'; 'illi . . . duae fuere filiae', etc. By 'relational displacement' such possessives were attached to nouns. The process may be seen clearly in the following example: 'quis est homo? :: amicus vobis' (Plt. *Poen.* 1213); cf. 'quis erat igitur? :: Philocomasio amator' (id. *Mil.* 1431). (On adnominal datives of purpose like *pabulum ovibus*, see below.

The dative of the personal pronouns was used frequently in colloquial speech to denote physical or emotional involvement in the action: 'animus mihi dolet'; 'ego tibi comminuam caput'; 'minatur mihi oculos exurere'; 'oculi splendent mihi'; 'quoi auro dentes iuncti escunt' (Twelve Tables). Such is the 'sympathetic dative' which was an inherited IE. usage. In meaning it is not far removed from the possessive genitive, and in Latin it is possible to say either 'nostris animus augetur' (Caesar) or 'ea animum eius non augebant' (Cic.). The difference between the two modes of expression is one of tone. The dative is more emotionally charged and it is preferred in popular speech. Thus in Petronius the majority of such datives occur in the 'vulgar' dialogue passages and the usage survives in Romance. The warmer tone of the dative made it also appropriate for poetical expression. Classical prose avoids this dative with nouns, but Caesar admits it for the pronouns, in which he is less fastidious than Cicero. The idea of possession is brought out further in popular speech by the use of the possessive adjective: e.g. 'meas mihi ancillas invito me eripis' (Plt.). Such habitual combinations of possessive adjective and sympathetic dative in the third person resulted in a fusion of *suus sibi*, which was used even where the reflexive pronoun was incorrect: 'reddam suom sibi' (Plt. *Trin.* 156); 'cum suo sibi gnato' (id. *Asin.* 825); 'priusquam tu suum sibi venderes' (Cic. *Philipp.* 2. 96).

The person (or thing) may be implicated not necessarily to his material advantage or disadvantage: the concern indicated may be of the weakest kind. By the use of the dative, especially of the second-person pronouns, the speaker as it were buttonholes the hearer and draws him into the orbit of the action, secures his interest and sympathy, and assures him that the event is his concern, as in the English 'there is a pretty kettle of fish for you!'. This is the so-called ethic dative, which is predominantly a feature of the warm, intimate, colloquial speech, e.g. 'em ergo hoc tibi' (Plt.); 'atque eccum tibi lupum in sermone' (id.). *mihi* is similarly used: 'quid mihi Celsus agit?' ('what is Celsus doing which is my concern?', Hor.). The interest or concern indicated may be that of a mere observer of the event referred to. This is the *dativus iudicantis*: e.g. 'quasi piscis est amator lenae' ('a lover is a sort of fish in the eyes of a *lena*', Plt.); 'ut me purgarem tibi' ('how could I clear myself in your eyes', id.); 'erit ille mihi semper deus' (Virg.). This dative was later particularly developed in participles with an indefinite reference in expressions of local orientation. This idiom, so frequent in Greek, is not found in Old Latin or Cicero, the first example being 'quod est oppidum primum Thessaliae venientibus ab Epiro' (Caes. *B.C.* 3. 80). It should be noted that Latin prefers the plural form and Greek the singular. This idiom, from Horace and especially Livy onwards, is extended to indicate the mental point of view: 'vere aestimanti Aetolium magis bellum fuit' (Livy).

With expressions denoting obligation the person concerned is envisaged as the agent: 'faciendum est tibi' ('something must be done and it's up to you', Plt.). Such datives are commonest with the gerundive (*abeundum est mihi*; *tibi cavendum censeo*; *virtus nobis est colenda*). The usage spread thence to the perfect participle passive (e.g. 'argenti quinquaginta mihi illa emptast minis' (id.), where the link with the dative of advantage is still evident; 'mihi decretumst remunerare omne aurum' (id.)), and finally to the finite forms of the verb including the *infectum* ('dissimillimis bestiis communiter cibus quaeritur', Cic. *N.D.* 2. 123). In Old Latin datives constructed with verbal abstracts, e.g. 'quid tibi hanc digito tactio est?', and 'quid tibi . . . hic . . . clamitatiost?' (Plt.), may be interpreted as agents but they show clear affinity to the category of 'possession'—'What's this shouting of yours here?'. Datives of the agent are also found with the verbal adjectives in *-bilis*: *amico exoptabilem* (Lucilius), but this may equally well be a *dativus iudicantis* 'desirable in the eyes of', or an analogical out-growth of the dative of advantage after *utilis*, etc. Such difficulties in drawing clear-cut distinctions may serve as a reminder of the essential functional unity of the dative in Latin.

Closely allied to the verbs of giving and taking away are the semantic groups comprising the expressions for bringing and send-ing: 'hominem alicui adducere' (Plt.); 'iussit Euclioni haec mit-tere' (Ter.), etc., and those for approaching and withdrawing (*occurro, appropinquo, cedo*). In such sentences the dative of the person has the usual function of expressing advantage or disadvan-tage. When, however, this usage was extended to nouns denoting things a fresh development took place: the concern of the thing in the action is construed as the purpose of the action. Such is the origin of the dative of purpose. Among the earliest of such uses are the datives of abstract nouns in *-tus*: e.g. 'receptui canere'; 'cibatui offas positas', a type of expression especially characteristic of military and agricultural special languages. Other examples are: 'ager oppositust pignori' (Ter.), 'arraboni dare', 'pecuniam doti dare', 'auxilio venire', 'succurrere', 'mittere', etc. Such datives may be combined with a personal dative of advantage: hence the familiar Latin idiom: 'dare alicui pecuniam faenori' (Cic.); 'emit eam dono mihi' (Ter.); 'Sabinis eunt subsidio'; 'res et fortunae tuae mihi maximae curae sunt' (Cic.), etc. By relational displacement in sentences as *satui semen dare, receptui signum dare* the final datives come to be used adnominally: 'pabulum ovibus, bubis medicamentum' (Cato), 'triumviri agris dandis adsignandis', etc.

The datives *commodi* with verbs of motion produced another 'fairy ring'—the dative of direction. It began with personal datives of the type 'tun mihi huc hostis venis' (Plt. *Stich.* 326). Here, too, the extension of the construction to non-personal nouns provided the basis for a new interpretation which was the germ of further development. The earliest example is the old formula *Quiris leto datus*, cf. 'me morti dabo' (Plt. *Merc.* 476). From *dare* there was an easy semantic link with *mittere*: hence 'morti mittere' (Plt.). Ennius allows himself 'conveniunt . . . tela tribuno'. An instructive example of development is provided by the dative constructions with the expression *manus tendere*. Classical prose authors confine themselves to a personal dative, e.g.: 'Romanis de muro manus tendebant' (Caes. *B.G.* 7. 48. 3); cf. 'manus diis immortalibus tendere' (Cic.). For *diis* Virgil substitutes *caelo*: 'caelo palmas tetendit'. This syntactical possibility once established in Latin, it was stimulated by the freer Greek use of such final local datives: hence Virgil's 'it clamor caelo', 'facilis descensus Averno', 'pelago dona praecipitare', etc.

So far we have considered the dative as expressing the concern or implication in a verbal action. Such usages spread to the corresponding verbal adjectives which acted as foci around which clustered a large number of Latin adjectives which take the dative. Prominent are the adjectives denoting proximity (*propinquus, adfinis, vicinus,* etc.), similarity (*similis, par, aequalis, congruens, aptus*, etc.), friendliness (*amicus, carus, benevolus, fidus*, etc.), and their opposites.

The ablative

The Latin ablative, as we have seen in the previous chapter, is a syncretistic case which has taken over the functions of the original ablative, instrumental and locative. Our analysis of Latin usage must therefore be arranged under these three headings.

The pure ablative

This case denotes the point of departure of an action. It may be represented thus: ⊢→. The plain ablative is preserved with the names of towns and certain islands, in the expressions *domo* and *rure*, and a few fixed formulae such as *manumittere, cedere loco*. But the local sense was in general reinforced by prepositions such as *ab, ex, de*, etc. If these coalesce with the verb to form compound verbs, the plain ablative may persist: 'patria hac ecfugiam', 'oppido eicere', 'portu exire', 'castris producit exercitum'. It is much rarer with simple verbs: 'primus cubitu surgat' (Cato), but this usage was, of course, affected by poetry which tends to strip itself of unnecessary words which of heir nature carry little emotional charge.

The ablative is employed, further, in expressions of source or origin: 'genere quo sim natus', 'sanguen dis oriundum', 'humana matre natus', etc. The pure ablative is preserved here, too, in poetry and Old Latin, but already in Old Latin we find the prepositions ('quo de genere natus est', Plt.) which were usual later. Relational displacement produced adnominal ablatives of origin: 'Periphanes Rhodo mercator dives' (id.), 'Philocratem ex Alide' (id.); 'video ibi hospitem Zacyntho' (id.).

The so-called ablative of separation is merely a lexical subvariety of the pure ablative. It is found with verbs of keeping away, taking away, etc.: 'ut te ara arceam' (Pac.); 'interdicere igni et aqua'; 'abstinere nupta, vidua, virgine'; 'anima privabo virum', etc. Such ablatives are also found after adjectives of corresponding meaning: 'expers metu'; 'virginem dote cassam' (Plt.); 'arce et urbe orba sum' (Enn.); 'Roma . . . recentes' (Cic.), cf. 'recentem caede locum' (Virg.).

The ablative of comparison developed from the pure ablative which expressed the standpoint from which another object was judged. Such ablatives are much rarer in Old Latin than the *quam* construction, being limited in the main (1) to the negative or virtually negative expressions of the types, *nihil hoc homine audacius* and *quis homo est me hominum miserior*; (2) to set expressions of the type *melle dulcior*; and (3) to numerical expressions after *plus*, *minus*, etc. In ordinary comparisons of the type 'Cicero is more eloquent than Caesar' the ablative of comparison is not used in Old Latin. Even in the classical prose writers the bulk of the examples are negative or quasi-negative expressions. The poets show some preference for the simple ablative as against the somewhat clumsy *quam* construction, although here, too, the influence of Greek models cannot be excluded. But throughout latinity there persists the tendency to express real comparisons by means of the *quam* construction and to reserve the ablative of comparison for elative expressions of the type *nive candidior*, which we should naturally render in English by an equative 'as white as snow'. In later Latin when phonetic developments had effaced the case distinctions, the ablative of comparison was replaced by prepositional phrases. *ab* occurs early: it is found after *secundus* in Horace and after *alter* in Virgil. An early example after a comparative is 'nec Priamost a te dignior ulla nurus' (Ovid, *Her.* 15. 98). Later when *ab* was confused with *ad*, *de* took its place in expressions of comparison. The first example of this construction, the ancestor of Romance idioms like *plus de*, occurs in the *Vitae Patrum*, 'plus facitis de nobis' (fourth to fifth century).

The instrumental-sociative

This case expresses 'togetherness'—being together, bringing together, etc. It may be symbolized thus: →←. This function is most transparent in the verbs of joining and mixing ('tignum iunctum aedibus' (XII Tab.); 'vinum miscere aqua'). From 'bringing together' the transition is easy to 'comparing', 'agreeing and disagreeing': 'oratio verbis discrepat sententiis congruens' (Cic.). 'Together with' leads on naturally to 'sharing with': e.g. 'quin sermone suo aliquem participaverit' (Plt. *Mil.* 263); 'communicabo semper te mensa mea' (ibid. 51). The sociative ablative is also used of the person or persons in whose company an action is performed. The plain ablative is still used in military expressions of the type *omnibus copiis* (e.g. 'exitum est maxuma copia,' Plt.). From the earliest times, however, the sociative ablatives were reinforced by the preposition *cum*, and this was regular in the case of personal substantives unaccompanied by an adjective.

A special instance is the ablative of concomitant circumstances: *Caesare duce, magno comitatu, clamore magno, luna silenti, inimico omine*, etc. Here, too, *cum* tends to be inserted: 'magno cum periculo optuma opportunitate advenis' (Plt.). Such ablatives of accompanying circumstances through relational displacement are attached more closely to nouns. Such is the origin of the ablatives of quality: e.g. 'summa virtute adulescens'; 'cano capite atque alba barba miserum me' (id.). They may be used predicatively: 'ut tu es gradibus grandibus' (id.), 'forma lepida et liberali est' (id.). Here, too, *cum* is found even in Old Latin: 'quis hic est homo cum conlativo ventre atque oculis herbeis' (id.); 'probo et fideli et fido et cum magna fide' (id.).

The instrumental uses of the ablative are closely connected with the sociative: thus 'nostro servire nos sibi censet cibo' (Plt. *Poen.* 810) may be interpreted 'he thinks we are his slaves, food and all'. Intrinsically the instrumental was possible with personal nouns. Latin, however, tended to reserve the plain instrumental ablative for things and to express personal instruments by *per* with the accusative: *virgis caedere, oculis cernere, senio confectus, maledictis deterrere*, etc. Certain lexical sub-varieties deserve special mention. Instrumental ablatives are found with verbs of filling, abounding in, and the like (*amore abundas, frumento affluere, vino scatere*, etc.) and the corresponding adjectives (*plenus, refertus, fecundus*, etc.). The instrumental is also found with verbs of feeding and enjoying, e.g. *vescor*; but it is uncertain whether this construction was inherited in the case of the verbs *fruor* and *utor* (the earliest examples of the accusative occur in Cato). *usus est* drew into its orbit the semantically associated *opus est*, with which a genitive would strictly be required. *potiri* was anciently constructed with the instrument 'make oneself master by means of'. In Old Latin it also takes the accusative (on the genitive see above). The IE. instrumental with *fungor* is not attested in Old Latin, where this verb takes the accusative. The influence of *utor* and *fruor* seems to have been responsible for the reintroduction (first in the *ad Herennium*) of the instrumental with *fungor*. The plain ablative of the instrument, too, in later latinity gradually acquired supporting prepositions: e.g. *ab, ex, cum, in,* and, above all, *de*.

Also to be classified as instrumental usages are the local ablatives of the 'route by which' (*recta porta invadam, ire publica via*: and with ellipse of *via, ea, hac, recta,* etc.) and the ablatives of money, etc., with which possessions are acquired ('quantillo argenti te conduxit' (Plt.) ; 'tribus nummis locavi', etc.). This province of usage suffered a limited encroachment from the genitival expressions of value (see above): *tanti, quanti, pluris,* and *minoris* are found in expressions of price. On the other hand, an ablative of value appears in late Latin with the verb *valeo*.

The instrumental appears with expressions of surpassing (by means of): e.g. 'divitiis superare'; 'cave sis te superare siris faciendo bene' (Plt.); 'vincere cervom cursu' (id.). From the instrumental in such phrases there developed ablatives of respect: 'numquam victus est virtutei' ('never surpassed in point of *virtus*', *CE* 9. 4) ; 'sicut ... praestitimus pulchritudine' (Plt. *Poen.* 1193), etc. This instrumental is found also with comparative adjectives as in the phrase *maior natu* which leads on naturally to *natu grandis,* etc. Some contribution to this category may have been made by ablatives of quality: e.g. 'nescio ut moribus sient vostrae' ('how your womenfolk are in character', id. *Most.* 708) can hardly be separated from 'antiquis adulescens moribus' (id. *Capt.* 105). From verbs denoting superiority, inferiority there is an obvious associational link with the verbs denoting distance from: 'alio intervallo distare' (Cic.). This formed the starting-point for the use in expressions of distance: e.g. 'milibus passuum sex a Caesaris castris sub monte consedit' (Caes. *B.G.* 1. 48. 1) ; a similar ablative is also used with *consisto* in *B.G.* 2. 23. 4. Later this usage was extended to verbs of motion (withdrawing) : e.g. 'XVII milibus passuum ab urbe secessit' (Plin. *Ep.* 2. 17. 2).

The ablative of manner is a lexical variety of the sociative of attendant circumstances or of the instrumental: *dolo* 'by a trick', *arte, astu, audacia, iniuria, vitio, silentio*; 'adire blandis verbis'; 'cum ea sermonem nec ioco, nec serio habeas' (Plt.). *cum* is frequently added to such ablatives of manner: 'cum clamore, cum invidia summa' (id.). In Classical Latin the rule was established making *cum* obligatory with an unsupported noun whereas a noun qualified by an adjective may dispense with the preposition. The apparent transgressions of this rule are due to the fact that some of the commonest ablatives of manner had become petrified as quasi-adverbs: *arte, modo, casu*, etc. An ancient stylistic device was the qualification of a verb by an etymologically related noun in the ablative of manner: 'aequo . . . censetur censu' (id.); 'fugit maxuma fugella' (Cato); 'curro curriculo' (Plt.), cf. 'curriculo sequi'. Such set formulae persisted in the special languages, in popular speech, and in the archaists.

The ablative of cause is traceable both to instrumental usages and to pure ablatives of origin: 'is aegritudine emortuost' (id.); 'amore perire'; 'lacrumare gaudio'; 'nimis sermone huius ira incendor' (id.). The ablatives of the 'material from which' may also have a double origin. Examples like 'cupam materia ulmea . . . facito' (Cato) and 'nescit quid faciat auro' (Plt.) suggest an instrumental origin. Such plain instrumentals were comparatively rare, and the more frequent classical insertion of the preposition *ex* (e.g. 'statua ex aere facta') suggests that for Roman *Sprachgefühl* at least the idiom ranked as an ablative of origin. The use with non-material nouns, as in 'quid eo fecisti puero?' (Plt.), 'de fratre quid fiet?' (Ter.), is colloquial.

The locative ablative

This case expresses 'place where' and 'time when'. The ancient locative ablatives were largely replaced in the pre-literary period by prepositional phrases with the ablative, the plain ablatives surviving chiefly with names of towns and with certain nouns denoting locality. The only certain examples in Old Latin concern the word *locus*: e.g. 'homo idem duobus locis ut simul sit' (Plt.). Later *parte* (Rhet. *ad Her.*) and *regione* (Caesar) follow the example of *loco*. These and nouns qualified by *medius, imus*, and *summus* exhaust classical usage in this respect, but the range of unsupported local ablatives was much enlarged in post-classical prose. Poetry and poetical prose permitted themselves greater freedom: e.g. 'densantur campis horrentia tela virorum' (Ennius), cf.

'nebula campo quam montibus densior sederat' (Livy). The ablative accompanied by *totus* is also used to denote 'place within which': e.g. 'toto me oppido exanimatum quaerere' (Ter.); 'omnes festinant intus totis aedibus' (Plt. *Cas.* 793). This usage fringes on the instrumentals of 'route by which' (see above).

Bare locative ablatives of time are frequent with nouns of temporal significance: *aestate, hieme, primulo crepusculo, mane, nocte, tertiis nundinis,* etc. The locative may also denote 'time within which', but it should be noted that nearly all the examples concern negative, or virtually negative, expressions: e.g. 'neque edes quicquam neque bibes his decem diebus' (Plt.); 'anno vix possum eloqui' (id.). When this construction was used in positive statements a new interpretation became possible: *me hoc triduo expecta* 'expect me three days from now'; and *hoc triduo venit* 'he came three days from now', i.e. three days ago. Early examples are 'emi istanc anno uxori meae' (id.); 'his annis paucis ex Asia missus est' (C. Gracchus). In negative expressions like '. . . ut triduo hoc perpetuo e lecto nequeat surgere' (Ter.) the ablative may be interpreted as signifying extent of time, 'cannot rise from his couch for the last three days'. Like the corresponding spatial idiom this development took place first where the noun was supported by the adjective *totus*: 'quoi bini custodes semper totis horis occubant' (Plt.); 'tota perducere vita . . . foedus amicitiae' (Catull.); cf. '. . . ut eo tempore omni Neapoli fuerit' (Cic.); 'tota nocte continenter ierunt' (Caes.). This usage gradually gained ground until *vixit annis* . . . became the predominant formula in epitaphs. Even Caesar has examples like 'hoc cum esset modo pugnatum continenter horis quinque' (*B.C.* 1. 46. 1). Note that here the durative force is underlined by *continenter* (cf. *perpetuo* in the Terence example above).

Nouns of non-temporal significance even in Old Latin normally required the support of the preposition *in*, though Plautus has both *nuptiis* and *in nuptiis*. This usage gradually spread in popular speech to the temporal nouns (e.g. Terence's *in tempore*) until in late Latin *in nocte*, etc., became the regular mode of expression. The preposition also occurs in expressions of 'time within which': 'illum confido domum in his diebus me reconciliassere' (Plt.); cf. 'in diebus paucis' (Ter.). The preposition is regular classical usage in distributive expressions: e.g. 'ter in anno' (Plt.); 'bis in die' (Cic.). But in non-classical and especially post-classical authors the type *bis die, septiens die* also occurs.

The ablative absolute

This construction originated in utterances where a noun in the ablative case was defined by an adjective, and in particular by a verbal adjective. The ablative could have any of the functions discussed above. The largest contribution was made by the instrumental-sociative of accompanying persons or circumstances: e.g. 'me quidem praesente numquam factumst' (Plt.); 'tute istic (dixisti), etiam astante hoc Sosia' (id.); 'Atticus quidam olim navi fracta ad Andrum eiectus est' (Ter.). But the ablatives of instrument, manner, cause, time, quality, etc., also played their part. The noun may be defined by an adjective (*me vivo*) or another noun (*me auctore, Caesare duce*). Of the participles the perfect predominates, the present being comparatively rare in Old Latin, except in fixed formulae like *me praesente, me absente*. Occasionally we find absolute constructions in which the subject is suppressed. Such usages show some affinity with the ablatives of manner of substantivized perfect participles such as *merito, consulto, sortito*, etc. *auspicato* in Plt. *Pers.* 607 is such an ablative of manner— 'auspiciously'. In Ter. *Andr.* 807, however, *haud auspicato* may be interpreted 'without taking the auspices'. The first indubitable example is Cl. Quadr. fr. 12: 'impetrato prius a consulibus ut in Gallum pugnare se permitterent'. The construction is rare in classical prose (never in Caesar), but it gains ground with Livy and subsequent authors.

THE VERB

The tenses

Indo-European, as we have seen in the previous chapter, had developed no grammatical category of tense, the so-called tense stems indicating different 'aspects' of the verbal action. Latin, however, evolved a comprehensive grammatical system of references to present, future, and past with each of its two aspectual stems and it was also meticulous in indicating the chronological relationships of events echeloned in time. This, too, was a Latin innovation, which is absent from Greek.

The durative stem

The present. The present tense indicates what is in progress at the moment of speaking even when the action may have started previously: e.g. 'iamdudum tacitus te sequor' (Plt.); 'triennium iam hinc abest' (id.). Past events may be represented as taking place before the eyes of the hearer, the temporal reference being supplied from the context. This 'present historic' is functionally equivalent to an aoristic perfect (see below) and it very rarely substitutes for an imperfect. Later, however (from Petronius on), more indiscriminate use is made of the present historic. This idiom was an ancient colloquial feature much utilized by the annalists. Its vividness and simplicity also made it suitable for poetry and it is particularly common in the dramatists, the temporal framework being fixed by introductory and concluding perfects. The future may similarly be referred to as present especially with verbs of motion: 'ego hos conveniam; post huc redeo' (Ter.); 'mane istic: iam exeo' (Plt.); 'in ius voco te :: non eo' (id.); cf. 'tuemini, inquit, castra . . .; ego reliquas portas circumeo et castrorum praesidia confirmo' (Caes. *B.C.* 3. 94. 5). Finally we have the so-called 'achronic' use of the present ('now and always'): 'facile omnes quom valemus recta consilia aegrotis damus' (Ter.); 'dulce et decorum est pro patria mori' (Hor.).

The imperfect. The preterite of the durative, the imperfect, had, strictly speaking, nothing to do with the actual duration of the event under reference, just as in English one and the same event may be referred to either as an item of history ('What did you plant in the garden yesterday?') or represented as in progress before the eyes of the hearer ('What were you planting in the garden yester-day?'). Thus the imperfect, being the preterite of the 'eyewitness' aspect, is used primarily in vivid descriptions, e.g. 'lacrimans tacitus auscultabat' (Plt.); 'ut trepidabat, ut festinabat!' (id.). From this basic function there developed the use to express habitual action ('optumi quique expectabant a me doctrinam sibi', id.), and repeated action ('cottidie accusabam', Ter.; but note the common *saepe dixi*). The use of the imperfect to express relative time, that is, action contemporaneous with another action, is also a secondary phenomenon. It is doubtful, too, whether we should set up the sub-categories of ingressive and conative imperfects. These are prompted by the difficulties of translation into languages which lack, or have developed differently, the grammatical categories of aspect. Thus *tunc dentes mihi cadebant primulum* means properly 'there I was with my teeth falling out' ('eyewitness' aspect). English translates 'my teeth began to fall out' and the grammars catalogue the usage as 'ingressive'. In the same way *eos captabant* means 'there they were in the process of catching them'. English renders 'they were trying to catch them' and the paragraph of the grammars is headed 'imperfectum de conatu'.

The future. The tense for factual reference to future events developed, as we saw, from old subjunctives and desideratives. We observe numerous survivals of the ancient modal force. Prospective force (see below) is evident in examples like: 'haec erit bono genere nata' ('she will turn out to be ...', Plt.); 'dicet aliquis' (Cic.); 'si viderit, gnatam non dabit' (Ter.). Such prospective futures are used in gnomic expressions: 'virgo atque mulier nulla erit quin sit mala' (Plt.). Voluntative usages also abound, especially in the colloquial language: 'tu, miles, apud me cenabis' (id.); 'tu cavebis ne me attingas' (id.); 'numquam edepol viva me inridebit' (id.); 'quae opus sunt dominus praebebit' (Cato). Sometimes this voluntative future alternates with the imperative: e.g. 'depsito bene ... postea magis depset' (id.).

Perfect stem

The Latin perfect combines the functions of the IE. aorist and perfect. As an aorist the perfect indicative refers to the event as an item of history without further qualification, regardless of its actual duration (e.g. 'hae permanserunt aquae dies complures', Caes.). It may even be used in predications of lasting qualities ('qui proximi Oceano fuerunt hi insulis sese occultaverunt', id.) and repeated actions (*saepe dixi*, etc.).

A gnomic use appears already in Plautus (e.g. *saepe is cautor captus est*), but this native growth was much stimulated by the example of Greek. In prose its chief exponents are Sallust, Seneca, and Tacitus (e.g. 'avaritia pecuniae studium habet quam nemo sapiens concupivit', Sall.).

The present perfect denotes the state resulting from an action. This is apparent in the ancient forms *memini, odi*, which have only present meaning: cf. *perii* 'I'm a dead man', etc. Often the perfect denotes that the action is over and done with: 'actum est, viximus, floruimus', cf. 'vixerunt!' (announcing the execution of the Catalinian conspirators) (Cic.), 'fuimus Troes, fuit Ilium' (Virg.). A future state may be vividly imagined as present: e.g. 'si offendero, periisti' (Ter.). On the periphrases for the perfect see pp. 166 f.

The pluperfect as the preterite of the perfect denotes the past state. In Latin, however, this function is observed only in the preterite forms of present perfects such as *memini, odi*. In the main the function of this tense is to express the priority of a past event over another past event: 'alium me fecisti: alius veneram' (Plt.). Such echeloning in time had no formal expression in Indo-European and it is often neglected in Latin: e.g. 'quam duxit uxorem ex ea natast haec' (id.). The use of perfect, too, even of prior events, is the regular classical usage in temporal clauses after the conjunctions *postquam, ubi, ut* (p. 332). The ellipse of the expression giving the *terminus ante quem* in utterances such as 'fugitivos ille, ut dixeram ante, vendidit' (id.), 'non te provideram' (id.) provided the starting-point for a gradual encroachment of the pluperfect on the perfect: e.g. 'eam osculantem hic videras' (id.); 'quanti hosce emeras' (id.). That this usage had a colloquial flavour is evident from the fact that Cicero rarely uses it except in his correspondence. Its growing frequency in later Latin was stimulated by the phonetic ambiguity of the inflexions in *vidit*, etc. (e.g. loss of final *-t*, see p. 159).

The future perfect rarely expresses the future state except as the future of the purely present perfects: *meminero, novero, odero*. It was mainly used to indicate the priority of a future event over some other future event, a usage which needs no exemplification. The distinction between the two futures is blurred even in Plautus, whose usage is often governed by metrical considerations, the endings of the future perfect providing a convenient close to a trimeter or septenarius: e.g. 'vos tamen cenabitis, | cena ubi erit cocta; ego ruri cenavero' (Plt. *Cas.* 780). As the future of an aorist stem the *futurum exactum* is sometimes clearly opposed in 'aspect' to the future of the *infectum*: e.g. 'hanc miserrimam vitam vel sustentabo vel, quod multo est melius, abiecero' (Cic.). This usage is colloquial and archaic. In the post-classical period we observe, further, the development of a deliberative use: 'occidi iussero?' ('shall I order him to be killed?', Seneca).

THE MOODS

The subjunctive

The IE. verb, as we saw in the previous chapter, had a number of morphological devices to express different modes of reference to events. In using the indicative mood the speaker made an objective reference to facts, stating that such-and-such is or was the case. The other moods expressed various attitudes towards the events or state of affairs referred to, the subjunctive expressing roughly (*a*) will (the voluntative subjunctive) and (*b*) likelihood or expectation (the prospective subjunctive); and the optative (*a*) wish and (*b*) contingency (the potential optative). These two moods, as we have seen, had in Latin become fused by a process of syncretism into a single mood, the subjunctive, which had morphological characteristics derived from the subjunctive and optative of the parent language with numerous innovations of its own. Such morphological variety would lead us to expect a functional multiplicity, and this is in fact apparent in the earliest texts. It is, therefore, merely an exercise in ingenuity to attempt to establish the 'unity of the Latin subjunctive' and by a plausible but arbitrary choice of examples to trace a chain of development from the 'primitive function'. This corresponds to the work of etymologists who derive the precise meanings of words in observed contexts from some vague 'Urbedeutung' of the root. Given the fact of relationship with other languages such as Greek and the evident morphological survivals of the IE. subjunctive and optative, it will be safer to assume that some functions of these moods survived in primitive Latin and to make these ancient functions the basis of our brief and summary analysis and classification, just as the manifold functions of the ablative case were arranged as ablative, locative, and instrumental. The functional distinction between will and wish and between prospective and potential is, of course, a delicate one, and many of the

examples allow of different interpretations. It will be recalled that
the 'tense' stems did not originally express time relations. But
what is particularly characteristic of Latin is its constant striving
towards precise differentiation of time relations in the moods.

1. *Voluntative (Commands, advice, etc.)*

The first person plural (e.g. *eamus* 'let us go', 'we must go') is
commoner than the singular: e.g. *ostende: inspiciam* 'show it: I
want to look at it', 'let me look at it' (Plt. *Poen.* 1075); cf.
'videam modo mercimonium' (id. *Pers.* 542); 'quod perdundumst
properem perdere' (id. *Bacch.* 1049).

In the second person singular the subjunctive is frequent in Old
Latin as a (perhaps milder?) equivalent of the imperative. Later
this type (*facias* 'you are to do it') is colloquial and poetical. In
Cicero it is practically confined to his correspondence (note also
'isto bono utare dum adsit, cum absit ne requiras', *de Sen.* 33).
The third person is common at all periods. Much rarer is the second
person plural: *velitis iubeatis Quirites*. The tense used is normally
the present; *perierint* (Plt. *Stich.* 385) is the imperative of the
'present perfect' *perii* 'I'm done for'. The perfect is somewhat more
common in the passive: 'hoc sit nobis dictum' (Cic. *de invent.* 2.
50). These jussive subjunctives in Old Latin are frequently introduced by *ut(i)*, which originally meant 'somehow': 'proin tu ab eo
ut caveas tibi' (Plt. *Bacch.* 739); 'sed uti adserventur' (id. *Capt.*
115). In this sphere of usage we find examples of the systematic Latin
development of temporal gradations. Thus the imperfect is used
for the past voluntative: e.g. 'si volebas participari, auferres dimidium domum' ('you ought to have taken', id. *Truc.* 748); cf.
Cic. *pro Rab. Post.* 29. The pluperfect is more frequent in Classical
Latin than the imperfect: e.g. 'quid facere debuisti? . . . rettu-
lisses', etc. (id. *in Verr.* 2. 3. 195). Once this usage was established
for the pluperfect, the imperfect by opposition came to be used for
present obligation.

For 'Prohibitions' Old Latin disposed of the following modes of
expression:

(i) *ne time*. This remained colloquial and poetical.

(ii) *ne facias* (*cave facias*). This, too, was a mark of colloquial
usage. The only certain example in classical prose is the passage

from the *de Senectute* quoted above, where it is to be explained by the careful concinnity and chiastic balance of the sentence. The more frequent occurrence of this type in Fronto and Apuleius is presumably one of their many archaizing mannerisms.

(iii) *ne feceris.* This type is rare in the third person singular although there are a number of examples with *nemo*: 'satui semen . . . mutuum dederit nemini' (Cat. *Agr.* 5. 3). The distinction between the present and perfect subjunctive in prohibitions may originally have been one of 'aspect': *ne facias* 'stop doing', *ne feceris* 'mind you don't do', but the distinction was already largely effaced in Old Latin. The perfect is not widely used in Classical Latin. Caesar avoids it and there is only one example in the speeches of Cicero, although it is commoner in the letters and in the philosophical and rhetorical works.

(iv) The expression characteristic of classical 'urbanity' *noli facere* was already well developed in Old Latin.

The subjunctive in questions is often difficult to classify. Thus Ernout and Thomas interpret 'an ego occasionem . . . amitterem?' (Ter. *Eun.* 604–6) as a subjunctive of possibility and translate 'pouvais-je laisser échapper l'occasion?' But questions commonly assume, by a sort of anticipatory assimilation, the form of the answer expected, or else are influenced by the form of the utterance which provokes the question. This consideration may guide our analysis. Thus *eloquar an sileam?* expects an answer of the type *sile* (*sileas*), i.e. a form of command or advice, not a forecast of events. Such dubitative subjunctives are, therefore, clearly voluntative in character. The same is true of the subjunctives prompted by a command: e.g. 'sequere :: quo sequar?' (Plt. *Bacch.* 406). The inherent voluntative force of the subjunctive may be brought out by an intercalated *vis*: 'redde huc sis :: quid tibi vis reddam?' In this usage, too, the imperfect is used to transpose the action into the past: 'quid agerem? :: adulescenti morem gestum oportuit' (Ter. *Adel.* 214); 'an tu tetigisti has aedis? :: cur non tangerem?' (Plt. *Most.* 454). The pluperfect in this sense is very rare: 'egone ut beneficium accepissem contumeliam' 'ought I to have received this insult as a favour?' (Cic. *ad Att.* 15. 11. 1). The voluntative future indicative sometimes substitutes for the present subjunctive: e.g. 'salta sic :: ego saltabo?' (Plt. *Men.* 198). The dubitative rejoinder to a command may be tinged with indignation and protest. Typical examples are: 'intus serva :: ego intus servem!' (id. *Aul.* 81) ; 'meum collum circumplecte :: ten complectatur!' (id. *Asin.* 696). This usage is also projected into the past: e.g. imperfect: 'ille daret illi!' (Ter. *Phor.* 120); perfect: 'ille aedis emerit!' (Plt. *Most.* 1026 d).

The note of indignation and protest arises from the context and the tone of voice and is not inherent in the subjunctive, which as we have seen is voluntative in character. Since, however, this type of expression came to be used in challenging not only commands but also statements, there is some justification for setting up a sub-category 'the repudiating subjunctive': 'vir ego tuos sim!' (id. *Amph.* 813); 'egon haec patiar aut taceam!' (id. *Asin.* 810); 'tecum fui :: tun mecum fueris!' (id. *Amph.* 818). In this way the usage gradually shades off into that of 'quotation', the 'oblique' subjunctive: 'quid fecit? :: quid ille fecerit . . .' 'you ask what he's done!' (Ter. *Ad.* 84).

Some examples quoted under this heading are ambiguous. Thus 'egone ut haec conclusa gestem clanculum? ut celem patrem . . . tua flagitia' (Plt. *Bacch.* 375) would be most naturally translated 'how could I hide your misdeeds', i.e. as potential. So, too, 'somnium! utine haec ignoraret suom patrem?' (Ter. *Phor.* 874) either 'nonsense! how could she not know her own father' (potential), or perhaps 'the suggestion that she did not know!' (repudiating).

Another offshoot of the voluntative subjunctive is the permissive usage: 'ubi illum quaeram gentium? :: dum sine me quaeras, quaeras mea causa vel medio in mari' ('you may look for him in the middle of the sea', Plt. *Epid.* 678). The closely related concessive use 'granted that . . .' is not fully developed until Classical Latin. The earliest example is 'sane sint superbi: quid id ad nos attinet' (Cato, p. 25. 4 (Jordan)). The corresponding use of the perfect subjunctive with reference to the past is found first in Cicero: e.g. 'fuerint cupidi, fuerint irati' ('granted that they were greedy . . .', *pro Q. Lig.* 18). Such concessive subjunctives are negatived by *ne*, a clear sign of their voluntative character.

2. *Optative (Wishes)*

The plain subjunctive is preserved in few formulae: *di te ament, di bene vortant, valeas, salvos sis,* etc.; but mostly such wishes are introduced by the particle *ut* (in OL.) or its strengthened form *uti-nam*, originally meaning 'somehow'. This is also the force of the rare form *qui*, the instrumental of the indefinite pronoun: 'qui illum di omnes deaeque perdant' (Plt. *Cas.* 279). The only Classical Latin example is 'qui illi di irati [sint]' (Cic. *ad Att.* 4. 7. 1). *si* and *sic* ('in this way') are occasionally found especially in poetry, but the occurrence of this particle in Petronius and the Romance languages suggests that it was a popular usage. The tense is most commonly the present subjunctive. In the first person it rarely occurs without *utinam*, although this omission is more frequent in imprecations, e.g. *moriar, peream*. The second person occurs rarely in classical prose. The perfect subjunctive is rare, most of the Old Latin examples being *s*-aorists: e.g. 'ita di faxint', 'di te servassint'. The *r*-forms of the perfect subjunctive are much rarer in Plautus ('ne di siverint', *Merc.* 323). Occasionally the perfect is a true 'present perfect': 'ut satis contemplata sis' (Ter. *H.T.* 617). The negative is normally *ne, utinam ne*; *non* also occurs, but not in Old Latin. In wishes, too, we occasionally find the voluntative future indicative doing duty for the subjunctive: 'dabunt di quae velitis vobis' (Plt. *Asin.* 623); 'di fortunabunt vostra consilia' (id. *Trin.* 576). The classical usage whereby 'unreal' or impossible wishes with present reference are expressed by the imperfect subjunctive and with past reference by the pluperfect is already well established in Old Latin. Examples are found, however, of the present subjunctive for present wishes ('utinam nunc stimulus in manu mihi sit', Plt. *Asin.* 418) and the imperfect for past wishes ('utinam te di prius perderent quam periisti e patria tua', id. *Capt.* 537). Unreal wishes are almost always introduced by *utinam*, the only exception being Catullus 2. 9.

3. *Prospective*

This ancient usage of the IE. subjunctive has left few traces and some scholars have denied its existence in Latin. The distinction between 'I rather think such-and-such will happen' and the potential 'such-and-such in given circumstances might happen' is, of course, a delicate one, while in the first person (e.g. 'quid ego cesso hos conloqui? sed maneam etiam opinor', Plt. *Trin.* 1135) the mood may be interpreted either as voluntative 'I will wait', or as prospective 'I think I'll wait'. A clear prospective use is 'ubi senex senserit sibi data esse verba, virgis dorsum dispoliet meum' (Plt. *Epid.* 92). But in the main the use of the Latin subjunctive of cautious assertion of future events is derivable from the ancient IE. potential optative. An ambiguous example is: 'nec me miserior femina est neque ulla videatur magis' (id. *Amph.* 1060).

4. *Potential (Optative)*

This mood is the expression of contingent events: such-and-such might, could, would happen or be the case in such-and-such circumstances. There are surprisingly few examples in Old Latin without an accompanying conditional clause and most of these are accounted for by the form *velim* and its compounds *nolim, malim*. This narrow restriction as compared with the much freer usage in Greek and Sanskrit has led some scholars (e.g. Kroll) to derive the Latin potential uses from expressions of will, wish, and 'futurity'. *velim*, according to this view, is merely a polite form of expression. But for it to be 'polite' the mood must express a different shade of meaning from the indicative as a downright statement of fact, i.e. the difference between 'I should like' and 'I want'. The explanation as 'politeness', in fact, concedes the whole position. That an ancient IE. usage should have survived only in a few tenacious idioms offers no theoretical difficulties. We may recall that the optative survived in late Greek chiefly in formulae such as χαίροις, μὴ γένοιτο. Our exposition, then, must take the form of a catalogue of the few pockets of usage. There is little point in separating a 'should/would' potential from a 'can' potential. The distinction is not inherent in the mood but prompted merely by translation into idioms lacking this piece of grammatical machinery. We may reverse the usual complaint and decry the tyranny of English grammar over Latin. The potential, then, occurs:

(*a*) in the forms *velim, malim, nolim*: examples passim.

(*b*) in the indefinite second person singular especially with verbs of knowing and perceiving: *videas, audias, cernas, scias, invenias, censeas, possis*, etc.

(*c*) The use of the third person singular is rare in Old Latin: 'id flagitium meum sit' (Plt. *Bacch.* 97) is followed by an infinitival expression equivalent to a protasis; 'quid sit hoc hominis?'

('What sort of a person might he be?', id. *Amph.* 576) is an offshoot of the repudiating subjunctive (cf. 'bonus est hic vir :: hic vir sit bonus?', Ter. *And.* 915). With verbs of saying and believing the earliest examples are quoted from Terence: 'roget quis'[1] (*Eun.* 511); 'quis non credat?' (*And.* 489). But in classical prose the perfect subjunctive was more frequent in this sense. The first example *dixerit aliquis* occurs in Cato, but it was developed by Cicero especially in the philosophical and rhetorical works and his letters as a Latin equivalent of the Greek optative (it is to be noted that it is avoided by Caesar), first in expressions of saying and thinking and then with other verbs: e.g. 'quis eum iure reprehenderit' (*de fin.* 1. 32). The usage was extended to subordinate clauses in post-classical latinity (see below).

For the potential, too, Latin devised a corresponding preterite expression. This use of the imperfect subjunctive is rare in Plautus except in full conditional sentences: 'scires' ('you might have known', Plt. *Curc.* 331), 'quo nunc ibas? :: exsulatum :: quid ibi faceres?' (id. *Merc.* 884); 'mare velis florere videres' (Cato 34. 4 J.). This use of the indefinite second person singular is still very rare in Plautus and becomes frequent only from Terence onwards. The first and third persons were at all times rare in unaccompanied main clauses: the type *quis crederet* is first found in Cicero. The perfect with past meaning was always rare: 'non illam vir prior attigerit' (Cat. 67. 20); 'hoc dixerit potius Ennius' (Cic. *de fin.* 2. 41). 'Themistocles nihil dixerit . . .' 'cannot have said' (id. *de off.* 1. 75); 'qui ambo saltus eum . . . deduxerint' (Livy 21. 38. 7).

The time gradations were developed most systematically in 'unreal' (that is, contrary to fact) potential statements. Indo-European possessed no separate means of expression for 'unreality' and the use of the present, imperfect, and pluperfect subjunctive respectively for future, present, and past is a Latin innovation corresponding to the similar series of expressions for wishes. At first the imperfect, as we have seen, was used as a preterite. Its

[1] The sense here being 'suppose someone asks', this example might well be taken as jussive. Precisely similar is 'atqui aliquis dicat' ('and yet suppose someone says', Ter. *And.* 640), with which we may compare 'vendat aedes vir bonus' ('suppose a man sells a house', Cic. *de off.* 3. 54). It is not insignificant for the jussive interpretation that the imperative figures in similar usages (see below). This usage, too, is transposed into the past: 'diceret "quid feci"' ('suppose he said . . .', Ter. *And.* 138).

shift to present reference came about by a process of rearrangement as a counterpoise to the pluperfect subjunctive, which is rare
in Old Latin especially outside full conditional sentences (see
below). Bennett quotes only two independent examples from
Plautus and six from Terence.

The 'unreal' indicative

In certain turns of phrase the indicative is used in an unreal
function. In the first place we have those rhetorical modes of
expression which vividly represent an event as taking place or
completed, the seemingly inevitable being prevented by unexpected
circumstances: e.g. 'praeclare viceramus, nisi spoliatum, inermem,
fugientem Lepidus recepisset Antonium' (Cic. *ad fam.* 12. 10. 3);
'at ille . . . ferrum . . . deferebat in pectus, ni proximi prensam dex-
tram vi attinuissent' (Tac. *Ann.* 1. 35). Here, too, we may classify
the example 'solus eram, si non saevus adesset Amor' ('I was
alone—except for Love', Ovid, *Am.* 1. 6. 34).

In other cases the apparent contradiction inherent in the 'unreal' indicative is accounted for by the greater precision of Latin,
for where a possibility, likelihood, obligation, propriety exists or
existed, a statement about it properly stands in the indicative:
possum 'I am able', *potui* 'I was able', 'I could have', etc. Hence
the 'unreal' use of the indicative with verbs like *possum, debeo,
oportet*, in phrases like *par, satius, melius est* and with the gerundive and the periphrastic *futurus fuit* 'he was likely to be'. On the
other hand, if the possibility depends or depended on an unfulfilled
condition, then the expression would appropriately assume the
'unreal' colouring of the subjunctive. It need hardly be said that
this fine logical distinction was not faithfully observed in Latin.
In practice *potui*, etc., and *potuissem*, etc., became interchangeable, the subjunctive being more frequent in classical prose: e.g.
'quid facere potuissem nisi consul fuissem? . . . consul esse qui
potui nisi eum vitae cursum tenuissem' (Cic.). In Old Latin the
use of the tenses is the logical one: *satius est* 'it would be better';
satius erat, fuit 'it would have been better'. But by classical times
the shift of tense reference had taken place which we have observed in the 'unreal' subjunctive. *satius erat* came to mean 'it
would be better'. For the past, however, the perfect was preferred

to the pluperfect. *par fuerat, aequum fuerat* occur in Plautus, and *potuerat* in Terence, but even in Ciceronian prose *potueram, debueram, oportuerat* still remained rare.

The imperative

On the distinction between the present and future imperative see 'Morphology' (pp. 276 f.).

The imperative has a wide range of meaning, being used in commands, advice, wishes (e.g. *bene ambula* 'have a nice walk'), prayers, etc. Of particular interest is its use to express a proviso or a supposition: 'ausculta, scies' ('listen and you will know', Plt. *Asin.* 350); 'verbum etiam adde unum: iam in cerebro colaphos apstrudam tuo' ('say another word and I'll brain you', id. *Rud.* 386); 'modo sis veni huc: invenies infortunium' ('just come over here and you'll be unlucky', id. *Amph.* 286); cf. 'lacesse: iam videbis furentem' (Cic. *Tusc.* 4. 54). It is this use of the imperative to express a supposition which lends plausibility to the interpretation of subjunctives like *aliquis dicat*, 'suppose someone says', as jussive rather than potential (see above).

THE VERBAL NOUNS

The infinitive

Morphologically the Latin infinitives are innovations having nothing in common with the infinitives of Greek or even Osco-Umbrian and Celtic. Thus the many resemblances in usage between Latin and Greek must be due to independent development. The Latin infinitives were in origin cases of verbal nouns which gradually divested themselves of some of their nominal functions and became more closely attached to the verbal system, acquiring in the process morphological distinctions for time and voice. In certain Latin usages the nominal character is still apparent: the infinitive simply names the action denoted by the verbal root. This is most apparent in the so-called historic infinitive which occurs where the narrative is drawn in rapid, broad strokes which leave the details of person and tense to be gathered from the context. Such nominal sentences are a primitive mode of expression of which even Plautus makes little use. It is not without significance that the historic infinitive is frequent in the archaizing historians, Sallust and Tacitus, whereas Caesar tends to avoid it.

Most of the Ciceronian examples occur in the early speeches. Among the earliest examples are: 'consonat terra, clamorem utrimque ecferunt, imperator utrimque Iovi vota suscipere, hortari exercitum' (Plt. *Amph.* 229); 'circumstabant navem venti, imbres atque procellae frangere malum, ruere antennas, scindere vela' (id. *Trin.* 836). This last example should suffice to refute the often repeated statement that the historic infinitive never has aoristic value but is always equivalent to an imperfect. It is, in fact, neutral, the type of action being determined by the meaning of the verb.

The infinitive, in naming the event, according to context and tone of voice, may be exclamatory or imperatival: 'vae misero mihi: propter meum caput labores homini evenisse' (Plt. *Capt.* 945) 'huncine hominem te amplexari' (id.; *Truc.* 953). The infinitive is used imperatively in a number of IE. languages, but in Latin it arose independently from the naming of the action in a tone of command. This was essentially a colloquial idiom and it does not occur in literature until Valerius Flaccus: 'tu socios adhibere sacris' (3. 412). Examples are abundant in the Vulgar prose authors and the usage has survived in Romance in prohibitions. The occurrence of the construction in ecclesiastical writers may well be numbered among the vulgarisms of Christian Latin, but the possibility of Greek influence cannot be excluded.

The substantival nature of the infinitive is clearly brought out by the use of qualifying pronouns: 'tuom conferto amare' (Plt. *Curc.* 28); 'istuc nihil dolere' (Cic. *Tusc.* 3. 6. 12); 'me hoc ipsum nihil agere et plane cessare delectat' (id. *de or.* 2. 24). This type of infinitive, which was convenient for rendering the Greek articular infinitive, had some vogue in philosophical literature. That it was colloquial in tone emerges from the fact that Cicero otherwise uses it mainly in his letters to Atticus and that it is frequent in Petronius. The substantival infinitive may even be governed by a preposition. The first example occurs in Cicero: 'inter optime valere et gravissime aegrotare nihil interesse' (*de fin.* 2. 43). In post-classical Latin the nominal functions are extended so that the infinitive may be qualified by a genitive ('cuius non dimicare vincere fuit', Val. Max. 7. 3. 7) and by an adjective instead of an adverb ('illud iners quidem, iucundum tamen nihil agere', Pliny, *Ep.* 8. 9. 1).

The infinitive as a verbal noun may function as the subject, predicate, or object of a verb.

Subject

'Petere honorem pro flagitio more fit' (Plt. *Trin.* 1035); 'quos omnes eadem cupere, eadem odisse, eadem metuere in unum coegit' (Sall. *J.* 31. 14). In this nominative function the infinitive figures most largely as the subject or complement of the impersonal verbs *decet, libet, licet, oportet, piget, pudet,* etc., and such phrases as *bonum est, aequom est, difficile est,* etc.

Object

'Hic vereri perdidit' ('he has lost all sense of shame', Plt. *Bacch.* 158); 'Gallia duas res persequitur, rem militarem et argute loqui' (Cato 9. 12 J.); 'hoc volo, meam rem agere' (Plt. *Curc.* 670). Such infinitives were particularly frequent as the object of *volo* and analogical influences extended this construction to a growing company of verbs denoting wish and effort (and their opposites): *cupio, studeo, cogito, experior, intendo, enitor, quaero, ardeo,* etc.; *nolo, dubito, cesso, vereor, omitto,* etc. *possum,* too, proved a fertile nucleus extending its construction to *scio, calleo, valeo,* etc. In these constructions the infinitive is normally in the present tense. In legal phraseology the perfect is sometimes found: e.g. 'neiquis eorum Bacanal habuise velet' (*Sen. Cons. de Bacch.*).

The infinitive after verbs of effort may also be traced to the original case function of the infinitives. These, as we saw, are formally either old datives or locatives and both these cases could express purpose. This function is apparent in the expression *dare bibere* which is frequent at all periods though, curiously enough, the corresponding *dare edere, manducare* do not occur until late Latin. Such infinitives of purpose are especially common in colloquial and poetical texts after verbs of motion: 'turbare qui huc it' (Plt. *Bacch.* 354); 'eamus visere' (Ter. *Phormio* 102); 'venerat aurum petere' (Plt. *Bacch.* 631). This construction was avoided in classical prose but was affected as an archaism by the poets from Lucretius on and by the archaizing prose writers. It survived in the colloquial language and is preserved in Romance.

The infinitive of purpose is also used after the causative verbs *iubeo, cogo, moneo, subigo* and other verbs of urging, persuading, compelling, though classical prose preferred the jussive subjunctive with many of these. It is from such sentences as *iussit eum manere*, where originally *eum* was the direct object of *iussit*, that the accusative and infinitive construction is believed to have arisen through 'relational displacement'—*iussit: eum manere*, in which *eum* was taken as the subject of the infinitive. The construction was gradually extended by the formation of analogical chains or 'fairy rings' (see pp. 284 f.) (*postulo, dehortor, decerno*, etc.). Some contribution was also made by those verbs which take a double accusative: 'quanti istuc unum me coquinare perdoces?' (Plt. *Pseud.* 874).

The nominative with the infinitive after verbs of saying and thinking does not occur in Old Latin. Its introduction into Latin is entirely due to Greek influence. The first example occurs in Catullus: 'phaselus ille... ait fuisse navium celerrimus' (4. 1–2). In Greek the infinitive may also define the application of an adjective (θέειν ἄριστος). This construction does not occur in Plautus except after participles in conjunction with the verb 'to be'. Thus 'animatust facere' (*Truc.* 966) is clearly synonymous with *vult, cupit facere*, etc. So, too, *potens* is linked closely with *potest* and *consuetus, insolitus, peritus* with *solet*. Thus by these analogical processes the native foundations were gradually laid for the bolder usage affected particularly by the Augustan poets in imitation of the Greek. The first purely adjectival Hellenizing example is Lucilius' 'solvere nulli lentus', but here the influence of *piget* may still be felt.

The infinitives may also be constructed with nouns. In sentences like 'nunc adest occasio bene facta cumulare' (Plt. *Capt.* 423), the infinitive is the complement of the phrase *adest occasio* (= *licet*). However, by 'relational displacement' it was felt to be governed by the noun *occasio*, whence such examples as 'ut haberent facultatem . . . pugnare' (Caes. *Bell. Afr.* 78. 4).

The gerund and gerundive

Since Latin possessed no article it could not make such flexible use of the substantival infinitive as Greek. Instead it used another verbal noun to serve as the oblique case of the infinitive—the gerund, e.g. *mittere*: *mittendum*, *mittendi*, *mittendo*. Throughout latinity there were severe restrictions on the use of this verbal noun and its employment must be considered together with the morphologically similar verbal adjective in *-ndus*. This signified 'capable of, prone to, susceptible of, ripe for' (killing, dying, rising, rolling, etc.). In some senses it is scarcely distinguishable from the present participle: e.g. *secundus*, *oriundus*, *volvendus*. This adjective was originally neutral as to voice and so could be formed from both transitive and intransitive verbs: e.g. *pereundus*, *placendus*, *caedendus*. It is, however, mostly passive in meaning, but a few intransitive examples occur in which the verbal adjective comes close in function to the future active participle, e.g. 'puppis pereunda est probe' (Plt. *Epid.* 74). The meaning of necessity and obligation was a secondary development which came about in certain contexts. Thus *agnus caedundus* meant 'lamb ready for slaughtering'; but in the predicative use *agnus est caedundus* the sense 'is for slaughter' passed easily to 'is to be slaughtered, must be slaughtered'. In combination with *esse* the gerundive forms a periphrastic tense. The neuter is frequently used as an impersonal (*agendum est*) and this may occasionally take a direct object in the accusative case: e.g. 'agitandumst vigilias' (Plt. *Trin.* 859), a construction which is found in later writers as an archaism (Lucretius, Catullus, Virgil; once in Cicero). On the gerundive as a future participle passive in late Latin see above (p. 167).

In its verbal character the gerund could intrinsically take a direct object in the accusative case, but this possibility was in fact little utilized. Caesar allows only a gerund in the genitive to govern a noun in the accusative case. Cicero allows this construction also after the ablative of the gerund. But in these cases, too, preference was given to the gerundival construction, the gerund being employed for particular reasons—clarity, emphasis on the verbal notion, and perhaps euphony. In Old Latin the gerund was used more freely than the gerundive, to which it gradually yielded as time went on. There are, however, traces of an older construction in which the noun is not governed by the gerund but stands in apposition with it: e.g. 'lucis das tuendi copiam' (Plt. *Capt.* 1008), where the noun *copia* 'supply, opportunity' is qualified by two genitives, *lucis* and *tuendi*, the second being as it were epexegetic, giving further precision to the expression—'opportunity of light, that is of seeing it'. If the noun were masculine or neuter (e.g. *operis fruendi causa*), then it was possible to interpret the gerund as a verbal adjective agreeing with the noun. Some scholars have suggested that the gerundive construction originated in this way. It might be adduced in support of this theory (1) that the 'gerundive' is invariable in Old Latin with the personal pronouns even when these refer to female persons, e.g. 'tui (*fem.*) videndi copiast' (Plt. *Truc.* 370); (2) that the genitive of the gerundive has a narrow semantic range in Old Latin, being found mainly with verbs of perceiving and knowing, searching and getting. There can, however, be no doubt about the antiquity of the verbal adjective. *secundus* is so old that it has cut adrift from the verb from which it was formed, while the gerundive construction is frequent in the ancient prayers preserved by Cato in his *de agri cultura*: 'te hoc ferto ommovendo bonas preces precor' (134. 2), etc. It should be noted, however, that in the attributive use the gerundive is practically confined to verbs expressing approval or disapproval; *mirandus, expetendus, pudendus, miserandus, amandus, contemnendus*, etc. The predicative use after verbs of giving and taking, asking and offering, and the like is still in its beginnings in Plautus (e.g. 'quos utendos dedi', *Asin.* 444), while the well-known classical construction after *curo* first appears in Terence.

The accusative case of the gerund is used only after certain prepositions: only after *ad* in Plautus, but Classical Latin admits also *in* (not in Caesar), while Cicero in legal phraseology has examples of *ob*, which first occurs in Cato. There are sporadic examples of other prepositions: *ante* (Virgil), *inter* (Ennius), *propter* (first in Varro), *circa* (post-classical, first in Quintilian). The gerund construction occurs after nouns ('canes ad venandum', Ter. *And.* 57), adjectives ('doctus ... ad male faciendum', Plt. *Epid.* 378), and verbs ('quo conductus venio :: ad furandum quidem', id. *Pseud.* 850). There is no certain example in Old Latin of the accusatival gerund governing a direct object. Varro is the first to venture this construction ('ad discernendum vocis verbi figuras', *L.L.* 9. 42), which in late Latin translation literature was found useful for rendering the Greek εἰς with the articular infinitive (*ad sanandum eos* = εἰς τὸ ἰᾶσθαι αὐτούς, Luke 5.17). Classical Latin like Old Latin used the gerundive in such constructions ('ad aquam praebendam', Plt. *Amph.* 669).

The genitive of the gerund is always adnominal in Old Latin, the governing nouns being a few abstract nouns—*occasio, tempus, copia, causa, gratia*, etc. (e.g. 'non enim nunc tibi dormitandi neque cunctandi copia est', Plt. *Epid.* 162). Classical Latin uses the genitive also after a few nouns denoting personal agents such as *auctor, dux, artifex*, etc. Certain adjectives also govern the genitive of these verbal nouns. The usage begins with Terence's *cupidus* (Plautus offers no examples), and the list was gradually extended but not greatly increased until post-classical times.

The genitive of the gerund and gerundive may also express purpose. The earliest example quoted is 'ne id adsentandi mage quam quo habeam gratum facere existumes' (Ter. *Ad.* 270), and on the strength of similar constructions in Osco-Umbrian the idiom is assigned to the 'Italic' period. Terence's example is, however, not free from the suspicion of being an anacoluthon, and since the construction is first used freely by Sallust it is more probably an independent Latin development. In *res evertendae reipublicae*, 'matters involving the overthrow of the state', the genitive has its normal defining function. When used predicatively (*res evertendae reipublicae sunt*) it comes close to a final meaning as in Cicero's 'quae res evertendae rei publicae sunt' (*in Verr.* 2. 132). The native foundations of a genitive of purpose once established, it proved a convenient equivalent for the Greek genitive of the articular infinitive in a final sense. Sallust introduced it into historical writing (note that it is not used by Caesar and Cicero) and he was followed by Livy, Tacitus, and others (e.g. 'Aegyptum proficiscitur cognoscendae antiquitatis', Tac. *Ann.* 2. 59).

The dative is used in a final sense after verbs like *studeo, operam do* (e.g. 'auscultando operam dare', Plt. *Amph.* 1006) and certain adjectives such as *natus, optimus, firmus*, etc. In this case the gerundive predominates over the gerund, which is rare. Plautus uses the gerund with a direct object ('hominem investigando operam . . . dabo', *Mil.* 260), but in Cicero it occurs only in traditional legal phraseology (*scribendo adesse, solvendo non esse*) and Caesar offers no example. Even the gerundive remained comparatively rare until Livy and Tacitus, in imitation of the poets, greatly extended the number of adjectives taking this construction (*intentus, promptus, exiguus, levis,* etc.).

The ablatival uses in Old Latin are practically confined to the instrumental, the gerund being more frequent than the gerundive ('legiones . . . vi pugnando cepimus', Plt. *Amph.* 414). With verbs denoting superiority the instrumental merges into the ablative of respect ('mendicum . . . mendicando vincere', id. *Bacch.* 514, whence freer examples such as 'astu et fallendo callet', Accius, *frg.* 475 W). The instrumental force is sometimes so slight that the gerund may express merely a concomitant action. Decisive examples are few in Old Latin ('hic expectando obdurui', Plt. *Truc.* 916) and even in Cicero. The usage did not make headway until Sallust and the Latin writers of the Empire, with whom it functions as an equivalent of the present participle, 'novi consules populando usque ad moenia pervenerunt' (Livy 8. 17. 1); 'exturbabant agris, captivos servos appellando' (Tac. *Ann.* 14. 31. 2). This usage also gained ground in the colloquial language and it is only in this form, functioning as a present participle, that the gerund has survived in the Romance languages.

The ablatives of the gerund and gerundive may be governed by prepositions. The most frequent are *in* and *de,* which are found in Plautus and admitted by Caesar. Cicero uses also *ex, pro* (these, too, in Plautus), and *ab,* which first occurs in Cato. This case of the gerund frequently takes a direct object in Old Latin, but Classical Latin shows greater reserve. The poets, Sallust, and Tacitus are less strict and full freedom is gained in late Latin. It is very rare for a prepositional ablative of the gerund to take a direct object. The first example is Varro's 'in supponendo ova' (*R.R.* 3. 9. 12).

The supines

The supines are remnants of verbal abstracts in -*tus* (see p. 280). The first supine is the accusative case used to express the goal or purpose of the action chiefly after verbs of motion: 'comissatum ibo' (Plt. *Most.* 317); 'abiit ambulatum' (id. *Mil.* 251). From verbs denoting 'sending' and the like there was an easy analogical link with the group 'giving', 'taking', which forms a second focus of usage: 'nuptum . . . daret' (id. *Aul.* 27); 'nuptum conlocet' (id. *Trin.* 735); 'coctum ego, non vapulatum, dudum conductus fui' (id. *Aul.* 457). Such uses persist in the archaizing writers, but the classical purists show greater reserve, Cicero hardly venturing outside common phrases such as *cubitum ire,* which persisted also in the spoken language down to late antiquity. This supine in Old Latin may take a direct object (e.g. 'it petitum . . . gratiam', Plt. *Aul.* 247), and examples occur in later writers including Caesar and Cicero. With *eo* the supine forms a periphrastic conjugation which provides in *-tum iri* the missing future infinitive passive. But this was always a comparatively rare form.

The morphology of the so-called second supine is ambiguous (see p. 280). Certain usages are clearly ablatival: e.g. 'primus cubitu surgat' (Cato, *agr.* 5. 5); 'ita dictu opus est' (Ter. *H.T.* 941). Others again are best explained as datives: 'hoc mihi factust optumum' (Plt. *Aul.* 582); 'dictu facilius' (Ter. *Phor.* 300). It is not without significance that Plautus once offers the form *-tui*: 'istaec lepida sunt memoratui' (*Bacch.* 62). It is, however, possible to interpret the *-tu* forms as ablatives of respect.

The participles

The participles are parts of speech which 'participate' in the nature both of the verb and the noun. The name, therefore, would strictly be applicable to the verbal nouns discussed above. It is used, however, especially with reference to the verbal adjectives which were attached more closely to the verbal conjugation. Of the IE. participles only the present active participle survived in Latin and even this had few verbal functions in Old Latin. In the perfect, Latin, like Osco-Umbrian, utilized the verbal adjective in *-to-* as a perfect participle but did not possess a corresponding active form. The future participle in *-turus* was a Latin creation (p. 281).

The present participle

In Old Latin this participle was practically confined to adjectival functions, appearing mainly in the nominative case: e.g. *vigilans* 'awake', *maerens* 'sorrowful', *sedens* 'seated', *sapiens, intellegens, cupiens,* etc. This is true of colloquial Latin throughout its history and in Romance, too, the present participles survive only as adjectives. On the gradual development of participial constructions in the literary language see p. 130.

Such adjectives may be used substantivally, but this usage is rare in the nominative singular until the time of Seneca. Early examples are 'quot amans ["a lover"] exemplis ludificetur' (Plt. *Truc.* 26); 'stulto intellegens quid inter est' (Ter. *Eun.* 232). The adjectives are also used predicatively with *esse* in a sort of periphrastic conjugation which lays emphasis on the durative aspect: 'tu ut sis sciens' (Plt. *Poen.* 1038); cf. 'utei scientes esetis' (*Sen. Cons. de Bacch.*); 'te carens dum hic fui' (Plt. *Capt.* 925).

As an adjective the 'present participle' originally merely described the circumstances in which the subject (and less often the object) of the main verb was placed. As such it had no explicit reference to time or any logical relationship, which had to be gathered from the context. Most frequently it refers to a simultaneous event or state, but occasionally, especially with verbs of arriving and departing, the participle has a past reference: 'puerum servos surpuit eumque hinc profugiens vendidit (Plt. *Capt.* 8 f.). Such examples are found also in Sallust and Cicero, but the present participle was not freely used in this way until Livy and still more Tacitus. In late Latin it proved a convenient substitute for the missing perfect participle active. In some contexts we must supply a future-final reference: 'dicto me emit audientem, haud imperatorem sibi' (Plt. *Men.* 444); 'missitare supplicantis legatos' (Sall. *Jug.* 31. 1). Other logical relationships (causal, modal, concessive, conditional, etc.) were left unexpressed in Old Latin. Not until Classical Latin do we find the present participle accompanied by particles such as *quamquam, etsi, ut,* etc., a development from which we can hardly exclude the influence of Greek models such as καίπερ, ὡς, ἅτε, etc.

The future participle evolved from an adjective having the meaning 'likely to, intending to, about to'. It is found in Old Latin only with *esse,* forming a periphrastic future tense: 'quid nunc es facturus' (Plt. *Bacch.* 716); 'immortalis est, vivit victuraque est' (id. *Trin.* 55). The detachment of the future participle from this close association with *esse* and its use attributively as an adjective was a long and slow process. Even Cicero only uses *futurus* and *venturus* (one example) in this way, and the emancipation was largely the work of Virgil and Ovid for poetry and of Livy for prose. In the predicative use the earliest example is from C.

Gracchus ('qui prodeunt dissuasuri'), but the text is not free from suspicion. Then follows Cicero with 'Servilius adest de te sententiam laturus' (*in Verr.* 2. 1. 56). Usage becomes freer with Virgil and Livy.

The perfect participle

The verbal adjectives in -*to*- refer to abiding qualities or states, e.g. *tacitus, doctus, scitus.* As such they were drawn into the orbit of the perfect tense. They were originally neutral as to voice and this still persists in such 'active' forms as *potus, pransus, cenatus, adultus, nupta, iuratus, lautus,* etc. Nor did this verbal adjective originally refer to past events. Present reference is frequent with such participles from deponent verbs: 'qui complexus cum Alcumena cubat' (Plt. *Amph.* 290). But present state implies past events and the Latin perfect system had this double reference. So it was that the perfect participle came to be used mainly of events taking place before that denoted by the main verb: e.g. 'acceptae bene . . . eximus' (Plt. *Cas.* 855). Certain examples have an ambiguous temporal reference owing to the nature of the verbal action: thus in 'coactus legibus eam uxorem ducet' (Ter. *And.* 780) the compulsion of the laws is a circumstance concomitant with the main action. From such examples this usage was developed to some extent in the Latin of the Empire so that the perfect participle served as a substitute for the missing present participle passive: 'quo saepe modo obsessi in obsidentes eruperunt' (Livy 9. 4. 9); 'servum sub furca caesum medio egerat circo' (id. 2. 36. 1); 'prae se actam praedam ostentantes' (id. 23. 1. 6).

Like the present and future participles the -*to*- adjective also combines with *esse* to form a periphrastic tense—the perfect passive of the type *ille est oneratus.* In the accusative it is also used predicatively after a variety of verbs, especially causative verbs: 'missum facio Teresiam senem' (Plt. *Amph.* 1145); 'tam frictum ego illum reddam' (id. *Bacch.* 767); 'factum et curatum dabo' (id *Cas.* 439). *habere* with the perfect participle often has its full force: 'abstrusam habebam' ('I kept her hidden', Plt. *Merc.* 360); 'domitos habere . . . oculos' (id. *Mil.* 564). Elsewhere such phrases are almost indistinguishable from the present perfect: 'hasce aedis conductas habet' (id. *Cist.* 319). On the substitution of this periphrasis for the present perfect in Romance see pp. 166 f.

Y

THE COMPLEX SENTENCE

The complex sentence is a comparatively recent growth in linguistic history. In the primitive state separate utterances were simply juxtaposed without explicit indication of their logical relationship. Such simple juxtaposition is known to grammarians as parataxis: e.g. *I know: he's coming.* In such an English sentence the absence of pause between the two parts is sufficient to fuse the utterance into a single whole and to indicate the subordination of the second part to the first. It will be convenient, however, to use the term parataxis also for such utterances in which there is no conjunction as an explicit mark of subordination. There are numerous traces in Latin of this primitive device of syntactical parataxis. *velim facias*, for instance, simply juxtaposes a potential subjunctive, *velim*, with a jussive *facias*, 'you are to do'; cf. *fac fidelis sis; sine amet; taceas oportet; licet abeas; servos iube hunc ad me ferant.* Now jussives and optatives were often accompanied by an adverbial *ut(i)*, originally meaning 'in some way' (occasionally also by *qui*, an instrumental 'by some means', e.g. *efficite qui detur tibi* 'get it given to you by some means'). This particle *uti*, becoming habitual, lost its full meaning and was weakened to a conjunction *ut*, which now was felt to 'govern' the subjunctive. This may serve as an example epitomizing the evolution of subordinate clauses in Latin. It follows that the moods in such clauses once had the same functions as those already discussed in main clauses. Thus in indirect questions Old Latin still largely maintained the distinction between the dubitative subjunctive and the indicative of fact. In many situations, however, both methods of expression were possible and there was a gradual effacement of the distinction. The association of the subordinating interrogative with the (originally dubitative) subjunctive became habitual and the introductory interrogative pronoun is now felt to 'govern' the subjunctive, a process analogous with the development of originally independent adverbs to prepositions 'governing' cases. This phenomenon we shall call 'habituation'. In the course of time such habituations produced series of semantically equivalent conjunctions with different constructions: e.g. *quamquam* with the indicative and *quamvis* with the 'concessive' subjunctive. Semantically equivalent expressions, however, tend towards assimilation and *quamquam* eventually yielded to the influence of *quamvis* and other concessive conjunctions and so came to 'govern' the subjunctive. The same tendencies persisted in other types of subordinate clause until the original distinctive functions of the subjunctive were largely obliterated and it became merely the mood of subordination—hence its Latin names *subjunctivus, conjunctivus*. In tracing the main outlines of this development we shall begin with some clear instances of (1) the voluntative-optative subjunctive, and (2) the prospective-potential subjunctive. Then, in view of the phenomena of habituation and governance, it will be convenient to discuss the functions of the various conjunctions and to examine their interactions under the heading of 'functional equivalence'.

Voluntative subjunctive

The jussive subjunctive is naturally seen at its clearest in indirect commands. It is found not only after verbs of ordering but also those of advising, requesting, permitting, contriving, and other related verbal expressions, e.g. 'lex est ut orbae nubant' (Ter.); 'optumum est ut loces' (Plt.); 'opus est ut lavem' (id.); 'fac Amphitruonem ut abigas' (id.); 'feci ut fierent' (Ter.); 'venit in mentem mihi argentum ut petam ('. . . I must somehow get some money', Plt.). The negative is *ne* as in the corresponding independent constructions (also occasionally *ut ne*).

Closely related to the jussive subjunctives after verbs of contriving (*efficio ut, curo ut*, etc.) are the subjunctives in clauses of purpose. Such clauses are also commonly introduced by *ut* (*ne*): 'me praemisit ut haec nuntiem' (Plt.); 'servate istum . . . ne quoquam pedem referat' (id.).

In clauses of result the subjunctives are of various origin. Thus in 'ut mentiar nullius patrimonium tanti facio' (Petronius) the repudiating subjunctive is still apparent—'I tell a lie!'. Then again a jussive after *efficio ut* is naturally extended to the perfect *ita effectum est ut* . . ., and for this a number of closely associated expressions may be substituted—*evenit ut, accidit ut*, e.g. 'evenit ut praeda onustus cederem' (Plt.). After verbs of willing and contriving, especially when they are accompanied by a correlative, it is difficult to distinguish purpose from result, e.g. 'sic in timorem dabo ut teneat', where the subjunctive may be voluntative or perhaps even prospective. In 'ita te ornatum amittam ut te non noveris' (Plt.) the subjunctive is potential. It was in such contexts that the habit of constructing *ut* with the subjunctive was established and then extended even to actual result. This habituation took place in Latin before the earliest texts, so that Latin could no longer make the distinction possible in Greek between actual and potential result.

The jussive subjunctive could be used in a stipulative sense: e.g. 'veniat quando volt atque ita: ne mihi sit mora' ('let him come when he wants and on this condition: I am not to be kept waiting', Plt.); cf. 'duae condiciones sunt: vel ut aurum perdas vel ut amator perierit' (id.). Closely related with the stipulative ('provided that') are the concessive ('granted that') uses of the voluntative-optative subjunctive. Such subjunctives are still rare in Old Latin in subordinate clauses ('licet laudem Fortunam: tamen ut ne Salutem culpem' (Plt.) and 'sint sane superbi: quid id ad nos attinet' (Cato) are still clearly paratactic) and the factotum conjunction *ut* does not introduce concessive clauses until Terence: 'iam in hac re, ut taceam, quoivis facile scitu est'.

The optative subjunctive

This function is clearly apparent in sentences such as the following: 'eveniant volo tibi quae optas'; 'ut ille te videat volo'; 'quaeso ut tua sors effugerit' (Plt.). It is also the source of the construction after verbs of fearing, for *metuo ne redeat* is readily analysed into 'I am afraid: may he not return'; cf. 'metuo ne techinae perierint' (Plt.). It follows that the Latin equivalent of the English 'I am afraid that the master will not return' takes the form 'I am afraid; may the master return': e.g. *metuo ut erus redeat.* This is the normal form in Old Latin: 'vereor ut placari possit' (Ter.); cf. 'id paves ne ducas: tu autem ut ducas' ('*you* are dreading the idea of marrying, *you* of not marrying', id.). Cicero, however, prefers *ne non* to *ut.*

The subjunctive in certain protases of conditional sentences is also optative in origin. This is apparent in paratactic examples, such as the following: 'virum me natam vellem: ego ostenderem' ('O that I had been born a man, I would show them', Ter.). Other cases may be traced to the use of the jussive in suppositions (see p. 315): 'prosit obsit, nil vident nisi quod lubet' ('suppose it helps or hinders . . .', Ter.). Such suppositions and wishes were introduced by the locative of the demonstrative *so-*, i.e. *si(c)*: e.g. 'sic: gladium quis apud te sana mente deposuerit, repetat insaniens, reddere peccatum sit' ('take the following case: suppose a man has deposited . . . suppose he asks for it back. . . . It would be a mistake . . .', Cic.); cf. 'meam rem non cures: sic recte facias' (Plt.), and the old formula quoted by Livy (10. 19. 17): 'Bellona, si hodie nobis victoriam duis, ast ego templum tibi voveo'. Other protases are derivable from prospective-potential subjunctives: thus 'si sapias, eas ac decumbas domi' (Plt.) breaks down most naturally into 'thus you would be wise: go and lie down at home'.

In Old Latin, as we have seen, the present subjunctive could refer both to the future and the present: e.g. (future) *si neget, amittat*; *si sciat, suscenseat*; (present) *si sit domi, dicam tibi*; *si habeat aurum, faciat*, *si nunc habeas quod des* (Plt.). The imperfect, on the other hand, could refer to the past: 'si esset unde fieret, faceremus' (Ter.); 'ni vellent, non fieret ('if they had not wished, it would not have been done', Plt.). There are survivals of this state of affairs even in Classical Latin. But the rearrangement whereby present subjunctive refers to the future, the imperfect to the present, and the pluperfect to the past had already begun in Old Latin: 'si equos esses, esses indomabilis' (Plt.); 'si appellasses, respondisset' (id.).

It was from this rearrangement of the time references of the different tenses of the subjunctive that the mood acquired its new 'unreal' function of expressing suppositions 'contrary to fact'. So subtle a set of distinctions established in the disciplined literary language could scarcely persist unblurred in popular usage. Plautus' usage fluctuates even in one and the same sentence (e.g. 'compellarem ni metuam'), and even classical usage is not so consistent as the school grammars suggest, for the present subjunctive often has present reference and the imperfect past reference; e.g. 'si ego cuperem ille vel plures [dies] fuisset' ('if I had wished he would have stayed longer', Cic.). In late Latin, as has already been pointed out, the pluperfect subjunctive gradually supplanted the imperfect.

Of the use of the indicative in certain types of 'potential' expressions we have already spoken (p. 316). Besides these we have the numerous changes of the mode of presentation within one and the same sentence resulting in the so-called mixed conditionals: 'ni hebes machaera foret, uno ictu occideras' (Plt.); 'praeclare viceramus nisi . . . fugientem Lepidus recepisset' ('a splendid victory was ours had not . . .', Cic.); 'perieramus si magistratus esset' ('we were as good as dead if . . .', Seneca). Such modes of expression became habitual in later Latin, with the result that the imperfect and pluperfect indicative tended to supplant the subjunctive in unreal apodoses.

THE CONJUNCTIONS

The first step in the evolution of conjunctions had been taken in Indo-European. In sentences such as *I saw shepherds: they were feeding their flocks*, this resumptive 'they' was expressed by the 'anaphoric' pronoun **i-* (Lat. *is*) and from this a relative stem **yo-* had been formed (Gk. ὅς). Latin, however, had abandoned this form of the relative and like Germanic made a new set of relative pronouns from the interrogative-indefinite stem *qui-, quo-*, etc. (see pp. 257 f.). It was from this interrogative-relative stem that the great majority of Latin conjunctions were formed: *quod, quia, quam, quando, quoniam, quom (cum), quamvis, quamquam, ubi, ut* (for the morphology of the last two see p. 282). The relative was the most loosely attached form of subordinate clause, being little more than the co-ordinated type 'and they . . .'. Consequently the moods and tenses in such subordinate clauses originally had the same values as in fully independent utterances. Hence we find consecutive, adversative, causal, and conditional relative clauses. Final, containing a voluntative subjunctive, are those of the familiar pattern *legatos miserunt qui pacem peterent*: e.g. 'gubernatorem arcessat qui nobiscum prandeat' (Plt.); 'perfodi parietem qua commeatus esset' (id.); 'eme lanam unde pallium conficiatur' (id.). It should be noted, however, that many of the examples often ranged under this heading are capable of a different interpretation: e.g. 'eam [rem] narrabo und' tu pergrande lucrum facias' is a 'generic' (see below) clause in which the subjunctive would be more naturally translated as 'you could make' (potential) rather than 'you are to make' (jussive).

The subjunctive in the so-called generic relative clauses, which is usually classified with the 'consecutive' uses, is clearly potential in origin: e.g. 'consilium dederim quod laudetis'; 'ecquis est qui possit'; 'quid est quod me velis'; 'pauci sunt qui certi sient'; 'mihi adsunt testes qui adsentiant'; 'conclave dedit quo nemo inferret pedem'; 'numquam hominem conveni unde abierim lubentius'; 'nihil est quo me recipiam' (all from Plautus).

The subjunctive in causal relative clauses may have grown out of the descriptive (generic) usages: e.g. 'ego inscitus [sum] qui postulem'; 'sanus tu non es qui furem me voces'; 'ego stultior qui credam'; 'ebriast quae compellet me', etc. (Plt.). But in many of these examples we may detect the tone of protest which recalls the 'repudiating' subjunctive (see p. 312): 'you're mad: to call me a thief!'. In such clauses usage in Old Latin and Classical Latin still fluctuates: 'sed sumne ego stultus qui rem curo publicam?' (Plt.); 'nos quidem contemnendi qui actorem odimus' (Cic.). These relative clauses might be preceded by *quippe*, which originated in an interjected question *quid pe?* 'why?', as is still apparent in: 'a te quidem apte. quippe? habes enim a rhetoribus' (Cic. *de fin.* 4. 7). In OL. *quippe qui* is mostly constructed with the indicative but the subjunctive is regular in Classical Latin. An example which still shows clearly the interjectional character of *quippe* is Cicero's '"Convivia cum patre non inibat": quippe qui ne in oppidum quidem nisi perraro veniret' ('. . . how could he a man who . . .', *Rosc. Am.* 18. 52).

It now remains to study the conjunctions which have evolved from the relative-interrogative stem.

quod, quia

The various functions assumed by *quod* in Latin syntax arose from relative sentences in which the neuter singular of the relative pronoun functioned as the subject or object. Thus in 'quod male feci, crucior' (Plt.), although *quod* is clearly the internal object of *feci* and a correlative *id* could easily be supplied with *crucior*, the sentence slides easily into a causal interpretation, 'because I have done wrong'. So too with the generic 'quid sit id quod sollicitere

ad hunc modum?' (Ter.), 'what is the reason why . . .'. Such was
the origin of *quod* as a causal conjunction. The distinction of moods,
which is to be explained as in other relative clauses (see above),
was obliterated in later times.

From other contexts in which the relative function of *quod* is
still apparent (e.g. 'gnatus quod se assimulat laetum, id dicis',
Plt.; 'adde huc quod caelestum pater prodigium misit', Acc.;
'mitte id quod scio', Ter.; 'istuc times quod ille operam amico
dat', id.) *quod* came to be used to introduce substantival clauses
after verbs of saying, thinking, knowing, etc. (e.g. 'scio iam filius
quod amet', Plt. *Asin.* 52). In 'id iam lucrum est quod vivis' the
relative clause is tantamount to 'the fact that you are alive'. In
'ego quod mala sum, matris opera mala sum' (Plt.), 'as for the
fact that . . .' passes imperceptibly to 'if I am a wicked girl'. The
similar 'quod dicat allatam epistulam' 'as for the fact that she says'
(id. *Asin.* 761) in the context is equivalent to 'although'. By such
manifold processes *quod* established itself in the course of time as a
universal conjunction, a colourless mark of subordination like the
Engl. *that* (Fr. *que*).

quia is in origin the neuter plural of the interrogative: cf.
quianam 'why'. It acquired its function as a causal conjunction
from its use in interjected questions: e.g. 'discrucior animi. quia?
abeundumst' 'I am in agony of mind. Why? I must go away' (cf.
the origin of Fr. *car* from an interjected *quare*). In Old Latin *quia*
is more frequent as a causal conjunction than *quod*, which, however, is preferred by classical authors. But *quia* regained its popularity in late Latin. *quia* parallels *quod* also in other functions: e.g.
'at nos pudet quia cum catenis sumus' (Plt.), 'we are ashamed
of the fact that . . .', cf. 'istuc acerbumst quia ero carendumst'
(id.), 'id doles quia non colunt' (id.). The use of *quia* to introduce noun clauses after verbs of saying and thinking emerged much
later than the corresponding use of *quod*: it is not found until the
time of Petronius.

cum (quom)

This conjunction was in origin the accusative masculine singular
of the relative stem and it still shows its origin in correlative expressions such as *tum . . . cum, eo tempore cum*. It, too, developed a range

of meanings apart from the purely temporal (causal, concessive), but in Plautus it governs the indicative in all its meanings. The indicative construction persisted into classical times after temporal *cum* when it is clearly relative (whether with an expressed antecedent *tum*, etc., or not), this including the loosely attached relative clauses known as *cum inversum* and the *cum interea* type: 'plus triginta annis natus sum quom interea loci numquam quicquam facinus feci peius' (Plt. *Men.* 446–7). The subjunctive came into use first in causal and concessive contexts. Its intrusion into circumstantial 'when' clauses is wrapped in obscurity, although there is some plausibility in the suggestion that the subjunctive in these clauses is analogous to the subjunctive in generic relative clauses— 'at *a* time when . . .' as opposed to 'at *the* time when'. The first example occurs in Terence: 'magistratus quom ibi adesset, occeptast agi' ('once the magistrate was present . . .', *Eun.* 22), and by the end of the Republican period the classical canon was established whereby *cum* 'when' takes the imperfect and pluperfect subjunctive except when it is clearly relative. However, exceptions are found to this rule even in the best authors: e.g. 'accepit agrum temporibus eis cum iacerent pretia' (Cic. *Q. Rosc.* 33) ; 'neque enim, si tibi tum cum peteres consulatum studui, nunc cum Murenam ipsum petas adiutor eodem pacto esse debeo' (id. *Mur.* 3. 8) ; 'fuit antea tempus cum Germanos Galli virtute superarent' (Caesar). Ingenuity may find a generic meaning here but the fact is that in *cum* constructions as elsewhere the subjunctive of subordination is gradually encroaching on the indicative of fact and even in classical times usage fluctuates.

dum

Though the etymological origin of this conjunction is obscure, its original sense seems to have been 'a while' (possibly connected with *durare*): e.g. *manedum* 'wait a while', *interdum* 'at times, between whiles', *nondum* 'not yet, not the while'. It developed many of the functions of the English word: e.g. 'while' = 'so long as', and 'while' = 'until' in dialect expressions such as 'wait while he comes'. It is worth noting in this connexion that *till* is also a conjunction derived from a Germanic word meaning 'time'. The purely temporal 'while', 'so long as' needs little comment:

conceivably it originated in correlative usages such as 'sic virgo, dum intacta manet, dum cara suis est' (Catullus). In expressions of the type 'during the time that such-and-such was taking place, something happened' an a-temporal durative present was used in the *dum* clause even with reference to the past. The more logical imperfect, however, occurs once in an early speech of Cicero (*Rosc. Am.* 32.91) and it became frequent in later authors. The functional equivalence of *dum* with *cum historicum* led to its construction with the subjunctive, especially in the usage of Livy and later prose authors.

Final clauses are also introduced by *dum*. This usage may have originated in juxtaposition such as *mane dum: scribam*, 'wait a while, I want to write', whence the progression was easy to the final sense 'wait for me to write'. This development is paralleled by the dialectal English use of 'while' in 'wait while he comes'. The usage is found from Old Latin onwards: 'observavit dum dormitarent canes' (Plt.); 'opperiar erum dum veniat' (id.).

Finally we find *dum* with stipulative subjunctives in much the same sense as the English 'so long as' = 'provided that': *oderint dum metuant* 'let them hate so long as they fear'. Examples occur already in Old Latin: 'me etiam vende dum saturum vendas' (Plt.); 'quid mea refert dum mihi recte serviant' (id.). Another such conjunction is *modo* = 'with the limitation': 'scies modo ut tacere possis' (Ter.). Both conjunctions may be combined: 'absit dum modo laude parta domum recipiat se' (Plt.).

The terminative sense of *dum* 'until' was more strongly rendered by *donec*. In Old Latin this conjunction is rarely used with the subjunctive, while it tends to be avoided altogether by the classical purists. Augustan and later prose authors, however, show a preference for *donec* over *dum* and construct it with the subjunctive. The partial functional equivalence with *dum* led to the use of *donec* in the sense 'as long as' (Lucretius and then Augustan and later prose and poetry). The mood used in this function was the indicative. On the iterative subjunctive see below.

quam (tamquam, quasi, priusquam, antequam)

quam is a case form of the interrogative-relative stem having the meaning 'in what (which) way', 'to what (which) degree'. As a relative it was employed with the correlative *tam* from the demonstrative stem: 'tam ille apud nos servit quam ego apud te servio' (Plt.). Subsequently the antecedent *tam* was omitted: 'non pisces expeto quam tui sermonis sum indigens' (Plt.). The two halves of the comparison being co-ordinated, *quam* naturally 'governed' the same mood as that of the preceding word: e.g. 'tam duim quam perduim' (Plt.).

tam . . . quam coalesced to form a single conjunction *tamquam*, which specialized in the introduction of assumed comparisons, 'as if it were'. In the earliest examples the subjunctive is clearly jussive: e.g. 'inde tamquam restim tractes facito'; 'facito tamquam faex fiat' (Cato). In this function *tamquam* competed with *quasi* (= *quam si*), the former being used by Cicero but not by Caesar. From the meaning 'as though' *tamquam* (and less frequently *quasi*) developed a causal usage to express the alleged reason after verbs of accusing, asserting, and fearing. The first example occurs in Livy: 'plus ira . . . valebat quia non ut hostibus modo sed tamquam indomitae et insociabili genti suscensebat' (37. 1. 4).

In such a sentence as *hic tam beatus est quam ille* the sense of *tam beatus* could equally be rendered by *non beatior*. It was presumably by the substitution of equivalent expressions ('contamination'), possibly first in negative expressions, that the illogical *quam* 'as' came to be used after comparatives. Whatever its origin, this usage is well established in Old Latin after the comparatives of both adjectives and adverbs: 'hau magis cupis quam ego te cupio'; 'citius abeunt quam in cursu rotula circumvortitur' (Plt.). Here, too, the same mood appears appropriately in the two halves of the comparison. Examples of the subjunctive are: 'plus viderem quam deceret'; 'hercle aufugerim potius quam redeam'; 'dem potius aurum quam illum corrumpi sinam' (Plt.). We may, however, detect a distinct 'fairy-ring' of usage—the semantic group clustering round *malo* 'I prefer' (< *magis volo*), among which are the verbs qualified by the adverb *potius*. After a verb of willing like *malo* it was right and proper to use a voluntative subjunctive: e.g. 'taceas malo quam tacere dicas' (Plt. *Pseud.* 209). This construction was then extended to the other members of the 'fairy-ring': e.g. 'quid mihi melius est quam opperiar erum?'; 'mussitabo potius quam inteream'; 'inopem optavit potius eum relinquere quam commonstraret' (Plt.). In other examples the repudiating subjunctive is clearly apparent: 'nam hercle ego quam illam anum inridere me ut sinam: satius mihi quovis exitio interire' (id. *Cist.* 662–3).

Once *quam* had acquired through its association with comparatives the new meaning 'than', it came to be used without a comparative, e.g. after *statuo, certum est,* and the like. An extreme example is '... quin vidua vivam quam tuos mores perferam' 'why shouldn't I live a widow (rather) than put up with your ways' (Plt. *Men.* 726) which is equivalent to 'I would rather be a widow than ...'. It was from such beginnings in sentences where the subjunctive was fully motivated that by 'habituation' this mood was introduced into comparative *quam* clauses where it had no such justification.

priusquam is merely a special instance of the *quam* construction after a comparative adverb (*antequam* appears first in Cato and Terence and is preferred by Cicero to *priusquam*, which, however, is favoured by Caesar). Consequently the use of the moods falls under the same headings as discussed in the preceding paragraphs. That the subjunctive where it appears is voluntative in origin emerges from the fact that in Old Latin, apart from examples of attraction and 'the oblique', it is found only after voluntative expressions: e.g. 'dicamus censeo priusquam abeamus' (Plt.); 'haec facito antequam incipias' (Cato); 'prius resicato quam ad arborem ponas' (id.). An apparent exception, 'animam omittunt priusquam loco demigrent' (Plt.), is clearly related to the *potius quam* construction just discussed. Thus there appear to be no grounds for regarding such subjunctives as eventual or anticipatory. 'Habituation' began at an early date (the subjunctive is frequently found even in Classical Latin with a purely temporal meaning) and the subjunctive became the regular construction in late Latin.

quamquam, quamvis

We have already discussed the use of the subjunctive in a concessive sense. In Old Latin, however, the most frequent concessive conjunction is *quamquam* (originally = 'however', 'in whatever way', 'to whatever extent') and it is constructed with the indicative as in Classical Latin: 'inde observabo . . . quamquam hic manere me erus sese iusserat' (Plt.). *quamvis* in Old Latin is still attached closely to an adjective or adverb: 'audacter quamvis dicito' (id.); 'locus hic . . . quamvis subito venias, semper liber est' ('come as suddenly as you like . . .', id. *Bacch.* 82). The first example without reference to an adjective or adverb occurs in Cicero: 'quamvis res mihi non placeat tamen . . . pugnare non potero' (*in Verr.* 2. 3. 209), but this conjunction is still avoided by Caesar and Livy. *licet*, too, remains rare as a concessive conjunction until the time of Martial and Juvenal and later prose authors. The functional equivalence of *quamvis* and *quamquam* resulted in some fluctuation in the mood employed, *quamvis* being sometimes used with the indicative (post-classical) and *quamquam* with the subjunctive (first in Nepos).

quominus and *quin*

Verbs of preventing were, in Old Latin, followed by the voluntative subjunctive introduced by *ne*. The characteristic classical conjunction *quominus* is hardly used at all by Plautus. The classical preference for *quominus* after verbs of preventing was perhaps a conscious device used in the interest of σαφήνεια to alleviate the overloading of *ne* (see p. 126 on this aspect of purism). It is a special instance of the use of the instrumental *quo* with comparatives in final relative clauses: e.g. 'id ea faciam gratia quo ille eam facilius ducat' (Plt.); 'si sensero hodie quicquam in his te nuptiis fallaciae conari quo fiant minus . . .' (Ter.). After negatived expressions of preventing Classical Latin used the conjunction *quin*. This originated in the instrumental of the interrogative—*quī ne*, meaning 'how not?' It could introduce independent impatient questions having imperatival force (*quin tu taces?*, 'Why don't you keep quiet?'), imperatives (*quin audi*), and also deliberative subjunctives (*quin rogem?*). That *quin* after expressions of preventing originated in dependent deliberatives is apparent from examples like: 'quin loquar, numquam me potes deterrere' 'Why shouldn't I speak? you will never deter me' (Plt.); 'quid causae est quin proficiscar' (Ter.); cf. 'quid obstat quor non fiant' (id.). Such *quin* clauses were appropriate after other expressions than those of preventing, notably after negatived expressions of doubt (*haud dubium est quin* . . .). The range of such negative expressions was extended by analogical processes until the original sense of *quin* was lost: e.g. 'numquam egredior quin conspicer' 'I never go out without being seen' (Plt.); cf. 'nec recedit loco quin statim rem gerat' (id.); 'nullum adhuc intermisi diem quin aliquid ad te litterarum darem' ('I never yet let a day pass without sending you some sort of letter', Cic.). Later the classical canon was disregarded and *quin* was used also after positive expressions of preventing and the like.

The subjunctive in oratio obliqua

In the preceding pages we have traced the use and origin of the subjunctive in subordinate clauses of command, question, alleged reason, and the like. From such beginnings, through processes of analogy and attraction, the subjunctive came to be used in all subordinate clauses of reported speech introduced by verbs of saying, asking, commanding, etc. This usage is regular in Classical Latin, the main exception being what may be described as explanatory footnotes inserted by the author which were not present in the original utterance: e.g. 'per exploratores certior factus est ex ea parte vici quam Gallis concesserat omnes noctu discessisse' (Caes.).

The iterative subjunctive

Latin had originally no explicit modal device for expressing repetition. In *saepe dixit* the fact of repetition is conveyed by the adverb and not by the mood or tense of the verb. So, too, in sentences like 'ut quisque acciderat eum necabam' (Plt.) the pluperfect, as expressing the past state, denotes the priority of the first event over the second, the element of repetition being denoted by *quisque*. Grammatically the pluperfect is no different from that in 'iam ut me conlocaverat, ventus exoritur' (Plt.), where it refers to a single action. In Classical Latin, however, the pluperfect indicative after *cum*, *ubi*, and *ut*, presumably first in sentences containing some explicit expression of iteration such as *quisque*, had developed the special function of denoting repeated events: e.g. 'Messanam ut quisque nostrum venerat, haec visere solebat' (Cic.); 'hostes ubi . . . conspexerant, adoriebantur' (Caes.).

In Augustan prose we observe a similar specialization of the pluperfect subjunctive. It is difficult to trace the genesis of this usage. The pluperfect subjunctive after *cum* in certain contexts refers to repeated events even in classical prose: 'cum cohortes ex acie procucurrissent, Numidae effugiebant' (Caes.). But here, as in the pluperfect indicatives just discussed, the iterative meaning is not an inherent function of the pluperfect subjunctive but is to be gathered from the context. Once, however, *ubi* had been drawn into the orbit of *cum* and came to be used with the subjunctive (first example in the Vulgar *Bell. Afr.* 78. 4), Latin possessed two constructions *ubi vidit* and *ubi vidisset*. It was the latter which from Livy onwards was specialized in the iterative function. It is not inconceivable that this use was in its beginnings a conscious literary artifice on the part of authors who seized on what was a Vulgar syntactical doublet to devise a Latin equivalent of the Greek optative in past iterative clauses. No such doublet existed in Latin for primary tenses and this may be the reason why an iterative subjunctive is not found with such tenses.

ADDENDUM

Gerund and Gerundive

In Hittite a genitive of the gerund does duty for the gerundive and such genitives are occasionally treated as adjectives with appropriate plural forms (H. Pedersen, *Hittitisch*, p. 149). Pedersen finds a similar development in Balto-Slavonic. In view of the 'invariable' gerundive (pp. 321 f.) it is conceivable that the Latin gerundive owes its origin to an interpretation of the adnominal genitive of the gerund.

BIBLIOGRAPHY

A comprehensive bibliography of works on the Latin language is:

J. Cousin: *Bibliographie de la langue latine. 1880–1948.* Paris. 1951.

OUTLINE HISTORIES OF THE LANGUAGE

A. Meillet: *Esquisse d'une histoire de la langue latine.* 5ᵉ ed. 1948.
P. Kretschmer: 'Die Sprache' in Gercke und Norden, *Einleitung in die Altertumswissenschaft.* 3rd ed. 1923.
F. Stolz–A. Debrunner: *Geschichte der lateinischen Sprache* (Sammlung Göschen). 3rd ed. 1953.
G. Devoto: *Storia della lingua di Roma.* 2nd ed. 1944.
J. Cousin: *Évolution et structure de la langue latine.* 1944.

CHAPTER I

A useful discussion of the affinities of Latin is D. M. Jones's article 'The Relation of Latin to Osco-Umbrian', *Transactions of the Philological Society,* 1950. The student may be referred to this article for the most important bibliographical references. See also the survey article by M. Lejeune, 'La position du latin sur le domaine indo-européen' in *Mémorial des études latines,* 1943, pp. 7 ff.

OSCO-UMBRIAN

C. D. Buck: *A Grammar of Oscan and Umbrian.* Boston. 2nd ed. 1928.

CHAPTER II

A useful guide to the prehistoric archaeology of Italy and its link-up with the linguistic evidence is:

J. Whatmough: *The Foundations of Roman Italy* (Methuen's Handbooks of Archaeology). 1937 (with a full bibliography).

More recent is:

Handbuch der Archäologie. 4te Lieferung, 1950 (= Müller's *Handbuch,* vi. 2. 1).

For more recent work see the articles by F. Matz in *Neue Jahrbücher für Antike und deutsche Bildung,* 1938, 385 ff., and 1939, 32 ff., and in *Klio,* xxxiii. 1940, 140 ff., and by J. Wiesner in *Die Welt als Geschichte,* viii, 1942, 197 ff.

THE INDO-EUROPEAN INVASIONS OF ITALY

H. Krahe: *Die Indogermanisierung Griechenlands und Italiens.* Heidelberg. 1949.

THE NON-ITALIC LANGUAGES OF ANCIENT ITALY (excluding Greek)

R. S. Conway, S. E. Johnson, and J. Whatmough: *The Prae-Italic Dialects of Italy.* Harvard U.P. 1933.
H. Krahe: *Das Venetische.* Heidelberg. 1950.
M. S. Beeler: *The Venetic Language.* Univ. of California. 1949.

ETRUSCAN

E. Fiesel: *Etruskisch* (= Geschichte der indogermanischen Sprachwissenschaft, v. 4). Berlin. 1931.
M. Renard: *Initiation à l'étruscologie*. 2nd ed. Brussels. 1943 (with a brief bibliography).
A. Ernout: 'Les éléments étrusques du vocabulaire latin', *BSL* 1929, 82 ff.
W. Schulze: *Zur Geschichte der lateinischen Eigennamen*. Berlin. 1904.
Corpus inscriptionum etruscarum. Leipzig. 1893– .

GREEK

B. Friedmann: *Die ionischen und attischen Wörter im Altlatein*. Helsinki. 1937.
O. Weise: *Die griechischen Wörter in der lateinischen Sprache*. Leipzig. 1882.
G. Pasquali: *Preistoria della poesia romana*. Florence. 1936.

CHAPTER III

A. Ernout: *Les éléments dialectaux du vocabulaire latin*. Paris. 1909.
—— 'Le Parler de Préneste d'après les inscriptions', *MSL* xiii. 283 ff.
—— *Textes latins archaïques*. Paris. 1947.
E. Stolte: *Der faliskische Dialekt*. Munich. 1926.
E. Norden: *Aus altrömischen Priesterbüchern*. Lund. 1939.

CHAPTER IV

J. B. Hofmann: *Lateinische Umgangssprache*. 2nd ed. Heidelberg. 1936.
H. Haffter: *Untersuchungen zur altlateinischen Dichtersprache*. Berlin. 1934.
E. Fraenkel: *Plautinisches im Plautus*. Berlin. 1922.
W. Jachmann: Article on Terence in Pauly–Wissowa, *Realenzyklopädie*, Ser. II, v A.1, 643 ff.

CHAPTER V

M. Leumann: 'Die lateinische Dichtersprache', in *Museum Helveticum*, iv, 1947, 116 ff.
A. Cordier: *Études sur le vocabulaire épique dans l'Énéide*. Paris. 1939.
E. Norden: *Die antike Kunstprosa*. 3rd ed. Leipzig. 1915–18.
——'Commentary on Virgil, *Aeneid* VI. 3rd ed. 1934.
W. Kroll: 'Die Entwicklung der lateinischen Schriftsprache', in *Glotta*, xxii, 1933, 1 ff.
—— Article on the language of Sallust, *Glotta*, xv, 1927, 280 ff.
J. Marouzeau: *Quelques aspects de la formation du latin littéraire*. Paris. 1948.
—— *Traité de stylistique latine*. 2nd ed. Paris. 1946.
—— Article 'Pour mieux comprendre les textes latins'. *Revue de Philologie*, xlv, 1921, 149 ff.
R. Till: *Die Sprache Catos* (= *Philologus* Supplement Band xxviii. 2). 1935.
S. F. Bonner: *Roman Declamation*. Liverpool. 1949. (Especially Chapter VIII on declamatory influence on the literature of the early Empire.)
A. W. de Groot: *La prose métrique des anciens*. Paris. 1937.

Z

CHAPTER VI

C. H. Grandgent: *An Introduction to Vulgar Latin*. Boston. 1907.

W. A. Baehrens: *Skizze der lateinischen Volkssprache* (= *Neue Wege zur Antike*, ii. 45–66).

M. Niedermann: 'Über einige Quellen unserer Kenntnis des späteren Vulgärlateinischen', in *Neue Jahrb. f. d. klass. Altertumswissenschaft*, xv, 1912, 313 ff.

E. Löfstedt: 'Spätlateinische und romanische Sprachentwicklung', in *Syntactica*, ii. 373 ff. (with a list of the more important works on Vulgar Latin).

—— *Philologischer Kommentar zur Peregrinatio Aetheriae*. Uppsala. 1911.

F. Marx: 'Die Beziehungen des Altlateins zum Spätlatein', in *Neue Jahrb.* xxiii, 1909, 434 ff.

H. F. Muller and P. Taylor: *A Chrestomathy of Vulgar Latin*. Boston. 1932.

G. Rohlfs: *Sermo vulgaris latinus*. Halle. 1951.

CHAPTER VII

J. Schrijnen: *Charakteristik des altchristlichen Lateins*. Nijmegen. 1932.

A critical survey of the work of Schrijnen and his school is:

J. de Ghellinck: 'Latin chrétien ou langue latine des chrétiens', in *Les Études classiques*, viii, 1939, 449 ff.

See especially the articles by Chr. Mohrmann in *Vigiliae Christianae*, i, 1947, 1 ff.; ii, 1948, 89 ff., 163 ff.; iii, 1949, 67 ff.; iv, 1950, 193 ff.

LATIN TRANSLATIONS OF THE BIBLE

F. Stummer: *Einführung in die lateinische Bibel*. 1928.

H. F. D. Sparks: 'The Latin Bible', in H. W. Robinson, *The Bible in its Ancient and English Versions*. Oxford. 1940.

H. Rönsch: *Itala und Vulgata*. 1875.

W. E. Platen and H. J. White: *A Grammar of the Vulgate*. Oxford. 1926.

PART II

The standard work of reference for the comparative-historical grammar of Latin is:

F. Stolz and J. H. Schmalz: *Lateinische Grammatik*. 5th ed. by M. Leumann and J. B. Hofmann (Müllers *Handbuch*). Munich. 1928.

W. Lindsay: *The Latin Language*. Oxford. 1894.

A descriptive grammar is:

R. Kühner: *Ausführliche Grammatik der lateinischen Sprache*. 2nd ed. of *Syntax*, by C. Stegmann. Hanover. 1912–14.

ETYMOLOGICAL DICTIONARIES

A. Ernout and A. Meillet: *Dictionnaire étymologique de la langue latine*. 3rd ed. Paris. 1951.

A. Walde: *Lateinisches etymologisches Wörterbuch*. 3rd ed. by J. B. Hofmann (in progress). Heidelberg. 1930– .

BIBLIOGRAPHY 345

PEDAGOGICAL WORKS

A. Meillet and J. Vendryes: *Traité de grammaire comparée des langues classiques.* 2nd ed. 1948.

C. D. Buck: *Comparative Grammar of Greek and Latin.* Chicago. 1948.

E. Kieckers: *Historische lateinische Grammatik,* i and ii. 1930–1.

W. Lindsay: *A Short Historical Latin Grammar.* 2nd ed. Oxford. 1915.

PHONOLOGY

R. G. Kent: *The Sounds of Latin.* 3rd ed. Baltimore. 1945.

M. Niedermann: *Phonétique historique du latin.* 3rd ed. Paris. 1953.

MORPHOLOGY

R. G. Kent: *The Forms of Latin.* Baltimore. 1946.

A. Ernout: *Morphologie historique du latin.* 3rd ed. Paris. 1953.

SYNTAX

A. Ernout and F. Thomas: *Syntaxe latine.* 2nd ed. Paris. 1953.

This work is intended to replace: O. Riemann: *Syntaxe latine.* 7th ed. by A. Ernout. 1925.

W. Kroll: *Die wissenschaftliche Syntax im lateinischen Unterricht.* 3rd ed. 1925.

C. E. Bennett: *Syntax of Early Latin,* i and ii. Boston. 1910–14.

E. Löfstedt: *Syntactica,* i. 2nd ed. Lund. 1942; ii, 1933.

J. Wackernagel: *Vorlesungen über Syntax,* i and ii. Basel. 1926–8.

APPENDIX

ARCHAIC LATIN TEXTS

A. EPIGRAPHIC

1. *CIL* i.² 3. E 1. Praenestine fibula. *circa* 600 B.C.

   Manios med vhe vhaked Numasioi

2. *CIL* i.² 4. E 3. Inscribed on a bowl with three compartments found on the Quirinal. Sixth century (?).

   iouesat deiuos qoi med mitat, nei ted endo cosmis uirco sied |
   asted noisi ope toitesiai pacari uois. |
   duenos med feced en manom einom dze noine med maao statod

3. *CIL* i.² 1. E 2. Cippus found in the Forum Romanum. *circa* 500 B.C.

   quoi hoi[...]
   [...] sakros : es-
   ed sorl[...]
   [...]ia[.]ias
   regei : ig[...]
   [...] euam
   quos : re[...]
   [...]m : kalato-
   rem : hai[...]
   [...]iod : iouxmen-
   ta : kapia : dotau[...]
   m : ite : ri[...]
   [...]m : quoi ha
   uelod : nequ[...]
   [...] od: iouestod
   loiuquiod [...]

4. *CIL* i.² 2. E 146. Hymn of the Fratres Arvales from the proceedings of the year A.D. 218. See above, pp. 63 f.

   enos Lases iuuate,
   [e]nos Lases iuuate,
   enos Lases iuuate.
   neue luae rue Marma   sins incurrere in pleores,
   neue lue rue Marmar   [si]ns incurrere in pleoris,
   neue lue rue Marmar   sers incurrere in pleoris.
   satur furere Mars,   limen [sal]i, sta berber,
   satur fu, fere Mars,   limen sali, sta berber,
   satur fu, fere Mars,   limen sa[l]i, s[t]a berber.
   [sem]unis alternei   aduocapit conctos,
   semunis alternei   aduocapit conctos,

simunis altern[ei]   aduocapit [conct]os.
enos Marmor iuuato,
enos Marmor iuuato,
enos Mamor iuuato.
triumpe triumpe triumpe   trium[pe tri]umpe

5. *CIL* i.² 366. E 64. Spoleto.

honce loucom | ne qu(i)s uiolatod | neque exuehito neque | exferto quod louci ‖ siet, neque cedito, | nesei quo die res deina | anua fiet. eod die, | quod rei dinai cau(s)a | [f]iat, sine dolo cedre ‖ [l]icetod. sei quis | uiolasit, Ioue bouid | piaclum datod. | sei quis scies | uiolasit dolo malo, ‖ Iouei bouid piaclum | datod et a. CCC | moltai suntod. | eius piacli | moltaique dicator[ei] ‖ exactio est[od]

6. *CIL* i.² 401. E 91. Luceria.

in hoce loucarid stircus | ne [qu]is fundatid neue cadauer | proiecitad neue parentatid. | sei quis aruorsu hac faxit, [in]. ium ‖ quis uolet pro ioudicatod n. [L] | manum iniect[i]o estod. seiue ˈmac[i]steratus uolet moltare, | [li]cetod

7. *CIL* i.² 361. Rome.

Iunone Loucinai | Diouis castud facitud

8. *CIL* i.² 581. E 126. Bronze tablet of 186 B.C. containing a copy of the *Senatus Consultum de Bacchanalibus*.

[Q.] Marcius L. f., S. Postumius L. f. cos. senatum consoluerunt n. Octob. apud aedem | Duelonai. sc. arf. M. Claudi. M. f., L. Valeri. P. f., Q. Minuci. C. f.

de Bacanalibus quei foideratei | esent, ita exdeicendum censuere: 'neiquis eorum ⟨B⟩acanal habuise uelet. sei ques | esent, quei sibe, deicerent necesus ese Bacanal habere, eeis utei ad pr. urbanum ‖ Romam uenirent, deque eeis rebus, ubei eorum u⟨e⟩r⟨b⟩a audita esenti utei senatus | noster decerneret, dum ne minus senatoribus C adesent, [quom e]a res cosoleretur. | Bacas uir nequis adiese uelet ceiuis Romanus neue nominus Latini neue socium | quisquam, nisei pr. urbanum adiesent, isque [d]e senatuos sententiad, dum ne | minus senatoribus C adesent, quom ea res cosoleretur, iousisent. ce[n]suere. ‖

sacerdos nequis uir eset. magister neque uir neque mulier quisquam eset. | neue pecuniam quisquam eorum comoine[m h]abuise ue[l]et. neue magistratum, | neue pro magistratu⟨d⟩, neque uirum [neque mul]ierem quiquam fecise uelet. | neue posthac inter sed conioura[se neu]e comuouise neue conspondise | neue conpromesise uelet, neue quisquam fidem inter sed dedise uelet. ‖ sacra in ⟨o⟩quoltod ne quisquam fecise uelet. neue in poplicod neue in | preiuatod neue exstrad urbem sacra quisquam fecise uelet, nisei | pr. urbanum adieset, isque de senatuos sententiad, dum ne minus | senatoribus C adesent, quom ea res cosoleretur, iousisent. censuere. |

homines plous V oinuorsei uirei atque mulieres sacra ne quisquam ‖
fecise uelet, neue inter ibei uirei plous duobus, mulieribus plous tribus |
arfuise uelent, nisei de pr. urbani senatuosque sententiad, utei suprad |
scriptum est.'

haice utei in couentionid exdeicatis ne minus trinum | noundinum,
senatuosque sententiam utei scientes esetis, — eorum | sententia ita
fuit: 'sei ques esent, quei aruorsum ead fecisent, quam suprad ‖ scriptum
est, eeis rem caputalem faciendam censuere'—atque utei | hoce in
tabolam ahenam inceideretis, ita senatus aiquom censuit, | uteique
eam figier ioubeatis, ubei facilumed gnoscier potisit. atque | utei ea
Bacanalia, sei qua sunt, exstrad quam sei quid ibei sacri est, | ita utei
suprad scriptum est, in diebus X, quibus uobeis tabelai datai ‖ erunt,
faciatis utei dismota sient. in agro Teurano

9. *CIL* i.² 614. E 125. Cadiz. 189 B.C.

L. Aimilius L. f. inpeirator decreiuit, | utei quei Hastensium seruei |
in turri Lascutana habitarent, | leiberei essent. agrum oppidumqu., |
quod ea tempestate posedisent, | item possidere habereque | iousit, dum
poplus senatusque | Romanus uellet. act. in castreis | a. d. XII k. Febr.

10. *CIL* i.² 586. E 127.

L. Cornelius Cn. f. pr. sen. cons. a. d. III nonas Maias sub aede
Kastorus. | scr. adf. A. Manlius A. f., Sex. Iulius [. . .], L. Postumius
S. f. |

quod Teiburtes u(erba) f(ecistis) quibusque de rebus uos purgauistis,
ea senatus | animum aduortit ita utei aequom fuit—nosque ea ita
audiueramus, ‖ ut uos deixsistis uobeis nontiata esse—: ea nos animum
nostrum | non indoucebamus ita facta esse, propterea quod scibamus, |
ea uos merito nostro facere non potuisse, neque uos dignos esse, | quei
ea faceretis, neque id uobeis neque rei poplicae uostrae | oitile esse
facere. et postquam uostra uerba senatus audiuit, ‖ tanto magis
animum nostrum indoucimus (ita utei ante | arbitrabamur), de eieis
rebus af uobeis peccatum non esse. | quonque de eieis rebus senatuei
purgati estis, credimus, uosque | animum uostrum indoucere oportet,
item uos populo | Romano purgatos fore

11. *CIL* i.² 25. E 147. Inscription of the *columna rostrata* of C. Duilius
restored or composed under Augustus or Claudius

. . . .
. . . . . [Secest]ano[sque . . . . op-]
[sidione]d exemet lecione[sque Cartaciniensis omnis]
[ma]ximosque macistr[a]tos l[uci palam post dies]
[n]ouem castreis exfociont, Macel[amque opidom]
[p]ucnandod cepet. enque eodem mac[istratud bene]
[r]em nauebos marid consol primos c[eset copiasque]
[c]lasesque nauales primos ornauet pa[rauetque],
cumque eis nauebos claseis Poenicas omn[is, item ma-]
[x]umas copias Cartaciniensis praesente[d Hanibaled]

dictatored ol[or]om in altod marid pucn[andod uicet]
[u]ique naue[is cepe]t cum socieis septer[esmom I quin-]
[queresm]osque triresmosque naueis X[XX, merset XIII].
[auro]m captom: numei ⊕⊕⊕ϴCIϽ
[arcen]tom captom praeda: numei   ⊕I [........]
[omne] captom aes ⊕⊕⊕⊕ ⊕⊕⊕⊕ [........]
[. . . .]   ⊕⊕⊕⊕⊕⊕⊕⊕⊕⊕⊕⊕⊕ [...... pri-]
[mos qu]oque naualed praedad poplom [donauet pri-]
[mosque] Cartacini[ens]is [ince]nuos d[uxit in]
[triumpod ......] eis [......] capt[......]

12. *CIL* i.² 6. 7. E 13. Sarcophagus of L. Cornelius Scipio Barbatus,
    consul in 298 B.C.

    [L. Corneli]o Cn. f. Scipio |
    Cornelius Lucius   Scipio Barbatus
    Gnaiuod patre | prognatus,   fortis uir sapiensque,
    quoius forma uirtutei   parisuma | fuit,
    consol, censor, aidilis   quei fuit apud uos,
    Taurasia, Cisauna | Samnio cepit,
    subigit omne Loucanam opsidesque abdoucit

13. *CIL* i.² 8 and 9. E 14. Sarcophagus of the consul of 259 B.C.

    L. Cornelio L. f. Scipio | aidiles, cosol, cesor
    honc oino ploirume   cosentiont R[omane]
    duonoro optumo   fuise uiro,
    Luciom Scipione.   filios Barbati
    consol, censor, aidilis hic fuet a[pud uos].
    hec cepit Corsica   Aleriaque urbe,
    dedet Tempestatebus   aide mereto[d]

14. *CIL* i.² 10. E 15. Sarcophagus of the augur of 180 B.C.

    quei apice insigne Dial[is   fl]aminis gesistei, |
    mors perfe[cit] tua ut essent   omnia | breuia,
    honos, fama uirtusque, | gloria atque ingenium.
    quibus sei | in longa licu[i]set   tibe utier uita, |
    facile facteis superases   gloriam | maiorum.
    qua re lubens te in gremiu, | Scipio, recip[i]t
    Terra, Publi, | prognatum   Publio, Corneli

15. *CIL* i.² 11. E 16. Possibly from sarcophagus of the brother of Cn.
    Scipio Hispanus (see no. 16).

    L. Cornelius Cn. f. Cn. n. Scipio
    magna sapientia | multasque uirtutes
    aetate quom parua | posidet hoc saxsum.
    quoiei uita defecit,   non | honos, honore,
    is hic situs, quei nunquam | uictus est uirtutei.
    annos gnatus (uiginti)   is | l[oc]eis mandatus,
    ne quairatis honore | quei minus sit mandatu[s]

16. *CIL* i.² 15. E 18. Sarcophagus of Cn. Scipio, praetor peregrinus in 139 B.C.

> Cn. Cornelius Cn. f. Scipio Hispanus | pr., aid. cur., q., tr. mil. II,
> Xuir sl. iudik., | Xuir sacr. fac. |
> uirtutes generis mieis moribus accumulaui,
> progeniem genui, facta patris petiei.
> maiorum optenui laudem, ut sibei me esse creatum
> laetentur: stirpem nobilitauit honor

17. *CIL* i.² 1861. E 134. Amiternum.

> Protogenes Cloul(i) | suauei heicei situst | mimus,
> plouruma que | fecit populo soueis || gaudia nuges

18. *CIL* i.² 1211. E 133. Rome.

> hospes quod deico, paullum est, asta ac pellege.
> heic est sepulcrum hau pulcrum pulcrai feminae.
> nomen parentes nominarunt Claudiam.
> suom mareitum corde deilexit souo.
> gnatos duos creauit. horunc alterum
> in terra linquit, alium sub terra locat.
> sermone lepido, tum autem incessu commodo.
> domum seruauit. lanam fecit. dixi. abei

19. *CIL* i.² 1202. E 135. Rome.

> hoc est factum monumentum | Maarco Caicilio. |
> hospes, gratum est, quom apud | meas restitistei seedes:
> bene rem geras et ualeas, | dormias sine qura

20. *CIL* i.² 1600. E 92. Capua.

> Pesceniaes | C. l. Laudicaes | ossa heic sita sunt

21. *CIL* i.² 1249. E 93. Rome.

> Aquilliaes C. l. Tertiae | C. Aquillius | Sosander l.

22. *CIL* i.² 37. E 24. Rome.

> M. Mindios L. fi., | P. Condetios Va. fi. | aidiles uicesma parti
> Apolones dederi

23. *CIL* i.² 59. E 22. Praeneste.

> Apolon[e C. Q. ?] | Metilio [C. f. ?] | magistere | coraueron. | C. Anicio
> l.(?) st|riando | [. . .]

24. *CIL* i.² 975. E 121. Trastevere.

> deuas | Corniscas | sacrum

25. *CIL* i.² 376. E 73. Pisaurum.

> Cesula | Atilia | donu | da Diane

26. *CIL* i.² 42. E 29. Nemi.

Poublilia Turpilia Cn. uxor | hoce seignum pro Cn. filiod | Dianai donum dedit

27. *CIL* i.² 610. Nemi. 202–200 B.C.

C. Aurilius C. f. | praitor | iterum didit, | eisdim consl || probauit

28. *CIL* i.² 48. E 31. Tusculum.

M. Fourio C. f. tribunos | [milita]re de praidad Fortune dedet

29. *CIL* i.² 60. E 34. Praeneste.

Orceuia Numeri (uxor) | nationu cratia | Fortuna, Diouo fileia | primocenia, || donom dedi

30. *CIL* i.² 980. E 123. Trastevere.

Forte Fo[rtunai] | uiolaries, | rosaries, | coronaries. || [m]ac[istres] coe[rauere]

31. *CIL* i.² 394. E 86.

T. Vetio | duno | didet | Herclo || Iouio | brat. | data

32. *CIL* i.² 30. E 21. Rome.

M. C. Pomplio No(ui) f(ilii) | dedron | Hercole

33. *CIL* i.² 62. E 37. Praeneste.

L. Gemenio L. f. Pelt[.] | Hercole dono | dat lubs merto | pro sed sueq. || ede leigibus | ara Salutus

34. *CIL* i.² 1531. E 128. Sora. *circa* 150 B.C.

M. P. Vertuleieis C. f.
quod re sua di[f]eidens   asper | afleicta
parens timens | heic uouit,   uoto hoc | solut[o]
[de]cuma facta | poloucta   leibereis lube|tes
donu danunt | Hercolei   maxsume | mereto.
semol te | orant, se [u]oti   crebro | condemnes

35. *CIL* i.² 626. E 129. Rome.

L. Mummi L. f. cos.
duct(u) | auspicio imperioque | eius Achaia capt(a),
Corinto | deleto   Romam redieit | triumphans.
ob hasce | res bene gestas quod | in bello uouerat, |
hanc aedem et signu | Herculis Victoris |
  imperator dedicat

36. *CIL* i.² 632. E 130. Reate.

sancte,
de decuma, Victor, tibei Lucius Munius donum
moribus antiqueis pro usura hoc dare sese
uisum animo suo perfecit, tua pace rogans te
cogendei dissoluendei tu ut facilia faxseis,

perficias decumam ut faciat uerae rationis,
proque hoc atque alieis donis des digna merent.

37. *CIL* i.² 360. E 61. Norba.

    P. Rutilius M. f. | Iunonei Loucina | dedit meretod | Diouos castud

38. *CIL* i.² 378. E 75. Pisaurum.

    Iunone rec(inai) | matrona | Pisaurese | dono dedrot

39. *CIL* i.² 364. E 62. Falerii.

    Iouei Iunonei Mineruai | Falesce, quei in Sardinia sunt, | donum dederunt. magistreis | L. Latrius K. f., C. Salu[e]na Voltai f. coiraueront

    gonlegium quod est   aciptum aetatei aged[ai],
      opiparum a[d] ueitam   quolundam festosque dies,
    quei soueis aastutieis   opidque Volgani
      gondecorant sai[pi]sume   comuiuia loidosque,
    ququei huc dederu[nt   i]nperatoribus summeis,
      utei sesed lubent[es   be]ne iouent optantis

40. *CIL* i.² 49. E 32. Tusculum.

    M. Fourio C. f. tribunos | militare de praidad Maurte dedet

41. *CIL* i.² 379. E 76.

    Matre | Matuta | dono dedro | matrona || M'. Curia, | Pola Liuia deda

42. *CIL* i.² 365. E 63. Falerii.

    Menerua sacru. | [L]a(rs) Cotena, La(rtis) f., pretod de | zenatuo sententiad uootum | dedet, cuando datu rected || cuncaptum

43. *CIL* i.² 675. E 94. Capua. 108 B.C.

N. Pumidius Q. f.	M. Raecius Q. f.
M. Cottius M. f.	N. Arrius M. f.
M. Eppilius M. f.	L. Heioleius P. f.
C. Antracius C. f.	C. Tuccius C. f.
L. Sempronius L. f.	Q. Vibius M. f.
P. Cicereius C. f.	M. Valerius L. f.

    heisce magistreis Venerus Iouiae murum | aedificandum coirauerunt ped. CCↃXX et | loidos fecerunt Ser. Sulpicio M. Aurelio co[s.]

44. *CIL* i.² 383. E 78. Firmum Picenum.

    L. Terentio L. f., | C. Aprufenio C. f., | L. Turpilio C. f., | M. Albani. L. f., || T. Munatio T. f. | quaistores | aire moltaticod | dederont

45. *CIL* i.² 1511. Cora.

    M. M[.]ţlius M. f., L. Turpilius L. f. duomuires de senatus | sente[n]-tia aedem faciendam coerauerunt eisdemque probauere

45. *CIL* i.² 1529. E 132. Aletri. Between 130 and 90 B.C.

L. Betilienus L. f. Vaarus | haec quae infera scripta | sont de senatu sententia | facienda coirauit: semitas ‖ in oppido omnis, porticum qua | in arcem eitur, campum ubei | ludunt, horologium, macelum, | basilicam calecandam, seedes, | [l]acum balinearium, lacum ad ‖ [p]ortam, aquam in opidum adqu. | arduom pedes CCCX↓, fornicesq. | fecit, fistulas soledas fecit. | ob hasce res censorem fecere bis, | senatus filio stipendia mereta ‖ ese iousit, populusque statuam | donauit Censorino

47. *CIL* i.² 1722. Aeclanum. Time of Cicero.

C. Quinctius C. f. Valg. patron. munic., | M. Magi. Min. f. Surus, A. Patlacius Q. f., | IIIIuir., d(e) s(enatus) s(ententia) portas, turreis moiros | turreisque aequas qum moiro ‖ faciundum coerauerunt

48. *CIL* i.² 1471. E 58. Praeneste.

M. Saufeius M. f. Rutilus, | C. Saufeius C. f. Flacus | q. | culinam f(aciendam) d(e) s(enatus) s(ententia) c(uraverunt), eisdem|q. locum emerunt de | L. Tondeio L. f. publicum.| est longu p. CX↓VIIIS, | latum af muro ad | L. Tondei uorsu p. XVI

49. *CIL* i.² 638. E 131. Forum Popillii (Lucania). 132 B.C.

uiam fecei ab Regio ad Capuam, et | in ea uia ponteis omneis, miliarios | tabelariosque poseiuei. hince sunt | Nouceriam meilia ↓I, Capuam XXCIIII, ‖ Muranum ↓XIIII, Cosentiam CXXIII, | Valentiam C↓XXX[.], | ad fretum ad | statuam CCXXXI[.], | Regium CCXXXVII. | suma af Capua Regium meilia CCCXXI[.]. | et eidem praetor in | Sicilia fugiteiuos Italicorum | conquaeisiuei redideique | homines ⊢CCCCXVII. eidemque | primus fecei, ut de agro poplico | aratoribus cederent paastores. | forum aedisque poplicas heic fecei

50. *CIL* i.² 584. E 138. Near Genoa. 117 B.C.

Q. M. Minucieis Q. f. Rufeis de controuorsieis inter | Genuateis et Veiturios in re praesente cognouerunt et coram inter eos controuosias composeiuerunt, | et, qua lege agrum possiderent et qua fineis fierent, dixserunt. eos fineis facere terminosque statui iuserunt; | ubei ea facta essent, Romam coram uenire iouserunt. Romae coram sententiam ex senati consulto dixerunt eidib. ‖ Decemb. L. Caecilio Q. f. Q. Muucio Q. f. cos.—qua ager priuatus casteli Vituriorum est, quem agrum eos uendere heredemque | sequi licet, is ager uectigal. nei siet.—Langatium fineis agri priuati: ab riuo infimo, qui oritur ab fontei in Mannicelo ad flouium | Edem; ibi terminus stat. inde flouio suso uorsum in flouium Lemurim. inde flouio Lemuri susum usque ad riuom Comberane(am). | inde riuo Comberanea susum usque ad comualem Caeptiemam; ibi termina duo stant circum uiam Postumiam. ex eis terminis recta | regione in riuo Vendupale. ex riuo Vindupale in flouium Neuiascam. inde dorsum fluio Neuiasca in flouium Procoberam. inde ‖ flouio Procoberam deorsum usque ad riuom Vinelascam infumum; ibei terminus stat. inde sursum riuo recto Vinelesca; | ibei terminus stat propter uiam Postumiam. inde alter trans uiam Postumiam terminus stat. ex eo termino, quei stat | trans uiam Postumiam, recta regione in fontem in Manicelum. inde deorsum riuo, quei oritur ab fonte en Manicelo | ad terminum, quei stat ad flouium Edem.—agri poplici quod Langenses posident, hisce finis uidentur esse: ubi comfluont | Edus et Procobera, ibei terminus stat. inde Ede flouio sursuorsum in montem Lemurino infumo; ibei terminus || stat. inde sursumuorsum iugo recto monte Lemurino; ibei termin(u)s stat. inde susum iugo recto Lemurino; ibi terminus | stat in monte pro cauo. inde sursum iugo recto in montem Lemurinum summum; ibi terminus stat. inde sursum iugo | recto in castelum, quei uocitatust Alianus; ibei terminus stat. inde sursum iugo recto in montem Iouentionem; ibi terminus | stat. inde sursum iugo recto in montem Apeninum, quei uocatur Boplo; ibei terminus stat. inde Apeninum iugo recto | in montem Tuledonem; ibei terminus stat. inde deorsum iugo recto in flouium Veraglascam in montem Berigiemam || infumo; ibi terminus stat. inde sursum iugo recto in montem Prenicum; ibi terminus stat. inde dorsum iugo recto in | flouium Tulelascam; ibi terminus stat. inde sursum iugo recto Blustiemelo in montem Claxelum; ibi terminus stat. inde | deorsum in fontem Lebriemelum; ibi terminus stat. inde recto riuo Eniseca in flouium Porcoberam; ibi terminus stat. | inde deorsum in flouiom Porcoberam, ubei conflouont floui Edus et Porcobera; ibi terminus stat.—quem agrum poplicum | iudicamus esse, eum agrum castelanos Langenses Veiturios po[si]dere fruique uidetur oportere. pro eo agro uectigal Langenses || Veituris in poplicum Genuam dent in anos singulos uic(toriatos) n(umos) CCCC. sei Langenses eam pequniam non dabunt neque satis | facient arbitratuu Genuatium, quod per Genuenses mo[r]a non fiat, quo setius eam pequniam acipiant: tum quod in eo agro | natum erit frumenti partem uicensumam, uini partem sextam Langenses in poplicum Genuam dare debento | in annos singolos.—quei intra eos fineis agrum posedet Genuas aut Viturius, quei eorum posedeit k. Sextil. Li Caicilio | Q. Muucio cos., eos ita posidere colereque liceat. e⟨i⟩s que. posidebunt, uectigal Langensibus pro portione dent ita, uti ceteri || Langenses, qui eorum in eo agro agrum posidebunt fruenturque. praeter ea in eo agro ni quis posideto nisi de maiore parte | Langensium Veituriorum sententia, dum ne alium intro mitat nisi Genuatem aut Veiturium colendi causa. quei eorum de maiore parte | Langensium Veiturium sententia ita non parebit, is eum agrum nei habeto niue fruimino.—quei | ager compascuos erit, in eo agro quo minus pecus [p]ascere Genuates Veituriosque liceat ita, utei in cetero agro | Genuati compascuo, niquis prohibeto, niue quis uim facito, neiue prohibeto, quomins ex eo agro ligna materiamque || sumant utanturque.— uectigal anni primi k. Ianuaris secundis Veturis Langenses in poplicum Genuam dare | debento. quod ante k. Ianuar. primas Langenses fructi sunt eruntque, uectigal inuitei dare nei debento.— | prata quae fuerunt proxuma faenisicei L. Caecilio Q. Muucio cos. in agro poplico, quem Vituries Langenses | posident et quem Odiates et quem Dectunines et quem Cauaturineis et quem   entouines posident, ea prata | inuitis Langensibus et Odiatibus et Dectuninebus et Cauaturines et Mentouines, quem quisque eorum agrum || posidebit, inuiteis eis niquis sicet niue pascat niue fruatur. sei Langenses aut Odiates aut Dectunines aut Cauaturines | aut Mentouines malent in eo agro alia prata inmittere, defendere, sicare, id uti facere liceat, dum ne ampliorem | modum pratorum habeant, quam proxuma aestate habuerunt fructique sunt. Vituries, que controuorsias | Genuensium ob iniourias iudicati aut damnati sunt, sei quis in uinculeis ob eas res est, eos omneis | soluei, mittei leiber(are)ique Genuenses uidetur oportere ante eidus Sextilis primas.—sei quoi de ea re || iniquom uidebitur esse, ad nos adeant primo quoque die et ab omnibus controuersis et hono. publ. li. | — leg(ati) Moco Meticanio Meticoni f., Plaucus Peliani. Pelioni f.

51. *CIL* i.² 1831. E 81. Cliternia.

uia inferior | priuatast | T. Vmbreni C. f., | precario itur. || pecus plostru | niquis agat

B. From LITERARY SOURCES

52. From Varro's *de lingua latina*.

(i) 5. 97. Hircus, quod Sabini fircus; quod illic fedus, in Latio rure hedus, qui in urbe ut in multis A addito haedus.

(ii) 5. 101. Lepus, quod Siculi, ut Aeolis quidam Graeci, dicunt λέποριν: a Roma quod orti Siculi, ut annales veteres nostri dicunt, fortasse hinc illuc tulerunt et hic reliquerunt id nomen.

(iii) 5. 159. Vicus Cyprius a cypro, quod ibi Sabini cives additi consederunt, qui a bono omine id appelarunt: nam cyprum Sabine bonum.

(iv) 5. 173. In argento nummi, id ab Siculis.

(v) 6. 2. Sic, inquam, consuetudo nostra multa declinavit a vetere, ut ab solu solum, ab Loebeso Liberum, ab Lasibus Lares.

(vi) 6. 4. Meridies ab eo quod medius dies. D antiqui, non R in hoc dicebant, ut Praeneste incisum in solario vidi.

(vii) 6. 13. Februm Sabini purgamentum, et id in sacris nostris verbum non ignotum.

(viii) 6. 28. Idus ab eo quod Tusci Itus, vel potius quod Sabini Idus dicunt.

(ix) 6. 68. Vicina horum quiritare, iubilare. Quiritare dicitur is qui Quiritum fidem clamans inplorat. Quirites a Curensibus; ab his cum Tatio rege in societatem venerunt civitatis. Ut quiritare urbanorum, sic iubilare rusticorum: Itaque hos imitans Aprissius ait:

Io bucco!—Quis me iubilat?
Vicinus tuus antiquus.

(x) 6. 86. Nunc primum ponam de Censoriis Tabulis:

Ubi noctu in templum censor auspicaverit atque de caelo nuntium erit, praeconi sic imperato ut viros vocet: 'Quod bonum fortunatum felix salutareque siet populo Romano Quiritibus reique publicae populi Romani Quiritium mihique collegaeque meo, fidei magistratuique nostro: omnes Quirites pedites armatos, privatosque, curatores omnium tribuum, si quis pro se sive pro altero rationem dari volet, voca inlicium huc ad me.'

87. Praeco in templo primum vocat, postea de moeris item vocat. Ubi lucet, censores scribae magistratus murra unguentisque unguentur. Ubi praetores tribunique plebei quique inlicium vocati sunt venerunt, censores inter se sortiuntur, uter lustrum faciat. Ubi templum factum est, post tum conventionem habet qui lustrum conditurus est.

88. In Commentariis Consularibus scriptum sic inveni: Qui exercitum imperaturus erit, accenso dicito: 'C. Calpurni, voca inlicium omnes Quirites huc ad me.' Accensus dicit sic: 'Omnes Quirites, inlicium vos ite huc ad iudices.' 'C. Calpurni,' cos. dicit, 'voca ad conventionem omnes Quirites huc ad me.' Accensus dicit sic: 'Omnes Quirites, ite ad conventionem huc ad iudices.' Dein consul eloquitur ad exercitum: 'Impero qua convenit ad comitia centuriata.'

(xi) 7. 29. Idem ostendit quod oppidum vocatur Casinum (hoc enim ab Sabinis orti Samnites tenuerunt) et nostri etiam nunc Forum Vetus appellant. Item significat in Atellanis aliquot Pappum, senem quod Osci casnar appellant.

(xii) 7. 42. Olli valet dictum illi ab olla et ollo, quod alterum comitiis cum recitatur a praecone dicitur olla centuria, non illa; alterum apparet in funeribus indictivis, quo dicitur
Ollus leto datus est.

53. The *Carmen Saliare*.

a divum empta cante! divum deo supplicate!
b quome tonas, Leucesie, prae tet tremonti
quot ibe tet e nubi deiscunt tonare
c cozeulodorieso. omnia vero adpatula coemisse. ian cusianes duonus ceruses. dunus Ianusve vet pom melios eum recum

a = Varro, *L.L.* 7. 27. For *empta* Bergk suggested *em pa* = 'in patrem'.
b Ter. *Scaur.*; *G.L.* vii. 28.
c = Varro, *L.L.* 7. 26.

54. Cato, *agr.* 141.

Mars pater, te precor quaesoque uti sies volens propitius mihi domo familiaeque nostrae, quoius rei ergo agrum terram fundumque meum suovitaurilia circumagi iussi, uti tu morbos visos invisosque, viduertatem vastitudinemque, calamitates intemperiasque prohibessis defendas averruncesque. utique tu fruges, frumenta, vineta virgultaque grandire beneque evenire siris, pastores pecuaque salva servassis duisque bonam salutem valetudinemque mihi domo familiaeque nostrae: harumce rerum ergo, fundi terrae agrique mei lustrandi lustrique faciendi ergo, sicuti dixi, macte hisce suovitaurilibus lactentibus inmolandis esto: Mars pater, eiusdem rei ergo macte hisce suovitaurilibus lactentibus esto!

55. Fragments of the *leges regiae*.

(i) Pellex aram Iunonis ne tangito. Si tagit, Iunoni crinibus demissis agnum feminam caedito.

(ii) (*a*) Si hominem fulmen Iovis occisit, ne supra genua tollito.
    (*b*) Homo si fulmine occisus est, ei iusta nulla fieri oportet.
(iii) Si qui(s) hominem liberum dolo sciens morti duit, paricidas esto.
(iv) Si quisquam aliuta faxit, ipsos Iovi sacer esto.
(v) Si parentem puer verberit ast olle plorassit paren⟨s⟩, puer divis parentum sacer esto.

56. Fragments of the Twelve Tables. E 114 ff.

(i) 1. Si in ius vocat, ito. Ni it, antestamino: igitur em capito. 2. Si calvitur pedemve struit, manum endo iacito. 3. Si morbus aevitasve vitium escit, [qui in ius vocabit] iumentum dato: si nolet, arceram ne sternito.

(ii) Adsiduo vindex adsiduos esto; proletario [iam civi] quis volet vindex esto.

(iii) Rem ubi pacunt orato. 2. Ni pacunt, in comitio aut in foro ante meridiem caussam coiciunto, cum peroranto ambo praesentes. 3. Post meridiem praesenti litem addicito. 4. Si ambo praesentes, sol occasus suprema tempestas esto.

(iv) Morbus sonticus . . . aut status dies cum hoste . . . quid horum fuit vitium iudici arbitrove reove, eo dies diffensus esto.

(v) Cui testimonium defuerit, is tertiis diebus ob portum obvagulatum ito.

(vi) Aeris confessi rebusque iure iudicatis triginta dies iusti sunto. 2. Post deinde manus iniectio esto. In ius ducito. 3. Ni iudicatum facit aut quis endo eo in iure vindicit, secum ducito. Vincito aut nervo aut compedibus. XV pondo ne minore aut si volet maiore vincito. 4. Si volet, suo vivito. Ni suo vivit, [qui eum vinctum habebit,] libras farris endo dies dato. Si volet, plus dato.

(vii) Tertiis nundinis partis secanto. si plus minusve secuerunt, se fraude esto.

(viii) Adversus hostem aeterna auctoritas esto.

(ix) Si pater filium ter venumdavit (?) filius a patre liber esto.

(x) uti legassit super pecunia tutelave suae rei, ita ius esto.

(xi) si intestato moritur, cui heres nec escit, adgnatus proximus familiam habeto. si adgnatus nec escit, gentiles familiam habento.

(xii) vias muniunto: ni sam delapidassint, qua volet, iumenta agito.

(xiii) qui malum carmen incantassit. occentassit.

(xiv) si membrum rupsit, ni cum eo pacit, talio esto.
    si iniuriam alteri faxsit, viginti quinque aeris poenae sunto.

(xv) si nox furtum faxsit, si im occisit, iure caesus esto.

(xvi) si adorat furto quod nec manifestum erit, duplione damnum decidito.

(xvii) patronus si clienti fraudem fecerit, sacer esto.

(xviii) qui se sierit testarier libripensve fuerit, ni testimonium fariatur, inprobus intestabilisque esto.

(xix) si telum manu fugit magis quam iecit, ⟨aries subicitur⟩.

(xx) neve aurum addito. at cui auro dentes iuncti escunt, ast im cum illo sepeliet uretve, se fraude esto.

(xxi) si servus furtum faxit noxiamve noxit.

SUBJECT INDEX

INDEX OF LATIN WORDS